ROAD HAULAGE BY MOTOR IN BRITAIN

Road Haulage by Motor in Britain

The first forty years

THOMAS GIBSON

Routledge
Taylor & Francis Group
LONDON AND NEW YORK

First published 2001 by Ashgate Publishing

Reissued 2018 by Routledge
2 Park Square, Milton Park, Abingdon, Oxon OX14 4RN
711 Third Avenue, New York, NY 10017, USA

Routledge is an imprint of the Taylor & Francis Group, an informa business

Typeset by Owain Hammonds, Bontgoch, Talybont, Ceredigion, Wales SY24 5DP.

A Library of Congress record exists under LC control number: 00052605

ISBN 13: 978-1-138-72825-7 (hbk)
ISBN 13: 978-1-138-72821-9 (pbk)
ISBN 13: 978-1-315-19057-0 (ebk)

Contents

Acknowledgements

While I was working on this book my wife, Marjorie, encouraged me all the way; and helped by indexing, sorting notes, typing part of, and re-reading most of it and in doing so, sometimes suggested how the meaning might be made clearer. I acknowledge my tremendous debt to her. I acknowledge also the help of my son, Geoffrey, in sorting out computer problems.

I am grateful to the members of staff of the Bodleian Library in Oxford, particularly those in the Lower Reading Room of the Old Library, who made my work easier.

In the early days of my research, now many years ago, the Chartered Institute of Transport kindly gave me a grant from the Rees Jeffries Fund to help defray the cost of travel. I am grateful to the Institute for that grant and for the implied encouragement that came with it.

I have made considerable use throughout the book of the valuable historical record contained in the pages of the weekly magazine *Commercial Motor*. In addition to this I have included an advertisement from the First World War years, and as appendices, Specifications of Vehicles from the year 1920, and extensive extracts from Cost Tables published regularly in the magazine. All of these are included by kind permission of *Commercial Motor* magazine.

I have used material, too from other sources and have sought to indicate the origin by end-of-chapter lists of references and a bibliography. I trust that this will be sufficient acknowledgement to the authors and publishers concerned.

TG

List of Abbreviations

AA	Automobile Association
AC	Automobile Club
ACVR	Automobile Commercial Vehicle Review
AEC	Associated Equipment Company
ASC(MT)	Army Service Corps (Motor Transport)
BRF	British Road Federation
C&D	Collected and delivered
CMUA	Commercial Motor Users' Association
DORA	Defence of the Realm Acts
FBI	Federation of British Industries
GWR	Great Western Railway Co.
HGV	Heavy goods vehicle
JCB	Joint Conciliation Board
JIC	Joint Industrial Council
LA	Licensing Authority
LCC	London County Council
LDRHA	Long Distance Road Haulage Association
LGB	Local Government Board
LGOC	London General Omnibus Co.
LMS	London Midland and Scottish Railway Co.
LNER	London and North Eastern Railway Co.
LNWR	London and North Western Railway Co.
MoM	Ministry of Munitions
MOT	Ministry of Transport
MVWUA	Motor Vehicle and Wagon Users' Association
NJCB	National Joint Conciliation Board
NER	North Eastern Railway Co.
NUR	National Union of Railwaymen
RAC	Royal Automobile Club
RASC	Royal Army Service Corps
RHA	Road Haulage Association
RRT	Railway Rates Tribunal
SMMT	Society of Motor Manufacturers and Traders
TAC	Transport Advisory Council
TUC	Trades Union Congress
WD	War Department

Preface

In the early years of the First World War, after some fifteen years of steady growth of the road haulage industry, the editor of *Commercial Motor* expressed the hope, or wish, that one day there would be an historian of the industry. Were he alive today, Shrapnell-Smith might be less hopeful, for the road freight industry has been neglected. If one reflected on the flood of books about railways – both popular and academic works - the conclusion might be drawn that road haulage has been shamefully neglected.

The present work is an introduction to the study of the history of the earlier years of road haulage. It is an outline only, for so much is still to be done. Topics come to mind readily – the study of individual firms, their competitive environment and their financial fortunes; the study of competition between the petrol vehicle and the horse, between petrol and steam, between petrol and diesel, between roads and railways. Bankruptcies, mergers, takeovers, the activities of clearing houses, the attempts to formulate standard rates, the problems of wage rates and labour relations, the impact of the licensing system through thirty-odd years – and much more. There is scope for scores of university theses; there is enough to keep the amateur historian busy for a very long time. Until this spadework is done the definitive history must needs wait.

In the meantime this book is offered to provide the background of the early years for the researcher and, it is hoped, it will suggest other themes not mentioned above.

T. Gibson

A note about money

Prior to 1971 the pound sterling was made up of twenty shillings, written 20s., or 240 pence, written 240d. Each shilling was made up of twelve pence (1s. = 12d.). So 2.4d. (old pence) were equivalent to one of our present-day pence (2.4d. = lp) and one shilling (1s.) was equivalent to five of our present pence (1s. = 5p).

CHAPTER ONE

A Most Important Improvement

The transport of freight has always been with us. Ever since the first savage hunter struggled homeward with the carcase of the wild animal he had killed, man has known that goods are more useful in one place than in another. So he laboured to move the dead beast to the hungry children. He toiled to move the branches and leaves and grasses to the place where he wanted his shelter. He carried the stones home to make his tool. He moved stones to make a rude hearth, and twigs and branches to burn for warmth. For many centuries man worked at his transport problem. When he learnt to grow crops he had to move the tools and the seeds to the field, the harvest home to the storehouse.

In those distant times man's muscle power was often unequal to the task. He discovered that things floated on water and could be made to carry a load. He tamed the wild horse and that wonderful creature eased his lot, improved his transport situation, raised his standard of living and carried him upward through the long centuries. That technological revolution – the domestication of the horse – was to have its effects right through to very recently. But it was not enough. All advances in technology move the human race forward materially, but man's wants always outgrow the means. He becomes discontented and looks for better ways of doing things. He looks especially hard when he has serious problems. Sometimes the solution is long postponed, but eventually the seeker finds.

Unfortunately in man's early days, when life was 'solitary, poor, nasty, brutish and short', the struggle to live dominated all. There was no time (nor means) for keeping records. Who now knows the name of the man who first noticed that a rolling log beneath a heavy load made the movement easier? Who now knows how (or whether) the transition was made from that to the wheel? Curiously, when we did get around to written records, we recorded the Tutankhamuns, the Nefertitis. We gaze today in awe at the great Pyramids and think of such rulers. We may glance at drawings of those herds of workers hauling massive stone blocks and ponder on the kings who wanted pyramids, but there is no thought for, no record of, the man who first put the roller beneath the stone, who made possible the building of the great monuments. There is no record of the Bronze Age man who made a wheel. These early people who have done more for the human race than all the Pharaohs together, are doomed forever to remain unknown.

Horses were domesticated. Wheels were made. The two were brought together, and in Mesopotamia 5000 years ago, wagons were made. Since then material well-being has improved apace. The forward movement was not at an even rate, nor was it without difficulties. Sometimes wheeled transport proved to be a nuisance. The Romans had to impose their speed restrictions, make laws about reckless driving of chariots – and about parking: but those same Romans knew well that for good transport one must have good roads. Not that the roads they built in Britain were intended for the transport of the wares of peaceful commerce. They were military in object (though that, too, involves much freight movement); but they demonstrated that wheeled transport must have adequate roads on which to run.

More than a thousand years on from that, when the inhabitants of these islands were stirring themselves, the need for roads became apparent. The population was growing. The feudal shackles were thrown off. The spark of desire for higher living standards was kindling to a flame. The first faint sounds of the coming Industrial Revolution were heard by those of keen ear. Packhorses and wagons were on the move; and as they moved they churned up the morass of red midland mud, or stiff Sussex clay, into a sometimes impassable slough. Not for the first time man's wishes for the transport of freight were frustrated by the poor quality of the roads. At first the legislators, having destroyed the only bodies organized to cope with road repairs – the monasteries – threw the responsibility back onto the inhabitants of the parish. An Act of 1555 required the people of the parish to elect from amongst themselves two honest men as Surveyors to inspect the roads in the parish and to organize the people into doing the necessary patching up. The parish residents were each required to give four (later six) days' work each year to this end. The surveyors – honest men as we see – were not required to have any technical knowledge. That they knew little about the work mattered not at all. That they were probably afraid to drive their co-parishioners too hard – they themselves might be on the receiving end the next year – mattered even less. The system, such as it was, was adequate only for a comparatively short time.

For freight transport was growing in volume. In the seventeenth century the carrier (for 'hire or reward' as we say in modern terms) was becoming a more common figure. In 1637 a Mr Taylor published his *Carriers' Cosmography*, listing some two hundred carriers – a sort of seventeenth-century ABC Goods Transport Guide – including such items as the regular Wednesday wagon from Oxford to London.[1] These wagons might have had as many as six horses but could cope with not much over a ton of freight on the appalling roads of the time. Of course, bulk freight could be moved by river if there happened to be one running in the right place. The increasing volume of freight generally is indicated by the building of locks on the rivers to get a greater depth of water – as on the Thames near Oxford in the 1620s.

The oft-amended 1555 Act proved inadequate to make the roads fit for the traffic. The legislators then did what they considered the next best thing. They attempted to make the traffic fit the roads. There is something depressingly familiar about all those seventeenth- and eighteenth-century Acts which limited the loads on wagons, or limited the horsepower with the same intention, or made rules about the width of wagon wheels so that they might not cut into the soft surfaces. There is something unpleasant about Acts which encouraged old ladies to make a living by informing the authorities when they saw heavily laden wagons having further horses added at the foot of steep hills.[2]

The constructive Act of 1555 and the later restrictive Acts alike were unable to cope with the growing traffic. Private enterprise took a hand and in 1663 the first Turnpike Act was passed, allowing a group of worthy yeomen to put turnpike gates on a stretch of road, charge tolls for the use of that road, and use the money raised to pay for proper maintenance. In the first half of the eighteenth century about four hundred such Acts were passed in England. By then the population was growing, and money made in trade with the 'Indies' was available to finance industrial developments to meet the needs of this population. Cotton and woollen goods were made in ever greater quantities. Mines were being opened up. Ironmasters' furnaces were changing that first trickle of molten metal into a stream in flood. Industry needed transport. The second half of the eighteenth century saw great pressure on transport facilities. Some sixteen hundred Turnpike Acts were passed in the forty years before the Napoleonic Wars. These were beneficial, in some places, and fast stage-coaches were able to run, e.g. from London to Bath. As often as not, though, a stretch of road poorly maintained by the parish would be followed by a turnpike stretch which was not much better. Each turnpike trust was free to build as it chose – or according to the abilities of the surveyor employed – and they were not all McAdams or Telfords or Metcalfes.

The rivers could not take much more despite many improvements, and they were not always in the right place. So canals were dug in great numbers. Historians talk of the 'Canal mania' but the mania referred to those who wished to buy shares in the companies. There is nothing maniacal about providing transport for the needs of industry. Then, as now, however, new facilities generated new traffic and still the pressure was on. Men in some places continued with experiments with iron rails to replace the ordinary roads, and with steam engines to replace the sorely tried muscles of those great horses which hauled the wagons or canal barges.

The carriers responded to the growing industrialization by expanding their services. In the late eighteenth century there was a network of wagon routes throughout the country. Over a hundred wagons worked out of Manchester each week to predetermined schedules (in addition to much packhorse traffic).

A four-day delivery to Bristol was advertised to Manchester merchants by carriers who had working arrangements with others to whom they transhipped the goods at Birmingham. The latter busy city had connecting services enabling it to send goods to 168 other towns in the kingdom. Collection and delivery services were available. Occasional through rates were in operation.[3] The much-improved main roads, were allowing fairly sizeable loads to be carried at this time. A Select Committee of the House of Commons in 1831 commented that 'the roads at present have to sustain waggons, weighing, at times, with their horses, nearly ten tons'.[4] Admittedly this reference to the included weight of the horses effectively reduces the possible weight of the load, but still we find one John MacNeill giving evidence to the Committee to the effect that an eight-horse wagon with load weighed 7 tons, though on average not more than 6 tons over the year.

The canals had dealt a severe blow to the road hauliers, for canal rates were only half or quarter of wagon rates in many cases. But canals, too, did not run everywhere, and as traffic increased they became more and more congested and there were allegations of monopoly practices. So there was still plenty of work for road hauliers. But eventually the vastly more efficient railways drove both canal and road carriers almost out of business, for railways were cheaper, faster, and could handle a much greater volume of traffic than the older modes of transport. Here and there enterprising carriers such as Pickford survived the onslaught by using the advantages of the railways to the benefit of their own businesses. Pickford adopted the simple (and modern-looking) practice of using the London and Birmingham Railway for trunking his freight, while maintaining his own collection and delivery services. There was still work for the local carrier, including carrying to and from the railway station.

For a long time before mechanical transport arrived in the form of railways there had been people, only too well aware of the deficiencies of horses, who sought to mechanize road transport. Not everyone thought in terms of railways, and, indeed, the first mechanical vehicles were road vehicles. The power of steam was well known. As early as 1687 Verbiest, a missionary in China, described a model in which steam jets blew on vanes fixed to the wheels.[5] Perhaps more interesting is the fact that even at that time the principle of internal combustion had been thought of. In 1680 Huyghens experimented with a piston in a cylinder, the explosive force being provided by gunpowder.[6] There were too many difficulties in the way of that particular experiment, but at least the germ of the idea was there to be developed two centuries later. The first mechanical vehicle actually to run on roads was built by Nicholas Joseph Cugnot, a French military engineer, in 1769.[7] It managed, by steam power, to reach a speed of 2¼ miles per hour though the boiler produced insufficient steam to keep the vehicle going for longer than 15 minutes. We are told, however, that 'the results ... showed so many possibilities that the French Government ordered the construction of a similar vehicle for the transport of artillery'.[8] Though the second vehicle was built, it was never used for the intended haulage job. There were other steam vehicles, however. Murdock ran one in England until Watt and his partner, Boulton, persuaded him to use his talents in other directions. Trevithick, encouraged by a trial run up Camborne Beacon with seven or eight passengers in a steam car, ran one in London in 1803, again with passengers, before turning his attention to vehicles on rails.[9]

The difficulty for Trevithick, as for others who tried out steam vehicles on road, was that the roads, other than some of the main highways under turnpike control, were poor, and the heavy unsprung vehicles took a fearful battering to add to their own vibrations from a not too-well-balanced engine movement. The manufacturing techniques of the early nineteenth century were just not up to the job of making engines which could stand all this. There were difficulties about the strength of the materials, and severe vibration and road shocks, transmitted through a very rigid chassis, quickly found weaknesses. Boilers sometimes did not withstand the necessary steam pressure. It was difficult, at first, to get pistons and cylinders made to such fine tolerances as to give a good working fit. Even if there were some successes, there was no such thing as mass-production turning out parts, one after another, all exactly alike. The loving craftsman often introduced his own slight variations. But many people persevered and some managed to get steam vehicles to work satisfactorily. In 1831, at the dawn of the railway age, Sir Charles Dance ran a road passenger service three times daily between Gloucester and Cheltenham for four months and in that time carried some three thousand passengers.[10] Others, such as Walter Hancock's service in London or Sir John Scott Russell's service between Glasgow and Paisley also worked successfully for a time in the early 1830s.[11]

These were all passenger services and so get only passing mention in a book on freight carriage, but two comments are necessary. First, fares from passengers yielded much more revenue than was obtainable from a comparable amount of freight, so experimental services were almost bound to concentrate on passengers. They might well have been extended to freight at a later date, had not practically all mechanized road transport to pay very heavy toll charges to turnpike trusts – heavier, that is, than comparable horse-drawn vehicles. Second, there was an assumption, general at the time, that nobody really wanted to send their goods at speed and it was only in the matter of speed that mechanical transport had any advantage. The Select Committee of the House of Commons, mentioned above, reported that at 4 m.p.h. horses were just as economical as steam vehicles. It was only beyond that speed that steam became more economical, for more horses had to be used, and changes made more frequently, at higher speeds. The Committee concluded, therefore, that it was unlikely that steam would be used as a propelling power on common roads for heavy wagons for a considerable period.

But if the Committee could not see much future for the haulage of freight by steam power on roads, their more famous witness, Trevithick, certainly did. He told the Committee (at a time when the Liverpool and Manchester Railway had been operating for some months): 'I have it in contemplation to do a great deal on common roads; railroads are useful for speed and for the sake of safety but not otherwise; every purpose could be answered by steam on common roads.' In answer to the question, 'You conceive Steam Carriages to be applicable to common purposes?' Trevithick replied, 'Yes, to every purpose a horse can effect.'[12] It is only fair to add that George Stephenson, so prominent in turning the planned Liverpool and Manchester Railway into practical reality, had a very different opinion. He just could not see steam engines on anything but rails.

The Select Committee of the House of Commons, mentioned above, had been set up to enquire into

> the proportion of tolls which ought to be imposed upon coaches and other vehicles propelled by steam or gas upon Turnpike Roads... the Rate of toll actually levied ... and ... generally into the present state and future prospect of Land Carriage by means of wheeled vehicles propelled by steam or gas on Common Roads and to report upon the probable utility which the Public may derive therefrom.

Trevithick may well have hoped that the Select Committee would have been able to do something about the very heavy tolls imposed by the turnpike trusts on steam vehicles. These tolls were, indeed, heavy and were one of the main factors stifling the advance of mechanized road transport at the time. The Committee accepted without question Mr Gurney's evidence that his steam carriages paid £2 on the Ashburnham – Totnes Road, whereas a four-horse coach paid only 3s. (3 shillings = 15p in modern terms). He paid £2.8s.0d. (£2.40) on the Liverpool – Prescot Road as compared with 4s. (20p) paid by the horse-drawn coach; and on the Teignmouth – Dawlish Road 12s. (60p) as compared with 2s. (10p). The Committee made no comment on the fact that the Appendix to their Report, listing the tolls authorized in various Turnpike Bills dealt with by the House of Commons in the 1830–31 Session, showed 2s.6d. (12½p) as a common rate. One of the items in that Appendix showed the toll on the Liverpool – Preston Road to be 6d. (2½p) per wheel up to one ton plus 6d. per wheel for each further ton.

The Committee approached, with much common sense, the question of what tolls ought reasonably to be charged.They noted that the turnpike trustees had two reasons for charging steam vehicles more than horse-drawn vehicles. First there was the point that as a steam vehicle carried more

Passengers than a horse-drawn one, fewer vehicles in total would pass, so turnpike revenues would suffer if all were charged alike. The Committee did not accept the possibility that there would be fewer vehicles, however. Second, the turnpike trusts claimed that steam vehicles did greater damage to roads. (We must remember here that in the 1830s roads did not have tarmac surfaces.) On this point the Select Committee made a remark that might well have served as a warning to future generations of legislators:

> and as to the second cause of increased charge, the Trustees, in framing their charge, have probably not minutely calculated the amount of injury to roads likely to arise from them [i.e. the steam vehicles]. Unless an experiment were instituted on two roads, one reserved solely for the use of Steam Coaches, the other for carriages drawn by horses, for the purposes of ascertaining accurately the relative wear of each, it would be quite impossible to fix with certainty the proportion, of Tolls to which, on the same road, each class of vehicle would be liable.

They made some enquiries, nevertheless: they noted the damage done by the flailing hooves of horses, the cutting into the road surface by extremely narrow coach and wagon tyres designed to cause minimal friction; and they compared the effects with the rolling action of the broad wheels of the steam vehicles which were designed to give adhesion. They had no hesitation in stating that the steam vehicles were less damaging to the road. It is a pity that the Committee's Report was not made compulsory reading for local authorities at the beginning of the nineteenth century.

The Committee went on to consider the basis on which tolls could be charged. Gross weight? Every vehicle differed and every load differed. There would be endless bother at the turnpike gates in deciding what the charge was to be. 'In fact, unless an accountant were placed at each [gate], the Committee cannot conceive how the proportions could be satisfactorily arranged.' To fix maximum weights of vehicles and maximum loads would require a licensing system which would be 'cramping the progress of improvement of a machine, the capabilities of which can be ascertained slowly and by continued experiment'. Another possible method was to charge on horsepower. 'Monstrous' they called one example of this, 'as if it were a national object to prevent the possibility of such engines being used.' Equally the Committee rejected tolls of so much per vehicle, or per wheel. In the end they devised a system in which the toll varied according to weight, width of wheels, and whether the load was spread over a trailer. Perhaps their system was too complicated, for it, too, might have required an accountant at every gate. But the situation never arose.

Despite the fact that this Committee of 1831 were of the opinion that 'the substitution of inanimate for animal power, in draught on common roads is one of the most important improvements in the means of internal communication ever introduced; its practicability ... fully established', no one took much notice of their Report and mechanized transport on roads seemed doomed to sink quietly into oblivion, crushed by heavy tolls, railway efficiency, and the opposition of coaching and farming interests.

Before leaving this brief account of the first attempts at mechanized road transport it is worthwhile noticing that when the road vehicle pioneers made their short bid for supremacy they used devices which were all copied later. Differentials, 'change-speed' gears and Ackerman steering were all developed by then. The propeller-shaft, or Cardan shaft, as it was then called (after a sixteenth-century Italian physician), with its universal joint had been used on some vehicles; and Hancock had tried out a front-wheel drive.[13]

So the years rolled on. In the crowded and growing towns the dark mills kept men, women and children alike, hard at work from before dawn until the darkness of the night hid their tired faces as they plodded their weary way homeward. The produce of their labours was carried to every part of the country by the triumphant railways; the operations being carried on with such pride by the most superior of working-class beings, the engine drivers and firemen, the stationmasters, goods agents and their cohorts of porters. Trains, too, carried everyone who was anyone about the country on business, pleasure, social duty or whatever their object was. Even Her Majesty herself was at last, persuaded to ride behind a steam engine; and the trains carried large numbers of people who were no one in particular.

But however hopefully people journeyed, however fast the freight moved, sooner or later it arrived – at a railway station. From there to their eventual destination people might walk if it were not too far. Otherwise they had to resort to road transport – a horse or horse-drawn vehicle. For freight there was no such choice. Road transport had to be provided; and so, when the smoke of the train had long since disappeared behind the hill, the station yard echoed to the cry of the carter, the stamping and whinnying of bewildered horses, the clatter of cart-wheels. Then came the heavy panting as the loads were hauled out of the yard and away to the mill, the factory, or through quiet country lanes to the farm.

But new sounds were echoing in the farmyards. Steam power was being applied to the heavy annual tasks of ploughing and of threshing the grain crop. Farmers did not usually own these steam-engines. They contracted with the owners to have the job done, and after the harvest threshing was done at one farm the steam-engine and the threshing machine were hauled away by a couple of horses to the next farm down the road. Inevitably people like Thomas Aveling thought of using steam power for both purposes. If it could be used for turning the wheels of the thresher could it not also be used for moving the whole apparatus from farm to farm? Indeed it could, and just exactly how was shown by Ransom and May of Ipswich when they won a prize with their self-propelling engine at an agricultural show at Bristol in 1842.[14] Although steam was initially applied to agricultural tasks, ploughing and threshing, and then to moving the apparatus around – 'portable', then 'self-propelling' – it was only a short step from that to the idea of hauling things generally, and more and more frequently true 'traction-engines' were being used.

Farmers were suspicious, though. Such engines were dangerous in the farmyard, with so much straw and dry grain around. There could easily be a fire; and the engines scared the animals or sank into soft ground. But animals got used to the engines. Care was taken to avoid fire; and as for sinking into soft ground, Boydell patented his 'endless railway' – great flat plates attached to the wheels so that the engines lumbered along as if on gigantic snow-shoes. The invention was unsatisfactory, being noisy, for one thing, and the plates were always breaking. Then it was discovered that wider wheels than usual fitted with strakes – diagonal bars across the width – would do all that was necessary. So the traction engine came into being, with its horizontal ('locomotive-type') boiler, flywheel, and pulley wheel for driving the farm machinery. Though none of these machines were at the Great Exhibition of 1851, within ten years they were becoming a common sight on the roads as firms such as Aveling, Burrell, Garrett, and Clayton & Shuttleworth began to perfect them. By the end of the 1850s a number of engines designed by and built for William Bray of Folkestone, for example, were in use. By the reported accounts of these it would appear that they were particularly useful for really heavy work that might have been difficult for horse teams. Much detail of these early engines and their jobs is recorded in *A Century of Traction Engines* by W.J. Hughes. We learn from that, for example, the interesting facts that as early as 1862 Aveling were supplying engines to a copper mine in Australia and to the Argentine, and that engines fitted with skis as well as wheels were going to Russia.

Quite a number of engines were on display at the Great Exhibition of 1862. Things were developing fast and Parliament by now had decided to intervene. Perhaps it was due to pressure from horse-breeding or horsedrawn-haulage interests, for steam was proving economical; perhaps it was because of awareness of the weight and speed of steam trains on rails; perhaps it was because of accidents such as Mr Hughes describes (when part of a roadway in Greenwich – being over cellars – subsided as an engine was passing over it). Whatever the reason, Parliament thought it was time to control the operations of the growing number of steam traction engines.

In 1861 the Locomotive Act was passed, imposing restrictions on this growing form of transport. The requirements in the Act were the first of an ever-growing volume of legislation about the construction or use of road haulage vehicles, though the small number of clauses in that Act might look like child's play to the modern transport manager. Tyres had to be 3 inches wide for the first 3 tons' weight of the engine, plus a further 1 inch for each ton above that. If a trailer were hauled, the minimum tyre width of the locomotive had to be 9 inches. A special licence had to be obtained from the surveyor in charge of the stretch of road concerned if the engine were more than 7 feet wide or weighed over 12 tons. Two lights were to be displayed at night – one on either side at the front; and the owner's name and the weight of the locomotive had to be shown. These were ordinary enough requirements, but there was worse to come.

Section 8 of the Act was a simple-looking requirement that every locomotive was to 'be constructed on the Principle of consuming and so as to consume its own smoke'. (Concern for the environment did not first arise in the 1980s.) This requirement had already been imposed thirty years earlier by the Directors of the Liverpool and Manchester Railway when laying down the specifications for the locomotives that would be tried out in the Rainhill competition.[15] Anyway, this was a near impossibility in the state of manufacturing and design techniques of the time (not to say anything of modern techniques!). A fine of £5 was incurred for every day on which an engine not meeting this requirement was used. There were other clauses, too, which gave the operator an uncomfortable time; if he were willing, that is, to take the risk of a fine for allowing his engine to produce smoke.

Section 5 provided that if the Secretary of State were of the opinion that the 'use of locomotives generally or of any particular description is dangerous or inconvenient to the public in certain districts or places', he could prohibit their use by an Order. Inconvenient!! If the Secretary of State did not wish to do anything about it the surveyor of the district perhaps could. Section 6 of the Act provided that it was illegal for

> the owner or driver of a locomotive to drive it over any suspension bridge, or over any bridge on which a conspicuous notice has been placed by the authority of the Surveyor or persons liable to the repair of the bridge, that the bridge is insufficient to carry weights beyond the Ordinary traffic of the District, without previously obtaining the consent of the Surveyor.

Even if the Surveyor or persons liable to the repair of the bridge were inclined to allow the locomotive to cross the bridge concerned, the driver had to take very good care to see that he did not damage the bridge; otherwise Section 7 might put him out Of business. This Section said that any damage due to the locomotive or its wagons passing over or coming into contact with the bridge or its supports had to be made good, or compensation paid for any 'obstruction, interruption or delay ... to any person'. If that were not bad enough the owner would have to make good 'all losses and expenses ... sustained or incurred ... by railways, vessels using streams or canals, proprietors of Turnpikes' – indeed, anyone – who suffered loss as a result of the damage.

So Parliament, by a few simple-looking clauses, provided that it would be technically almost impossible for steam locomotives to run on the roads; and that if they did they would be subject to restrictions which did not apply to wagons drawn by horses, however heavy those wagons might be. If this were not already enough, road locomotives might be made uneconomic for, by Section 9, at least two persons had to be there to drive and conduct the locomotive. If more than two wagons were being hauled, a third man had to be present to see to those. Finally, Section 11 limited the speed to 10 m.p.h. in the country and 5 m.p.h. in towns.

Perhaps Parliament, by all these restrictions, was trying to make amends for Section 1 of the Act, in which they had tried to ameliorate the lot of the engine-owners by relating the tolls charged on steam engines to those on horse-drawn vehicles. Each 2 tons of the locomotive weight was to be treated as equal to each horse of a wagon. In the case of trailers drawn by the engine, the charge for each two wheels was not to exceed the charge for 'two horses drawing any wagon'. Having saved the operator from wildly excessive charges for tolls, Parliament had apparently panicked and balanced the thing by imposing the various restrictions outlined above.

In view of this Act, it is not clear whether Parliament realized that traction engines might be, or might become, useful. The Earl of Caithness, in proposing a Second Reading of the Bill in the House of Lords, sounded almost favourable. He described how he had recently seen the crank-shaft for the *Black Prince* drawn from Mr Penn's factory by one of Mr Bray's engines. The total gross weight was 38 tons, yet a single engine did the job with ease. Had horses been used, a great number of animals with their attendants would have been needed. The Duke of Montrose, on the other hand, did not seem to be bothered by the proceedings at all. He thought that there was not much probability of these locomotives coming into general use.[16] *Hansard* does not record whether he was smiling cynically as he gave this opinion.

The good duke was clearly wrong, however. Businessmen have an awkward way of persisting with their business, and they did want their freight moved. Parliament was obliged to return to the attack with the notorious 'Red Flag' Act of 1865, even though the Earl of Hardwick, moving the Second Reading in the Lords, complained that the Secretary of State had been appealed to so frequently to exercise his powers under the 1861 Act that 'a valuable mode of traction was now almost entirely put a stop to'. In the debates on both Bills many of their Lordships apparently thought favourably of steam haulage, but yet Acts were passed imposing crippling restrictions on its operation.

The 'red flag' provision of the Locomotive Act, 1865, is known to everyone – how a man had to walk in front of every locomotive with a red flag in his hand to warn road users of the approach of these dangerous engines –

but it is perhaps worthwhile to quote a few more passages from the Act to make it clear that the red flag requirement was by no means the only, or the worst, imposition. Section 3 starts off by stipulating that at least three persons had to be employed to drive or conduct the locomotive – so the man with the red flag was clearly additional to the two men required under the 1861 Act. The requirement of that Act of another person to look after the wagons if there were more than two was re-enacted in the 1865 Act, so there could be as many as four people in all. The Act then goes on:

> Secondly, one of such Persons, While any locomotive is in motion, shall precede such Locomotive on Foot by not less than sixty yards, and shall carry a Red Flag constantly displayed, and shall warn the Riders and Drivers of Horses of the Approach of such Locomotives, and shall signal the driver thereof when it shall be necessary to stop, and shall assist Horses, and Carriages drawn by Horses, passing the same ... No steam shall blow off when the Locomotive is on the road; ... Every such Locomotive shall be instantly stopped, or the person preceding the same, or any other person with a Horse, or Carriage drawn by a Horse, putting up his hand as a Signal to require such Locomotive to be stopped,

(Well, that's a bit worse than having to stop at the request of a policeman or a vehicle examiner.)

Parliament was clearly jealous of the Secretary of State's power to prohibit the use of road locomotives in certain cases under the 1861 Act, so they now repealed that section. They gave the same power to people at the local level. (How different from legislation of recent years.) In Section 4 of the 1865 Act speed limits were now reduced to 4 m.p.h. in the country and 2 m.p.h. in any 'City, Town or Village' and Section 8 added a bit more trouble for the operators. That section provided that the Court of the Lord Mayor and Aldermen of the City of London, the Metropolitan Board of Works, and Borough Councils, if the borough had over 5000 people, could restrict the times during which locomotives could pass through their areas. This restriction had to be advertised in some newspaper circulating within the jurisdiction of the council. The Act, however, made one small concession. The maximum width could now be 9 feet and the maximum weight 14 tons, subject to certain conditions about the wheels. It looks as if the traction engines were becoming bigger and more powerful.

There would seem to be no doubt that Parliament – and the people in general, for that matter – were afraid that steam locomotives on roads would frighten horses, perhaps causing them to bolt and injure people or damage their loads; and after all there were large numbers of horses around at the time. The House of Commons chose to ignore Mr Henley when he told them, during the Committee Stage of the Bill, that only low-bred horses became timid on seeing these locomotives. High-bred horses possessed pluck enough to go ahead.[17] Mr Henley may well have been wrong as to the reasons for high-bred horses going ahead. Maybe it was simply that their high-bred owners knew enough about the law to hold up their hands and stop the approaching steam engines.

Parliament clearly did not imagine that the 1865 Act was the last word on the subject, for they did not make the Act a permanent one. It was to last for two years initially – possibly on a 'wait-and-see' basis. Then it was extended for a further year by the Expiring Laws (Continuance) Act, 1867. After that a series of these Acts, year by year, continued the 1865 Act in force right through till 1878, when Parliament had another look at the problem. It was not merely the Red Flag Act which was extended in this manner. The 'Continuance' Acts, in a few brief sentences, merely stated that the Acts listed in the Schedule attached would continue in force until a date mentioned. The Schedules generally listed half a dozen or more Acts and included the 1865 Act. But debate on these seems to have been absolutely minimal, no more than the necessary formalities for getting a chore attended to. Not even an attempt in 1871 to have the Red Flag requirement repealed disturbed the calm of Parliament through these years.

The Highways and Locomotives (Amendment) Act, 1878 consolidated the legislation and made a few changes. Perhaps the most interesting of these is that the Act dispensed with the need for the man walking in front of the locomotive to carry a red flag. Motoring enthusiasts nearly always hail the 1896 Act as the one that got rid of the red flag requirement, but in fact the 1878 Act did it. (Admittedly it has been stated that some local authorities reimposed the red flag rule through their own bye-laws. That has not been researched by this writer.) There still had to be the man walking in front, however, even if Section 29 reduced the distance the man had to be ahead from 'not less than sixty yards' to 'at least twenty yards'.

But if there was some gain to the operators in this respect there were other sections which imposed new burdens. There was Section 32, for instance, which empowered county councils to make, alter or repeal by-laws for granting annual licences within the county. The maximum fee for the licence was to be £10 and, needless to say, that was what was charged. This licensing system did not apply to locomotives used for agricultural purposes. The worst feature of it, however, was that a county council, in issuing a licence for £10, was only authorizing the use of the locomotive within that county. If the operator wished to go into an adjoining county he had to get a licence there too.

The section which seems most unfair, and which gave most trouble in subsequent years was Section 23:

> Where by the certificate of their surveyor it appears to the Authority ... that having regard to the average expenses of repairing highways in the neighborhood, extraordinary expenses have been incurred ... in repairing

> such highway by reason of the damage caused by excessive weight passing along the same, or extraordinary traffic thereon, such Authority may recover in a summary manner from any person by whose order such weight or traffic has been conducted, the amount of such expenses ... [and the Section went on to provide] that any person against whom expenses are or may be recoverable ... may enter into an agreement with such authority ... to pay them a composition in respect of such weight or traffic.

The net result of this was that so long as the authority maintained the road sufficiently well to cater for the normal traffic of the district, it need make no provision whatever to enable the roads to bear the occasional engine. Indeed, almost as a matter of course traction engines with their loads would be assumed to be of excessive weight or to be 'extraordinary traffic' and their owners would be asked to pay substantial sums to make good the road damage. The owners complained that not only were they expected to make good the damage they caused, but also that councils would often let roads deteriorate and when the odd engine happened to come along the owner would be expected to pay for bringing the road up to a reasonable standard.

As the number of traction engines increased towards the end of the century the owners, and their Association – the National Association of Traction Engine Owners and Users – argued strongly that their engines were not 'extraordinary traffic' and that roads should be brought up to standards sufficiently high to accommodate this 'usual' traffic. Later they were joined by the Commercial Motor Users' Association and the Automobile Club in their fight for better roads. It is not surprising that these very heavy engines did cause damage to the roads at times for even the cyclists formed an organization which, among other things, was to campaign to get roads fit to carry them! Another cause of grievance to the traction-engine owners was that nobody ever seemed to bother to claim for repairs from owners of horse-drawn wagons. These were considered 'normal' whatever their weight.

Although it was traction-engines that suffered under these three Acts of Parliament – for there was no other mechanical transport on the roads at the time the Acts were passed – it should be noted that the rather circular definition of a locomotive in the 1878 Act covered anything mechanical. According to this a locomotive was 'a locomotive propelled by steam or by other than animal power'. Well, a locomotive is a locomotive, undoubtedly, but the mention of propulsion 'by other than animal power' could cover, as someone subsequently pointed out, bicycles or tricycles propelled by small electric or petrol motors. That form of transport, strictly, would have needed the man walking in front, the £10 licence fee and all the rest. The position, then, in the last quarter of the nineteenth century was that any mechanical transport whatever was subject to a heavy burden of legislation. In summary: at least three persons to manage the vehicle, one to be 20 yards in front ready to stop the vehicle on the sight of a horse, a licence fee of £10 in each county, maximum weight of 14 tons, minimum tyre widths, maximum speed only a walking pace, the vehicle to emit no smoke, powers in the hands of the County Council to regulate the use of mechanical vehicles, for example the hours when they might be used, possible prohibition of movement over certain bridges, liability for damage to bridges and for losses ensuing to railway companies, canal companies and so on, and, liability to compensate road authorities who had to make good damage caused by the mechanical transport.

All this might well have kept motor transport of passengers and goods off the roads, preventing the motor age from ever dawning. (In the language of the time 'motor' included steam engines.) The advantages of mechanized road haulage were clearly considerable, however, and by the 1890s it was clearly time to move forward.

Yet, if the politicians from the mid-century onward took little interest in mechanical road transport, other than to attempt to suppress it, presumably quite happy that the great British invention – the railways – and the great British friend – the noble horse – could cope with all the country's transport needs, there were others who were not so sure. Indeed, one way or another, there was a fair amount of dissatisfaction with the railways. Freight was often delayed or damaged, the charges were often considered to be too high, and when people complained to the companies they were often very high-handed in their replies.

A considerable public outcry arose, indeed, over the matter of railway rates. Even in those days of the market economy the State was well aware of the monopolistic position held by the railways, so that right from the beginning railways had been subjected to a great deal of controlling legislation. The latest of many Acts – one in 1888 – had set out the basis for the maximum rates that railways could charge, and these were generally above the rates that were, in fact, then being charged. On the passing of the Act the railways had to set about preparing new rate books to show separately for each class of goods and for each of some seven thousand stations in the kingdom the maximum rates chargeable from the given station to every other one. This required an examination of many thousands of special rates that had been in operation before the 1888 Act. The companies were quite unable to perform this mammoth task by the stipulated date from which the new rates were to apply, so they took the simple way out – they cancelled all the special rates and applied the maximum allowed by Parliament right across the board, thus increasing most rates. There was a tremendous howl of rage, or panic, from industrial, commercial and agricultural interests.

Parliament hurriedly resolved that the revised rates which had come into operation at the beginning of 1893 were prejudicial to the railways' customers and the general interests of the country. They appointed a Select Committee and the outcome was another Act of Parliament. This came into effect in August 1894 and provided that where a railway company had raised its rates since 31 December 1892 and a trader complained that the increase was unreasonable, the railway was required to justify the increase. (Even if it was an increase within the limits set down by Parliament!). One problem was that, in those days of neither radio nor television, news was slow to travel and not many people seemed to know that they could object to the increases. The date originally set by which complaints had to be made – 25 February 1895 – had to be twice extended. Whatever the original reasons or outcome, the whole episode was scarcely calculated to endear the railways to their customers.

Another area where the relationships were soured was in respect of the rates quoted for the carriage of goods imported into Britain. People generally regarded these as being definitely preferential to the foreigner as compared to the British producer. The railways might, and did, argue that the foreigners provided the goods in full wagon-loads, better packed, and going straight through from a port to a large city. This was cheaper to handle than the small baskets from the British farmers picked up by stopping trains at many small country stations. The complaints persisted, though, and we see many comments such as those by Mr Aubrey Spencer, an Assistant Commissioner, in a report to the Royal Commission on Agriculture. 'Everywhere railway rates are complained of', he wrote, 'both because they are too high, and because railway companies unduly favour the foreign producer'.[18]

There is no doubt that the British farmer was having a rather rough time. Since the 1870s a flood of wheat and meat from the American prairies had poured into the country. Railways had opened up these new lands and as the West developed, exports to Britain increased, the British consumer benefiting from the lower prices and the British farming industry suffering a long and agonizing depression. The Royal Commission on Agriculture had been set up to study the problem, and much of the evidence to the Commission indicates how acutely aware was the farming community of the low railway rates afforded to already cheap imports while local produce usually had to pay much higher rates. It was claimed, for example, that grain could be hauled 1600 miles overland by rail in America and then carried 3000 miles by sea to Liverpool, all for 11½d. a bushel (a measure of capacity equal to 8 gallons) or less than a British farmer would pay to send his grain to Liverpool from 200 miles away.[19] A Mr Berry told the Commission that in his opinion the high railway rates were an important factor among the causes of the depression in agriculture. Another Assistant Commissioner, Mr Hunter Pringle, reported[20] that bitter complaints were raised against the excessive rates and he gave several instances of ill-proportioned charges as between long and short distances, as follows:

Rate on corn

		s. d.	
Cardiff to Birmingham	110 miles	8 4	per ton (41p)
Cambridge to Birmingham	110 miles	12 6	per ton (62½p)
Isham to Birmingham	60 miles	8 4	per ton (41p)
Rate on 4-ton lots of potatoes			
Boston to London	128 miles	10 2	per ton (51p)
Sandy to London	48 miles	7 6	per ton (37½p)

The Times reported on 31 January 1895 that the previous day 'an influential deputation representing farmers and merchants' had seen Mr Bryce, President of the Board of Trade, 'to complain of the high railway rates upon agricultural produce'. Mr Bryce's reply shows the tone of the time. 'If they could make any suggestion as to what could be done to relieve agriculture, short of interfering with the free trade policy of the country, the government would listen to it with pleasure and attention.' The government would not do anything about railway rates apart from specifying maximum charges, and as yet there was no alternative form of transport to turn to.

Even the man in the street – or at least the gentleman in the country estate – joined in the protests. A Lt General Drury-Lowe wrote from Bath to *The Times* complaining that rail charges were often more than the value of the goods. A bill which he had just received asked him to pay as follows:

Coal	7T. 13	@ 8s. 3d. per ton (41p)	£3 3 1 (£3.15)
Rail carriage		@ 11s. per ton (55 p)	£4 4 2 (£4.21)
			Total £7 7 3 (£7.36)

This coal was carried by rail from Denby Colliery (near Derby) to Rowland Castle on the London and South Western Railway.[21]

So the complaints went on about both passenger and freight service and charges, and the railways, safely monopolistic, were often loftily indifferent in their replies. The railways had plenty of pins pricking them. There was the Mansion House Association of traders and agricultural interests, whose chairman could say, in May 1895, that since they were formed as an association they had had one continuous struggle with the railway companies.[22] There was the Railway Reform Association which, in its annual meeting in January 1895, called for nationalization and reform of the railways on the grounds that 'cheap carriage for goods is essential to enable us to compete with other countries' and 'to protect trading, productive, and industrial interests against sudden and arbitrary increases in rates or fares'. Nationalization, they estimated, would save the nation over £40 millions per annum. (This was before the formation of the Labour Party.)[23] There were endless meetings, like that of the Derbyshire Farmers' Association, in January 1895, in which speakers stressed the need for farmers to unite, as the individual farmer was powerless against companies as large as railway companies.[24] The railways certainly were by far the largest commercial organizations of the time. Not many other companies approached them in size, and it is not surprising that the farmer, the shopkeeper, even the millowner, often felt a sense of frustration in attacking these great mountains, equipped only with their teaspoons. How often must they have wished for some alternative mode of conveyance for their goods!

Railway rates pervaded the whole economy and when a Member of Parliament complained in the House about parcel post charges the trouble emerged as being in railway rates. The member drew attention to the high charges especially for the heavier parcels as compared with other countries. The minister replying for the Post Office said 'the chief difficulty in the way of a reduction in this country lies in the large payments which the Post Office is compelled to make to the railway companies under the agreement made in 1884 which does not expire for several years'.[25] The agreement, in fact, was made under Section 2 of the Post Office Parcels Act of 1882, which required the Post Office to pay to the railways for carriage 55 per cent of the gross revenue obtained for the postage of any parcels carried by rail. In this case, too, the government stuck to its *laissez-faire* philosophy and showed no great desire to intervene.

So widespread was the dissatisfaction during the late 1880s and the 1890s that the railways had, eventually, to take notice. They persuaded a well-known economist of the time, Mr W.M. Acworth, to write a book setting out their side of the argument. He wrote *The Railways and the Traders,* in which he demonstrated the railway case for discrimination between home-produced and foreign-produced goods on the grounds of quantity, packing, length of haul and so on. He did a thorough-going job and showed the causes of the so-called anomalies in rates. But perhaps he missed the whole point. It did not matter whether the farmers and traders had justification for their complaints. So long as they thought they had, they would be dissatisfied – and Mr Acworth did not persuade everyone – and so there would be opportunity for any new form of transport to make inroads on railway traffic.

Whatever Mr Acworth's arguments about the justification for the railway case, there is some evidence that the railways were becoming less economic than they had been. The point was expressed by a Mr Jeffards, writing to *The Times* in April 1895. He asked why British farmers were not able to beat off American competition.

> There is only one answer, and that is that he is handicapped with ancient and expensive methods of handling inland transportation. Modern appliances introduced upon American railways have reduced working expenses 65% from what they were thirty years ago ... while today the working expenses of English lines are, if anything, more than they were thirty years ago.

He then quoted the figures mentioned above about the cost of carrying bulk grain. Perhaps this is not good evidence for it is difficult to compare costs in two countries with their own special circumstances, and in any case he ignored the point that modern appliances could be used for handling bulk commodities but not necessarily for the great variety of items carried by British lines.

Costs had been rising for Britain's railways. The Board of Trade had been enforcing stringent safety requirements – automatic brakes, better signalling, and so on, and this cost money. Wages had been increased recently and this too was adding to the companies' troubles. Further, their arteries were beginning to be clogged up by the sheer volume of traffic carried. The tremendous job of sorting millions of packages and tens of thousands of wagons at great numbers of freight depots and marshalling yards was becoming increasingly difficult, expensive and slow. A carefully considered view of the railways at this time was put forward by E.H. Phelps-Brown and S.J. Handfield-Jones in an article entitled 'The Climacteric of the 1890s', published in *Oxford Economic Papers,* vol.4, 1952. The authors had been seeking causes for the relative decline in Britain's fortunes after the 1890s. In the nineteenth century Britain had been ahead of most nations in most respects, but by the end of the century it was beginning to lose momentum. The authors sought some common factor in the levelling off or decline of British industries in and after the 1890s. 'Such common factors', they wrote (p.282) 'may reasonably be sought in the declining rate of extension at this time of the techniques of power, transport and machinery comprised beneath the name of Steam and Steel.' They had drawn this conclusion after pointing out, amongst other things, that

> Two industries stand out as reaching their highest output per operative early on, and considerably declining thereinafter. The first of these is transport by rail ... the traffic, measured by a combined index of passengers and freight which the railways carried per operative employed reached its maximum in the early seventies and then declined for twenty years. This can scarcely be due to any lack of the economies of scale, for traffic continued to rise faster than the occupied population... The cause must be sought on the opposite side, in diminishing returns; or in the competitive increase of amenities offered to the public or in improvements in the working hours and conditions of work of the railwaymen. (p.275)

Much more recently Professor D. Aldcroft has made the same point about diminishing returns in his book *British Railways In Transition.*

It is perhaps worth suggesting at this stage that the dissatisfaction which traders felt towards the railways in the late nineteenth and early twentieth centuries was a symptom of a much wider and unseen malaise that pervaded many parts of British industry. Just as the railways were handling a very considerable volume of traffic but suffering behind the scenes from diminishing returns, so, too, were many other sectors of British industry slipping in relative terms. Perhaps mesmerized by being first in the field in so many ways and having become the 'workshop of the world', perhaps content with ever-growing output and exports, perhaps satisfied with earning a very comfortable living, some of Britain's industrial leaders lost sight of what was happening elsewhere. They did not see that countries like Germany and the United States had overtaken Britain in output in a number of industries. More to the point, British industrialists did not seem to notice the new techniques and inventions that were giving other countries the edge. Indeed, in some cases, the British attitude was one of resistance to new ideas. Sidney Pollard, in the first few pages of his book *The Development of the British Economy, 1914–1967*, writes of the relative stagnation or backwardness of some of Britain's industry. Fortunately the picture was never completely gloomy and there was still much life in the old dog. There were go-ahead entrepreneurs and thriving activity also described by Pollard. Amongst these was the road haulage industry.

If the hardening of the railway arteries gave opportunity for new transport to evolve, there was a further factor in the general need for transport in rural areas. This crops up repeatedly in evidence given to the Royal Commission on Agriculture. Farms were often isolated, and much of their production had to go to the nearest railway station, be it three or four or perhaps ten miles distant. It was all very well, the farmers knew, to talk of the great network of railways over the country and that no place was more than ten miles, or whatever, distance from a station. But we can sympathize with the farmer who wrote to *The Times* in January 1895 with a cry from the heart about the cost of carting 2000 tons of potatoes to his nearest station, six miles away. There had been a great deal of talk about building light railways through these rural areas to link remote villages and farms to main-line stations. Costs of construction and operation of ordinary railways, to the very high safety standards laid down by the Board of Trade with Parliament's blessing, were prohibitive, and there was insufficient traffic in sparsely populated areas to justify the expenditure by the main-line railway companies. So it was considered that 'light railways', built to much less rigorous standards, might help. After all, they had been moderately successful in France, Belgium, Ireland and other places. However, to build railways at lower standards required the express authority of a new Act of Parliament.

The Board of Trade called a conference of interested parties early in December 1894, from which a committee was set up to report in detail. This committee, in due course, reported that

1. Railway development in rural districts was hindered by antiquated and unnecessary restrictions, both legislative and administrative.
2. The work of investigating and sanctioning new railway lines of purely local interest should be transferred to the county councils.

The Board of Trade also called for *Reports from Her Majesty's Representatives Abroad on Light Railways,* which were duly published under that title. The Royal Agricultural Society, too, had been busy, issuing 11,500 copies of a circular asking its members what benefits would arise from the construction of light railways in their districts. Perhaps, surprisingly, only 420 replies were received, but from these the Society compiled and submitted to the Board of Trade Committee a *Memorandum on the Light Railway Requirements of Rural Districts.* These were all in favour of the construction of light railways.[26]

Despite this apparent unanimity, however, there were occasional voices putting forward other ideas. We find *The Times* report on the Council Meeting of the Central Association of Chambers of Agriculture on 5 February 1895 saying 'A long discussion ensued ... while some members of the Council warmly advocated light railways, others spoke in favour of steam trams and haulage by traction engines.' A little later a gentleman who signed himself 'Road Loco' entered the debate. In response to a correspondent who discussed the difficulty of collecting farm produce into bulk lots, he wrote to *The Times* (10 September 1895)

> The use of steam on common roads is growing in many districts. ... A service of steam road locomotives making regular rounds among farmers ... would go a great way towards helping farmers send regular supplies to ... large provision merchants. ... By using the right wagons the produce would be loaded at the farmyard and not touched until unloaded at the shop door.

(There was the vision of the twentieth century transport revolution.) He went on, 'Those who make use of the much abused traction engine find it eminently useful and doing their work at a much lower cost than could be done by railways.'

But most people put their faith in railways, and in the Queen's Speech in February 1895 the government announced their intention of submitting a bill to facilitate the construction of light railways. After repeated requests by Members of Parliament, the Bill was eventually introduced on 24 April.[27] Under the Bill any proposal for a light railway would have to be submitted to the appropriate county or county borough council. If the council thought a *prima facie* case existed for such a railway, they would set up a sub-committee which would examine the proposal in detail and before whom objectors and sponsors would argue their cases. If the council accepted the scheme, then it would go to the Board of Trade which would examine it in regard to

1. Length or importance – for it was not the intention of the government to deprive Parliament of its right to oversee major railway construction.
2. Safety
3. Protection of landowners who might object to compulsory purchase of their land.

There was to be no financial assistance from the government and councils were not to subsidize such railways from the rates. Farmers had, in fact, argued very strongly that in their financial position they would not be able to face rate increases.

Lower constructional standards would be permitted, and it was hoped that the construction costs would be no more than £3000–£3500 per mile as compared with the £10,000 or so which a light railway would cost under existing legislation and compared with the £50,000 per mile for main-line railways at the time. All went well until, in the Second Reading on 10 June, a Mr Strachey moved a proposal which almost proved the death knell of the Bill. Light railways were subsidized in Ireland (then entirely ruled from London) but the Bill would not allow subsidies in England. Mr Strachey moved that there should be no subsidies in one without the other. A week later, on 18 June, *The Times* in its 'Political Notes' commented that the government might decide not to proceed with the Bill. Pressure had been brought to bear on Mr Strachey not to take his amendment to a division. So far, no compromise had been arranged and it was believed that rather than risk a trial of strength on the issue, the government would drop the Bill. The minister declined to give a pledge that English light railways would be subsidized like the Irish and Scottish. That was nearly the end of the Bill. The debate on Mr Strachey's amendment was adjourned at midnight in deference to a rule of the House and it was months before it was revived.

The Act passed later that year, however, provided the framework which allowed the construction, over the next twenty years or so, of 468 lines totalling 2352 miles. These lines were anything between one and twenty miles in length and were variously worked by horse, steam, electricity or by oil engines. An example of a freight line lay on a farm of 900 acres adjacent to Littleworth station on the Peterborough–Boston branch of the G.N. Railway. There was a line of just over two miles to the station and a 'branch' line of one mile. This light railway handled some 5000 tons of farm produce or farm supplies per annum. The *Twenty-third Annual Report of the Light Railway Commissioners*, in January 1920, to the newly founded Ministry of Transport, from which these facts are taken, also tells us that though the Act had provided

£1 million for 'advances' for the construction of light railways, in fact only some £400,000 was taken up. This may, perhaps, be indicative of a serious deficiency of light railways – that they are very specific to the particular place and so are rather inflexible. It may be that people preferred to put their money into the new, flexible, form of transport which began in this period.

So, the scene was set. The railways were becoming firm in their monopolistic ways; their lines and goods sheds were becoming congested, their costs were rising for various reasons. The little bit of enterprise then being shown was in the 'Race to the North'; but while the companies would have preferred the public to concentrate on the speeds being achieved by the passenger expresses, the vociferous part of the public, the London commuters, were outdoing each other in letters to *The Times* about lower and lower average speed records being set in the 'Crawl to the South'. From the point of view of this book, however, the important aspect was in many parts of the country traders were uneasy with existing modes of transport of goods or, so far as farmers were concerned, a virtual absence of services. Whether it was rates, or delays, in straightforward cases, or in the charges, or damage occurring at frequent transhipments, or the time taken for roundabout journeys between points that were only a few miles apart across country, there was considerable dissatisfaction. This was always present, although *Commercial Motor* could say 20 years on that 'The railways of this country have served our industries at large much better than it is the rule for traders to admit' (No. 513, 7 Jan. 1915, p.335). But there *were* great gaps in the provision of freight transport. The time was ripe for the new form.

Notes

1. Jackman,W.T., *The Development of Transportation in Modern England.*
2. Ibid., p.62.
3. Ibid., p.307.
4. Select Committee on ... Tolls to be charged ..., 1831, p.11.
5. Chas. St. Clair Davison, *History of Steam Road Vehicles,* p.4.
6. Ibid., p.4.
7. Ibid.
8. Ibid., pp.4 and 5.
9. Ibid., p.6.
10. Ibid., p.34.
11. Ibid., pp.36 and 37.
12. Select Committee on ... Tolls, p.59.
13. Davison, *History,* pp.9–11.
14. Ibid., p.14.
15. Samuel Smiles, *Lives of George and Robert Stephenson,* Folio Society, London, 1975, p.176.

16. Lords 2nd Reading, 1861. Parl. Debates, 3rd Series. Vol. CLXIV p.286.
17. Commons Committee,1865. Vol. CLXXVII, col. 1063.
18. *The Times,* 16/1/1895, p.11.
19. *The Times,* 20/4/1895, p.14, letters.
20. *The Times,* 18/7/1895, p.13.
21. *The Times,* 14/3/1895, p.7.
22. *The Times,* 30/5/1895, p.14.
23. *The Times,* 8/1/1895, p.3.
24. *The Times,* 26/1/1895, p.7.
25. Parl. Debates, 4th Series. Vol. XXXI, Feb–Mar 1895, col. 41.
26. *The Times,* 7/2/1895, p.10.
27. Light Railways Bill, 1895.

CHAPTER TWO

To Fill a Great Void

By the third quarter of the nineteenth century the problem of creating motive power by exploding a mixture in a cylinder, which Huyghens had tinkered with almost two hundred years earlier, had been solved. In 1860 Etienne Lenoir patented a gas engine. Then, when in 1876 Dr Otto patented his four-stroke cycle, the way was open for the application of the engine to transport purposes. Carl Benz made a three-wheeled car in 1885 and the next year Gottlieb Daimler built a four-wheeler. From then onward there could be no holding back the progress of internal-combustion engines, and speed records were quickly made and broken, going from a Peugeot clocking up 11.5 m.p.h. in 1894 to a Darracq achieving 104.5 m.p.h. just ten years later. Steam was still the recognized agent of mechanical power, however, and developments were made in that direction, too. As late as 1902 Serpollet held the world's land-speed record of 75.06 m.p.h. (=120.1 km per hour) (over 1 km) with a steam car. Whether steam, or internal combustion, or electric, in the mid-1890s the developments in applying non-animal power to carriages were nearly all taking place on the Continent, where there was no restrictive legislation such as the British, a nation of horse-lovers, had imposed on mechanical transport. Many people found this very odd indeed. Even Edison commented on the fact that the development ought to have been British – a great industrial and engineering country had tied its own hands with restrictive legislation and had let the lead go to France.

So far had things progressed in that country that they were able to hold a road race for cars from Paris to Rouen in 1894. This was won by a de Dion–Bouton steam car. In the next year petrol-driven vehicles had their revenge and in a much longer race from Paris to Bordeaux the steam carriages were beaten convincingly. Since there was a fair amount of coming and going of diplomats, politicians and wealthy classes generally between England and France, news of these vehicles soon got around. Carriages propelled by petrol or gas engines, by electricity or steam, were more and more frequently encountered in the streets of Paris and on the roads to country estates. In due course Parliament in London had its attention drawn to what was going on, and a not inconsiderable number of influential people started to agitate for the repeal of the Acts which practically prohibited the use of mechanically propelled vehicles in Britain.

Letters began to appear in the leading newspapers. Here and there a strong character imported his new car from France and ignored the law, though sometimes it overtook him as he chugged along at 15 m.p.h.; he was subsequently fined. Sir David Salomons, Mayor of Tunbridge Wells, organized a 'Horseless Carriage Exhibition' in the Agricultural Showground there on Tuesday 15 October 1895. Six vehicles were advertised as taking part, including one of the type that had won the Paris-Bordeaux race. Salomons's poster, somewhat apologetically, stated that 'Every effort has been made to collect as many carriages as possible, but as the few which are in use are widely scattered, it is very difficult to obtain the loan of them, but the carriages exhibited fairly illustrate the development of this means of locomotion to the present date.' Just in case any spectators were disappointed, he added a remark that 'The ground selected for this Exhibition being soft, the trial is scarcely fair, since the carriages travel admirably on a hard road.'[1]

Interest was generated, too, by the publication of a new periodical, *The Autocar*, in November 1895. In a sense this points to the growing interest since the publishers clearly felt that there would be a sufficient market for a magazine on 'horseless' carriages. The next month Salomons, again demonstrating his active interest, played a big part in the founding of a 'Self-Propelled Traffic Association' which was 'to deal with a subject which closely affects agriculture, trade and private interests'.[2]

It must not be assumed that the authorities had dug in their heels and were resisting to the last the encroachment of modern times. Far from it. A Bill to ease the stranglehold of legislation had been introduced by the Government in the House of Commons on 17 June 1895, and the Government had already had discussions with bodies concerned, such as the County Councils Association. That Association, however, had wanted more time to think about it, so the Bill did not contain any very complex clauses, or, for that matter, many clauses at all. The detail would come later, when people saw how it was all working out in practice and what difficulties were arising. In fact the Bill contained only one clause. That simply said that none of the restrictive legislation would apply to vehicles under 2 tons in weight. Such vehicles would have to pay only the normal taxes that all carriages were subject to as a matter of course.

The effect of this Bill would have been to distinguish quite clearly between light private cars on the one hand and traction engines on the other. (There was, as yet, no other category.) But it is certain that the 2 ton limit would have been a major deterrent in the way of the development of vehicles for freight haulage, such as steam lorries and petrol lorries, which became common within the next ten years. This particular aspect was not even mentioned in the House of Commons. Certainly, Mr Shaw Lefevre, introducing the Bill, gave no indication that such a thing as freight existed at all. He was more concerned to save private cars from the inevitable criticism. These carriages, he said, were completely under command, and horses were not frightened by them any more than by ordinary traffic.

The First Reading of a bill is very much a formality since discussion of the Bill's purpose takes place on the Second Reading and the wrangling over detail in the Committee Stage. But this particular Bill never got to a Second Reading although a date had been fixed for it. It was swept away when Lord Rosebery's government resigned just after the First Reading. It was not over this particular Bill that the Government resigned, but on one about ammunition for the forces. Locomotive or motor-car bills were certainly not so important as to cause a government to fall. The outgoing Prime Minister, Rosebery, was then able to go and give his full attention to raising good horse flesh. (His horse had won the Derby that year.) When the new Parliament opened after a general election the Conservatives under Lord Salisbury had displaced the Liberals; but that made no difference so far as 'Locomotives on Highways' were concerned, for transport was not, mercifully, a matter of party politics at that time. Nobody bothered to mention it in the Queen's Speech, nor in the subsequent debate. It obviously took a degree of priority a long way behind foreign affairs.

Very soon afterwards things began to happen. Formal leave to introduce a bill was given in the Commons on 14 February 1896, just as a deputation from the Self-Propelled Traffic Association was pressing the Local Government Board to have the 1878 Act repealed. The formal First Reading of the new Bill in the Lords on 23 March was followed by the more serious business of the Second Reading on 23 April. Lord Harris explained that pressure had been brought to bear on the late government and the present one, and therefore he, as the mouthpiece of the Local Government Board, had introduced the Bill. With disarming frankness he admitted that they were 'legislating in the dark' as they had no experience of these light locomotives in Britain. It had been thought, he said, that farmers would be able to depend on these light locomotives for the carriage of their goods to the market and they would become practically independent of the light railways or feeder railways then so much talked about. He expressed a cautionary view, though:

> There were enthusiasts who believed that as soon as the law was altered, our whole system of conveyance of persons and goods was to be changed ... that the farmer was going to take his produce to the nearest market town on a wagon with a motor of some sort on it ... [He did] not imagine that these improvements would come as rapidly as enthusiasts suggested.

Lord Clifden pinpointed the need for motor transport facilities in rural areas: 'If the Bill facilitated the transit of farm produce to the market town or railway station it would fill a great void and meet a great want.'

In committee on 19 May, Lord Harris announced that the maximum tare weight would be raised from the 2 tons in the original Bill to 4 tons, thus opening the way for vehicles which could carry a load. Lord Thring wanted a maximum *gross* weight to be inserted but Lord Harris dismissed that by pointing out that the erection of a large number of weighing machines would be necessary all over the country. 'It would be ridiculous to expect carriages carrying persons to be weighed whenever a policeman or someone else demanded it.' The Bill reached the Commons Second Reading on 30 June 1896, and when Sir Henry Chaplin, President of the Local Government Board, gave his opinion that it was even possible that these motor cars might become a rival to light railways, the *Hansard* report of that sentence concluded with the word: [Laughter].

The usual vested interests made their appearance: county ratepayers worried about the cost of road repairs, Irish horsebreeders concerned about the possible elimination of their industry, farmers who thought that motor transport would not do enough for them 'seeing that the cost of one of these machines was £250 and it was bound to break down in a fortnight' (Dr Tanner, Mid-Cork). The Commons, however, did not oppose the measure, though there was a fair amount of discussion about speed limits. The main difficulty, the Members saw, was that in specifying a limit they would be quite unable to take into account all the varying road and traffic conditions so that a general speed limit might be too low for convenience in some cases and too high for safety in others. The summer vacation was approaching, however, so time for discussion on this and other bills was limited. On 14 August Her Majesty signed it as the Locomotives on Highways Act, 1896'.

Though the Act had grown somewhat from the one clause of the original Bill, it was still a fairly short one. Section 1 defined a new category of carriage – a light locomotive – propelled by mechanical power, being under 3 tons unladen (a compromise?) and not used for the purpose of drawing more than one vehicle. This class of locomotive, as with previous categories, was to be 'so constructed that no smoke or visible vapour is emitted therefrom except from any temporary or accidental cause'. The exciting thing, for which many had been campaigning for years, was that this new category was free of all the other restrictive legislation which had so impeded both technical and commercial development. Gone was the requirement that a man should walk in front. Out went the rule about stopping when someone with a horse signalled. No longer would the team of people be required to manage it. Perhaps it was too much to hope that all restrictions would go, for Section 1 did provide that county or county borough councils could still make by-laws to prevent or restrict the use of these light locomotives on any bridge within their area.

The next few clauses were not too onerous. Sections 2 and 3 respectively required a lamp to be attached to the locomotive from an hour after sunset to an hour before sunrise, and the fitting of a bell or other instrument to give an audible warning of approach. The next Section set a speed limit of 14 m.p.h. – or any lesser speed that the Local Government Board might prescribe by regulations. Section 5 made the keeping and use of petrol or other inflammable liquid subject to regulations too. None of this was exceptional, but there followed a clause which may since have caused many a manufacturer or operator to react strongly. Section 6 empowered the Board to make regulations 'with respect to the use of light locomotives on highways, and their construction, and the conditions under which they may be used'. Such regulations could be of a purely local nature if the Department thought fit. If the regulations were not observed the offender could be fined up to £10 under Section 7. Ever mindful of the possibilities of adding to state revenues Parliament wrote into the Act, too, Section 8, providing for new impositions to operate on and after 1 January 1897. The new taxes, which were in addition to those payable by ordinary carriages under an Act of 1888, were:

£2.2.0 (i.e. £2.10) if weight over 1 ton but not over 2
£3.3.0 (i.e. £3.15) if weight over 2 tons but not over 3

The remaining four sections of the Act covered topics such as the application of the Act to Scotland and Ireland, the Short Title, and allowed certain parts of the 1878 Act to be varied by order of the Board. One little sting in this tail was that the Act would not come into operation for three months – not until 14 November 1896. This was presumably to give time to get the 'Regulations' sorted out. When they did emerge, on 9 November 1896, these Regulations contained little that calls for comment except that the maximum speed limit had been reduced to 12 m.p.h. generally, with the added proviso that in no case might a light locomotive go 'faster than was reasonable and proper, having regard to the traffic on the highway'. Given the extra month or two since the Bill had been debated it was inevitable that someone would think of this way to overcome the difficulty of a fixed speed limit. It is interesting to note that neither the Act nor these early Regulations contained anything whatever about licensing or registration of vehicles nor about licences for drivers. Clearly the legislators were entering a new world where much had to be learnt by experience.

'As every schoolboy knows', the effective repeal, so far as light vehicles were concerned, of the notorious 'Red Flag Act' was a matter for celebration. The Motor Car Club, already in existence, decided that their form of celebration would be a great run to Brighton of as many cars as could be persuaded to participate. The event was fixed for a date in October, but with an English official's scrupulous regard for the letter of the law, whatever its spirit, the Chief Constable of Sussex refused to allow any anticipation of the change in the law. The Brighton run had, therefore, to wait until the officially decreed date for the Act to come into operation – 14 November.

Not only did the 1896 Act free motorists, but at the same time it allowed light haulage vehicles to operate unencumbered by the previous very severe restrictions. This at once released the talents of several builders and generated interest amongst the many who could benefit from a new mode of transport. Three weeks before the Act became operative, Sir David Salomons, ever active, addressed a meeting inaugurating the public activities of the Liverpool Self-Propelled Traffic Association, a body which was to play a crucial role in the early years of road haulage by lorry.[3] A year later, on 16 November 1897, to be precise, this Association was able to announce that it would conduct trials of commercial freight vehicles the following May. There were to be two classes, carrying respectively a minimum of 2 tons of freight and a minimum of 5 tons. Tests would consist of runs for a minimum distance of 30 miles on each of four successive days, no run being greater than forty miles, and there would be certain hill-climbing and manoeuvring requirements to be checked. The entry fee was 5 guineas and prizes were to be £100, £75 and £50, to be awarded at the discretion of the Judges.

Bearing in mind that up to this time there had been no such thing as manufacturers of commercial freight vehicles (only steam traction-engine builders), and even until fairly recently there were not even car manufacturers, the pioneers should be congratulated for managing to get anything built at all. They were virtually starting from scratch – and without assembly lines – and the six months' notice of the trials proved a little short. Nevertheless ten entries were received; but this may have been an indication of the scramble and the hope, for on the day – the morning of Tuesday, 24 May 1898 – only four vehicles, completed and ready, presented themselves at the starting-point. These were a 2-ton LIFU (Liquid Fuel Engineering Co Ltd, East Cowes) lorry, a 3-ton Thornycroft lorry, a 5-ton, six-wheeled, articulated, Thornycroft, and a 4-ton Leyland lorry. All were steam driven, the LIFU and the Leyland both using oil firing. It may be because steam technology was well known that these vehicles could be presented, whereas the newer, internal-combustion engines were not as easily prepared.[4]

Two circular routes had been chosen in the neighbourhood of Liverpool, each being traversed once in each direction, and this provided 143 miles over a variety of road surfaces which included 'granite sets, boulders [!], macadam, and incidental lengths of other varieties'. The 'macadam' of those days was quite definitely not the 'tarmac' of our times, for there was no tarred binding of the material. The Judges, in their report, commented on 'the imperfections of the common roads' which, they thought, were 'the principal causes of the heavy maintenance and depreciation charges, and of the element of uncertainty which at present attaches to any service of motor vehicles'. Yet the roads during the tests were not at their worst, for the judges, commenting on fuel and water consumption, anticipated that these 'would be very considerably increased when the vehicles have to run over wet, muddy, or exceptionally heavy roads'.

There were tribulations, as might be expected. The LIFU suffered the indignity of having 'a light carriage run into the rear oil tank at stopping point', though, we are told, 'the hole was plugged up'. Worse, the head of the low-pressure cylinder was blown off and the vehicle continued working on the high-pressure cylinder only. Delays were recorded of 'five minutes to despatch telegram respecting damaged cylinder', and 'two minutes delay in raising pressure to climb canal bridge'. (Perhaps it was one of those hump-backed ones.) On the second day the LIFU started late through having to replace the damaged cylinder by a new one but this would have enabled the vehicle to do better than on the first day.

The Thornycroft 'artic', too, had its troubles. A great many minutes were lost here and there getting extra water and attending to the fire. But there were also delays, such as the 12 minutes in which the crew 'removed back valve cover of donkey pump and filed wing of valve'; 'six minutes tightening bolts of gear-case and brake brackets' and the tragic '25 minutes getting out of fallen culvert'. That says something about the road. Eventually the 'artic' had to give it up for the first day because of a loose tyre on the nearside driving wheel. Even the heroic 'cut up a spanner to make rivets' did not save the day, and the vehicle was unable to run during the second day of the trials. Subsequently, when it resumed the battle, it suffered more delays – to take up a fan belt (this fan was to provide forced draught to the firebox), replace chain to pumps, and tighten studs of driving pinions. The Thornycroft lorry, perhaps, fared a little better, though it, too, had trouble with the fan belt and had to have split tubes plugged. What would a vehicle examiner of today make, one wonders, of the three minutes delay 'to tie the brakes, a bolt having fallen out'? The Leyland had trouble with tyres and was unable to finish the run on one of the days.

After studying the observers' notes in the logs in which the above-quoted examples were recorded, the five judges – Sir David Salomons, Mr S.B. Cottrell, Dr H.S. Hele-Shaw, Mr Beverton Redwood and Mr Henry H. West – awarded the First Prize of £100 to the Leyland, the Second Prize of £75 to the LIFU, and the £50 Third Prize to the 3-ton Thornycroft lorry. Though some of the faults and troubles mentioned above might appear, at this distance in time, to suggest that the whole thing was a comic opera, in fact it was a very serious business indeed. The Judges had taken into consideration a great many factors, including:

- Cost – economy of working;
- Control – stopping, starting, changing speed, steering and reversing, particularly under adverse conditions such as on hills or in confined spaces;
- working – noise, smell, visible vapour, dust or other nuisance when

travelling (maybe the ecology/pollution band-wagon was not rolling in those days, but people thought about these things just the same), number of mechanical operations required of the driver, brake efficiency, time occupied in preparing vehicle for the road, distance run without refuelling;

- construction – Strength of frame and working parts, quality of workmanship, freedom from complications or over-refined parts, facility with which repairs could be effected, ratio of 'available' to 'total' platform area, relationship of power of motor to tare weight, ratio of tare weight to freight carried and there were other points specifically concerned with engine efficiency.

The judges noted two other important features in their report. The first of these was that the 3-ton maximum tare imposed by the 1896 Act was a real handicap so far as commercial freight vehicles were concerned. It 'seriously tends to reduce the strength of the working parts and practically precludes the possibility of constructing a really satisfactory motor vehicle capable of carrying five tons and upward, except, perhaps, at such an increase of prime cost as would be commercially prohibitive'. This remark pin-pointed the major fault in the Act, a fault which was to be as crippling to potential road haulage operation as ever the 'Red Flag' was. Fortunately it did not take thirty years to get this impediment removed. The other point was about wheels. The judges, with perception, noted where the trouble lay. 'The form of wheels and tyres adopted by all the manufacturers', they pointed out, 'though probably perfectly efficient as carriers, were all structurally more or less inefficient as drivers.' This plagued manufacturers and customers for quite a few years.[5]

So the first Liverpool Trials, watched with interest by large numbers, including representatives from the War Office and the Post Office, were over: four days of activity to demonstrate the possibilities of the road vehicle, which was destined to change the whole transport scene in Britain. The change was to come, not painlessly, totally and immediately, it is true, nor without mistakes, but inevitably. It is not, perhaps, a matter of great surprise that two of the manufacturers involved in these Trials, who were enterprising enough to 'have a go' right at the beginning, subsequently played a leading role in the production of fine vehicles right through to modern days. Leyland, for example, had been formed as a private company in 1895 – The Lancashire Steam Motor Co. Ltd – and had that year produced a steam van for the Post Office. They had, too, won first prizes with other steam vehicles in the Royal Agricultural Society's trials at Crewe in 1897 (said to be the very first trials of road haulage vehicles)[6] and Birmingham in 1898. This experimental work was in addition to their production of steam lawn-mowers.[7]

The Liverpool Trials cost the Association somewhat more than £3000, of which the entry fees covered under £250. Practically all of the remainder came from private subscriptions, including 100 guineas (£105) each from the Earl of Derby, Sir Alfred L. Jones and Sir David Salomons.[8]

By this time the Automobile Club (later the RAC) was in existence and had organized a show of vehicles, tyres and accessories to take place in Richmond in June 1899. As an additional feature the Club arranged for a trial of freight vehicles to be held shortly beforehand. This consisted of an out and home run along ten miles of the Uxbridge Road, 20 miles in all. The main point here was the appearance of the internal-combustion engine in freight vehicles. By this time it had been extensively employed in what were then called 'pleasure cars'. Of the five vehicles entered, there were two steam lorries – a Thornycroft and a steamer designed by Mr Sidney Straker to carry 3.25 tons. The other three had internal-combustion engines. One of these was a Post Office van, built by Daimler, Coventry on the lines of their heavier touring car, for the chassis of such car was clearly capable of carrying a van body. The other two were German-built Daimlers entered by Mr Frederick Sims, who was then the English agent of the company. Both these were commended by the judges as having performed with conspicuous success and for good manoeuvrability. One of them, a 6-tonner (which carried between 3½ and 5 tons in the trial) ran the 20 miles on 4 gallons of petrol, and the other, carrying 1½–2 tons, did the round trip on 2.75 gallons. The judges, incidentally, included three of the Liverpool Judges – Dr Hele-Shaw, Mr B. Redwood, and Sir David Salomons; another pioneering name, that of Mr E. Shrapnell-Smith (Secretary of the Liverpool Self-Propelled Traffic Association (SPTA), appears with the observers.[9]

A little later that summer the Liverpool SPTA held their second trials, this time in connection with the Annual Show of the Royal Lancashire Agricultural Society.[10] Again ten competitors entered (eleven vehicles in all) but again not all turned up. Only six appeared for the preliminary measurement of the vehicles and checking of the capacity of the tanks on Friday and Saturday, 28 and 29 July 1899. All were steamers, the Leyland and Clarkson vehicles burning liquid fuel.

Hill-climbing and manoeuvring tests were carried out on Monday 31 July over granite sets, cobbles and macadam, with vehicles both light and laden. Vehicles were required to stop on both the ascent and descent of the hills, which had a maximum gradient of 1 in 9 (about 11 per cent). The running tests were carried out over two of the previous routes, a distance of 71.5 miles being run. This time there were four classes, for maximum loads of 2 tons, 3½ tons, 5 tons, and 6½ tons respectively. Thornycrofts came out of these Trials with the two gold medals that were awarded.

The judges reiterated their condemnation of the roads and suggested that if vehicles worked over such roads, about 15 per cent depreciation per annum would have to be provided; that is, just under a seven-year working life for the vehicles. The weight limitations in the prevailing legislation also came under fire again. So far as the vehicles themselves were concerned the judges commended their manoeuvrability – the vehicles could stop sideways on, alongside a platform, within a space of only one-and-a-half times their own length, and the judges had nice things to say about hill-climbing which put motor vehicles at a clear advantage over horses. Many improvements had been made as compared with the 1898 vehicles; for example, in distances run before refuelling, improved fuel consumption, lower first cost, improved ratio of tare to payload, and a better distribution of weight – off the steering and on to the rear axles to give better adhesion.

Official interest was greater than ever. The Local Government Board (LGB), as the Department responsible for roads and road traffic, were represented, and, as before, so were the War Department and the GPO. Officials from some twenty English and Scottish local authorities, from the Mersey Docks and Harbours Board, the Liverpool Chamber of Commerce, the Liverpool Cotton Association, the Liverpool Corn Trade Association, all watched closely. There is no doubt that these latter commercial bodies had a real concern for road transport, whatever justification Acworth had offered a few years earlier for the railway case. Henry Fowler of the Mechanical Engineering side of the Midland Railway was there – as, indeed, he was at all three Liverpool Trials. Whether those present included any of the commercial or operating people from the railways was not recorded, but they were probably there too. Certainly they would have learnt something to their advantage.

The 1898 and 1899 Liverpool Trials had amply shown that the self-contained motor-lorry-carrying goods had inherent merit and a real future. The transport world would never be the same again, though the war against the railways was certainly not yet over; indeed, it had hardly begun. Yet those Trials were the opening shots in a struggle that would go on for decades before road haulage finally won the spoils of the bulk of the nation's freight. But there was still that 3-ton tare limit which the Legislature had imposed in 1896; this, even given the minister's disarming admission of ignorance of motor vehicles, nevertheless was the law. The organizers of the Liverpool Trials wondered whether manufacturers, given plenty of time, could produce worthwhile vehicles within the limit. So another set of trials was arranged for June 1901 with a year's notice of the event.[11] Classes were provided for 4- and 5-ton loads with no maximum tare weight stated. The other two classes were for 1½-ton load, maximum tare 2 tons, and 5-ton load, maximum tare 3 tons.

The routes on this occasion spread out from Liverpool further than formerly, taking in Manchester and Blackburn in the total of 168.5 miles. Honorary local secretaries were appointed to help out at a number of towns en route and Manchester, as befitted an important commercial metropolis, had the honour of a local committee representative of its trading and commercial interests. This Manchester committee included the Lord Mayors of Manchester and Salford as well as top-ranking representatives from a number of commercial firms and bodies such as the Bleachers' Association and the Calico Printers' Association.[12]

A change was made in the loads carried. Whereas in the first trials only gravel ballast had been carried on the lorries and in the second set bags of maize only were loaded up, this third occasion saw a variety of goods made available by Liverpool merchants and shipowners – canned goods, cement, flour, grain, leather, machinery, motor spirit, soap and sugar. On the return journey to Liverpool there was manufactured cotton, blocks and pulleys, paper and spinning machinery. One load of cloth from Manchester was reputed to have been built up to 17½ feet from the ground. The freight carried was a good enough representation of the raw materials and the output of English industry of the time. Two vehicles were entered in Class A (2-ton tare), one in Class B (5-ton load, 3-ton tare), four in Class C (5-ton load, no tare specified), and six in Class D (4-ton load, no tare specified). That there should have been only three vehicles entered in the classes which were within legal limits whilst ten lorries were entered in categories which could fall outside the law suggests that in the minds of manufacturers the 3-ton legal maximum did not offer much scope for operators to carry paying loads. In the event one of the Class C and one of the Class D vehicles failed to put in an appearance.

Again a great deal of meticulous recording of performance was carried out. In the hill-climbing tests, for example, considerably greater care than previously was taken to record precisely what was happening, and from the information obtained it was possible to draw graphs showing a vehicle's speed every ten feet up to seventy feet from the start upward on the hills, and similarly when drivers were anticipating signals to stop. Again the vehicles showed improvement over previous trials and this time practically no involuntary stops occurred apart from what was necessary in traffic. The only petrol lorries, on this occasion, were the two 1½-ton Milnes in Class A and both received gold medals although the judges did comment on the high cost of fuel per ton-mile as compared with the steamers. Other golds were won by one Leyland in Class B, the Thornycroft in Class C, and a Thornycroft and a Coulthard in Class D.[13]

Mr Walter Long, the President of the Local Government Board, who happened to be MP for one of the Liverpool constituencies, was keenly interested in the Trials and he travelled up to Liverpool to attend a meeting of the Chamber of Commerce to hear the judges' report at the end of this third Trial.[14] Not surprisingly, the totally unsatisfactory nature of the 3-ton limit was again emphasized. This now became the issue for manufacturers and users alike to press. Owners of private cars were happy enough with the 1896 Act, and the development of 'pleasure cars' went on apace. Commercial operators – or rather potential commercial operators were in a spot. The law allowed only vehicles with a tare maximum of 3 tons to run free of all the restrictive rules of the 1865 and 1878 Acts. There was not much choice, therefore. Below 3 tons one could have something like a 1-ton or 30 cwt van built on an ordinary car chassis and driven by a petrol engine or an electric motor. People, naturally enough, tried to get a bit more on to the car chassis, with the obvious consequences, and the early transport magazines constantly warned people not to overload the 'pleasure-car' chassis. Apart from what the chassis would stand, the tyres were a problem and the early pneumatics could not take too much extra weight. For greater payloads it was necessary to get a heavier chassis and that meant steam power too; in any case, it was not possible to get more than about 3 or 4 tons' payload on a 3-ton tare. Going beyond that meant that the vehicle would be in exactly the same category as traction engines, that is 'heavy locomotives' which were still governed by the earlier legislation. In effect, then, the much-vaunted repeal of the so-called 'Red Flag' Act set only the private motorist free and allowed small vans. (It did, admittedly, also allow passenger buses under the 3 tons but they are outside our scope.) There were always people who would take a chance, though, and some freight carrying vehicles of over 3 tons did masquerade as 'light locomotives'.

Knowledge of the difficulties imposed by the 3-ton tare did not stop pioneering spirits who were willing to invest their reputations, their time and their money in trying to prove that road haulage by lorry was a viable proposition.

One such company was the Road Carrying Company, set up in Liverpool in the spring of 1902 by Lord Derby, Sir Arthur Stanley, MP, and Mr E. Shrapnell-Smith, and some of their friends, who jointly put up £20,000 capital.[15] They had watched the series of three trials with careful attention and had concurred with the judges about the tare weight. Nevertheless Shrapnell-Smith and his colleagues decided that trials were not enough; what was needed was a sustained period of actual operation under commercial conditions. Practically the first decision they had to take was whether to ignore the law and have some chance of making a profit or to stick to the legal tare. Bravely, they kept to the law, weighing all their vehicles on railway weighbridges to make sure that they did not exceed three tons, though they must have known that they had only a slim chance of breaking even. Had they decided to contravene the law, they would have been in the company of many or most of the lorry operators who were running the one-hundred-odd vehicles at this time. The problem was that a steam lorry was basically a heavy vehicle. To get it down to 3-ton tare meant that wheels had to be narrow, axles had to be light, and in general, the chassis had to be made lighter than was regarded advisable. The result was that narrow wheels cut into the soft roads and vehicles became bogged down, 'axles snapped like carrots', chassis parts broke, and it became a hazardous undertaking to load up with any sort of reasonable payload.

'We worked them round Liverpool', Shrapnell-Smith told the LGB's Departmental Committee investigating the whole question in February 1904:

> picking up goods from the docks, carrying everything, from bananas to pig-iron, cotton, large quantities of petrol, and various goods that were considered dangerous, we handled with safety. We ran these machines for about eight months; they gave endless trouble through their lightness, and on the soft roads; there were certain strips of road where we used to go through the crust, three or four wagons a night, and had endless delays in jacking them out, owing to the fact that we could not specify our tyres more than six inches on the back wheel, because, if we had, we should have been several hundredweight more than the legal weight. After working with these for a year we had to lay the wagons off as being completely useless – we lost too much money.[16]

So this enterprise, which had started off so valiantly with fourteen machines, bought between July and November 1902, had to be called off in the Liverpool area, though some work was still carried on for a time on the somewhat better road surfaces in London. The machines which Shrapnell-Smith operated would, typically, have had between three and four tons on the platform and perhaps another couple of tons on a trailer.

There were other pioneers. F.J. Bretherton, who later worked as an engineer with Clayton and with Robey, started as a haulage contractor in London in 1899 with a couple of Mann steam-wagons. He claimed to be the first contractor to use mechanical vehicles, although there were a Thornycroft and a couple of Leyland steamers also working in the metropolis. Bretherton had his troubles, carrying on a running battle with the authorities. He suffered his first prosecution for taking a steamer through Blackwell Tunnel, because the vehicle emitted vapour, that is, steam. An injunction was placed on him to stop his wagons going over Westminster Bridge – an injunction lifted only when the London County Council (LCC) wished to run trams over the bridge. Worse was to come in later years. Mr Bretherton fought twenty-three cases in 1904 and had to pay up some £2000.[17]

Although the 3 ton load on a 3-ton tare was, perhaps, the safe limit for the vehicles, there were operators who were willing to try a greater weight, for, as Mr J.E. Thornycroft told the same Departmental Committee, 'Experience has shown that loads of less than four tons cannot be worked successfully.'[18] (Profitably, he undoubtedly meant.) Mr J.H. Toulmin, Managing Director of T. Coulthard & Co. Ltd, told of a vehicle made by his company which, at the time of the hearing, was carrying seven or eight tons of stone to the new War Office buildings. This was on a tare (illegal) of about 3 tons 15 cwt, but he pointed out that the road between Chelsea and the War Office site was extremely good.[19] The case to which Mr Toulmin referred was certainly not the only example of illegal operation. Other operators, too, worked well above the legal tare and the appropriate payload, though it was customary to mark all the vehicles, whatever their weight, as being 2 tons 19 cwt 3 qrs.

By this time the light passenger car had being going for some six years and was drawing a great deal of unwelcome attention to itself – roaring through villages at fearsome speeds, 15, 16, or even 20 m.p.h., throwing the village 'bobby' head over heels into the duck pond and leaving a layer of dust over everything. Action was needed. There had to be some means of identifying the vehicles so that their dreadful owners could be traced and duly fined for treating peaceable folk in such a cavalier manner. Thus the Motor Car Act to provide for registration, number plates, licensing of drivers, fines for reckless driving and endorsement of licences in appropriate cases came in 1903. It was that same Act which really gave birth to the road haulage industry, though, the 1896 Act had permitted the operation of light delivery vans.

While the main part of the 1903 Act was designed to deal with the annoyance caused by private cars, the opportunity was taken to amend the onerous conditions under which the heavier freight vehicle had to operate. The Liverpool Self-Propelled Traffic Association, operators such as the Road Carrying Company, the British Army, and various others, had demonstrated beyond any argument that the 3-ton tare was hopelessly inadequate. Certainly it did lead to narrow wheels cutting into roads and getting vehicles stuck, and heavy rates of depreciation as the lightweight vehicles groaned or shivered over rough surfaces, but even though the vehicle might have survived this, a 3-ton load was just not economic. There was a demand for vehicles which would carry 6 tons. As was the case in 1896 when the earlier restrictive legislation was swept away, no one could say that the President of the Local Government Board (LGB) was against the new transport.

Section 12 of the 1903 Act simply empowered the LGB to make regulations which would increase the maximum tare mentioned in the 1896 Act, and to make the lorries subject to any further conditions as to construction and use which might be in the regulations. Finally the powers granted to the LGB included that of making regulations about the speed of any motor car exceeding two tons in weight (that is, buses and freight vehicles generally). This, then was what the previously mentioned Committee was all about. It was to investigate matters in connection with the regulations to be made under this Section 12. The enquiry revolved around three issues:

1. What was the maximum tare to be?
2. What was the appropriate mixture of wheel diameter, tyre width and axle load?
3. At what speed should these heavy vehicles be allowed to run?

An incidental point which concerned several members of this (Hobhouse)

Committee was whether the tyres should be smooth or have steel strakes or transverse grooves (for we are talking about steel tyres).

As was to be expected, the manufacturers (via the Society of Motor Manufacturers and Traders (SMMT), already in existence since 1902) and the users (via the Automobile Club and its associated Motor Vehicle and Wagon Users' Association – MVWUA) wanted a 6-ton tare. This, with a 6-ton or more payload and a ton or more of water and fuel, would gross out at, perhaps, 14 tons. Mr H. Burford of Milnes-Daimler volunteered the information that 'we are building five ton lorries, and a large number of them. Then we are infringing the 1896 Act by our tare weight.'[20] Mr Toulmin of Coulthard's, who had described a lorry built by them when working on the War Office construction job, also related how he had gone to sell a vehicle to a firm. 'I offered a vehicle with a four ton tare. The manager would not look at that; he must have a vehicle that would carry at least five or six tons, that is, to make it a commercially paying load'.[21] Other witnesses such as Sydney Straker argued that horse-drawn vehicles often carried 10 tons while people objected to motors doing so.

Oddly (or maybe not), the traffic superintendent of the Caledonian Railway, Guy Calthrop, wanted to go even further than the road carriers. He wanted lorries legalized to carry the contents of a railway wagon – 10 tons. He looked to such vehicles to open up new areas and act as feeders for the railways.[22] One of the judges at the Liverpool Trials, E.R. Calthrop, supported this view, but nobody, presumably, thought of a time when large lorries might supplant railway wagons altogether instead of merely being feeders. The Departmental Committee was convinced that the 3-ton tare was too low and would have to be raised substantially if road haulage was to be economic. But the 6 tons requested by the SMMT and the MVWUA (CMUA) would come to 14 tons gross. To allow that would mean that many traction engines, registered under the Locomotives Acts 1861–98 as 'Heavy Locomotives', would fall under the Motor Car Acts instead. This would have had the effect of depriving county councils of the £10 annual licence fee as well as the control they had over these heavy engines. The Committee could not accept that either of these should be allowed to happen so they settled for a compromise and recommended a maximum 5-ton tare – or 6 tons if a trailer were included. Needless to say the recommendation was welcomed by road haulage interests.

Several of the witnesses had argued that all the talk about gross weight was misguided. What really mattered was the weight pressing on the road at any one spot, so that it really was a question of axle load and tyre width. One member of the Committee, possibly remembering the Thornycroft of the 1898 Liverpool Trials, asked several manufacturers about the possibility of six-wheelers to spread the load, but he got very little joy out of that. Toulmin thought that 'a two-wheeled trailer with a connection to the framework of the motor vehicle' might be possible in the future but 'we have not gone into it'. Straker did not anticipate building a vehicle with more than four wheels, and Thornycroft sounded a bit rueful with his remark that his firm had tried them, 'but the difficulties in construction and other complications have led us to abandon them so far'.[23]

Most of the county council and other road authority representatives who gave evidence were not too much against the new transport. Some were even using mechanical road transport themselves. (Chelsea Vestry – later Borough – had started making enquiries at the time the 1896 Act was being prepared, hired a dust cart from Thornycroft in March 1898 for a trial period and had bought and used a steam tipper from that firm from February 1900 onward.) The main concern of the county authorities was the cost of keeping their roads in decent condition. Mr W.B. Hulton, Chairman of the Main Roads Committee of Lancashire County, told of his troubles. There was the main Blackburn–Preston Road, for example. It had previously cost about £210 per annum to keep it fit for horse-drawn traffic. Then, in the last year, thirty-eight steam lorries had begun to run about one hundred trips a day back and forwards between Blackburn and Preston Port. These lorries were usually labelled with the tare of 2 tons 19 cwt 3 qrs, but from what he could learn from the drivers they were up to ten tons gross. The result was that the road had had to be resurfaced with 'best Penmaenmawr granite' at 12s. a ton – a total cost to the council of about £8000 (which included a bit for making up an alternative road after motors switched to it when the main road deteriorated). The rub was that the vehicles were registered in the cities and made no contribution to the county rates, and the county had to maintain the road. He was straight enough to admit that nothing could be recovered under the 'extraordinary traffic' rule for as soon as the traffic became regular enough and heavy enough to cause damage to the roads it was no longer extraordinary – and the county ought to bring the roads up to a standard to cope with such traffic. He took the same view about side roads – so long as traffic was light, no great expense was involved, but as soon as the traffic became regular and heavy, it was the duty of the council to bring the road up to standard.[24]

At least one witness did not bat an eyelid at the thought of 14 tons gross. The City Engineer of Liverpool, Mr J.A. Brodie, pointed out that the usual weight of a horse-drawn cotton lorry in Liverpool was 12 tons, that traction engines with 30 tons behind were a daily occurrence in Liverpool, and, indeed, he claimed to know of many examples of 80 ton loads being hauled on four wheels.[25]

Following the Departmental Committee's Report, new regulations were issued under Section 12 of the Motor Car Act, 1903, and these came into operation on 1 March 1905, though vehicles which had been earlier registered were given until 1 September to comply. The new regulations – The Heavy Motor Car Order, 1904 – took the class of vehicles mentioned under the 1896 law as 'Light Locomotives' and in the 1903 Act as 'Motor Cars (Up to 3-ton Tare)' and divided these into two new classes. These were light motor cars (up to 2 tons unladen) and heavy motor cars (over 2 tons but not exceeding 5 tons), the latter being the new maximum. These two classes were, in effect, passenger cars ('pleasure cars') and light delivery vans on the one hand, and the heavier freight vehicles on the other. The latter were restricted to a maximum of 8 tons on each axle, but there were complex requirements about the relationship between axle load, wheel diameter and tyre width. Only one trailer could be hauled and the total tare of wagon and trailer could not exceed 6½ tons. The legal maximum gross weight was 12 tons. Speed limits were also set down:

Unladen weight	*Axle weight (tons)*	*Maximum speed (tons)*	*m.p.h.*
On metal tyres	3	6	8*
On metal tyres	5	8	5
On rubber tyres	3	6	12
On rubber tyres	5	8	8

*5 m.p.h. if trailer hauled.

The light motor cars which included delivery vans were now allowed to go at 20 m.p.h.

So the way was now clear for the road transport industry to begin its attack on rail and horse-drawn traffic. Coinciding with the new, liberating regulations, magazines appeared on the newsagents' counters. There was, firstly, the *Automobile Commercial Vehicle Review,* but a longer-lasting one was to champion the cause of motor haulage and to preach with missionary zeal to the unconverted who stuck to rail or horse transport. Under the proprietorship of Edmund Dangerfield, the enthusiastic editor (Shrapnell-Smith, the man who, at Liverpool, had practised what he preached), in the first issue of *Commercial Motor* on 16 March 1905, wrote an article prophetically headed 'The Coming Great Home Industry'. He said that

> nine years of trial, of experiment and unremitting effort, have resulted, at last, in the unloosening of the legislative bonds which so long retarded the outcome of our engineering genius in relation to mechanised road transport. [Since the Trials of 1898, he went on] sustained pressure has been exerted on the government of the day, through the local Government Board and other channels to secure the freedom for construction and circulation which has tardily been granted. The effect of this prolonged uncertainty as to speeds, tyres, weights, width of vehicle and other detail – has been to hinder that regular output which is the measure of cheap manufacture, and to keep prices at a level which has been unattractive to the great body of prospective users.

There were, at this stage, up to 3000 commercial motors in use, from 5 cwt delivery vans to buses and 6-ton wagons. 'When so fine a record has been achieved despite such great drawbacks and disadvantages, can human foresight gauge the future?'

It is, perhaps, understandable that Shrapnell-Smith should have considered the government tardy. When one puts in great efforts to hold trials, when one loses money in a costly pioneering experiment, every week that passes is of consequence. But to be fair to the governments, they had had a war in South Africa to think about and had had to cope with a completely new form of transport. In the circumstances perhaps two Acts of Parliament, one Departmental Committee, and two sets of construction and use regulations was not a bad record for eight and a half years. It is hard to see how they could have had a Motor Car Act any sooner than 1903 -some time had been needed to get experience, and even then parliamentary time was limited; and following the 1903 Act, March 1905 was probably as early as could be expected to hold an enquiry and have a set of regulations in operation. That was all now past, however, and people could turn to the future. Could any human foresight, indeed, gauge that future?

Notes

1. *The Times,* 16/10/1895, p.9.
2. *The Times,* 11/12/1895, p.12.
3. *The Times,* 11/12/1895, p.12.
4. Liverpool Self-Propelled Traffic Association, *Judges' Report on Liverpool Trials, 1898* by E. Shrapnell-Smith.
5. Ibid.; *CM,* 11/7/1907, p.467.
6. *CM,* 1/5/1913, p.189, 30/3/1905.
7. Ibid.
8. *CM,* 25/7/1907, p.498 and 2/11/1911, p.182.
9. *CM,* 18/7/1907, p.488.
10. Liverpool Self-Propelled Traffic Association, *Judges' Report on Liverpool Trials, 1899* by E. Shrapnell-Smith.
11. *CM,* 13/2/1913, p.518.
12. Ibid.
13. *Judges' Report 1901.*
14. *CM,* 16/1/1908, p.425.
15. *CM,* 11/12/1913, p.326.
16. Local Govt. Board. Departmental Committee on Motor Cars, 1904 – Minutes of Evidence. Cmnd 2070. Question 893.
17. *CM,* 8/7/1919, p.462, and *CM,* 7/3/1912 re small firms.
18. Departmental Committee Evidence Question 31.
19. Ibid., Questions 151–155.
20. Ibid., Question 285.
21. Ibid., Question 165.
22. Ibid., Questions 2132–37.
23. Ibid., Questions 3/207.
24. Ibid., Questions 314–328.
25. Ibid., Question 525.

CHAPTER THREE

The Coming Great Home Industry

Now that the legislative decks were cleared, motor freight transport could take on its opponents. The railways were there, carrying the bulk of the country's goods and having the advantage of established and known (if at times doubtful) performance. They had been a key factor in helping to make Britain into the 'workshop of the world', so it is not surprising that a tradition-bound country did not immediately cast them aside. Then there were the horse-drawn freights. Horses were cheap and the British loved them; they, too, had an established place in the scheme of things. Horses, indeed, were intelligent – not like the new vehicles – and could be trusted to move on to the next delivery point even when their driver was not at his best. There were conservation interests too, as has been mentioned, trying to keep down noise and vibration, escaping steam and smoke. Inevitably there were accidents with mechanized transport, as indeed there had been with horses. There were ratepayers and some councils who objected to the heavy wear on the roads which had to be made good at the expense of those citizens who gained little or nothing from road transport. Finally, there was the ordinary citizen, the man (or woman) in the street or on top of the Clapham omnibus, who was incensed at the loutish behaviour of some private car drivers. Unfortunately some of the opprobrium was dealt out to freight transport as well. So there were half a dozen groups of opponents to be defeated or converted.

The most obvious place for road transport to encroach on rail was in short-distance work, especially across country, and in collection and delivery from stations. So long as a destination was on the same line of railway as the despatching station, the railways did not do too badly in transit times, but much of the traffic was not for stations on the direct line and had, therefore, to be re-marshalled at one or more junction points, or transhipped if there were less than full wagon-loads. The result was that delivery of a substantial amount of traffic for destinations between ten and twenty miles distant could not be guaranteed the following day, and sometimes not even on the day after that. The railway companies themselves regarded three days, including the day of despatch and the day of delivery, as 'reasonable'. The trouble was in the roundabout routes and consequent tranships or re-marshalling. Typical was the writer to a magazine who complained that 'from Potters Bar to High Barnet by rail via East Goods Yard is 23 miles; by road 3½ miles.[1] The customer had to pay for the distance traversed. There was clearly great opportunity here, particularly for delivery in areas adjacent to London, for road transport to cut across country and save all this excess mileage and its attendant expense, and save a great deal of time too. Not only that, but road transport could cut out some of the repeated handlings and avoid damage or loss of the goods.

Though it was not, perhaps, a 'fault' of the railways for which they could be blamed, short-distance traffic was expensive to deal with. The costs of the loading and unloading, and of collection and delivery, were disproportionately large when set against a small transit charge. The railway rates system took these factors into account. We take the charges in operation in the early 1900s on the Great Northern as an example. Beer in casks was Class 1 traffic and as such incurred a charge of 2.2d (just under lp) per ton per mile for the first twenty miles. A ton carried for twenty miles therefore would cost 44d. (l8p). To this would be added 1s. 6d. (7½p) per ton for 'Station Terminals', that is, for the use of the stations. There was then a further 5d. per ton for loading and the same for unloading. If the goods were carried in an open wagon there could be a further 1½d. at each end for covering (with a tarpaulin) and uncovering respectively. But assuming that this latter charge might not arise, this twenty-mile journey could still cost 6s. per ton on a 'station-to-station' basis. A great many rates, however, were normally quoted on a 'collected and delivered' (C&D) basis, so that cartage charges at each end would be added to the already-mentioned 6s. The 'cartage' would be 1s. (5p) or more per ton at each end, depending on the size of the town concerned and therefore the radius within which delivery would be performed. So the twenty-mile haul of a ton of beer could end up costing in the region of 8s. per ton, or more.

Whether road transport was competitive would depend on individual circumstances. A steam wagon used fairly steadily throughout the year would need a charge of 1s. (5p) per vehicle mile to be worthwhile at all. Given a 5-ton load over twenty miles, returning light, it would just about break even with the railway charge. But one could see why the 3-ton tare pre-1905 was unacceptable, for with only a 3-ton payload the steamer was still costing much the same to run. On the other hand, though, the terminals, handling, collection and delivery charges would have made the railway rate for half the distance much less attractive. The beer rate for ten miles would have been 22d. less, that is, 6s 2d. (31p). So a 5-ton lot would have cost 30s. 10d. whereas the road cost for the twenty miles' round trip would have been 20s. (100p or £l). There were the other points in favour of road: saving in time, delivery at a specified time; and fewer breakages.

One of the many complaints levelled at the railways was that whereas they had started out by quoting most rates on a 'Station to Station' basis, adding the collection and delivery charge when required, in the twenty years or so before the time we are discussing they had fallen into the habit of quoting many rates on a 'collected and delivered' basis and asking no questions about whether the trader really wanted the cartage services. Worse, they quoted rates as C&D even for stations where they did not operate a delivery service. Worse still, where a trader hoped to save a few pence by performing the collection or delivery services himself and claiming a rebate, the railways were less than generous. They would not refund the full amount that they had added into the rate for the service. Where they had included 1s. 3d. (6p) for delivery they might give a rebate of say 10d. (4p) per ton when the trader himself lifted the goods at the station, and would argue that they had had to provide the facilities and this had cost money even if the trader chose not to use them.

Another cause of irritation at the time was that when traders did attempt to perform the cartage themselves, seeking even the meagre rewards for so doing, or trying to get their goods a bit earlier in the day, the railway staff were alleged to have been very obstructive, making the traders' carters wait unduly at the station while railway carts were given preference; and when mechanized road transport put in an appearance at the railway sheds the local railway agents were quick to argue the dangers of fire. If this is true, it strikes one as somewhat unreasonable since the motive power complained about was often exactly the same as the railways used – steam.

Diversion of traffic began very early, though not, of course, on a very large scale. A letter from C. Vaux & Sons, Sunderland, to the editor of *Commercial Motor* in April 1905 told how they had used a 3-ton Thornycroft steamer to carry bottled beer between their brewery and Annfield Plain since May 1902, even though the road had two long hills of 1 in 6½ gradient and in winter was 'apparently bottomless'. The journeys 'are done at a considerable saving on the cost of carriage by rail, and also at a very great convenience to our customers in comparison with the latter mode of conveyance, owing to the delays which occur in railway deliveries at busy times and to the frequent pilferage which occurs'. Watkins Brothers, Imperial Flour Mills, Hereford were, at the same time (1905) delivering 'with ease' up to twenty-five miles round their mills. 'We ... find it an immense advantage in approaching customers to whom, in the old days, we used to deliver by rail, and offer them flour and goods delivered directly by steam wagon into their warehouse or bakehouse.[2] A.&G. Little, County Roller Mills, Hexham – in very hilly country – could say that ' A large proportion of the goods now delivered by motor were previously sent by rail.'[3] Lt Col. Mark Mayhew, Vice-Chairman of the Automobile Club, had used road transport in connection with his milling business since 1900 and by 1905 was thoroughly convinced of the merits of mechanized transport.[4]

Others, who could not individually afford lorries, wished to gain some of the advantage too. Barham and District Fruit Growers' Association, Bognor, were anxious to hear 'from some firm for conveying their produce to Covent Garden by motor van'.[5] Whether they were successful is not known to this writer but a witness told a committee studying the home fruit industry that so far as the Swanley district was concerned railway carriage was dispensed with almost entirely.[6] Admittedly it is not certain that the railways really regretted the loss of some of this fruit traffic in the palmy days of 1905, for it was small in quantity, intermittent, and difficult to carry. Of course it would not be right to claim that road transport had it all its own way. Cox's Milling Co. Ltd at Weybridge, for example, had a private siding connected to the railway. They said then that 'the cost of delivery by motor to places that can be easily reached by railway puts the former right out of the running in those cases: but we find the lorry handy for cross-country work where it is difficult to deliver either by horse traction or by rail'.[7]

The costs of working steam wagons in 1905 clearly varied with the mileage run and the type of roads over which the wagon worked, for the latter could have quite severe consequences both for fuel consumption and for the repair bills; and to be economic at all raised the question of the minimum amount of work necessary to allow the overheads to be spread. The following costs were given by Willesden Urban District Council in March 1905[8] for the conveyance of road materials from local railway stations or canal wharves. On a capital cost of £680–£700 (which allowed two bodies – one for carrying materials, the other for water):

	£ per annum
Sinking fund and interest on loan	84
Repairs	65
Wages	100
Fuel	80
Lubricants and sundries	10
Insurance	7
	TOTAL £346

At 30 to 35 miles per day, working 260 days per annum, this works out at roughly 3d. (a bit over 1p) per ton per mile. Even allowing that this machine would have been working over fairly good roads and used fairly intensively (seven or eight hours running per day as well as loading and unloading) the 3d. per ton per mile gives a charge which is in many cases competitive with rail. But not many firms would be in a position to work vehicles as intensively as that. Some machines would cost less than the £680 which Willesden UDC paid. Steam wagons at the Park Royal Show in the summer of 1905 were listed at from £500 to £550 for capacities between 4 tons 17 cwt and 4 tons 19 cwt (Allchin, Foden, Mann and St Pancras makes).

The limitation in competitive power of these steam-wagons was clearly in their slow speed. At 5 m.p.h. their daily run was rather severely limited and this necessarily handicapped them badly, a handicap which was not to be removed so long as they were running on steel wheels. For this was the essence of the matter. Steel wheels on rough roads and absence of shock absorbers meant serious vibration at anything over 5 m.p.h. with consequent high depreciation charges and high repair bills. Even if the law had allowed higher speeds it is doubtful whether the steamers would have stood it.

But even at 5 m.p.h. they were faster than horse-drawn wagons, the other main area of competition. The very high capital cost of the steam-wagon (£500 at least – and we saw that Willesden UDC paid more) required that the vehicle should be used fairly intensively. This cut out a large number of smaller firms which had not the required minimum of work to be done. At the same time delivery work in urban areas was the strong point of the horse, where constant starting and stopping and very short distances between the 'drops' with a comparatively low daily mileage would have made the motor uneconomic. The steamer, therefore, would have to pick up those instances where there was a prospect of a reasonable mileage before the first delivery, not too many deliveries, and then the 'long' run home again. If they could get, say, fifteen miles out to the first delivery point then they could clearly save time over the horse-drawn vehicle.

For the longer run of twenty miles or more with heavy loads the horse had another disadvantage. This was simply that after hauling a full load for this distance and returning, say with empty casks, the horse team would usually have to be rested the following day so that a second team had to be provided. Four horses, working in pairs on alternate days, would clearly add considerably to the cost of heavy goods transport in the early 1900s. Costs of as much as £400 per annum for a four-horse set working in these circumstances have been quoted though that may have been excessive. However, Messrs C.H. Witherington, Sonning Mills, Near Reading, gave some figures which are useful for comparison:[9]

1902 – 7 horses				1903 – one Foden 5-tonner			
	£.	s.	d		£.	s.	d
Food	271	0	0	Wages – driver	91	0	0
Wages 2 men	124	16	0	Wages – asst.	67	12	0
Shoeing	30	14	8	Repairs	44	7	0
Vet's bill	8	10	6	Oil	16	12	10
Repairs – van & harness	11	2	9	41½ tons coal	49	0	0
Interest on capital**	20	10	0	Insurance	11	18	0
Deprec. on vans	50	0	0	Interest on cost	25	0	0
Incidentals	3	6	1	Depreciation	70	0	0
				Incidentals	4	10	2
Total	£520	0	0	Total	£380	0	0

** Interest @ 5% on capital of
7 horses @ £50 = £350
2 vans = 60

These figures illustrate one or two points: horses sometimes needed veterinary attention; the life of the steamer was usually considered to be six or seven years; and carrying 5 tons on a 3-ton tare involved a great many repairs (almost 12 per cent of the total cost). The Foden carried 3870 tons in the 301 working days for which these figures are given, but unfortunately no ton-mile nor wagon-mile data are given. Nor indeed are there any figures for the work done by the horses, but the implication is that the two sets of costs are for roughly comparable work.

About this time probably only some forty heavy vehicles were in use by local authorities throughout the country, but far more would have been employed by brewers, millers, and similar firms having regular bulk loads for delivery. So far as can be established, about mid-1905 some sixty-two breweries and allied trades operated one or more vehicles each, and transport companies were then running some 130 vehicles of all kinds. Some idea of the amount of work done in general can be got from the following details of four vehicles of W.T. Farmiloe's fleet, quoted in *Commercial Motor* in June 1906:

		1904			*1905*	
Make	*Working Days*	*Miles Run*	*Tonnage Moved*	*Working Days*	*Miles Run*	*Tonnage Moved*
Straker	244	4854	1453	208	4006	1178
Straker	222	4620	1191	259	5314	1347
Thornycroft	226	5827	1220	225	5509	1165
Straker	170	3733	1047	248	4468	1334

This table shows just over five tons moved each working day on average and the mileage per day is around twenty: but again they give no clear idea of ton-mileage, which would be a much better indicator of the work done. Some people were arguing for this measure at the time but few operators kept records in such detail.

The steam wagon in 1905, then was already making a niche for itself in'heavy' haulage – up to a 5-ton load or so, at least with the wagon alone,wherever an initial run of ten miles or more could be obtained or wherever there was sufficient volume of work for intensive usage. Steam lorries cost much more per hour than horse transport and so delays or waiting times were crucial. As we have seen, such wagons could compete successfully with the railways over the cross-country routes where the railway journey was circuitous, and in many cases were more economical for the shortest distance where the terminal charges made the railway rate disproportionately heavy.

The total usage of steam wagons at this time was, of course, very small indeed in modern terms. They had not been notoriously reliable or economic before the abolition of the 3-ton tare limit, so there was plenty of reason for the horse user to distrust them. In any case generations of employees of business firms had been used to the ways of horses. Their tricks were known, their abilities and potential in a given situation were common knowledge – not like these steam wagons and petrol-engined vans whose possibilities had to be learnt the hard way. The capital cost of a horse was low – between £50 and £100, depending on the quality, so that another one could easily be added to the stable, or, for that matter, sold off when trade fluctuations warranted it. The whole way of life was geared to horse usage – supplies of feeding stuffs, drinking troughs in the streets, frequent sales where the beasts could be seen before purchase, a large 'supply' of suitable labour; and horses had the reputation of being much better able to keep their footing on frost-bound roads.

Steel-wheeled wagons often did not manage to beat the icy surfaces. They needed lots of water, too, and occasional arguments arose as the drivers filled the tanks from the horse troughs or the village pond. Steam and petrol enthusiasts were quick to point out that their machines did not need any attention on Sundays, did not get tired after long runs, thus needing to rest for a day, and certainly did not get colds or fevers.

Whatever the tribulations of the early steam wagon another type of motorized transport was making rapid strides – in light delivery work where the petrol-engined, rubber-tyred van was now well established. In this field the matter of legal tare weight was no problem. Hard on the heels of the success of the private car, many firms, freed by the 1896 Act, tried to use delivery vans as early as 1899 or 1900. At first there was a certain lack of success, partly due to the initial problems of the petrol engine, but mainly due to overloading. Nearly all vans at the beginning had the bodies built on to a 'pleasure car' chassis – and a chassis intended for use in a private car was able to carry, perhaps, 5 or 6 cwt (250–300 kilos). Once a body of 2 or 3 cwt and the payload were added, trouble was inevitable. It took time to learn this lesson. Manufacturers were not unduly hasty in making chassis for delivery vans, for they had all the work they could cope with in providing 'pleasure cars'. Up to 1901 it had not been possible to get anything other than these private car chassis for the lighter end of the work; the Milnes-Daimler 30 cwt vehicle which did well in the trials of that year was really the first to be manufactured strictly as a freight-carrying chassis. It was not, perhaps, until about 1904 that other manufacturers seriously turned their thoughts in the direction of light delivery vans of 10 cwt to 1 ton capacity. Then a number of major builders emerged – Albion, Arrol-Johnston, Napier, Simms, Wolseley, and so on. The problem of overloading was not immediately solved, for then (as now) the capital costs were high – twice as much as a horse and van – and users naturally wanted to get the maximum amount of work from the vehicle. Halfway through the first decade of the new century – and indeed later – commercial motoring magazines were still preaching the inadvisability of overloading. It was not only that the chassis was not strong enough. The new pneumatic tyres were also a problem – but more on that topic later.

The obvious users of delivery vans were the large department stores and provision merchants, and they built up their fleets quite steadily in the years leading up to the First World War. One well-known London firm of the time, Shoolbreds, which had about three hundred horses originally on delivery work, started with a Lacre van in mid-1905 on an experimental basis. In a six weeks trial period this van ran a distance of 1483 miles, averaging 41.2 per day with a maximum on any one day of 70 miles. It made 1429 deliveries, averaging 39.7 per day with a maximum of 60 on one day. The actual time taken in running and delivery during this period was about 250 hours which works out at 5.9 miles per hour overall. The overall petrol consumption was 10.9 miles per gallon (m.p.g.), though on some trips with only a few stops 15.25 m.p.g. was achieved. This was clearly better than a horse could do and, seeing the encouraging results from the first van, Shoolbreds soon added a second one.

They now discovered that the much greater mileage possible with motor vans allowed them to open up a considerably wider area of custom than was possible with horses. New districts were brought in and by mid-1911, when the first two vans had accumulated about 100,000 miles each, Shoolbreds' fleet had grown to 56 Lacre vans and the number of horses in their employment had fallen to 120. Each van was then doing a round of something of the order of 45 miles a day.[10]

While the bulk of these trips were run comparatively close to home, there were adventurous souls even in those early days. One firm sent a 15 cwt load in a Lacre van from London to Swansea in March 1905 – '213½ miles plus 8 or 10 for detours', we are told, taking 17 hours 56 minutes. It says a good deal for the progress made in the petrol engine in the eight-and-a-half years since the 1896 Act that in this case the engine was said not to have stopped during the entire journey. (Would there have been some switching of drivers? Did they stop for a meal?) The only difficulty encountered was that at one stage the throttle would not open fully because a wire was stretched. However, 'a piece of string was attached' and that was that. The journey to Swansea cost 14 gals 3½ pints of petrol which was near enough to 15.2 m.p.g.[11]

It was with fair pride, too, that Shoolbreds' transport manager could describe, in March 1908, how they were now ranging further afield. Recently, he said, two vans 'in one day, delivered 3½ tons furniture from Tottenham House [London] to a few miles beyond Abingdon [near Oxford]. This was a sixty miles run out, fully loaded, with three hours stop at the house, and a sixty mile run home, after which both vans were out as usual next morning.' This latter point, no doubt, was a reference to a difficulty of horse transport.[12]

Even by the end of the first decade of the twentieth century, then, motor transport was making a distinct impression on the economics of business firms by allowing the already-mentioned widening of the effective trading area. It is worth noting one particular firm's experience in this respect. Maples & Co. Ltd were long established as furniture retailers. Up to about 1889 they did their deliveries by horse van within a radius of fifteen miles of their main London store in Tottenham Court Road. Thereafter, to extend operations, they established six sub-depots at about eight miles out from the city centre – for example at Pinner, Barnet, Lewisham, and so on. At each depot they placed a driver and porter together with a van and three horses. Each morning a van would arrive at a sub-depot at about nine o'clock and the previous day's empty van would be taken back to Tottenham Court Road. The load on the newly arrived van would then be transhipped for local delivery. By this means Maples' range was now extended to a radius of some twenty-three miles. More sub-depots were added and by 1899, with nine of these, the practical limit of horse operation was reached – a radius of some thirty miles from the centre. This was just at the time when motor transport was putting in an appearance, so a couple of steam wagons were purchased (a Thornycroft and a Hindley) and in 1906 two Lacre 2-tonners were added to the fleet. In 1908 when the firm had ten Lacres, the directors gave instructions for exhaustive tests and studies of the leading makes. As a result of this, four 2-ton and two 3-ton Leylands, and five 2-ton Dennis vans were added to the fleet. The firm was then able to establish motor depots at Guildford, Kingston, Maidenhead, Ware and Berkhamsted, and also to replace horses by motor vans at some of the inner depots. By 1911 the firm had 33 motor vehicles and had an effective delivery radius with their own resources of 55 miles from the centre. Of course, the large trade which they had, anyway, contributed to the success of the motors for with the Dennis vans averaging 71 miles per day, the cost per mile was well below the average for the time.[13]

Harrods, too, started fairly early on with motor delivery, and by the autumn of 1907 their 23 Lacres were doing an average round of about seventy miles a day. They were able to close a depot at Shepperton which had required nine men and thirteen horses and, instead, to do the work by three vans running from London. In January 1913 the Lacre Company (Albion) was advertising that Harrods then had 63 of their chassis in use, with an accumulated mileage of two millions odd. They claimed, too, that the average life of a van was at least 150,000 miles. Although Lacres were a very well-known type of vehicle, Harrods used others and early in 1912 they also had 31 Dennis vans in use.[14] Other stores were equally enthusiastic. William Whiteley had thirteen Lacres in use by the beginning of 1908.

One very striking development as a result of motor transport was the weekly, fortnightly or monthly delivery to the large country house. A growing number of well-to-do folk, perhaps dissatisfied with local facilities, gave substantial orders for groceries and provisions – totalling as much as £70 for a single order, quite something in those days – and the stores were now able to deliver these direct to 'the big house' by motor van, whereas for distances of thirty miles or so the horse van would just not have coped. Needless to say, the stores were able to deliver the odd package to other addresses in the vicinity on the same run as the main consignment of anything up to a ton. The comfortable gentry of the country mansions were able to extract some social prestige, too, from having a motor van deliver directly to them. There are many accounts in the trade press during these early years of the century of trips out through leafy lanes, up well-kept drives, to pleasant, even stately, homes.

While the large stores in London and the bigger cities played an important part in the early delivery van work in the 'up to 1 ton' category there were several long-established parcels carriers such as Carter Paterson, Pickford and McNamara which also found motor transport of benefit to them. Carter Paterson, at the turn of the century, operated something like 1250 horse vans with some 3000 horses. They had made some experiments with motorized road transport from about 1897 and bought their first motor van in 1898. Their experience with this first one, it seems, was a bit unfortunate, for the van caught fire and burnt down a sorting depot. However, undismayed, the firm bought four Straker steam wagons between November 1903 and July 1904 to serve their outlying London depots. These carried three tons on the platform and a further two tons on the trailer, and each ran 48 miles a day. So far were they encouraged by this, and seeing the progress in petrol vans generally, the firm decided, early in 1906, to buy 40 petrol vans of 15–20 cwt capacity, mostly Lacres. They set up two new subsidiary companies – London Motor Parcel Express Ltd and London and Provincial Despatch Co. Ltd – to work them. By late 1912, when merger with Pickford was being discussed, Carter Paterson could boast of a complete parcels delivery service by motor over an area of 420 square miles in and around London. They then had 500 delivery 'districts'. Their fleet, at this time, according to a Leyland advertisement, included 60 Leyland 3-tonners, too. It my be relevant to note the rates they charged for the parcels service. The charges were flat rates based on weight only:

Weight not exceeding	7 lb	14 lb	28 lb	56 lb	84 lb	112 lb	Over 112 lbs
Charge	6d.	8d.	10d.	1s.0d.	ls.3d.	1s.6d.	3d. for each extra 28 lbs

They had, at this time, too, a 'Passengers' Luggage' service operating to some seaside towns, like Margate – to which a 4-ton Leyland ran in the summer.[15] By the end of 1913 Carter Paterson's fleet was not far short of 300 petrol vehicles, including Dennis, Lacre, Leyland, Napier, Straker-Squire and Thornycroft makes.[16]

Entry by a different route into the parcels business was possible. W.&G. du Cros Ltd, which operated a fleet of taxis in the London area, afflicted by strikes, decided that they needed some sort of standby; so early in 1913 they started up as parcels carriers with sixteen old Napier cabs converted to vans. Their idea was that West End and suburban gentry who came shopping in the morning could have their purchases delivered by motor van in the afternoon.[17]

The Royal Commission on Motor Cars, 1906, in Appendix A to the published evidence, tells us something about the number of mechanically propelled vehicles in use at that time. It listed the numbers of vehicles registered up to the end of 1904 in the various counties and county boroughs, and though it does not say whether they were all still in operation, most probably were, since registration had been going on only for a short time. In addition to the headings 'Private Use' and 'Public Conveyances', it also listed registrations of vehicles 'intended for trade purposes' and it is probable that these would have been mainly freight vehicles. The numbers in this latter class, then, were:

NUMBER OF VEHICLES REGISTERED
'Intended for Trade Purposes'

Unladen weight	England & Wales	of which, London	Scotland
Under 1 ton	2,599	723	180
1 and under 2 tons	410	190	36
2 and under 3 tons	608	161	42
3 and under 4 tons	210	38	5
4 and under 5 tons	532	87	17
5 tons and upwards	201	30	1
Totals	4,560	1,229	281

Unfortunately no breakdown is given as between petrol and steam propulsion – and indeed there were some electrics included as well. Petrol, though, would have accounted for the bulk of the 2779 vehicles up to a ton and probably most of the 446 between 1 and 2 tons. At the other end of the scale the 751 from four tons up would have been mostly steamers, for petrol still had to prove itself in the bigger vehicles. The figures, incidentally, refer only to vehicles registered under the Motor Car Act and not to Heavy Locomotives (traction engines and tractors) registered under the Locomotives Acts, 1861–98.

If the assumption is made that the average unladen weight of the vehicles in the 'under 1 ton' class was 0.75 ton, that in the '5 tons and upward' class it was 6 tons, and that in the other classes the average unladen weight was the middle point of the class, then we have a gross unladen tonnage of about 8800 tons. Beyond that it becomes 'guesstimate' rather than estimate, The assumption could be made that the carrying capacity was not much more than the unladen weight, and if something were added for trailers, which are not mentioned in the table, then in 1904 there was a carrying capacity in the 'Motor Car' categories of rather less than 10,000 tons, possibly not much over 9000. Estimates of ton-mileage would be foolhardy, for we know nothing about whether full loads were carried, or for what mileage or how much of the mileage was light. Given that so many of the vehicles would have been 'own-account' delivery vans there must have been a fair proportion of empty mileage on the homeward run as well as gradually reducing loads on the outward trip. Even in the higher tonnage categories flour millers, furniture removers and the like would have had substantial light mileage. If we guess at 25 miles laden per day with an average load of half the capacity, we end up with something like 112,500 ton-miles per day in 1904 and that must be recognized as a crude guess following from a number of assumptions.

The general picture, then, in the decade leading up to the First World War, was of a gradually expanding road haulage industry. The number of vehicles was not yet large, and lorries might still be infrequent visitors to some of the more out-of-the-way villages. In most places schoolboys would stop to stare at these symbols of the modern progress of the new century and greybeards would shake their heads in disbelief at the way their world was changing. Not large numbers of vehicles were to be seen but the numbers were growing steadily and most people, at least in the more populated areas, would have seen a road vehicle with a load before the War changed society even more dramatically.

The pre-war period was a proving period, a time of experiment, a time of learning, a time of development. There was much discussion of the best type of fuel for the internal-combustion engine – petrol or benzole or alcohol; of the best type of drive to the back axle – worm drive, bevel gears, chain drive; of the merits of pneumatics versus solid rubber versus steel tyres; of clutches; of differentials; of magnetos and carburettors, and all the rest.

The steam lorry owners, drivers and enthusiasts debated the merits of vertical boilers as compared with 'locomotive type'; of fire-tube boilers versus water-tube boilers, and worried about the ever-present problem of obtaining water when away from the main centres of population. The village duck-pond or a suitable stream had often to provide the supply, and a length of stout hose-pipe was a standard part of the equipment, but horse owners certainly took exception to any attempt of the drivers of the 'steamers' to obtain water from the horse-troughs which were then a common feature of street furniture. Probably Westminster City Council's Works Committee were not the only local authority to take action when, in the spring of 1907, they decided to put notices up at the troughs cautioning people against taking water from the troughs for any purpose other than slaking the thirst of the horses. The Highways Committee backed them up by instructing the Town Clerk to take proceedings against anyone who ignored the notices.[18] Canal companies posted men to prevent the extraction of water from their waterways. Water supplies continued to be a problem, particularly for steam-wagons – for the more water they took on at the start, the smaller the payload they could carry within their maximum gross weight of twelve tons. Indeed only a few months after it began publication *Commercial Motor* carried an article (14 September 1905) advocating the provision of slot machines which would deliver a given quantity of water on the insertion of the appropriate payment. Unfortunately that did not come to fruition until many years later. In the meantime the magazine came to the aid of its readers by awarding prizes for lists of watering places. Reporting on the competition, the editor expressed satisfaction that 'many competitors have gone into careful detail as to the exact location of the watering places, and point out the best places on stream banks, the depth of water from the road, pools where deeper and cleaner water can be obtained, and so on'.[19]

Though there were still many problems to be resolved by the time the war started nevertheless great progress had been made. The uncertainties of the 1898–1901 Trials were gone, and by 1914 petrol and steam lorries alike had become fairly reliable and had taken their place confidently beside the heavy workhorses – the traction-engines – which had by then fifty years experience behind them. Here and there, too, were electrics or petrol-electrics on short-distance delivery work.

So far as the development of the petrol engine is concerned it must be pointed out that a very great contribution to knowledge came from experience with passenger buses. The first double-deckers were licensed in London in 1904 and within about four years there were a thousand of these in use on the streets of the metropolis. The heavy punishment that such a vehicle would endure with constant stopping and starting would test any vehicle and engine, and the manufacturers and mechanics quickly learnt a great deal. By the end of 1911 the couple of thousand horse-buses previously in use in the capital had gone and some 25,000 horses no longer hauled passengers in London; many were getting a respite from freight haulage.

In the early days of petrol vehicles there had been problems aplenty, ranging from radiator failures and leaking petrol tanks to ignition and lubrication failures – apart altogether from wear of parts, overloading problems and tyre troubles. By 1907 the Lacre Company could advertise proudly with a photostat of a letter from Shoolbreds. The firm had 23 Lacres then in use. Two of these had been going for nineteen months and had each clocked up 25, 000 miles. Another one, sixteen months in use, had run 21,000 miles, and three others, thirteen months old, had completed 18,000 miles each. They were, according to the letter, 'absolutely reliable, and practically foolproof as regards driving'. From 15 March that year until 26 April not one of their vehicles had been off the road for any part of a day.[20] Similarly the Belsize Company, well known for their 3-tonners, advertised early in the war 'the worm that turned for

60,000 miles', the worm in question being the form of drive to the rear axle, and the vehicle referred to being a 3-ton mail van running nightly between Manchester and Birmingham for the previous three years.[21]

The Post Office was involved in mechanical transport right from the start. As we saw, their representatives had been at the first Liverpool Trials, watching with keen interest what was going on. They had, of course, an enormous volume of mail to move in the early 1900s; indeed, they were amongst the biggest customers of the railways. Much of their traffic would flow in the direction of the main lines of railways, but there was also a very large quantity moving on what were circuitous or cross-country routes. For an organization which prided itself on next-day deliveries, these cross-country routes were a problem. So once the 1903 Act had let motor haulage develop, the Post Office was seeking tenders for the carriage of mails. When the annual report for the year ended 5 April 1913 was published, it referred to over 150 services or 'sets of services' performed by motor mail van.[22] These services were operated by contractors and the PO continued subsequently to seek tenders for a number of routes. In September 1913, for example, tenders were being sought for Doncaster–Rotherham–Sheffield route. This was for 255 miles a week with loads of 13 cwt.[23] In the summer of 1914 the surveyor of the N. Midlands district at Leicester was advertising a three-year contract for a minimum capacity of 10 cwt between Peterborough and Folkingham; the surveyor at Shrewsbury was inviting tenders for the Chester–Crewe (24 miles each way) and the Stoke–Nottingham (52 miles each way) routes; and the Cardiff official sought a contractor to take 3 cwt loads between Llanelli and Penygroes and to carry loads of 12 cwt to and from Llanelli station. This last pair would be on a three-year contract too. That was quite usual. At the time there were many more requests for tenders just like these; for example: Sheffield–Leeds, London–Cambridge, Sunderland–Newcastle, Northampton –Hitchin, and so on.

But it may be that the Post Office people were very conscious of the deal with the railways mentioned in Chapter One, for they had no intention of allowing any road haulier to make a fortune. An enquirer was told by the editor of *Commercial Motor* in March 1914 that 'Our knowledge of competitive rates leads us to the conclusion that you will have no chance of getting the contract if you ask more than 9d. a mile'. This was at a time when a 10 cwt van would be just profitable on a charge of 6d per mile run -provided it was worked fairly intensively, say 300 miles per week. A 1-tonner, though, would need a charge of 1s. (5p) per mile and a 3-tonner 1s. 3d.[24] The rub was in whether the contract would allow the operator to get the necessary mileage. In the summer of 1914, two or three weeks before Europe erupted in ghastly war, *Commercial Motor* warned any readers thinking of responding to the Glasgow Surveyor's request for tenders that mileage contracts could be a snare.

> In this connection we would very strongly warn any intending contractors to protect themselves against the experiences which befell McNamara & Co. Ltd. This can alone be done by a fair guarantee of a minimum payment per hour, because delays at the post offices sometimes render a paying mileage impossible of attainment ... There has, of late, been evidence that motor mail contractors are not making much profit.[25]

A little later they gave a similar warning about tenders for 'extensive contracts' at Edinburgh, again referring to the McNamara example and adding that 'There is risk, on the mileage basis, of big losses, without an hourly minimum.'[26]

A contractor taking on a Post Office contract had other things to worry about – it was not just a case of throwing a few mail bags on any old lorry and doing one's best. As befits a large organization, the Post Office protected itself by fairly stringent conditions in its contracts. When the weekly *Automobile Commercial Vehicle Review* (later called the *Industrial Motor Review*) published, in April 1905, Post Office advertisements for contracts between London, Tunbridge Wells and Hastings, and London, Tunbridge Wells and Eastbourne, the paper followed up a couple of weeks later with three pages setting out the requirements of the contracts. Obviously the vehicles had to be in accordance with the Motor Car Act, 1903 and the LGB regulations, but the Second Schedule to the contracts set out many more detailed requirements relating to the size of the van and its carrying capacity, hooks for hanging mailbags, a speaking tube between driver and guard, the doors, the painting of the vehicle, the GPO insignia, lights, a waterproof apron to protect the driver and guard, and more. Then the drivers had to be 'competent, steady, sober and careful' and of good character, and had to be between 25 and 50 years of age. They were required to wear GPO uniforms. The vehicle must be kept in thorough repair and any damage made good with 'all convenient speed'. The vehicle must not be used for any other purpose and a spare van had to be kept in reserve. Strict timetables were laid down: departure from London, Mount Pleasant, at 10.30 p.m. and arrival at Eastbourne 6. 15 a.m. On the Hastings run a stop was booked at Sevenoaks from 1.25 a.m. until 1.29 a.m. The vehicles had to go by the routes laid down by the Post Office; there was to be no stop at any house or place except to collect or deliver mails. If, through any neglect or default of the contractors, any of the mail vans were twice or more often in one week more than ten minutes late in arriving at their destination, the contractors, in respect of every such default except the first one, would have to 'forfeit and pay' the sum of 5s. (25p), and if more than 30 minutes late, the sum of 10s. (50p). Wages had to be in accordance with those current in the trade in the district where the work was carried out. There was to be no assignment of the contract, no subcontracting, and the contractor had to enter into, or arrange, a bond of £1000 for the Hastings contract, or £500 for the

Eastbourne one. Payment for the work would be made monthly. The contract was terminable on six months' notice in writing by either side.[27]

Going back to McNamara & Co. Ltd, they had, indeed, been unfortunate, but this only shows that though technical/mechanical problems were being solved, there were still financial and legal lessons to be learnt the hard way – even by big companies. They had been one of the biggest horse-van contractors for the Post Office and were changing over to motors by the end of 1906. *Commercial Motor* published details in the issue of 16 October 1913 of a Report from McNamara issued on the first of that month. A 'disastrous change has come over the fortunes of the company since the commencement of the new Post Office contract for the London Mail service'. This state of affairs was partly due to the increased price of petrol and the refusal of the GPO to revise the rates, but there was more to it than that. Directors of the haulage firm complained of getting only 2.25 revenue-earning miles for each hour of use with the Post Office because of detentions without payment. 'It is possible for an expensive motor car to be kept for 25 minutes and then dispatched on a journey occupying 2 minutes, and kept for another 25 minutes, with the result that for the whole period of 52 minutes the company received a remuneration of 4½d.' (just under 2p). This particular contract was for five years until June 1917, although McNamara had the option of terminating it at the end of June 1914 if they were willing to pay a penalty. Their report said, rather ruefully, 'the loss for the year ended 30th June last was no less than £25,000' but it is not clear without further research whether this was solely on the Post Office contract or overall on all their operations, probably the former.[28]

If the mails were conveyed by contractor, the Post Office did use motor vehicles for some of their internal work. They had bought a Wallis & Stevens steam-tractor in 1905 and a Maudslay 3-ton lorry in 1907 for the purpose of conveying heavy cable drums and stores. In 1910 they bought a couple of 30 cwt vehicles for miscellaneous stores and then in 1913 they added five more Allday & Onions 30 cwt vehicles.[29]

Apart from contractors such as Carter Paterson and McNamara, big stores such as Harrods and Shoolbreds, brewers and flour millers, and large organizations such as the Post Office, another substantial group which made use of motor transport in this first experimental decade was made up of local authorities – town and county councils. They were responsible for a range of services which included maintenance of streets and roads, emptying of dustbins, and the cleansing of the streets. This last must have been quite a job in the bigger cities. One has only to think of those 25,000 horses which pulled London buses, not to mention the thousands pulling bread or milk vans, brewers' drays, private carriages and so on. The Medical Officer of Health in Battersea said in his Annual Report early in 1905 that an estimated 363 tons of solid and 25,377 gallons of liquid horse manure were deposited in the streets of London each day.[30] While we might wonder how estimates could be so remarkably precise, nevertheless we have to admit that there would have been a lot of the stuff to be cleared. I do not have available any estimates, precise or otherwise, of the quantity of household rubbish to be removed, but that, too, was clearly a substantial haulage job. Then there were the great quantities of stone and chippings to be moved from railway stations to various spots around the county where road repairs were being undertaken. The local authorities, then, were 'own-account' operators in a big way.

As was mentioned in the previous chapter, Chelsea Borough Council were using road motors very soon after the 1896 Act was passed. After trying out that first Thornycroft dustcart in 1898 and ordering three vehicles very soon after, they built up their fleet gradually – the Thornycroft steam-tipper in February 1900 (at a price of £550, including a cartage body and a tank body), a couple of Leyland steam wagons the following August for £950, two more in September 1903, again each with two bodies, and another one of the same in June 1905. By this time the merits of the steam wagons had convinced the council officials, so their next order doubled their fleet. They ordered ten Leyland steamers in 1906 with cartage bodies plus five water tanks for the round sum of £5550.[31] Willesden, too, has already been mentioned earlier in the chapter as running steam wagons.

One noteworthy aspect of these early purchases is that the buyer often contracted with the manufacturer to do an annual check and overhaul of the vehicles. When Westminster City Council sought tenders for three wagons in the summer of 1908 the Leyland quotation of £580 each (plus £85 if rubber tyres were fitted) carried the additional information that the company would maintain the vehicles free of charge for the first year and for the following four years at £68 15s. 0d. per annum. Similarly Kensington Borough Council's purchase of two Thornycrofts in 1912 was accompanied by a maintenance contract: the first year was free, years two to five would be £65 p.a., years six to eight, £70, and the ninth and tenth years would be £90 p.a. Obviously these contracts did not include tyres.[32] Week by week throughout those pre-First World War years *Commercial Motor* listed various local authorities which had bought or ordered or had resolved to order, motor vehicles. By 1913 some forty local authorities owned about 200 vehicles in total but, admittedly. these were not all – perhaps not even mainly – road haulage vehicles. The list included fire engines, ambulances, prison vans, tower wagons, sweepers and similar utility vehicles. The experience of Chelsea was not uncommon – a single vehicle at first, one or two more added over a few years and then a quite substantial order. Liverpool started using motors in 1910 and, just before the war, in June 1914, they ordered eight Halley 6-tonners to add to their existing twelve. They were said to have had purchases of a further 24 Halleys in hand just as the war started. The Halleys cost about £700 apiece.[33]

Though road motors meant competition for the railways, some of the companies soon learnt that road transport had its merits. They quickly started using motors for collection and delivery work at the bigger stations and in some areas they used motors instead of undertaking the much greater expense of building branch lines or even the much-discussed light railways. The GWR had a 5-ton 'Yorkshire' steam-wagon with a couple of trailers at Henwick Station near Worcester in the summer of 1905 and were doing a daily twelve-mile run along the Teme Valley, calling at various depots of the Teme Valley Agricultural Association. This service carried 556 tons in the first five months of 1905 and 1114 tons in 1909, but it was withdrawn in 1909 since working costs were exceeding receipts by about 60 per cent.[34] The NER similarly were operating by road from Tollerton (Notts) and the Brandsby and Northallerton areas of Yorkshire. The last two were started to 'assist agriculture' but often had to rely on the carting of roadstone for the councils. They were withdrawn at the start of the Great War.[35] By the end of 1905, too, the LNWR had a couple of 5-ton Foden steamers doing feeder work in the hilly areas of North Wales.[36]

In the spring of 1906 there were no less than six private Bills of various railway companies before Parliament, seeking powers to operate road vehicles. The Bill brought forward by the London, Brighton and South Coast Railway, for example, sought powers simply to carry goods, parcels and passengers by road. But that really was asking for a significant extension of their function and it is not surprising that it was opposed by firms such as Carter Paterson and bodies such as the London Master Carmen's Association. In the event the Bill was amended in committee and the opposition withdrew, leaving the company with new powers only to carry by road goods 'which have been, or are to be, conveyed by rail'.[37] That limited the railway company to collection and delivery rather than allowing them general powers to convey goods by road. Had the latter been allowed, it would have enabled the large and powerful companies – which the railways were – to run struggling road haulage firms right out of business.

Immediately before the First World War there were over one hundred railway companies operating in Britain, though most of them were small. Most were set in their ways and their road transport fleets listed in the *Railways Directory* for 1914 (data for 1913) were mostly in the form of horses and carts. However, the GWR had 67 motor lorries, the L&NW 43, the NE 23, the Midland 18, and the L&SW 16. No other had as many as 10, and the total for the twelve companies having motor lorries was 190.

It is only to be expected that if a new, fast and flexible system of transport had come on the scene the newspaper companies would be among the first to take advantage of it – and so they did. Pickfords, we are told, were now [i.e. August 1906] carrying the *Daily Mail* and the *Daily Mirror* to various South Coast watering-places, including Brighton, Newhaven, Seaford and Margate. 'The service rendered is proving highly acceptable to all the interested parties including members of the public, who get their papers much earlier.' The 2-ton 'James & Brown' van left the *Daily Mail* premises at 1.20 a.m., got to Brighton at 4.00 a.m., Lewes at 5.00, Newhaven at 5.20, whence it went on to a couple of military camps. After a break the van set out from Seaford Camp at 9.00 a.m getting back to the Hammersmith depot at 12.30. The trials for this service covered nine days' operations – 160 miles a day for a consumption of just under 12 gallons petrol at 9d. (3.7p).[38] These were not the first deliveries by road, for some months earlier *Commercial Motor* had reported that the *Newcastle Chronicle* had six Clement-Talbot 2-cylinder vans of 10-12 hp each capable of carrying 15 cwt of newspapers. A seventh van was held in reserve. The paper had bought the first of these vans in October 1903. By 1912 the *London Chronicle* was reported to have had 29 1-ton vans in use.[39]

In this first decade of road haulage much that we might consider very modern was already in place. As early as 1905 a company was registered in Bury to supply vehicles both on lease and on hire purchase. In 1908 *Commercial Motor* carried an article describing in detail the method of hire purchase; vehicles could generally be had on payment over three years. The manufacturers themselves had sold a great many vehicles on deferred payments systems, but by the summer of 1911 trade was 'in such a healthy state that they [could] afford to decline such business and leave it to London stores and dealers whose organizations [were] specially suited for it'.[40] Quite a number of companies supplied vehicles on hire. Trade was good, indeed. An enquirer seeking in 1912 to hire a vehicle and driver for odd loads was told, 'the demand for motor vans on hire is so great at present that few contracting owners entertain work on odd days in the manner which you mention'. By 1910 at least nine bodies were on record as hiring out vehicles – though in all probability there were many more.[41]

While petrol-lorries were handling with fair comfort loads of up to five tons by the start of the Great War in 1914, and steam wagons, particularly with trailers attached, could do even better, some attention must be given to traction engines. As has been seen in previous chapters, these had come into use from the middle of the nineteenth century and had been, up to the early years of the twentieth century, the only mechanical means of road transport. They hauled a variety of heavy loads such as grain and flour, road-stone, machinery, furniture and, as modern readers are aware, fairground and circus equipment. They were particularly useful for outsize loads which the railways could not handle. They could cope with loads of 60 tons or more at a time. However, with the advent of the steam wagon and the heavier petrol lorry, the traction engines lost some ground in the area of smaller payloads of five or ten tons. Despite this the number of traction engines was increasing up to the war. John Allen, Chairman of the National Traction Engine Owners' and Users' Association, told a Departmental Committee of the Local Government Board in October 1915 that the number of engines in haulage work had increased by about 25 per cent over the previous twenty years. At the time he spoke there were some 1400 engines in such work in England and Wales, but he did not give any figures for Scotland.[42] The number in haulage work was small in comparison with the 8400 or so used for steam ploughing, threshing, and so on.

Mr Allen distinguished between the south of the country and the north. In the south, he said, traction-engines were used mainly in hauling road materials for councils. (His own company's engines, based at Cowley, Oxford, did little else, he said.) In the north of the country, on the other hand, 'they are used for moving heavy machinery'. This was obviously a generalization, for we know, for example, of traction engines hauling logs from many miles around the neighbouring counties to the furniture manufacturers in High Wycombe.[43] Other witnesses before the Departmental Committee also added some different detail. Mr George Arnold of Wm Arnold and Sons, Paddock Wood, Kent, said his firm used eleven traction engines in their flour milling business,[44] and he mentioned a gas company which he knew also employed these 'heavy locomotives'. Similarly, a representative of Barnsley Co-operative Society talked of deliveries of flour and foodstuffs from their mills. Interestingly, both of these gentlemen referred to other mechanical transport. As well as their eleven traction engines in haulage, Arnold's had two steam-wagons, one steam-tractor, and a petrol-lorry. The Barnsley Co-op. had a couple of 'motors' as well – a 7-tonner and a 3-tonner.[45] Though the matter being dealt with by the Committee was damage to road surfaces, these three witnesses mentioned financial matters in passing. Allen always employed engines of the maximum legal size – 14 tons – since they were capable of hauling 25–30 tons at practically the same cost as a smaller engine hauling 18–20 tons; just slightly more for fuel. But while an engine would last for twenty years or more and could do the work of thirty horses, nevertheless there was so much competition that there was little profit in haulage. 'I have never known a man who owned hauling engines alone who died worth much money.' Maybe he was anxious to convince the committee of hauliers' poverty in the face of prohibitions by highway and bridge authorities and heavy charges for 'extraordinary traffic'. Mr Arnold, on the other hand, said that the gas company had reduced haulage costs by 50 per cent by substituting traction engines for horses. The man from the Co-operative gave no explanatory detail at all in saying that their deliveries the previous year had cost 2s. 9d. per ton (14p) by traction engine and 3s. 6d. by motor.

Traction-engine-owners were peculiarly subject to claims from highway authorities for road damage said to be due to 'extraordinary traffic'. Mr Fearnley, the Barnsley Co-operative Society witness, might have been forgiven if he had sounded bitter about his experience. His engines had for a long time regularly used a macadamized main road. Then tram lines were laid and the road resurfaced with granite setts. These were rather slippery and on one occasion, when an engine with several wagons in tow was descending a steep curved hill, the rake got out of control and slithered about the road. The wagons jack-knifed and the whole lot came to rest, fortunately, within a few feet of a tram-car. The Co-op decided that that was enough, and switched their route to a minor road. Then they got the bill for £284 for repairs to the minor road. They took the matter to Court but the judge was not interested in why they were using the minor road. It would have been all the same if the sea had risen up to wash the main road away. Their use of the minor road did constitute 'extraordinary traffic' and the Co-op had to pay £150.[46]

Notes

1. *CM*, 31/5/1906, p.275.
2. *CM*, 8/6/1905, p.259;
3. Ibid., p.260.
4. Ibid., p.253.
5. *CM*, 15/6/1905, p.287.
6. *CM*, 20/7/1905, p.365.
7. *CM*, 8/6/1905, p.260.
8. *CM*, 23/3/1905.
9. *CM*, 8/6/1905, p.255.
10. *CM*, 29/6/1911, pp.341–2.
11. *CM*, 13/4/1905.
12. *CM*, 26/3/1908, p.59.
13. *CM*, 20/7/1911, pp.421–3 and 27/7/1911, pp.438, 439.
14. *CM*, 3/10/1907; 22/2/1912, p.529; and 30/1/1913, ads pp.xvi,xvii.
15. *CM*, 26/8/1909, p.505 and 22/2/1912, p.529.
16. *CM*, 12/6/13, p.339; 8/3/1906, p.512; 15/3/1906, p.415; 17/10/1912.
17. *CM*, 13/2/1913 and 24/4/1913.
18. *CM*, 25/04/1907, p.201.
19. *CM*, 10/10/1912.
20. *CM*, 23/5/1907, p.302.
21. *CM*, 12/8/1915.
22. *CM*, 25/9/1913, p.86.
23. *CM*, 25/9/13, p.86.
24. *CM*, 5/3/1914, p.22.
25. *CM*, 16/7/1914, p.494.
26. *CM*, 8/4/1915, p.112.
27. Automobile Commercial Vehicle Review, Vol. III, No.11, 26/4/1905, pp.170–172.
28. *CM*, 16/10/1913, p.148.
29. *CM*, 11/9/1913, p.44.

30. *CM*, 17/8/1905, p.437.
31. *CM*, 5/8/1915, p.471 and 486–7.
32. *CM*, 28/3/1912, p.74.
33. *CM*, 25/6/1914, and 3/9/1914, p.9.
34. *CM*, 18/1/1905, p.386.
35. Ibid; and Select Committee on Transport, 1918, Minutes of Evidence, Question 1446.
36. *CM*, 14/12/1905, p.286.
37. *CM*, 12/4/1906, p.122.
38. *CM*, 16/8/1906, p.496; 30/8/1906, p.539; and 27/9/06, p.53.
39. *CM*, 29/3/1906, p.86 and 24/10/1912.
40. *CM*, 13/4/1905; 14/9/05; 14/5/08, pp.2274–5; 3/8/1911.
41. *CM*, 15/7/1909, p.400; 28/7/1910, p.439 and 17/10/1912.
42. Departmental Committee on Construction and Use of Road Locomotives and Heavy Motor Cars. Minutes of Evidence, Question 5278.
43. Royal Commission on Motor Cars, 1906. Cmd. 3081.
44. Departmental Committee. Minutes of Evidence, Questions 5778–83.
45. Ibid., Questions 5659–702.
46. Ibid.

CHAPTER FOUR

Ways and Means

On the eve of the bloodbath which the First World War was to be, the haulage industry had almost completed its first decade. Some motor users had been operating a little longer but, as we have seen, the Heavy Motor Car Order of 1904 signalled the real beginning. While it could not be claimed that mechanical traction had despatched the competition – very far from it – the writing was on the wall clearly enough to point to a healthy future for the new industry. In regard to one element of the competition the *Municipal Year Book* of 1914 (p.655) could say:

> In this issue ... we are able to cite a few instances of the relative cost and output of work of horse and motor traction which leave no room for doubt that even in detached cases – that is when the horse and motor are working together, and on a comparatively small scale – all the advantages under every condition of full and partial employment and weather are in favour of the motor.

Perhaps that was overstating the case, for all those thousands of people who went on using horse and cart for the next twenty or thirty years were not complete fools. Their capital costs were low. But motor transport was effective and efficient and the *Year Book* went on:

> One thing is abundantly clear, that municipal bodies are now fully alive to the advantages of the motor, for orders are being distributed all round very largely in excess of last year, and more particularly the year before, but as long as the service is divided between the horse and the motor, it will be impossible to derive the full benefits from the motor.

Numerous municipalities were listed as having distributed orders 'all around' to Leyland, Thornycroft, Foden, Commer, Albion, Hallfords, Karrier, and so on, but it certainly did not include all the local authorities in the country.

The other competitors – the railway companies – had already lost some traffic, to road, but road haulage had hardly made a dent in the 400 or 500 million tons of freight being carried annually by the railways in three-quarters of a million wagons. The railways hardly noticed what they had lost; perhaps it eased things a little – a very little – for them.

Road vehicles need roads to run on and this had proved a thorny problem in the first decade and a half of motor transport. After the series of turnpike acts in the seventeenth century had produced some reasonable roads and allowed the speeding up of stage-coaches, the process was killed by the advent of railways. With the bulk of the nation's passengers and freight carried by rail – the 'iron road' – little attention was given to roads, and right through the nineteenth century it was mainly in the towns that reasonable conditions for vehicles were enjoyed. Outside the urban areas the roads did not need to be of a very high standard, since only farm carts and occasional deliveries passed over them. In many rural areas the practice was simply to dump some gravel in the potholes or softer stretches of the road and allow the traffic to roll it down. Some authorities did have steam-rollers to do the job, but not by any means all of them. These country roads were usually rough, often muddy, and frequently very dusty in the summer. Where there was need for better roads they would be treated according to McAdam's methods – small stones of granite or similar durable material filling in the gaps between the larger stones underneath. This would be sprayed with water to help to bed down the small stuff, and the road would usually be rolled to produce a fairly smooth surface. In the first decade of the century private cars, vans, buses and freight vehicles increased rapidly in number and the roads suffered. Reference has already been made to the early battles about demands for payment for damage done to roads by 'extraordinary traffic'. By the time the Royal Commission on Motor Cars was taking evidence in 1905 it was clear that serious action was required to cope with the problem of roads.

Some of those who gave evidence – such as the Motor Vehicle and Wagon Users' Association (MVWUA) – were prepared to accept a tax to be administered by a central authority for bringing roads up to a prescribed standard[1], and the Royal Commission's Report published at the end of July 1906 carried such a recommendation in its Paragraph 74. A year and a half later when it was likely that the Chancellor was going to include taxation of motor vehicles in his next budget the Commercial Motor Users' Association, as the MVWUA had now become, had no objection to a reasonable tax, 'if there is a guarantee that the proceeds will be spent on the roads'. They went to see the Chancellor all the same, in February 1908, to inform him that 'There is no precedent for the imposition of a burden on trade and industry.' They had told the Royal Commission what they considered a reasonable tax, 5s. (25p) per annum per ton of registered axle weight.[2] The government then set up – by the Development and Road Improvement Funds Act, 1909 a Road Board, 'for the purposes of improving the facilities for road traffic [a clear recognition that road traffic was growing] ... in the United Kingdom and the administration of the road improvement grant'. This grant was authorized by Section 90 of the Finance (1909–10) Act, which provided for the net proceeds of a 3d. (about 1.25p) per gallon duty on 'motor spirit' and of the licence fees for motor cars affected by the Act (that is, not buses and hackneys) to be paid into a Road Improvement Fund. From the road haulage point of view it is worth noting that half the duty on motor spirit would be refunded where the vehicle was 'constructed or adapted for use, and [was] used solely for the conveyance of any goods or burden in the course of trade or husbandry'. Motor buses and hackney cabs got the rebate too.

But in May 1909, when the Commercial Motor Users' Association (CMUA) heard of the proposed taxes, they immediately passed a resolution saying:

> That this Committee views with consternation the proposed tax of 1½d per gallon upon petrol for use in commercial vehicles which is equal to an increase of 25% on the fuel bill, and is of the opinion that this contemplated handicap upon this country's internal transport and communication compares very unfavourably with the practice in Germany, Switzerland and Italy, and other continental countries whose governments encourage by substantial subsidies motorbus and other motor services. The Committee is also of the opinion that the proposal to tax one class of transport for the benefit of all other users of the highway is inequitable and contrary to the accepted principles of taxation.[3]

The Times of 7 May had thought it 'hard that a new industry and a new method of locomotion should be practically taxed out of existence', and *Commercial Motor* asked why horse-drawn transport was not also subjected to a tax, as it would gain benefits; 'and what about private carriages, tradesmen's vans, farm carts?' It might have added the 5-ton steam-wagons which paid no tax either, and traction-engines which got away fairly lightly on £10 per annum. The editor was in no doubt that:

> commercial motoring is nothing short of a necessity to our continued industrial existence; it is a case of life or death to the manufacturer that his goods should be promptly conveyed from point to point, and not subjected to railway delays and uncertainties, and any deterrent which the government may place upon this new branch of transport is a hindrance to the commercial prosperity of the country as a whole.[4]

The government went ahead with the tax.[5] The effect of the duty on petrol was to increase running costs slightly. A 1-ton motor van doing 13 m.p.g. would cost an additional 0.115d per mile (about one-twentieth of 1p), some £9 12s. 0d. per annum on an average 20,000 miles. A 3-tonner doing 6.5 m.p.g. would cost an extra 0.23d per mile (one-tenth of lp).

The Licence duties to be paid into the Road Improvement Fund were raised under Sec. 86 of the Finance Act but did not at that time affect commercial vehicles. They were charged on private cars on a horsepower basis and ranged from £2 2s. 0d. for cars up to 6½ h.p. to £42 for over 60 h.p. Since there were very many more private cars around – paying 3d. per gallon on fuel plus the licence fee -than there were freight vehicles paying the 1½d. on petrol, the haulage industry was, perhaps, not too hard done by. Once the industry had got over its shock, it realized that good roads were a real benefit and *Commercial Motor* was soon estimating that £20 per annum would be saved in repair bills for a 2-ton van.[6] There was still a little niggle in that operators had to pay the 3d. duty when buying petrol and then submit a claim to the Excise for refund of 1½d. It was alleged that the Excise officials often took over six months after the claim was made to pay the rebate.[7]

So far as the Road Board was concerned, Section 8 of the 1909 Act gave it power:

> with the approval of the Treasury,
> (a) to make advances to County Councils and other highway authorities in respect of the construction of new roads or the improvement of existing roads,
> (b) to construct and maintain any new roads which appear to the Board to be required for facilitating road traffic,

The term 'improvement' was defined in Section 5 of the Act to include widening, cutting corners, altering steep gradients, and 'the treatment of a road for mitigating the nuisance of dust'. The term 'road' included bridges, viaducts and subways and the new roads which might be constructed included 'by-pass roads'. While it is not surprising that the disposal of funds should have been subject to the approval of the Treasury, it is interesting that that powerful wing of government should have been made responsible for appointing the Board members. It might have been thought that the Local Government Board, which was responsible for overseeing local authorities, and for roads and road traffic, would have been the appointing body. The Treasury it was, though, and for a start they named Sir George Gibb (a railway director) as Chairman. Perhaps reflecting the spirit of the times, too, the Treasury appointed several worthy Lords as Board members on what appears to have been a regional basis. It is not surprising that, as well as the chairman, one other member was a railway director, for before the First World War some 45 railway directors sat in the House of Lords and in the Commons another thirty-five represented their companies – that is, as well as representing their constituents. The Secretary of the Board was W. Rees Jeffreys; the Chief Engineer was H.P. Maybury, the County Surveyor of Kent; and the Consulting Engineer Colonel R.E. Crompton. The Board was assisted by an Advisory Engineering Committee which, as well as the Chairman, Chief Engineer and Consulting Engineer of the main body, included Mr John Brodie, Chief Engineer of the City of Liverpool, and Mr John Willmot, County Surveyor of Warwickshire.

The Board began operations in the middle of May 1910, in temporary offices at 4 Cowley St, London, better known today as the headquarters of one of our political parties, but soon moved to 'permanent' offices in Queen Anne's Chambers, Broadway, Westminster. It did not lose any time getting a circular out to county councils and other highway authorities saying that the Board was prepared to receive applications for advances but stressing that at the outset it wanted applications only in respect of work of 'the most important and urgent nature'. The circular suggested to the highway authorities that preference would be given to applications which had been the result of conferences between the county surveyor concerned and the surveyors of the non-county boroughs, urban and rural districts in the county. The response to this invitation tells us something of how the highway authorities saw their priorities. According to the First Report of the Road Board, the initial applications were as follows:

Purpose	Amounts requested England & Wales	Scotland
	£	£
Improvement of road crusts	1,745,000	724,891
Road widening and improvement of curves and corners	2,422,287	126,904
Road diversions	464,055	29,176
Reconstruction – improvement of bridges	666,251	48,365
New roads and bridges	342,166	–

As might be expected, the more populous areas around London generated a large part of the requests, at least for the second and third categories above. Of the £2½ million requested for road widening, and so on, London sought some £550,000, Middlesex £612,000, and Surrey £165,000. All the other county boroughs in England and Wales asked, in total, for £440,000. Outside of these, four counties asked for amounts around £50,000. One of these four, Glamorgan, was top in the road diversions field, asking for £135,000.

The Board had to decide quickly how it was going to share out the available money, for, as it pointed out on page five of that first report, 'actual and immediate requirements ... [are] ... far in excess of the moneys available, and consequently no apportionment could at the present time practically be made on the grounds of the comparative importance of the requirements'. So it made an initial distribution to the four countries of the kingdom purely on the basis of population, even though it was well aware that 'the burden of motor traffic' had fallen more heavily on England, and to a lesser extent on Scotland, than on Ireland. The Board decided, too, as a matter of principle, that 'it would not be advisable to begin by selecting for assistance a few large works in a limited number of places [but rather] to distribute grants widely'. It would not, itself, 'at present' undertake the direct construction of new roads but would try to make the most of the existing roads, 'to improve and utilize these to the best advantage'. It felt, too, that it would be better to deal with approach roads to cities rather than to try to relieve congestion in the city streets. Finally, in recognizing that the most urgent problem was in the condition of road crusts, the Board announced that it would favour projects to apply 'bituminous binding material', that is, tar.

The general procedure adopted was that after considering an application the Board would, if satisfied, 'indicate' its general approval and the promise of a grant. It would then go into detailed examination of the proposal with the technical officers of the authority concerned. Only then would the final amount be decided. The Board members were wise enough in the ways of this world to realize that 'if the Local Authorities could obtain from the ... Fund the whole cost of the proposed works they would be less careful in designing, proposing and executing these works than if they have to pay a proportion' (First Report, p.7). So the grant, as a general rule, was 75 per cent of the cost.

The Board got going right away in another direction by asking the Treasury for permission to set up a laboratory for the testing of road materials within the National Physical Laboratory at Teddington, and to enter into working arrangements with H.M. Geological Survey for reports on rock samples. The road haulage aspect, however, is more important to readers of this book. Here the Road Board's members and advisers were well aware that, expert as was their own knowledge, they had very little hard evidence about the volume of traffic on most roads throughout the country. They suspected that surveyors in the counties were in a similar position and it was clearly desirable that requests for grants be backed up by sound information. So the Board immediately suggested to the highway authorities that they should start doing some traffic counts in the areas they controlled using the Board's *pro forma* to record the information. Unfortunately, from our point of view, the published information does not distinguish between private cars, buses and freight vehicles. Being concerned only with the wear and tear on roads, the Board merely asked for numbers of motor vehicles and the gross weight passing over a given stretch of road and similar data about horsedrawn vehicles. The *pro forma* suggested an 'assumed average weight' for each type of vehicle. For horse-drawn vehicles the lowest figure – for a light, one-horse vehicle – was 0.4 tons and the maximum – for a heavy, two- or more horse vehicles – 3 tons.

For mechanical vehicles the weights were:

Motor cycles	0.13 tons	Light tractors	5.0 tons
Motor cars	1.6 tons	Their trailers	5.0 tons
Motor vans	2.5 tons	Traction-engines	12.0 tons
Motor lorries		Their trailers	8.0 tons
(rubber tyres)	6.0 tons	Motor bus	6.0 tons
(steel tyres)	10.0 tons		
Their trailers	5.0 tons		

East Sussex, for example, did counts at 100 points on their 416 miles of road during the months of October 1910 and September 1911, and recorded data for seven-day periods. The counts were made for sixteen hours each day, for in those days apparently sensible people stayed in bed at nights and there was thought to be little worth recording between 10.00 p.m. and 6.00 a.m. The figures were detailed in the Second Annual Report of the Road Board in 1912. The lowest figures recorded showed an average of only 39 vehicles passing per day of which 17 were mechanical, and the average total for all vehicles was only 59 tons. This point (between Hawkhurst and Seddlescombe) does not appear to have been very busy and such vehicles as used it were obviously the lighter types. At the other extreme was Preston Road, Brighton, where an average of 955 vehicles passed daily, of which 346 were mechanical. The average daily gross weight was 1898 tons. Midway between these two figures was that of a point between Godstone and Turners Hill, where an average of 150 vehicles passed daily. Of these only 50 were mechanical. The average daily gross weight in this case was 248 tons. Of the 100 counts recorded, 33 were done in October 1910 and these show only six cases with more than 100 mechanical vehicles daily. Only the Brighton case mentioned above showed more than 200.

The other two-thirds of the counts were done in September 1911 and showed 22 cases of more than 100 mechanical vehicles daily, of which five cases were in the 101–200 vehicle category and a couple more with more than 300 mechanical vehicles per day. To make any worthwhile judgment about changes in traffic volume we have to select the ten instances where counts were done at the same point in each of the two years. At the very least these showed a doubling of the number of motor vehicles over the eleven months and in most cases a three- or four-fold increase, and all ten cases showed substantial increases in the proportion of mechanical traffic to all traffic. Naturally enough the greatest volumes of traffic were on routes to or from the larger towns – Brighton, Eastbourne, Lewes, Hailsham,Crawley. The average daily weights suggest that there was a heavy preponderance of private cars but, equally, a high rate of increase probably applies to commercial freight vehicles too. In setting out a specimen to illustrate how the returns should be compiled the Road Board's Third Report showed figures for the London–Petersfield road, near Farnborough, for the week ended 1 September 1912. It is not certain whether this was an actual return but it gives some idea of the proportions. The daily averages given were:

Motor cycles	84	Lorries	
Motor cars	268	(rubber tyres)	9
Motor vans	11	(steel tyres)	5
		with trailers	2
Light tractors		Traction-engines	
with trailers	8	with trailers	1

Kent, too, was among the first counties to do traffic counts, and recorded as early as September 1910 a daily average of 147 mechanical vehicles using the Canterbury–Dover road and 189 using the Ashford–Canterbury road. A year later the Eltham–Sidcup road was used by an average 318 mechanical vehicles daily (though that was in the whole 24 hours). Between September 1910 and March 1912 nineteen cases were recorded where the daily average of mechanical vehicles exceeded one hundred. In eight of these, motor vehicles comprised over half the total number of vehicles and in six others the proportion of motor vehicles was between 40 and 50 per cent. Unfortunately, unlike the East Sussex authorities, the Kent people did not do repeat counts at any given spot.[8]

Good roads could clearly contribute to smoother and more economical running, but so also could good rubber tyres. The heavier vehicles – the steam-wagons – stuck to steel tyres, as did traction-engines and tractors. But for the lighter vehicles rubber was very attractive. Initially, however, rubber – whether solid or pneumatic – was unreliable and expensive, though the improvement over the period up to, and even during, the First World War was dramatic. Without such progress road haulage would have had a much longer way to travel before achieving superiority.

Although a pneumatic tyre had been invented by a Scotsman, R.W. Thompson, in 1845 and tried for a time on horse-drawn vehicles, nothing much came of that. Another Scot, John Boyd Dunlop, while practising as a veterinary surgeon in Belfast, produced a much better article in 1888 and this was quickly put to use on bicycles by, for example, Mr Du Cros, who would be the driving force behind the Dunlop Tyre Company; the pneumatics demonstrated not only much greater comfort but also a considerable saving in effort by the rider. The Michelin Company in France came up with the first pneumatic tyre for motor cars in 1895. In those early days rubber was mainly collected from the wild trees in the rainforests of the Amazon and similar areas of Africa and the East Indies. A number of different varieties of rubber was collected in this way and it was highly likely to contain grit or other impurities. Prices fluctuated considerably, depending on the arrival of consignments. *Commercial Motor* pointed out in the issue of 29 July 1909 that 'Hard Cure Para rubber, normally 4s. 6d. to 5s. per lb [22½–25p] fell to 2s. 9d. in February 1908 due to the arrival of a surplus from USA.' It was now 8s. (40p) due to a shortage. 'Relief may be expected early in October when shipments from S. American harvests will begin to come in.' The mixed quality of the wild rubber, coupled with the uncertainties of manufacturing processes in which the makers were slowly feeling their way forward, resulted in tyres of rather uncertain performance in the first few years of the twentieth century. In 1904, for example, the Liverpool City Engineer (and later Road Board Advisory Engineering Committee member also), Mr J. Brodie, told a Local Government Board Departmental Committee on Motor Cars: 'I know from recent experience that there is a great variation in the wear of rubber tyres doing the same work and looking exactly the same.'[9] But that year saw the addition of 'carbon black' to the mix to harden the rubber and such improvements continued apace. The advent of the motor vehicle obviously created a growing demand, and it was hardly coincidental that the passing of the Act of 1896 came just at the time the first commercial plantations were started in Malaya. Despite the kind of fluctuations mentioned above, the London price of rubber fell from 6s. (30p) a pound in 1904–5 to 2s. 6d (12½p) in 1913–14.[10]

In general, pneumatic tyres were suitable only for cars and light vans with, at first, the tyres carrying only about 15 cwt. By 1905 one manufacturer, Palmer, was displaying a tyre at Olympia with the claim that it could carry a wheel load of 25 cwt. A 10 h.p. eight-seater bus fitted with these was said to have run for three and a half months without tyre trouble. At the same show the Continental Tyre Co. displayed tyres said to be able to carry a wheel load of 1 ton.[11]

Solid rubber tyres would be used for the heavier vehicles, of 2 to 4 tons, and we find the Managing Director of Milnes-Daimler telling the Royal Commission on Motor Cars in 1905 that tyre manufacturers were supplying tyres to bus companies at 2½d. per car-mile. It was not until 1908 or thereabouts that the state of the art allowed solid rubbers on 5-tonners,[12] though it was said as early as January 1907 that in the USA solid rubbers were usual for 5-tonners.[13] At the beginning of 1909 there were two common ways of fitting solids. The first was described as 'grip section', where the rubber tyre was wedged into the steel channel of the wheel. These were said to suffer from 'creep', with resultant wear at the base, and were liable to come away from the rim before they were fully worn. For a chassis for loads of 3 or 4 tons a set of these would cost about £70 and would give anything between 2500 and 6000 miles. At a life of 5,000 miles this would work out at 3.36d. per mile (just over 1¼p). The second method was more expensive. It was known as 'band section', in which the tyre was moulded and vulcanized to a steel band which was then hydraulically compressed on to the wheel. A set of these would cost £100 or more, depending on sizes, and would run between 9000 and 17,000 miles. If an average of 12,000, say, is taken, the cost per mile for tyres would be 2d. (rather less than 1p). We find *Commercial Motor* reporting towards the end of 1911 that:

> on a Milnes-Daimler van which first undertook the Liverpool–Manchester motor mail in 1902 tire cost was in the vicinity of 8d per mile run. A year later upon the Eastbourne motor buses ... the cost had been reduced to 4d per mile run. Now, as is generally well-known a five ton petrol lorry can be run at a cost for tires but little in excess of 2d.[14] [The spelling had not yet settled on 'tyres'.]

While the quality of tyres improved rapidly in the first decade of the twentieth century, lorry owners still had problems. In early 1907, we are told, few towns had any facilities for the repair or renewal of rubber tyres. Wheels usually had to be sent to London, which might mean two days by rail in each direction. Well might editors of transport journals encourage readers to provide themselves with spare wheels for their vehicles.[15] Users had to learn other lessons, too. What was the best size of tyre to use for a particular size of vehicle? Readers of *Commercial Motor* were told (27 Feb 1913, p.576) that 'the increase, for example, from 120mm to 140mm [width] on a 3-tonner frequently yields 14,000 miles compared with 8,000'. The article went on to set out 'present day practice for band tires' – a table of sizes for various axle weights ranging from 56 mm width x 44 mm depth for axle weight of 10cwt, through 110 x 75 (single) or 75 x 60 (twin) for 2 tons, to 120 x 80 (twin) for 5 tons. The next week, in a sort of unconfirmed gossip column, 'One Hears'; the journal said that the tyre people wished to standardize loading at about 1½–2 pounds per cubic inch of mass. Issues at the same time carried advertisements of the Avon Rubber Co. listing retail prices of their tyres for particular vehicle capacities but without mention of tyre sizes. These ranged upward from £39 for a set of 'clinched-on' tyres, single front, twin rear, for a 10 cwt vehicle.

One of the problems in these early years was, indeed, lack of standardization generally, and there seemed to be a fair bit of uncertainty. One engineer, writing to *Commercial Motor* at the end of 1905, said:

> If I use too thick a tyre I shall waste engine power and the tyre will heat; if I use too thin a tyre I shall not absorb the vibration due to road shocks; if I use too wide a tyre I shall have to use a heavier wheel; if I use too narrow a tyre it will wear out very quickly. I must, accordingly strike a happy medium amongst this choice of evils.

But the trade press advocated the heavier tyres, as we saw in the previous paragraph.[16] British Standard rim sizes did not come until 1915.

There was lack of knowledge, too, and vehicle owners were accused in 1914 of thinking that solid rubber tyres would stand anything. There was no awareness, it was said, of the need for ample 'section, exact tracking, frequent inspection, and the need for replacement when the tyre was down to within 1 inch of the steel'.[17] By this time the tyre manufacturers were issuing booklets with their recommendations for appropriate tyres according to load and type of road surface – 'best city roads', 'best macadamized main roads', 'average provincial roads', and so on. While guarantees of 10,000 miles had been given by some firms since 1908 or 1909 (sometimes at a slightly increased price) by the beginning of the war, all the twenty or so manufacturers were giving such guarantees (maximum one year) but often with provisos about vehicle maintenance, avoidance of skidding and so on.[18] Even by the beginning of 1916, however, the Avon Company was pointing out in its advertisements that 'flats' occurring in solid rubber tyres were not the responsibility of the manufacturer. They were entirely due to some mechanical defect and could not be caused by any fault in the tyre itself. They listed the possibilities, including play in the steering gear, slackness in front-wheel bearings, lack of proper wheel alignment, bent axles, eccentricity in the wheel, and bad driving – for example, sudden applications of the brakes.[19]

The advantages of rubber tyres, whether solid or pneumatic (or the ones that were around for a time filled with a spongey 'rubberine' substance) were obvious. The vehicles ran more quietly and were fairly well insulated from road shocks, so that maintenance and depreciation costs were reduced substantially. Admittedly there was a great deal of debate in the pre-1914 press as to whether rubbers exercised suction on the road surface, throwing up clouds of dust and fine grit. The heavier vehicles with their steel wheels did not have the advantages, but neither did they earn reproach, for their wheels were claimed to roll the surface down. They did, however, have the disadvantage of the lower permissible speeds mentioned in Chapter Two.

In the last year or so of the war, tyre manufacturers generally gave guarantees of 10,000 miles for their solid tyres and pointed with pride to the many cases where 10,000 was exceeded. Even in unfavourable conditions the guaranteed mileage could be achieved and in favourable conditions it was said that mileages of three or four times the guarantee were possible. So common, indeed, did good mileages become that within a couple of months of the end of the war, while a couple of companies increased their guarantees to 12,000 miles, some twenty other companies jointly decided to abandon the idea of giving specific mileage guarantees.[20] There was still a lot to be done, of course. One aspect related to standardization of sizes. Early in 1919 the tyre manufacturers began discussions with a view to eliminating some of the less popular sizes, while the trade press was calling on vehicle manufacturers to adopt a short-list of standard tyre sizes. The position, then, at the end of the 1914–18 War was that the haulage industry could rely fairly heavily on the tyres they were getting. Pneumatics were general for the light delivery van of up to 1-ton capacity. Solids were used from that up to lorries of 5- or 6-ton capacity (both petrol and steam) and steel wheels still reigned supreme on anything above that weight. Since there were few regulations to worry about, a vehicle might have quite different tyres on the front from those on the twin rear wheels. Tyre costs set out in *Commercial Motor* of 20 March 1919 ranged from about 0.75d. per mile for a tiny 5 cwt parcel van, through 1.87d. for a 3-tonner, to 2.88d. for a 5-ton petrol lorry. Rubber tyres on steamers would cost a bit more – as much as 3.6d. per mile (1.5p) on a 5-tonner.

Notes

1. *CM*, 16/11/1905, p.195.
2. *CM*, 20/2/1908, p.521.
3. *CM*, 13/5/1909, p.196.
4. *CM*, 6/5/1909, p.165.
5. Sec.84–86, 90 of Finance (1909–10) Act, 1910.
6. *CM*, 23/9/1909, p.43.
7. *CM*, 1/12/1910, p.256.
8. Road Board, Second Report.
9. Departmental Committee on Motor Cars. Cmd 2070 1904.
10. *Economic History Review*, Vol. XXIV, No. 4, Nov 1971.
11. *CM*, 23/11/1905, p.222.
12. *CM*, 25/2/09, p.523.
13. *CM*, 3/1/1907, p.378.
14. *CM*, 2/11/1911, p.173.
15. *CM*, 14/3/07, p.2.
16. *CM*, 27/2/1913, p.576.
17. *CM*, 24/12/1914, p.308.
18. *CM*, 22/4/1915, p.157.
19. *CM*, 27/1/1916, ads p.25.
20. *CM*, 27/2/1919, p.4.

CHAPTER FIVE

Wars and Rumours of Wars

We have already seen in Chapter One that the French government of the late eighteenth century, not long after the end of the war with England, saw the possibilities for the transport of artillery of Cugnot's steam carriage, though they did not follow it up. Perhaps they had too much on hand considering the country's chaotic finances and a restless peasantry which in a few years would sweep Louis XVI and his colleagues away. Mechanized military transport was not to come yet, even though Trevithick was convinced that steam could do anything that horses could do in the field of transport. Long years were to elapse in which heavy wagons and heavy guns would be hauled to or from the battle scene by horse, often aided by the weary infantry struggling to get the equipment across rivers, through mud, and up and down hillsides. At the time of the end of the Crimean War in the mid-1850s steam power on roads was just beginning, with people such as Mr Bray designing traction engines and engaging in haulage operations to earn an honest penny. It is on record that one of his engines was on loan to the Royal Artillery for trial as a gun tractor in 1858, but what impact that made on military thinking is not at all clear.[1] Probably it was not forgotten, for in 1869 *The Illustrated London News* reported that two Aveling and Porter traction-engines were used in a combined land and sea exercise – an assault on Dover Castle. At least they were in the 'land' part, hauling a battery of guns up Castle Hill.[2]

In his *Century of Traction Engines*, Mr Hughes gives a great deal more information about military use of steam tractors. He tells how a Lt R.E. Crompton who was then at regimental workshops at Rawalpindi, submitted proposals at this time to the military authorities for the haulage of troops, stores and guns. Crompton, who was later to become well known by the road haulage industry, was put in charge of a small depot with a Ransomes 'Thompson' engine for experimental work. A couple of years later he was in England on behalf of the Indian Army to find better engines. Mr Hughes recounts Crompton's trials and tribulations as he tried out a couple of Ransomes engines which had been given appropriate Indian names. The 'trials' part of it included a run from Ipswich to Edinburgh and back in the autumn of 1871 with one of the engines, which was fitted with rubber tyres.

Mr Hughes tells, too, how in 1871 the Aveling Company designed and built a lightweight engine – 5 tons in working order – to meet the requirements of an Army committee set up to consider the possibilities of steam in military service. It is clear that the performance of steam generally, whether in military trials or in civilian use (we are now in the 'Red Flag' era), impressed many people and during the Franco-Prussian War the Germans used a couple of traction engines for moving stores and evacuating wounded in the Metz area.[3] Traction engines went to war again in a squabble between Russia and Turkey 1876–78.[4] By the time that Britain became involved in a war with the Boers in South Africa (1899–1901) the War Office had already been experimenting with different engines for several years. Lord Roberts called Crompton in to organize the mechanical transport aspect of operations and at least fifteen engines were in use early on in South Africa.[5]

A trial between Ipswich and Edinburgh was one thing – with ample supplies of fuel readily at hand and any number of streams and canals en route to provide essential water. South Africa was something quite different, with great areas of veldt having very little water, and coal available only near the railways. Giving evidence to the Royal Commission on the War in South Africa[6], Major-General Paget talked of the problems of maintaining supplies to Lindley from Kroonstad – forty miles away. 'The traction engines were employed – it was the first time I had seen them – for bringing me out supplies.' Asked what he thought of them, he said:

> They did exceedingly well, but the difficulty was coal. As an example: when they came to Lindley the first time they got there with 50 or 60 tons of forage, but their coal had given out ... They require to be used along a route where there are coal depots, otherwise they are practically useless.

Paget had to pull down some old houses to get timber to burn in the traction engine fireboxes. He added his opinion that they burned too much coal to make it worthwhile for them to carry their own. Lord Kitchener was a little more enthusiastic, but, in general, he confirmed Paget's view:

> We had about 45 steam road transport trains. As a rule they did useful work, but questions of weather, roads, water and coal limited their employment, as compared with animal transport, to which they can only be regarded as a supplement.[7]

There were some steam wagons in use in South Africa too, though details are sketchy. Lord Kitchener, continuing, said, 'The motor lorries [that is, steamers] did well. Thornycrofts are the best. They will, in the future, be found superior to steam road trains as field transport.'

One interesting possibility came from an officer of the Royal Engineers – Sir Elliott Wood. Saying that 'the electrical engineers came out with traction engines to carry searchlights', he went on to express his preference for 'motor-car searchlights'. But although 'I had a most excellent offer for motor-cars, the very thing that would have suited us, from a French firm, and the prices were very good', the whole thing came to naught. He had to put his order in via the War Department. They ignored the very suitable French cars at good prices and put the matter out to tender in Britain. That took time and no (or not many) motor-cars ever got to South Africa. Wood, however, anxious to get on with his project, bought some cars in South Africa and proceeded to have them adapted in Army workshops. Alas, 'They were just ready when the war ended.'[8]

The Royal Commission had been set up to try to discover what bungling and incompetence lay behind the fact that the mighty British Empire had to make such inordinate efforts – and suffered not a few defeats- in bringing 70,000 Boers to heel.

Transport was an important issue; the British were very unprepared in this as in other directions. But apart from the few remarks about mechanical transport which are quoted above, and apart from the railways, the whole emphasis is on the use of animals (as Paget's remarks about forage confirm). Over half a million horses, over 150,000 mules and donkeys, and, in the first fifteen months, some 150,000 oxen, were employed, with appalling mortality.

When government plans were announced in 1904 for the reorganization of the War Department and Army, the main concerns were administrative. Anyway, railways and animal transport were the order of things at the beginning of the twentieth century, and it is hardly surprising that no mention was made of specific detail such as mechanical transport. But it had not been forgotten. While the South African war had been going on a Mechanical Transport Committee had been set up at the War Office to look at the use of steam transport in South Africa and to consider the extent to which mechanical transport could usefully be employed for military purposes. The relative cost of such transport and of other means then in use had to be considered and, in addition, the committee was to make recommendations as to suitable engines and vehicles, organization and personnel.

A couple of familiar names appeared among the membership of this committee. Very soon after its inauguration Lord Stanley (the later Lord Derby) became its Secretary. He had close connections with the early transport industry, having been involved with the Liverpool Trials and one of the first road haulage companies. Major (as he now was) Crompton was a member too. Before the end of 1901 the Committee had arranged trials on a fairly substantial scale, though their rules excluded petrol-driven vehicles. Only one internal-combustion-engined vehicle was entered – a Milnes-Daimler – which used petrol to start the engine and then switched over to run on paraffin. The two best machines in these trials turned out to be a Foden and a Thornycroft and these were bought by the War Department and sent to South Africa for further testing.[9] It may have been these that Kitchener was referring to.

From the time it was set up the Committee took a close interest in what was going on in terms of development of self-propelled road vehicles whether in buses (which could be used for moving troops), cars (movement of officers), tractors and lorries (movement of supplies, guns, ammunition, even troops), or motor-cycles. Wherever trials of commercial vehicles were being held throughout the length and breadth of the country, a member of the Committee would be there, and of course, the War Department itself carried out more tests. A big problem was that the needs of the Forces were not necessarily met by a lorry designed for commercial purposes and vice versa.

The year 1903 saw a Volunteer Motor Corps – civilian vehicles and drivers – taking part in the annual army manoeuvres; the setting up of an Inspectorate of Mechanical Transport to supervise the growing number of military vehicles and act as technical advisers to the War Department; and, most significantly, the setting up of the first mechanized transport unit – No.77 Company of the Army Service Corps. From 1904 onward a few internal-combustion-engined lorries were bought each year. In 1906, the end of the first decade since the repeal of the Red Flag Act was fittingly marked by the inclusion, for the first time, of provision for the use of mechanized transport in the general 'Mobilization Instructions for the Field Army'. According to these Instructions the supplies and provisions for one cavalry division and six other divisions were to be staged forward from railheads by mechanized transport. It was assumed that by using motor transport, twice the distance covered by horse transport in a day could be achieved.[10]

The members of the Mechanical Transport Committee were gradually coming to the conclusion that internal combustion would be more likely to meet military needs than would steam, but there was a problem in that no one could be certain, in the first few years of the century, at least, of the reliability of petrol supplies. The bulk of oil from wells was then used for producing paraffin – a major source of household and business lighting – and for lubricants. There were not as yet furnace or diesel uses. So, while the War Office was interested enough in internal combustion, the main interest was in paraffin. We are told that Colonel (again promoted) Crompton spent £5000 of army money in an effort to produce to his design a satisfactory long-range medium-sized tractor for army purposes.[11] The sticking point was a useful paraffin carburettor. The sum of £5000 does not seem much in our present-day society, but before the First World War it would have provided a week's wages for perhaps three thousand unskilled men. The £30,000 spent by the Mechanical Transport Committee in the first decade of the century on experimental work has to be judged in the same light.

Whatever might be said about the Edwardians, they did not believe in being rash with money (the Treasury had taken a lot of abuse for the Boer War fiasco). So there was little prospect of substantial amounts being spent to provide for all the Army's needs in motor transport. One good old system which had provided the first 14,000 horses for the South African theatre of war was that of paying subsidies to civilian owners who registered their animals with the War Department in return for a small annual fee. The owners then undertook to hand over the animals on demand at the start of a war and they would be paid a fair sum. This seemed to offer a way forward in respect of motor vehicles, too. It would meet the needs of the peacetime army, enabling it to try out vehicles on manoeuvres at no great expense without saddling it with large numbers of vehicles not being used fully. At the same time it would instantly provide, it was hoped, a substantial number of vehicles at the outbreak of war. From a civilian point of view a subsidy would help those who were struggling to make a go of a new form of transport.

As early as 1902 Edmund Dangerfield, later proprietor of *Commercial Motor*, and E. Shrapnell-Smith, who would be his editor, were among those invited to the War Office to discuss the possibilities of a subsidy scheme. Nothing much came of it, for the War Office people thought that the £20 per annum subsidy demanded by the vehicle users was too much. In any case it is doubtful whether much could have come of it in the conditions obtaining before the Heavy Motor Car Order of 1904. By the beginning of 1906, though, with the use of motor transport about to be written into Army Mobilization Instructions, the time was ripe and *Commercial Motor*, mentioning that the idea had been reconsidered for several weeks, thought that a £10 annual subsidy with a generous scale of purchase might be satisfactory. Six weeks later, on 22 February, the journal reported that the War Department had written to the MVWUA proposing the outlines of a subsidy scheme for discussion. Owners, in return for the subsidy, would undertake to make their vehicles and drivers available for peacetime manoeuvres. They would be paid a hire charge. In the event of war the vehicles might be bought for home use and sold back to the owner after the war, or might be bought outright for use abroad. In no case would there be any compensation for disturbance to the owner's trade. The following week the journal was arguing that, apart from anything else, a registration subsidy of £3–£10 should be paid. It warned that owners would incur extra costs through heavy wear and tear to vehicles on the manoeuvres and through having to use horses instead. In the event of war owners would find difficulty in replacing vehicles quickly.[12]

After a year's negotiation with the MVWUA, the War Office produced its scheme in January 1907 – much as the Users had asked. Vehicles were divided into classes for which appropriate registration fees would be paid. Class A – 'Traction train units' – (that is, a heavy locomotive plus three trailers and a water cart) would get £2 2s. 0d. (£2.10p) plus 2s. 6d. (12½p) for each additional trailer. Class B2 (wagons of a capacity of 3 tons plus) would get £2 and vans of 20–30 cwt (Class B4) only £1. The full registration fees would be paid only if the vehicle were available for purchase by the War Office, but only a percentage would be paid if the vehicle were only available for hire. When (and if) the vehicles were required for hire, 30 days' notice would be given and the hiring period (stipulated by the owner on registration) would be continuous in categories of 5–14 days, 15–30 days, or 5–30 days in any one year. Hiring rates for Class A were £4 per day with additions for extra trailers, £4 for Class B2 and £2 per day for B4. These rates covered not only the vehicles but their crews as well. The owners had to provide for the pay, upkeep and accommodation of their men hired to the War Department (WD), and the men would be subject to military orders. The hiring rates also had to cover upkeep of the vehicle, petty stores and spare parts. The WD generously undertook to provide water, fuel, lubricating oil and grease, and paraffin for the lamps – but they disclaimed liability for 'any derangement of mechanism' while the vehicle was employed under normal conditions and in circumstances similar to those in which it was usually employed.

In the event of the Secretary of State for War certifying that there was a 'state of national danger', the WD would be entitled to exercise its purchase option. Class B vehicles had to be delivered to a specified site within five days of notice. The vehicle might be rejected if unserviceable but otherwise the owner would be paid 'the then value' plus 25 per cent to allow for disturbance to his trade. 'The then value' was the original purchase price minus a specified rate of depreciation – 12 per cent per annum for a B2 vehicle, for example, or 15 per cent for a B4. The minimum paid would never be less than 30 per cent of the original.[13]

Three months later the journal advanced the opinion that the registration scheme was 'a sound proposition for any commercial motor user'. There had been some response by then, but the editor expected an increase in registrations once 'the business advantages of the scheme are appreciated'.[14] Nevertheless the editor did complain subsequently of the niggardly nature of the scheme and compared it unfavourably with the German version which was 'generous to a degree'. It appeared that the latter seemed to be designed so as to permit the use of vehicles by companies in rural areas where normal commercial demand was insufficient'. By the autumn of 1908 the Germans had about one hundred vehicles under subvention. 'At this rate', said *Commercial Motor*, 'the year 1913 will see the German War Office in quasi-possession of 500 first class lorries'.[15] But perhaps the British scheme was not as unfavourable as all that. By March 1909 some 200 wagons and tractors were registered, and, according to Col. R.H. Beadon, historian of the Royal Army Service Corps, this had grown to about 700 vehicles registered under the main subsidy scheme by the outbreak of war in August 1914. This 'main' scheme was for vehicles which met the WD's specifications ('subsidy type' vehicles). There was also a 'provisional' scheme for reasonably suitable vehicles which did not measure up to the 'subsidy type' specifications. Beadon attributes the (in his view) poor response to the shortness of time since the scheme was inaugurated and to the 'smallness of the subsidy' which did not make it a commercial proposition for civilian users to buy 'subsidy type' lorries. Beadon, too, comments on the Germans – that they had gone into a scheme 'almost regardless of expense'.[16]

We are getting a little too far ahead though. Trials continued to be held throughout the intervening years, some under the auspices of the WD; some by bodies like the RAC which attracted WD interest. The RAC, for example, held trials in the summer of 1907, the object of which was 'to demonstrate in a convincing manner the advantages of mechanical haulage over horse haulage for the transport of freight'. A long list of criteria was published on which vehicles would be judged – accessibility for repair, adequacy of platform area and convenience for loading, adhesion, cost of carriage per net ton-mile, freedom from nuisance to the public and so on.

In the event, several War Department Diplomas were awarded in addition to the RAC's recognition. In Class C a Thornycroft 24 h.p. paraffin-engined lorry was adjudged the winner by the RAC and it also got the War Department Diploma. In Class E the first two got the War Office's award. The winners were a 30–40 h.p. miller's dray entered by Maudslay and a 30–38 h. p. lorry made by J.&E. Hall. Considering present-day prices, those of the Edwardian era are noteworthy. They ranged from the winning small van in Class A – a 10 h.p. Mann & Overton priced at £315 – through the Thornycroft already mentioned, priced at £595, to the bigger Maudslay at £860.[17]

In 1909, the WD held trials of its own for tractors, but the conditions laid down effectively ruled out steam, for the tractor had to be no more than 7 tons gross and to be able to carry fuel and water for 100-mile trips. There were to be eight days of tests and these would include braking, speed, manoeuvring, and hill climbing. An 8-ton gross load had to be hauled and an average speed of 5 m.p.h. had to be attained. The tractor had to be capable of being driven through 2 feet of water without the motive power being seriously affected; and a winding drum had to be fitted to haul the 8 tons up a 1 in 6 gradient.

The virtual exclusion of steam clearly presented problems to the manufacturers for although seven or eight months' notice had been given, only three tractors turned up on the occasion. The numbering of these in the competition – 3, 4 and 10 – suggests that there were other hopefuls entered which were not able to make it. Perhaps the first ten days of March was rather early in the year, for the weather was not altogether wonderful. But then freight transport by lorry is not just a fine-weather operation, so the trials went ahead. The day of the tests, on a measured mile at Harford Bridge on the London–Basingstoke road, produced fun and games. There was, we are told, 'a regular blizzard of snow and sleet raging incessantly until about noon, after which the downfall changed to one of sleet and rain'. It fell to the Thornycroft, 'owing to its superior running powers', to 'make the tracks' through the snow ahead of the others to get to the site. This machine was, indeed, 'the first tractor to return to the depot being many hours ahead of its competitors'. It had taken nine minutes to do the measured mile with its load.[18] That Thornycroft – described as a 50 h.p. heavy oil tractor – eventually won the competition and was purchased by the Mechanical Transport Committee for £975. According to *Commercial Motor* the tractor could not 'of course, be regarded as an experimental machine because the company had already turned out a number of paraffin-engined tractors'. The other two competitors had their merits. The Broom and Wade tractor 'proved itself capable of unlooked-for effectiveness when it came to winding the eight ton load through the bog at Claycart Bottom' . It appeared to have been a bit overloaded, however, with 8 tons. On the hill-climbing test it showed considerable power in low gear though it was rather slow. The one steamer in the competition -manufactured by Stewarts – was at a great disadvantage in comparison with either of the two internal combustion motors. 'It was hard pushed to get the unladen weight down to 6 tons' (that is, to keep within 7 tons with its water and fuel). It was a bit unfortunate, too, in that just before attempting the hill climb – a rise of 300 feet in 2200 yards up 'Hungry Hill' – it got the rear wheels of its trailer into a soft ditch. One sad feature of the early history of road haulage is that so many of the heroes remain 'unsung'. In respect of these trials, though, it is on record that 'at the end of the one mile stretch, Tom Baker, the Thornycroft driver whose record in road trials dates back to the first Liverpool competition of 1898 if, not to earlier days, gave a masterful display of smart manipulation'.

Commercial Motor, as was its custom, fired a broadside at the War Department, criticizing 'the Financial Secretary's branch' which by 'its ruthless manner [was] seriously hampering the advancement of transport organisation for the British Army'. The trials, it seems, had been delayed while a 'paltry vote' of £500 was discussed and in the end the India Office put up another £250 to make the £750 prize.[19] The real nub of the matter was that the War Department was happy to agree on specifications for its subsidy model and to let whoever would, register. (In the summer of 1908 they sent out letters to municipal authorities, which were operating at least a couple of hundred vehicles at the time, inviting them to register.) It gave the manufacturers no direct encouragement in financial terms to go to the bother of developing suitable military vehicles, nor did it place any large orders which would have perhaps compensated manufacturers for development costs. *Commercial Motor* argued, at the time, for a payment of £2000 each to several manufacturers to enable them to undertake development work. The subsidy models, too, were widely alleged to be unsuitable for commercial work. A respected modern historian comments that 'the Army never went over thoroughly to mechanized transport and failed to encourage the mass manufacture of automobiles'.[20]

As might have been expected, the War Department people was concerned with moving troops as well as supplies. With the help of London General Omnibus Company (LGOC) a large-scale exercise was carried out just before Christmas 1908, when 94 buses were used to concentrate troops at Shoeburyness to repel 'invaders'. Immediately after the tractor tests described above, a battalion of Guards was moved from London to Hastings and back in some 400 cars – that includes about 100 for Press, officials and visitors. From the point of view of freight transport the move of the necessary gear was carried out by means of 21 light Napier chassis with platform bodies, 5 de Dion 40 h.p. similarly constructed and 2 Fiat 3-tonners of 35–40 h.p. In case of breakdown these were accompanied by a Commer covered van and an unspecified 20 h.p. 2-tonner as spare vehicles. Perhaps with tongue in cheek *Commercial Motor* commented, 'It is open to doubt whether anything likely to be really useful in case of war was definitely proved. The Guards had the time of their lives and nobody was hurt.'[21] More to the point is that in that same March the Army Estimates were discussed in the House of Commons, during which the Secretary of State for War announced that cuts were to be made in the horse-transport branch of the Army Service Corps (ASC) while more funds for additional mechanical units would be forthcoming. In 1909, too, a Base Mechanical Transport Depot for the ASC, complete with workshops, was set up near Bisley. There was now no going back.

In December 1910 General Paul submitted a memorandum to the General Staff in which he said that 'There can be no doubt that our existing supply system is obsolete.' He was referring to a system where ammunition, foodstuffs, and all the impedimenta of war were moved forward from railheads in two or three stages by horse-drawn wagons. That system, incidentally, was totally incapable of supplying fresh food to any large number of troops and carried with it the nineteenth-century assumption that soldiers either lived off the land they were occupying or, at best, were provided with 'preserved' foodstuffs. General Paul proposed that units be replenished daily from the railway by mechanical transport convoys of fast motor lorries. Three-tonners would be employed for non-cavalry units and, presumably because cavalry formations might be expected to move forward faster, they would be supplied by 30 cwt vehicles.[22] Thereafter rather larger numbers of internal-combustion lorries were introduced into the Army.[23] Nevertheless horse transport was still there in a large degree and although the decision was made to abandon steam, too, a number of traction engines and steam wagons certainly found their way to France. They did good work, but what the 1910 Trials had shown was soon confirmed – if they ventured too close to the front line the plumes of smoke from their funnels quickly drew the attention of enemy artillery.

General Paul's ideas were taken up and the Field Service Regulations issued just before the war provided for the movement of all ammunition and supplies from seaports or base depots by rail to stations a little way short of the front. From there motor transport columns would move the material to 'refilling points' where it would be collected by the horse-drawn transport of the fighting units. Since a war of movement was expected, the 'refilling points' would be changed frequently and consequently the Quarter-Master General's Office would specify 'rendezvous' points to which the motor transport would head after leaving the railhead. There they would be met by guides to conduct them to the 'refilling points'.[24]

While it was envisaged that some 1400 lorries would be needed for a six-division expeditionary force, by the time the war started in August 1914, only about 700 vehicles were registered under the subsidy scheme and not all of those might be fit for military service. Quite contrary to the British reputation for 'muddling through', the call-up of vehicles went like clockwork. Telegrams went out the day war was declared and the mobilization of the vehicles was completed within the five days specified in the subsidy scheme. Such was the enthusiasm that 'among the numbers of impressed vehicles, it was found that some 300 arrived at Liverpool [one of the four collecting points] mechanically unfit from various causes, the principal of which were due to the over-anxiety of the civilian drivers to reach their destinations in the shortest possible time'.[25] These were sent to Bulford for repair. About 950 lorries went to France in the first days and this number was soon made up to 1200 – comprising both the Army's own vehicles and civilian subsidy lorries. The system set down in the Field Regulations broke down virtually from the first moment of contact with the advancing German forces because of the impossibility of keeping up with a rapidly changing situation. But within a month or two the opposing armies got bogged down in trenches and little substantial change was made in the lines for the next three years. Mechanized road transport could then play a major part.

In a book about commercial transport the fine detail of transport operations in France or in other theatres of war is not generally relevant but some points must be made here. The first of these is that just as the intensive operation of early petrol-engined buses by LGOC encouraged the development of reliable engines, so too did the intensive working of lorries in the war situation weed out weaker designs and ensured the development of a sound freight vehicle. War 'fronts' do not fall conveniently where good road and rail links had been developed for civilian needs. Much of wartime road transport was over narrow unsurfaced country roads in France and Belgium which had seen little more than the occasional farm cart passing. The roads quickly became morasses under intensive military operation and occasional shellfire or bombing. Such conditions were very testing indeed. The better roads and streets were pavé, that is, paved with stone blocks or wooden blocks – in effect cobblestones –

and these, too, gave the vehicles a hammering. Both roads and vehicles needed constant attention. Initially the French were responsible for road maintenance in their own country while the British Army dealt with roads in Belgium, but from the end of 1915 the British became responsible for all roads in their sectors. Since there was little road stone in Northern France, supplies of granite had to be brought in from Guernsey and conveyed by rail and road to wherever it was needed. At the time of the battle of the Somme in the summer of 1916 the best part of 5000 tons of stone a day were being used along the 12-mile front. Road stone continued to be a big item to be hauled by lorries, and, as was noted by the authorities, this haulage, too, was part of the problem of deteriorating roads. By the beginning of 1918 the General Staff was pointing out to the Armies the serious shortage of roadstone.[26]

More and more lorries were coming into use and when big offensives were in hand there were heavy tonnages to be moved. The Somme again may be taken as an example. Some 500–600 tons of heavy or medium ammunition were used up daily on each mile of the 12-mile front. The greater part of this was moved by lorry from railhead to the batteries, and some of it by motor to dumps from which light railways took it forward. Slightly more than that tonnage in light ammunition plus 270 tons of rations, ordnance stores, and so on (again per front-mile per day) were moved by lorry to the refilling points as described above. At this time the 4th Army had 1200 or 1300 lorries on ammunition supply alone, out of some 4670 which it had altogether. While there was only this one major offensive in 1916, there were four the following year with obviously increasing road traffic and congestion such as the M25 never saw. A Census of Traffic passing Fricourt Cemetery on 22 July 1916 recorded 7300 vehicles (both horse and motor) in the 24 hours.[27] That was five vehicles per minute on average and between 9.00 a.m. and 3.00 p.m. the density reached eight per minute.

Similarly, it was claimed that the French defence of Verdun in the first half of 1916 'was fought completely on petrol transport', as artillery and bombing had destroyed all other communication lines. The American Society of Engineers was told afterwards that 'during the height of the Verdun battle there was a 90 mile circuit over which trucks passed day and night for a period of several weeks, at average intervals of 20 seconds between each vehicle. At times traffic was as dense as it is on Lower Broadway during the rush hours.'[28]

When vehicles are heavily worked over poor roads they suffer and there were repair problems aplenty. One of the difficulties was that in these still early days of road freight transport there was no standardization of parts and, worse, there was not even standardization of name for any given component. Since the Army had acquired a motley collection of requisitioned civilian vehicles as well as the 'subsidy types', there was a ghastly spare-part problem – made worse by the fact that some of the vehicles were obsolete so far as the manufacturers were concerned. It took, the Army Service Corps (ASC) the best part of two years beginning in 1915 to achieve the degree of standardization they wanted. Part of the credit for keeping the Army's motor transport operating must go to the staff of the 'Home Mechanical Transport Depot'. From a dozen men in 1914 the depot eventually had 2431, their job being 'to supply all stores for the equipment and maintenance of all War Department vehicles'. Their growing expertise kept the supply of appropriate parts flowing. In addition they kept detailed records of issues to all types of vehicles in all types of environments. The knowledge in these men and their records found its way to manufacturers through the agency of ASC Inspectors who visited the factories in connection with testing of vehicles being bought for the Army. This must have been a major influence on the design of new components for lorries.[29]

Road transport in France and Belgium grew steadily and the Army had to prepare maps for the lorrymen – marking roads in different colours to indicate whether they could be used in both directions, whether they could be used by all traffic, or indeed whether they could be used by any lorries at all. By the summer of 1917 working was being examined carefully to see whether new railheads could be used a little nearer to horse transport, whether circular routes could be used – out one way and back another – and so on – in order to relieve road congestion. But though very substantial reliefs were achieved the fact was that demands kept growing. Apart from sheer traffic volume there were all sorts of problems. An example was in the matter of finding hard standing for vehicle parking overnight. It is recorded, for example, that lorries of the XV Corps at Bussy ran 14 miles light to the railhead, carried their load a distance of five miles and then ran 17 miles back to the park.[30]

One other point illustrates a difficulty of early transport. Among all the loads carried – ammunition, foodstuffs, engineering stores, roadstone, troops, civilian evacuees, even a couple of steam launches from Arras – one very important item was petrol. At the beginning of the war about 250,000 gallons a month were supplied mostly in flimsy 'cases' of 4 x 2 gallon tins mainly from Portishead, where the Asiatic Petroleum Company imported the petrol and filled up the tins. Sometimes the cases had 2 x 4 gallon tins. By the end of 1915 heroic efforts achieved the filling of 100,000 gallons a month. Consumption grew rapidly as motorized transport, tanks and aircraft increased consumption month by month. By the beginning of 1918 monthly consumption was about eight million gallons for general transport and about three-quarters of a million for aircraft. The Asiatic Petroleum Co. had opened a depot in Rouen in late 1917 where the filling was carried on by some 3000 workers. That was a lot of tins to be handled by train and lorry. Yet it was not until someone noticed the ludicrous procedure of using twenty men to pour 700 tins (1400 gallons) into the tanks of large bombers like the Handley Page that underground tanks and pumps came into use – in some places. Before the war ended there were 180 road tankers each of 600 gallons' capacity in use in France. With 150 rail tankers of 3000 gallons capacity they met about 15 per cent of needs. It is perhaps surprising that more tankers were not in use earlier in the war. The War Department had strongly supported the efforts of the petrol companies and the trade press to get the use of tankers legalized in Britain. There had not actually been any legislation banning them but a Departmental Committee on Petroleum Spirit appointed in February 1909 had recommended, in its First Report in May 1910, that there should be such legislation. That rather put a damper on things. The Committee was persuaded, however, and in its Final Report in February 1913 it recommended that road tankers should be allowed. A year later *Commercial Motor* commented caustically that the petrol companies could not be 'accused of any remarkable alacrity in turning this to account'. BP and Shell were getting going by the start of the war.[31]

Something must be said briefly about lorry drivers, mechanics and all those who made the transport system work. With heavy demand for men to fight in the trenches, the decision was made in 1916 to transfer into the infantry some 80,000 men of top grade physical fitness from whatever services they were performing behind the lines. They were 'replaced by men less skilled and of a comparatively low medical category'. This decree, of course, affected the transport workers. It

> inevitably had a marked effect on the efficient operation of the mechanical transport ... a heavy multiplication of accidents and abuse of the mechanism of the vehicles . . serious financial loss through increased demand for spare parts, increased strain on the repairing facilities, and a rise in the number of men evacuated as sick.

While it would be unfair to blame the men who were thrust into the situation without previous experience or adequate training, nevertheless one must go along with one comment that ' it may be doubted whether the full extent of the mental and physical strain to which drivers of the mechanical transport were normally subjected in the field was fully appreciated'.[32] Certainly the hours of driving over poor roads or dealing on the spot with breakdowns could be exhausting: and while lorry-driving was not quite the same as going 'over the top' towards the enemy machine-guns, the vehicles were usually the subject of special attention of enemy artillery or aircraft when they were near the front. Sometimes the men were not quite up to what was needed; there was one report from France in the second year of the war of a lorry which was burnt out. The driver, peering into his petrol tank to see how much fuel he had left, decided to strike a match in order to see better. It is a wonder there were not more such mishaps. There was often considerable difficulty in getting lorries started in the icy conditions of winter. Tips were passed from man to man, but some drivers found placing warm rags on the petrol inlet pipes a bit slow and uncertain. It is reported that some preferred to warm the petrol directly – by placing some of it in a basin, setting it alight, and then smothering the flames when the fuel was sufficiently warm. A reader of *Commercial Motor* at home in England responded to this report with his own 'tip'. His idea was to lower an electric light bulb into the container, switch it on and wait for the heat of the bulb to do the trick.[33]

There can be no doubt that lorries contributed substantially to the victorious outcome of the Great War for the Allies, but few histories ever mention the transport aspects. They are content with simple statements that Field-Marshal X moved 10,000 men from A to B and it is left to the reader to assume that tens of thousands of tons of guns, ammunition, food, etc were spirited there by good fairies. General Ludendorff on the German side, writing his memoirs at the end of the war, left no doubt that a German weakness in motor transport was a contributory factor in his defeat.

This short account of the war has been confined to France and Belgium, but it must not be forgotten that vehicles – and the men – were tested and proven in arduous conditions in other places – over the Alps to help the Italians, in the deserts of the Middle East, in the savannah-land of East Africa, and so on.

One somewhat bizarre episode in the War Department's operations must be recorded, even though its effects on road haulage were only slight and indirect. Indeed, those effects were in the creation of uncertainty rather than anything worse. The motor transport sections of the armed forces had their workshops in France and elsewhere. But perhaps in about 1916, with tens of thousands of vehicles in use, owned not only by the Forces but by virtually every department of government, the idea arose that a major workshop for repair and maintenance in England was necessary. The WD pondered this for a while and came up with some concrete proposals in early August 1917. According to one account, the proposals were then 'locked up within the four walls of the War Office' and 'escaped' to reach the War Cabinet in May of 1918.[34] It may be that the 'escape' had something to do with the German Spring Offensive which had raised the possibility of the loss of some of the British workshop facilities in France.

The scheme then went ahead. Under the Defence of the Realm Acts (DORA), some six hundred acres of 'valuable land' were commandeered at Cippenham, Slough, and workshops were erected and plant installed. Thousands of workers were involved including large numbers of German prisoners of war. A Select Committee on National Expenditure[35] recommended that the work be carried out in self-contained stages – particularly in view of the changed military situation following the collapse of the German offensive. But as the War obviously neared its end, work went ahead on all aspects of the full-blown scheme. Expenditure was running £¾ million ahead of the original £1 million estimate (without parliamentary authority) and people began asking questions about the purpose of the 'Slough Depot'. Could it be simply the repair and maintenance of government vehicles, the numbers of which were going to be drastically reduced in the near future? Or was it simply the repair of many of these vehicles so that they could be sold off to the public for a reasonable price once the demands of war abated? But for the latter purpose there would soon be available hundreds of engineering workshops throughout the country which could do the work. Did the government intend to flood the market with thousands of refurbished cars and lorries to the detriment of vehicle manufacturers? Worst of all, though, was the horrible thought – in an atmosphere of state control, with talk of nationalization of the railways – was the government thinking of retaining their surplus war lorries to form a gigantic state-owned road transport organization? Why else would such an enormous repair and maintenance depot be needed in peacetime? Hundreds of small haulage contractors who had had to suffer the vicissitudes of fuel shortages, of an absence of new lorries and vans, shortage of repair materials and spare parts, and direction by the Ministries of Food and Munitions, went about their work uneasily.

In Parliament ministers fended off questions. A couple of weeks before the end of the war the Under-Secretary stonewalled.[36] Yes, the recommendations of the Select Committee had been attended to. Yes, the possibility of using munitions factories had been considered. Yes, the offer of the vehicle manufacturers had been considered but had been rejected by the War Office as unsatisfactory. (The manufacturers had proposed, with the aid of a government loan of £1¼ million, to repair vehicles of their own make, and sell them for the government on a cost plus commission basis.) No, there was no point in submitting the whole question to any new enquiry. There were not many straight answers forthcoming and questions continued – as did the work on the Slough Depot (but not yet on any vehicles) – and as did the expenditure.

Notes

1. W.J. Hughes, *A Century of Traction Engines,* p.48.
2. Ibid., p.99.
3. Ibid.
4. Ibid., p.125.
5. Ibid., p.192 and Ian Hogg, *The British Army in 20th Century,* p.68.
6. Royal Commission on War in S. Africa, 1904. Minutes of Evidence, Vol. II. Cd.1791. Minutes 16411–13.
7. Royal Commission on War in S. Africa, 1904. Minutes of Evidence, Vol. I. Cd.1790. p.12, para. 219.

8. W.T. Stead, *How Britain Goes to War,* p.129.
9. R.H. Beadon, *Royal Army Service Corps,* Vol. II, p.26.
10. Ibid., p.29.
11. Ibid., p.32.
12. *CM,* 1/3/06, p.493.
13. *CM,* 13/1/1907, p.469.
14. *CM,* 11/4/1907, p.133.
15. *CM,* 8/10/08, p.91.
16. R.H. Beadon, *Royal Army Service Corps,* pp.37–40, 43 and 414.
17. *CM,* 7/11/07, p.232 et seq.
18. *CM,* 11/3/1909, p.13.
19. *CM,* 18/3/1909, p.23.
20. A.J.P. Taylor, *English History 1914–1945,* London, 1977, p.122.
21. *CM,* 25/3/1909, p.62.
22. R.H. Beadon, *Royal Army Service Corps,* p.52.
23. R.H. Beadon, Ibid., p.34.
24. Field Service Regulations,1913 and A.M. Henniker, *Transportation on the Western Front,1914–18,* pp.1, 2.
25. R.H. Beadon, *Royal Army Service Corps,* p.414.
26. Henniker, *Transportation,* pp.343/44.
27. Ibid., p.157.
28. *CM,* 3/8/1916, p.595; and Parl.Debates, Commons Vol. LXXXV, Aug.1916, Col. 130.
29. Beadon, *Royal Army Service Corps,* p.429 and *CM,* 11/11/1915, p.213.
30. Henniker, *Transportation,* pp.156/157.
31. *CM,* 19/3/1914, p.52.
32. Beadon, *Royal Army Service Corps,* pp.420/421.
33. *CM,* 22/2/1917, pp.555/556 and 563.
34. *CM,* 15/7/1919, p.471.
35. *CM,* 26/9/1918, p.89 and 10th Report of Select Committee on National Expenditure, 1918.
36. *CM,* 29/8/1918, pp.2, 3; 31/10/1918, p.199; 14/11/1918, p.244; and 21/11/1918, p.266.

CHAPTER SIX

Keeping the Home Wheels Turning

In Britain conventional wisdom thought that the war would be over and done with by Christmas, 1914. But as time went on and Britain suffered early reverses that idea had to be abandoned. Under a Liberal government with a *laissez-faire* philosophy matured over long years, the attitude to industry and commerce during the war continued, initially at least, to be one of non-intervention, and people generally echoed the politician's cry of 'business as usual'. It was not until three months after the start of the war that the first Defence of the Realm Act (DORA) allowed the Army to take over the output of factories producing whatever was needed for war. Before long most vehicle producers were deemed to fall into that category. Oddly, control was exercised by more than one government department or agency. The War Department took over the whole of a controlled firm's output but, at intervals, and for a short time, would allow a small percentage of the output to be 'released' for delivery directly to buyers serving the government – who had to be prepared to give these vehicles up to the War Office at any time they were demanded. On the other hand the Ministry of Munitions (MOM), which applied control to all manufacturers of steam wagons and some 'petrol' makes, had a system under which the majority of the output was sold directly to traders who had obtained permits from the Ministry. Prospective buyers of vehicles had to apply to the MOM stating very precisely the make and model they wished to buy and the purpose for which it was required. The Ministry had its priority system depending on the goods to be carried (for example, munitions), whether it would relieve railway or dock congestion, release labour, and so on. The Ministry then supplied lists to the manufacturers in which every applicant was given a serial number and a priority rating, and the manufacturer supplied the vehicles to the applicants strictly in conformity with that.[1]

Under the DORA 1914, the government was soon taking virtually the whole output of sixteen major manufacturers: 3-tonners from Albion, British Berna, Daimler, Dennis, Hallford, Karrier, Leyland, Maudslay, Napier, Pagefield, Thornycroft and Wolseley; and 30 cwt vehicles from Belsize, Daimler, Napier and Straker-Squire. Overall output was pushed up from about ninety lorries a week in 1914 to about 250 a week in July 1915.[2] Civilian operators just had to do without these makes until, from October 1915 when output was beginning to match the Army's demands, some 'releases' were allowed. It was always possible to buy second-hand vehicles, of course. Even before the war there had been a thriving market, fed by such things as the sale of a large number of chassis by the LGOC when they introduced their famous 'B'-Type bus in 1910. Faced with a railway strike in the autumn of 1913, operators no doubt were glad to read advertisements for second-hand 'B' Types. At that time, too, we see models like 'Straker-Squire 3–4 tons, new tires' going for £185 but with no details of age or mileage in the advertisement.[3] Part of the strong demand, then, was probably from people making a first essay into transport but not wanting to put too much capital into the trial. Sadly, but as we might expect, things did not always work according to plan, and that last pre-war autumn also saw an advertisement, by the liquidators of a Manchester transport company, of 29 4-ton Milnes-Daimler petrol lorries.[4]

The 3-ton petrol lorry continued to be the Army's preferred vehicle, though as was seen above, steamers like the Foden 5-tonner were in heavy demand, too. One interesting aspect of this is that although the manoeuvres in 1910 had been held to be the death-knell of steam, so far as the Army was concerned – because steamers would disclose their whereabouts to the enemy, and because of difficulties in the supply of coal and water – nevertheless the Army was now getting hold of any vehicles it could, whether petrol or steam.

Even before being subjected to the powers under the Act, manufacturers tried hard to do their bit, but they had their problems. There was a shortage of magnetos, for example. Pre-war these had invariably been imported from Germany, where they were produced with the aid of government subsidies. Britain, being a free-trade country, happily imported tens of thousands of these a year and developed no resources at home. Even the drawings issued by the WD for their subsidy models specified Bosch magnetos. In the event America saved the situation but Britain had to get down to making its own and by the middle of the war about 2000 a week were being produced domestically.[5] A rather similar story applied to cast-steel wheels which were imported from Belgium.

Nevertheless, we find among manufacturers the same enthusiasm as among the drivers of the impressed vehicles mentioned above. One example will illustrate this. Mr A.H. Scammell was called to the War Office at 1.00 p.m. on a Saturday in September, a few weeks after the outbreak of war. He was asked to provide 28 5-ton Foden steam wagons, six trailers, all the necessary stores and equipment, and a travelling workshop with its own electric lighting, by Tuesday. The whole column was to be self-contained and capable of maintaining itself for some months under war conditions. Not only were the vehicles provided on time but they were accompanied by drivers, five mechanics (artificers), a couple of wheelwrights, a couple of boilermakers, and a cook. That his efforts were appreciated is shown by the fact that soon afterwards he was asked for another 31 steam wagons.[6]

The difficulties of hauliers and tradespeople generally were not simply that they had lost to the Army any vehicles registered under the subsidy scheme. Those, plus the output of the controlled factories, were insufficient in number to meet the Army's needs and right away the government ordered the commandeering of any civilian vehicles that would suit. Regular officers of the ASC who had been involved with the subsidy scheme now went about the country seeking whatever serviceable lorries they could find. Each ASC officer was accompanied by a newly commissioned officer who had been connected with the motor trade. If a vehicle were fairly new, the price paid would be according to the War Office price lists. Otherwise the two officers would make an assessment of the age and condition of the vehicle and determine a price on the spot. Naturally enough there were complaints. The owner of an 'impressed' lorry was given a docket by the impressing officers and on presentation of this to the Army Paymaster in the district it would be met by immediate cash payment.[7] There were fairly general grouses from the owners of registered subsidy vehicles that these non-registered owners got paid first. The complaints were more usually about the price, in particular about the depreciation set off against the original capital cost. The method was to calculate depreciation in half-yearly periods at 7½ per cent per half-year (15 per cent per annum was the standard figure applied by the Army even though many operators were now depreciating lorries on a basis of 10 per cent per annum). From the point of view of the owner the worst feature was that if the age of a vehicle had just gone over a half year mark – even by a few days – it would be counted as having reached the next half year (a year and a half plus one week would be counted as two years). Some complaints were also made that the impressing officers sometimes adopted a 20 per cent depreciation rate. There was rage, too, that no allowance was made for 'disturbance to trade', for the vehicles had to go immediately they were commandeered. The owners of registered vehicles got a 25 per cent bonus on the assessed value in this respect, though they were never paid more than the original cost of the vehicle. One disgruntled owner wrote to *Commercial Motor* of his dismay at finding that one of the two officers impressing his vehicles had been, a few weeks earlier, his main competitor.[8]

Occasional arguments arose about the cost price. Buyers had not always paid the list price. Sometimes they had managed to get a discount on single vehicles, more usually so when a number were bought at a time, and often they had bought the vehicle on hire purchase. As often as not, some special body would have been added or other modification undertaken. An aggrieved owner could always take the matter up through the Courts. According to *Commercial Motor* in 1914, the 'War Department and the Treasury will take a neutral attitude and regard the judges as undertaking arbitration. Neither ... will enter an appearance unless suspecting something in the nature of deliberate unfairness on the part of the claimant'.[9] The Courts had to sort out the complexities of normal commercial dealings, as in the case of a vehicle bought on hire purchase which was impressed before the final instalments of the purchase price were paid, and the tyres of which belonged to a tyre manufacturer who had supplied them on a payment-per-mile basis.

Despite the disruption to business caused by the call-up of vehicles, one notes again that enthusiasm – almost an excitement – in rising to the occasion. Waring and Gillow were proud to relate that one of their nine Leyland 3-tonners was at Worthing when the War Department's telegram reached head office (at 9.15 p.m. on the day the war started). The vehicle made a (then astonishing) 102-mile non-stop run back home to be able to go with the others to the Army concentration point in the west of England. Commercial common sense did not evaporate in all this enthusiasm, though. Mechanics had got to work immediately on receipt of the call-up orders to remove the electric-light installations from the vehicles and restore the original oil side-lights. The mechanics had to replace the paraffin carburettors on four of the machines by petrol carburettors, too.[10]

So, from all over the country vehicles were going off for military service. Lever Brothers lost no fewer than 72 machines in the first days.[11] A photograph in *Commercial Motor* on 13 August 1914 showed a fleet of Carter Paterson lorries at one assembly point – 15 Leyland 3-tonners, 3 Thornycroft 4-tonners, and 15 lighter Thornycrofts. So far as the parcels firm W.&G. was concerned, vans were said to be 'leaving their Acton premises by the dozen'. Some firms were luckier than others. A mineral-water firm in Camden Town, London – Idris & Co. – had 21 vehicles at the start of the war: 3 Foden steamers, 2 Dennis 5-tonners, 15 Wolseleys, and 1 vehicle made by Thames Ironworks. Only the two Dennis 5-tonners were taken. Others were less fortunate. Motor Services Ltd of Huddersfield and Motor Hiring Co. (Manchester) Ltd were among those that went into voluntary liquidation through loss of their vehicles. Dove & Dove, furniture removers and haulage contractors of Nottingham, had two 3-ton Commers impressed. So they bought a 4-ton Albion. It went the way of the Commers. Next they got a 2-ton Albion and it was impressed; then a Star, then a Durham-Churchill. For a while they were back to horses and the railways.[12]

Firms were paid for the impressed lorries but that did not mean that they could just buy replacements and carry on as if nothing had happened. Since the State had taken over the output of most major producers, no British replacements for these makes were to be had. Some went in for smaller vehicles, say 2-tonners, which were not generally being impressed. Some went for steam lorries (and the steam manufacturers, too, were coming under government control), and some reverted to horse transport. In general, however, prices of new vehicles were raised by about 10 per cent within a week or two of the outbreak of war since the manufacturers were now competing for materials with munition factories and all other makers of military goods. Whatever an owner of an impressed vehicle received for his depreciated lorry, it often was not enough to allow the purchase of a higher-priced replacement.

Many people then turned to American makes (expensive in British terms) and soon there was an influx of American and Canadian vehicles – 'trucks' as the press called them – the quotation marks remaining in use for a long time. So the trade press reviewed the newcomers – Pierce-Arrows, Jeffreys, Packards, Whites and so on. Some 400 had arrived within three months of the outbreak of hostilities and the flow kept on steadily for years, though importation became subject to a licensing system in June 1916. This was to save shipping space. The CMUA had to battle with the government to get sanction for the import of spares for American vehicles already in Britain. One noticeable absentee from the early arrivals was Ford, though subsequently Fords did sterling service, both in civilian and military use. By the middle of the war the Ford van was the standard delivery vehicle for department stores and the like, and by the end of the war, it had established such a position in commercial life that *Commercial Motor* devoted a weekly page to its upkeep and maintenance – the only specific make to enjoy that privilege. The Ford car had possibilities, too. It could be converted into something sturdier. We see, for example, the tantalizing advertisement of a London firm in May 1917 calling on readers to 'CONVERT your FORD into a ONE-TON Chain-Driven Lorry with the SMITH FORM-A-TRUCK'. This was done by a 'convertor' which was bolted on to the original frame to make a longer, wider chassis with new rear wheels and drive, all fit for the carriage of goods.[13]

The American vehicles were left-hand drive and American manufacturers were not particularly interested in adapting their models to the British market. While most of these lorries were acknowledged to be excellent machines, the trade press did carry warnings about 'truck trash' from time to time. Over a period, too, the press carried discussion about the relative merits of the British and American manufacturing methods. In Britain the manufacturers built the entire vehicle from their own resources, except for tyres, whereas the Americans assembled their machines from parts bought in from a number of suppliers. The general tone of the discussion suggested that the British vehicle was designed and built as a whole unit whilst American vehicles were simply collections of bits which might not necessarily be compatible with each other. The American manufacturer, it was hinted, if he did not have the right back axle or whatever, might simply substitute whatever he could lay his hands on at the time. Whatever the truth of that, large numbers of American trucks performed perfectly satisfactorily in Europe.

As mentioned earlier there was a second-hand market, with many vehicles coming, no doubt, from owners who had given up the battle in the face of wartime difficulties – disruption of trade, shortage of fuel, spares and labour – for the difficulties of both manufacturers and operators were accentuated by shortages of skilled labour. There was no conscription of men at the beginning of the war, but large numbers of men were in the Reserves and they were called up immediately. Within a couple of weeks of the start of war *Commercial Motor* was reporting that 'About 10% of Maudslay employees have been withdrawn to the Colours'; '50 men from the Star Works have been called up'; 'Several hundreds of Thornycrofts' employees have been called up'; 'About 65 men of the Foden staff have gone'; 'Between 300 and 400 men from the Leiston Works [i.e. Garretts] have been called up'; 'About 1000 employees of the Dunlop Rubber Co have been called up'.[14] Apart from those who had volunteered for the Reserves there were many who felt strong social pressures on them, and before long schemes were being devised whereby men were being given badges by their employers to indicate that they were in important war work and doing a more useful task than they could do at the front.

Operators, too, suffered labour problems. Very frequently when vehicles were registered under the subsidy schemes the drivers joined the Reserves and many joined anyway from patriotism and a sense of adventure. There had been an Army Service Corps Reserve in existence for several years before 1914. It is well known that on the railways, in munition factories and other industrial jobs women very quickly began taking the place of the men who had gone to the war, but this was not without considerable heart-searching by the men who remained. The London Metropolitan Police, for example, refused to allow women to drive taxis at the beginning of the war; they did not feel that the public would accept such a thing. Public opinion certainly did change, for the Police relented before long. But a year and a half after the war started the editor of *Commercial Motor* was saying 'We must rid ourselves of this artificial attitude to the new if we are sanely to consider the suitability of women for many of the wartime jobs'. He went on:

> we have frequently expressed the opinion that they may drive vehicles under suitable circumstances. We summarize our opinion – a strong, healthy, single woman may quite suitably be established as the driver of any of the lighter types of van. She is obviously unfitted physically, and in many cases, temperamentally, for the control of a steam wagon, a tractor, or a heavy lorry. We doubt her ability to do more than clip the tickets on a motorbus, particularly on a city service. She must have shorter hours of work and she must not be expected to undertake any but the simplest and least fatiguing of adjustments, She may admirably combine the duties of driver and saleswoman in many businesses, perhaps even better than the man she has displaced. Few women of gentler birth are suited for such duties. The ephemeral enthusiasm of the ex-hockey girl is better directed on to something less monotonously utilitarian ... she is

> unlikely to take her work seriously for long. It is not bread and butter to her and essentially matters little ... But for the hard, healthy woman who is accustomed to work hard for her living ... the lighter forms of commercial driving are far from unsuitable.[15]

There were, however, a number of women driving by this time. A director of Hammersmith Distillery Co. pointed out at the end of 1915 that he had two women driving Hallford 4-tonners. 'Although, I admit, it was only an experiment in the first place the results obtained have proved to be entirely successful ... the women handle the machines with wonderful ease and ... are an unqualified success ... compare favourably with men'. These vehicles would normally have had two men on them and a woman driver was accompanied by a man whose job it was to unload the heavy hogsheads – 14 cwt each – and to 'crank the engine' which the woman could not do.[16] Similarly a London brewer wrote in response to the Editorial that 'It may surprise you that I employ women drivers ... On the vehicles which my women drive I have had suitable weather screens fitted, which, of course, protect them from various atmospheric changes'. Here, too, the drivers were accompanied by men to handle the load and start the lorry by using the crank. 'I am entirely satisfied', said the letter writer.[17] One manager, commenting on how well women could do the job, said that, for him, women drivers had an advantage over men – they did not waste time chatting up the servant girls at the 'big houses'. Nevertheless, by the beginning of 1918 McNamara's had only six women drivers – and those were on light vans. But the firm had some difficulty in keeping the women, for they seemed to prefer driving tractors on farms.[18]

Times were changing, and despite the 'business as usual' slogan some things could not be as usual. The Road Board had, by the start of the war, achieved a considerable amount of good work by helping the highway authorities in resurfacing and reconstruction of the more important roads. They now had to call a virtual halt, however, to the distribution of grants in the manner they had followed up to that time. On 17 March 1915, some seven months after the war started, they sent a circular letter to the county councils advising them that henceforward grants would be on a much reduced scale and only for the most important roads. The plan now adopted was that the LGB would advise the Road Board of 'distress areas' where, 'owing to the existence of unemployment, it would be desirable that works of road construction or road improvement should be initiated'. Some £200,000 was provided for this purpose. This was clearly a socio-political decision and the Board further demonstrated its concern by negotiating with a large number of highway authorities provisional plans for works to be undertaken in the event of a trade recession.[19] Keynes must have been happy to see £1 million being earmarked for this purpose more than twenty years before he published his famous book. There seems to have been some expectation that the war was going to result in such a disruption of the commercial life of the country that there would actually be recession.

In so far as the Board continued to give grants, they laid more stress than ever on tarmacadam for road surfaces for it was learnt that the distillation of tar produced other materials which were highly useful in the manufacture of high explosives.

Because of its expertise and its links with local authorities the Road Board was now called upon to help the Army Council. With military camps being set up all over the country it fell to the Road Board to supervise and arrange for the construction and maintenance of some new roads and improvements of certain private roads – all at the expense of the Army Council. A number of public roads similarly had to be improved, and finally the Board had to settle, by negotiation between the Army Council and the highway authorities, payments to the latter in respect of damage caused by 'extraordinary traffic' in connection with military movement.[20] Before the next Report appeared in mid-1916 the Admiralty, the MoM and a Department of Timber Supply had been brought into the scheme too. With some of its staff gone 'to the Colours', the Board could not do all it wanted, though, and in August 1914 it had to advise highway authorities to abandon traffic counts until further notice. The proposals for the classification of roads were filed away.

Despite its impressive record in the few short years of its existence the Road Board was now in danger. In the first place, the Finance Act of 1915 provided that no further payments would be made into the Road Improvement Fund. The petrol duty and the licence fees would continue to be collected, but would go into general government funds. The Board had, however, substantial investments by this time and was receiving a steady income from them, which was allowed to continue. Worse was to come. With the cost of the war increasing rapidly, the Treasury had appointed a Retrenchment Committee to look at all possible ways of saving money. In September 1915, it came up with the recommendation that

> In view of the altered position of the public finances and the urgent necessity of utilizing all available resources of revenue for meeting the charges resulting from the War, [they] feel bound to recommend that the activities of the Road Board should be suspended during the war and that the proceeds of the taxes earmarked for the service of the Board should be retained in the Exchequer.

Naturally enough, the highway authorities did not wish to see this source of funds being abolished, particularly as roads were being subjected to more and more freight traffic, and they objected. So the Retrenchment Committee in its Final Report (21 Feb. 1916) accepted that the Road Board could continue – with its much-reduced resources – but only to make grants necessary 'to prevent the serious deterioration of roads of real importance'. The eventual demise of the Road Board had been signalled, but that was still in the future, and in mid-1917 the Board was still looking forward. They pointed out that despite the improvements in roads achieved since the Board was set up, and despite the expenditure of £1½ million by the Army, the Admiralty, and MOM, and so on, on roads,

> the heavy motor traffic directly or indirectly connected with military movements and the transit of warlike stores, has caused a great deal of damage to many miles of road ... There can be no doubt that a considerable amount of expenditure will have to be incurred on these roads after the war. Many other roads have also suffered damage by the substitution of motor traffic for horse-drawn traffic in connection with agricultural operations in some counties.

So there were a lot of arrears to be made good after the war.[21]

By the middle of the war the road haulage industry had completed a decade-and-a-half of development. *Commercial Motor* reported on 6 April 1916 that it had supplied the Treasury with its estimate of the number of goods vehicles in use. The editor supplied the figures without knowing why they were wanted and understandably expressed some anger when he learnt why. The Treasury was proposing to increase the taxes on transport, for example by raising the petrol duty. As it so happened, the proposals came to naught, but the bitter feeling of having been 'conned' remained. The figures supplied were:

Petrol driven – up to 2 tons unladen	24,000	vehicles
Petrol-driven – above 2 tons unladen	18,000	vehicles
	42, 000	
Steam lorries and tractors, other than heavy traction engines	4,800	
Total goods vehicles	46,800	

There are no details of the division of these vehicles between those run by businesses 'on their own account' and those run 'for hire or reward'. Undoubtedly the former predominated and we have already mentioned industrial owners such as Lever Brothers, retail stores like Harrods (103 Albion vans in 1917) and Waring and Gillow, breweries, flourmills, laundries, largish shops, railways, local authorities and gas-works. Wandsworth, Wimbledon and Epsom District Gas Co. had sixteen steam wagons and nine petrol vehicles (converted cars) in mid-1916. An advertisement for a Leyland 6-ton steam wagon in *Commercial Motor* of 18 May 1916 said that the depicted vehicle was one of eleven in use by, or on order for, Joseph Appleby & Sons, Millers, Liverpool. Textile factories in Lancashire were moving by road a fair quantity of raw materials and partly finished or finished goods between the mills and between the mill-towns and the ports of Liverpool and Manchester. The Calico Printers' Association Ltd of Manchester sent 30 to 40 tons weekly to London.[22] (Their problem was in getting return loads.) Another advertisement about a month later by Straker-Squire claimed that John Walker Ltd of Bolton had been unable eight or nine months earlier to get 300 bales of cotton goods forwarded because of railway congestion. They bought a Straker-Squire petrol 5-tonner and had nine of them at the time of the advertisement. The figures above suggest, too, that retail delivery vans were not unimportant. There were even the first examples of 'mobile shops' going around villages.

On the other hand, there were haulage contractors. *Commercial Motor* every week printed a couple of pages of 'Useful names for Users'. In August 1917 that included a section headed 'Motor Haulage Contractors' with 64 firms' names listed, including the well-known ones like Box, Carter Paterson, Du Cros, McNamara, Pickford and Thomas Tilling. Twenty-seven of those were limited companies. There were other firms not listed, of course. Ed Nelson & Co. Ltd of Peckham had a fleet of twelve vehicles collecting meat from the docks or distributing it to 100-odd shops around London. This was on contract for the British and Argentine Meat Co. and the work had begun in 1903. By 1917 these hauliers were doing 100,000 miles a year on this traffic.[23] At the other end of the scale were small firms like J. Leatherbarrow of Salford ('a great believer in rubber tyres'), whose two Mann steam wagons each did three round trips (80 miles) a week to Liverpool with a 9-ton load (that is, with trailer) and brought raw cotton back. (They left Manchester at midnight and got back at 7.30 p.m.)[24]

It is not always easy, at this stage in the development of road transport, to decide just what an operator's main business was. Commercial transport journals generally listed new company registrations week by week, but rarely did these indicate road haulage as the one and only purpose. More often the stated objects of the new companies covered a range of activities – haulage, bus and taxi operation, vehicle sales, repair, and so on. One thing is sure, though, there were not very many owner-drivers. By the beginning of 1918 the magazines were receiving a great many enquiries from servicemen about the prospects for small haulage businesses after the war. One writer commented: 'There are, of course, quite a number of driver-owners of steam wagons – quite sound financially ... [but] ... I only know of a few instances of driver-owners of petrol lorries and I cannot recall a single one of a small petrol van, although, no doubt, he exists.' It was a month after that article before 'he' did write to confirm that he did indeed exist – and owned a converted 1906 Humber. That swallow, however, did not make a summer.[25]

The list of haulage contractors published in *Commercial Motor*, which had contained over sixty firms in the summer of 1917, grew shorter over succeeding weeks and was down to about a dozen at the beginning of the winter. The reasons are not clear. The journal was having to limit its pages because of paper shortages, but road haulage was having difficulties -shortage of staff, shortage of spares (British manufacturers had been accused of assuming that their products would not need spares), shortage of fuel. Just one further specific problem might be mentioned. Once the war had become a serious business, controls of all sorts crept in. Even such things as getting repairs done to motor vehicles or parts were not permissible without a permit issued by the MOM, the Army Council, or the Admiralty. Fortunately there were some exemptions. Vehicles used for the collection and delivery of goods, for example, did not require a permit where the repair did not cost more than £10.[26] Admittedly £10 would have bought a good deal of repair work in the middle of the war.

Road transport of both passengers and goods had been growing: and in the war theatres – on land and in the air, demands for fuel increased enormously. That, coupled with ever-increasing German submarine activity, resulted in petrol supplies now beginning to be a serious problem. The immediate effect of the submarines was that War Risks Insurance premiums were increased, and so the price of petrol doubled by the middle of the war – from 1s. a gallon at the start of the war to 2s. 2½d. including tax in 1916. The problem was exacerbated by the commandeering by the government of about half the fleet of tank steamers. While it was appreciated that needs of the forces came first, road haulage interests were not too pleased to see several of the tankers being used simply as reserve stores at the ports. They argued vociferously to get those ships moving. Eventually the inevitable came – rationing.

In the spring of 1916 the government set up a Petrol Control Committee. It got off to a bad start. After a month's silence it announced that owners must register their vehicles and details of their petrol usage with the Committee, which would then issue licences for petrol. The closing date for applications was quite soon afterwards. Not surprisingly many owners did not know anything about the scheme. An announcement was made in *The Times* on 15 August 1916 – apparently on the strength of a press release – that 'no fewer than 24,000 owners of motor vehicles *neglected* to make returns during the stated period'. The late applications were set aside temporarily, but 'now that all the applicants [keeping to the regulations] have received their permits, the *negligent people* can receive attention'.

The rationing system may seem odd to our day, for it put a heavy reliance on people's honesty. Vehicle and car owners having stated what they needed, the Petrol Committee simply added up the total, compared it with what petrol was available and issued licences on the basis of a percentage of what people had asked for. Commercial goods vehicle operators were licensed to get 60 per cent of what they had asked for, buses and taxis 50 per cent, doctors and vets would get their full request up to a maximum of 50 gallons per month, while private cars would get 25 per cent with a maximum of 30 gallons.[27] While there was criticism of the scheme in the trade press, for example, for not realizing that private motorists might well use less in winter than in summer, there was little more than passing comment on the principle of asking people what they wanted. *Commercial Motor* permitted itself to comment that since 110 million gallons had been used in 1915, the 153 million gallons asked for under the scheme might be regarded as an 'optimistic inaccuracy'. But it added that there had been an enormous increase in (genuine) commercial demand.

To get a licence was one thing, but to get the petrol was another. Right at the registration stage the Petrol Control Committee was instructing distributors to supply petrol on a priority system. Munitions transport, medical users, police and fire brigades got top priority. Ordinary goods transport and buses came second in the queue and private cars and charabancs behind that again. Mistakes were made, too, and in a Commons debate on 1 August an MP raised the case of a Dorsetshire Co-operative Dairy whose two lorries collected some 6000 gallons of milk daily from farms within a 10- to 12-mile radius. The dairy had asked for 600 gallons of petrol a month – its normal usage – and was licensed for 60 gallons. With the help of the CMUA and similar bodies complaints were eventually attended to, growth of traffic allowed for, and supplementary licences given.[28]

The supply position did not get much easier, though, and on 1 September 1916 charabancs were banned from using petrol – they were the vehicles that carried Sunday School groups, or members of clubs, off to the seaside for the day. A month or two later the press was confidently assuring commercial users that they would be getting 85 per cent of their needs by Christmas. It did not work out quite like that, for the new licences at the beginning of November gave only a 10 per cent increase on what the users had been getting – that is, an increase from 60 to 66 per cent of their needs. The submarines kept going, however, and military needs kept growing. In May 1917 a cut of one-third was made, so goods vehicle operators were then only getting 44 per cent of what they had requested a year earlier. But by the end of that summer there were alleged to be 50,000 public service vehicles and goods vehicles laid up for want of petrol.

As might be expected, the industry made every effort to keep going, and the technical press revealed the regular and frequent filing of patents for new carburettors – either allowing a switch from petrol to paraffin as soon as the engine had warmed up, or working solely on paraffin, alcohol, benzole or whatever. One co-operative society said early in 1917 that they had had reasonable results using a mixture of one gallon of mineral turpentine (white spirit) to two gallons of petrol! None of their seven lorries, they said, 'showed any appreciable difference in the power developed and there was only the faintest trace of pinking when pulling hard on hills'. All they had done was to attach small weights to the carburettor floats to make the needle valves cut off later. A 3½-ton Signal lorry of theirs had just completed 800 miles using a ratio of 2¾ petrol to 1¼ white spirit. The cylinders showed only a very slight carbon deposit – 'about 1/32 in. thick – certainly no more than for petrol alone'.[29] Users of paraffin were warned by the press to watch their lubrication. Engines ran hotter with paraffin and the fuel in the cylinders tended to escape past the pistons and mix with the oil.

Whatever the merits of paraffin, and so on, the editor of *Commercial Motor* began and continued a campaign to convert people to the use of coal-gas as a fuel. Since that was available in virtually every town in the country, it was well suited to the needs of transport. Gas quality and price varied from town to town but on average 1000 cubic feet of gas was sold for 3s. and this would be the equivalent of 3 to 3½ gallons of petrol. With petrol at over 2s. a gallon gas was, even at its most expensive, clearly cheaper than petrol, even when allowance was made for the weight of the gas containers on the vehicle. Tests were carried out, for example by Dennis Brothers at Guildford. No changes were necessary in the engines and Dennis's were said to be at an advantage there because their engines worked on a higher compression than most. Barton Brothers at Beeston began running their buses on town gas, which, as a large user, they bought for 1s. 4d. per 1000 cubic feet. They developed a gas-bag for the roof of the bus and subsequently did a profitable trade selling such bags to other users.

But it was not all pure gain. For one thing, the gas-bags suffered quite a bit of wind resistance. Then there was the capital cost – about £23 plus another £5 for the structure to carry it plus 10s. to 15s. to make the connection to the carburettors.[30] Rather more serious, however, was the fact that the bag would only last eight or nine months and then begin to leak. Furthermore, it could not hold much at atmospheric pressure – perhaps 400 or 450 cubic feet – and that was enough to take a 3-tonner only ten or twelve miles.[31]

To get more would entail compressing the gas and that meant pumps and steel bottles rather than bags. Steel was in short supply and needed a licence, steel bottles were heavy and reduced the payload. Potential buyers were told to get a vehicle with one ton more capacity than the payload they intended to carry. Despite these disadvantages, the idea gradually took hold – even when gas companies stripped the gas of any and every constituent which could be used otherwise in the war effort. It was said in early 1917 that the 'present attenuated gas' was showing a loss of 15 to 20 per cent of power.[32] However, gas was a good fuel in that it could be readily 'enriched by allowing it to bubble through petrol, solvent naptha, solar oil, or other hydrocarbon before it reaches the induction pipe of the engine'. So it took on; and in October 1917 a demonstration of heavy commercial vehicles and light vans fitted for gas, arranged by *Commercial Motor* at Thornycroft's premises in Grosvenor Road, London, attracted some 1700 people.

The authorities in a way encouraged the move to gas by calling on the nation to save 50 million gallons of petrol a year from October 1917. That would have needed perhaps 12,500 million extra cubic feet of gas. But no steps were taken to provide it. Indeed the opposite occurred, with 50,000 miners being called up early in 1918 and, in consequence, coal becoming scarce. Inevitably gas became scarce, too, and in the spring of 1918 a number of towns were instructing their Gas Departments not to supply gas for transport purposes. Hauliers who had changed over to gas in Sheffield, Dudley, Stockport, Stockton-on-Tees and Tottenham, to name a few, were regretting their decision. Since the beginning of the year national regulations had required them to surrender one-third of their petrol allowance if they had gone over to gas.

Another way out of the fuel difficulty – especially for users of small vans – was to change to electric vans. These had been around for some time, of course. What was claimed to be the 'largest and most powerful motor truck in the world' had been demonstrated in America in 1905. It had a 3½ b.h.p. electric motor on each wheel and could carry a payload of 6 tons.[33] But, in general, electric vans were not thought to be practicable in Britain at that time. Batteries had a short life and the transmission systems were unsatisfactory. The majority of vehicle users in Britain displayed a resolute lack of interest, but here and there people impressed by what was going on in America decided to try them. The RAC had carried out a week's test of an Edison 10 cwt van in February 1913 with varying loads and showed a usage of 192 units of electricity to charge the batteries for the 312 miles run. There were said to be about 150 electric vans in use in Britain at the start of the war in 1914.

Among those experimenting at that time were Harrods and the Midland Railway. Sir Woodman Burbidge, the managing director of Harrods, had visited the United States in 1913 and had seen electric vans at work. He was impressed and right away ordered ten vehicles of between 10 cwt and 2 tons capacity. By the summer of 1917 the firm had about sixty in use, all of American manufacture (in addition to their 100 petrol vehicles). The electrics did an average of 20 miles per day and although they could get up to 25 m.p.h. they normally ran much more slowly. The firm delivered some 8000 parcels a day by this means and admitted that overloading was frequent. The only consequence of that was broken springs. A spokesman at this time told *Commercial Motor* that the life of the battery remained an unknown quantity but that depreciation charges for the vehicles were constantly being revised downwards.[34] Sir Woodman told the Select Committee on Transport in the last week of the war in 1918 that the electric vans cost 1½d. per vehicle-mile as compared with the 3d. the petrol vans cost. But the firm had its own power plant and admitted that its power cost was well below that prevailing elsewhere.

The Midland Railway had completed their initial enquiries about the feasibility of electrics for collection and delivery work just before the war started, and they tried out some electrics during the Christmas rush in 1914.[35] Satisfied, they introduced some 30 cwt vans in June 1915. By the beginning of 1918 they had 54 electrics working in London, where their comparatively slow speed and easy acceleration were suitable for the congested city streets. About half of these electrics were in the 15 cwt to 1½ tons capacity range and dealt with parcels carried by passenger train. The rest were mainly 2- and 3½-tonners, but included six 5-tonners. These larger vehicles dealt with loads carried by goods train. That railway company had another 22 operating in other large cities. The Chief Goods Manager of the London & North Western Railway (LNWR) told the Select Committee that his company's experiments with electrics in London rather confirmed them in their use of horses. The problem with electrics was in getting the batteries recharged. This indeed was a problem which severely limited the operating range of this type of vehicle. At this time, electricity stations were local and had not been linked into a national grid. Costs and facilities, therefore, varied from place to place. The *Electrical Review* had to publish maps early in 1917 showing towns where vehicles could be recharged.

There were other users – Hayes Wharf, for example, which had been doing meat deliveries with electrics in 1915, and Joseph Lyons. The Park Coal Co. (Cardiff) Ltd bought a Walker 2-ton electric lorry in June 1917 for retail deliveries of coal. This vehicle was said to have done about 500 to 600 miles per month with work done reaching a maximum on occasions of 75 tons per week.[36]

One potentially important development came almost at the end of the War. While railway tracks were a little removed from the general gaze of the public and, anyway, it was not obvious to those who watched the trains go by whether the majority of railway wagons were loaded or empty, the same was not true of lorries. They were right in among the public and a great many empty or partly loaded vehicles were noted by concerned citizens. The fact, too, that brewers' vehicles from perhaps fifty miles away were seen delivering to public houses quite close to competing breweries raised many hackles. Petrol companies and millers, also, came in for a great deal of criticism for their 'parallel deliveries'. By 1917 there were fairly general complaints about the wasteful methods of road transport and calls came for control – not least from the road haulage press. With the ever-growing demands of the land and air forces for men and petrol, these had been scarce at home and transport had suffered. Indeed many vehicles in non-essential trades had been laid up; but with expectations of a great German offensive in the spring of 1918 things took a turn for the worse. The Petrol Controller feared that the transport needs of the Ministries of Food and Munitions would not be met. Something had to be done quickly and eyes were turned to those activities of road transport that were considered wasteful.

So, on 18 February 1918, under the DORA Regulations the Board of Trade appointed a Road Transport Board (RTB) whose Chairman, Sir Evan Jones, was also Petrol Controller. This was an interdepartmental body, the remainder of its members coming from the War Office, the Ministries of Munitions and Food, the Post Office, the Board of Trade, and the Road Board, and they all had to do with transport in one way or another. Not surprisingly, the composition of the RTB came in for criticism. *Commercial Motor,* while expressing some relief that the Chairman of the Board was not a railwayman, was none too happy with the representation generally – the Post Office 'owns not a single motor vehicle and all its work is done by contract'; the War Office – 'it is notorious that all branches of the Army seek to keep their own transport to themselves wherever possible' and were guilty of much wasteful running.[37] Agenda and minutes of the fortnightly meetings were circulated to a number of other ministries and bodies who were not represented on the RTB. These included, for example, the Railway Executive Committee. The Board's terms of reference were:

> To co-ordinate the work of existing Government Departments in connection with road transport; to determine what further measures are necessary to ensure the most economic use of road transport vehicles, and their efficient allocation for meeting such requirements as may arise from time to time for the transport of food, munitions and other war material, and for the essential needs of the trade and industry of the country, and ... to give executive effect thereto.

The latter was achieved by an organization comprising 13 Divisional Road Transport Boards each of which included, *inter alia,* 'a representative of road transport trade interests in the division'. Below the Divisional Boards came 84 Area Committees each of which comprised four representatives of food transport; four representatives of transport other than food, and of general local interests; two representatives of horse transport; and one representative of munitions transport. The Road Transport Board took over the work of some 300 local transport sub-committees of the Food Control Committees and became the only controlling body for road transport. In addition to the full-time organization there was a central Advisory Committee whose Chairman was from Pickford and whose remaining members were from the National Alliance of Commercial Road Transport Associations, the CMUA, the National Traction Engine Association, the London retail distributing firms, Hayes Wharf Cartage Co. Ltd, Thomas Tilling, and the Association of

Chambers of Commerce. This Committee representing operators and users met just before the Road Transport Board meetings so that the Board was in possession of the views of the Committee on any given topic. At the Divisional level there were similar advisory committees.

As a first step in organizing road transport the Board ordered the registration of road vehicles. All goods-carrying road transport vehicles on 4 June 1918, other than those used wholly or mainly in agriculture and horse-drawn vehicles of under 15 cwt capacity, had to be registered by the end of July. In the records the vehicles were classified according to their use and given a priority rating for emergency work and, in the case of petrol vans and lorries, petrol licences. Note was taken, too, of those laid up or for sale. Permits were then issued, without which a vehicle could not legally be operated. For good measure the vehicles had to carry the registration markings showing that they were, say, petrol lorries, the area number, the owner's registered number and a number to indicate that the one in question was the second or third or fifth or whatever in that owner's fleet. Purchase of new vehicles and of spare parts had to be authorized by the Board's staff too, and they often referred prospective buyers to owners of vehicles recorded as laid up or for sale.

Not every owner apparently rushed to get registered, and expressions of surprise were uttered that, despite all the publicity, 'owners are only now registering' in early September (and even later). The RTB was to operate only during the war and by the time the initial formalities had been completed, the war was nearing its end. Most permits, for example, had been issued on 1 September 1918, just nine weeks before the Armistice; and only about six weeks before hostilities ceased did the RTB take over the issue of petrol licences (1 October 1918). It was intended that by the time these licences came up for renewal the Board would have got a clear picture of the transport job to be done and of the means to do it.

Though its wartime work lasted only a few months, it is worthwhile looking at what the RTB was doing before the end of the war brought the large sale of army-surplus vehicles to increase substantially the number of goods vehicles on the road. In evidence to the Select Committee on Transport on 30 October 1918 Sir Evan Jones, the Chairman of the Road Transport Board, submitted a paper which, among other things, described wartime developments. It drew attention to:

> an enormous increase in road traffic from the establishment of munitions and allied works. A large number of road vehicles have also been employed in the extensive constructional work for Government factories, aerodromes,etc, The Timber Supplies Department have also used road transport for the haulage of timber required not only for use in this country but for the use of the Forces overseas. [He went on to

> refer to the] shortage of stocks and materials of all kinds. This shortage has necessitated in many instances the adoption of the speediest method of transport available, irrespective of economy, and during railway congestion road transport has in certain localities been the only means of rapid distribution.

An example of the kind of thing intended was in May 1918 – before the RTB had got going – when the CMUA had assembled, at the request of the Divisional Food Commissioner of the North West, a fleet of 60 mechanically propelled wagons (with 350 tons' capacity) to move that part of foodstuffs arriving in shipping convoys at Manchester and Liverpool Docks which the railways could not cope with.[38]

In regard to rationing, Sir Evan wrote that

> One of the main factors in the success of any scheme of rationing is the equitable distribution of the rationed article. It has consequently been necessary for the Ministry of Food to secure that ample supplies of sugar, butter, meat and margarine shall be available in every part of the country ... At times delays on railways have precluded the carriage of goods by rail, and road transport has therefore been called on to carry the goods to their destination with the minimum amount of delay.

To make the country self-supporting, 'The produce of the land has been carried by road either to the nearest market or to the nearest railway centre.' Again and again he came back to railway congestion.

> The railways have notoriously been overloaded, and recourse to road traffic has become greater and greater as the war has progressed ... Our main roads, especially those leading to the principal ports, show daily an almost continuous procession of convoys of mechanical vehicles, and in all parts of the country a considerable quantity of goods traffic that in pre-war days would naturally have been rail-borne now travels by road. [His conclusion from this was that] It may be postulated that in this country, in common with other belligerent countries, the efficient conduct of the war has quite appreciably hinged on the speedy transport of material, which has very largely been dependent on the provision of mechanical transport by road.

So much for the general scene. In the last months of the war the RTB set out to make road transport 'more efficient'. The first area for attention was general collection and delivery work. Sir Evan Jones's paper said that

> in some divisions it has been possible already to secure co-ordination of delivery. In Birmingham, Exeter, Cheltenham and Gloucester the restriction of retail delivery of bread has been voluntarily accepted by the trade and schemes are working satisfactorily. In other parts of the country attention is being given to the delivery of milk and the delivery of newspapers; the dyers and bleaching trade, the brewers, and the preserved fruits trades; and new schemes of economy in the use of road transport vehicles are rapidly taking shape.

The RTB worked closely with the Railway Executive and between them they agreed that 'goods shall be carried by road up to a distance of 10 miles and by rail for distances over 10 miles wherever conditions of traffic permit'. One aspect of particular importance was that of 'return loads'. At the beginning of September 1918 an experimental office was opened in Bristol and was soon seen to be successful. Sir Evan's paper told the Select Committee that 'over 5,000 tons of goods have been moved by using vehicles which would otherwise have travelled empty or light'. So schemes were set up by the MOM in Birmingham, Coventry and the West Riding. An agreement was reached with Furniture Warehousemen and Removers' Association to provide back loads for their vehicles where possible. The Manchester Chamber of Commerce, too, set up a Motor Transport Department to provide for back loads in that area.

This question of back loads had exercised a number of minds ever since the war started. Within days the *Commercial Motor* magazine had set up its own 'freight exchange' to put those who sought return loads in touch with those who wanted transport. A minimum load of 3 tons was specified and a minimum distance 30 miles. In the event the scheme did not succeed although the journal made no charge for the service, and after five or six weeks it was wound up. The explanation given was that after the initial dislocation of railways caused by mobilization, the railways soon settled down again (though maybe 3-ton loads for over 30 miles were not all that common). Requests from readers kept coming in but the editor declined to try again and advised enquirers to put small advertisements in the daily newspapers. *The Times* carried classified advertisements of this nature for a time but all in all nothing much seemed to come of it. In general there seemed to be far more vehicles offering than loads. As the war went on the railways became more and more congested and even by a year after the start of the war freight was said to be 'offering in unheard of quantities'. At that time a firm called Interfreight Exchange in London was running full-page advertisements claiming to have 200 or more agents – in all the principal towns. No details of tonnage handled are available but that firm seems to have done all right. It was taken over at the end of 1915 by Commercial Car Hirers Ltd and continued to operate as 'Motor Freight Exchange Ltd'.[39] The Manchester Chamber of Commerce scheme which handled its first traffic in August 1917 was said to have provided 2225 tons of return loads up to the end of 1917 and 12,530 tons between January and August 1918.[40] Right at the end of the war we see 'small ads' by Boots, the Manufacturing Chemists, offering to provide loads from Nottingham to the principal towns in the UK but again no details are available to this writer. Sir Evan's paper looked ahead to the post war situation:

> Pending the adoption of some permanent road transport system, if such is likely to come about, it seems desirable that the Return Loads Bureau set up by the Road Transport Board should be continued on a voluntary basis at those centres where their existence has been justified ... *It is necessary to guard against these bureaux, which are established for purposes of economy, developing into instruments of competition with canals, railways or common carriers*. [italics added].

It is hard to see why Sir Evan felt it necessary to protect the railways for, a couple of paragraphs later, he said

> So far as the development of road transport as an independent through or trunk service for the carriage of goods is concerned, I am not able to speak with any degree of special knowledge, but I cannot conceive the possibility of development in this direction where railway or water carriage is available ... Neither can Motor transport compete in restricted areas with horse transport ... The future of commercial motor road transport is, I think, restricted to its use as an independent local service in areas of fairly extended character and deficient in railway facilities, for the internal traffic of the area itself, and as an auxiliary feeder service to the railways or canals for extra-area traffic. Even for this work ... services must be co-ordinated and terminal delays eliminated,

The basis of Sir Evan's argument was, he explained, that 'The petrol-driven motor, as we know it today, is not economical either in first cost or running cost. As a preliminary to any well-designed schemes for cheap road transport, there must be evolved a standardized type of motor vehicle, with its spare parts all standardized also.' But it was clear that he just did not like the idea of multitudes of vehicles running all over the place, often light or partly loaded, picking up loads wherever possible. It was untidy, wasteful and uneconomic. He was not the only one. The Chairman of the Select Committee asked him (Minute 3274)

> I am sure that you are of the opinion, looking at the matter from a scientific view, that the conditions of road transport which existed before the war, and which you have been changing during the war to some extent, however convenient they may have been to individuals, have really been extremely wasteful and unscientific?

Sir Evan replied, 'Yes, there is no doubt about that.' In response to another question he described his work as 'very largely educational'. When he was asked (Min. 3281) 'Do you find the ideas of the people whom you have been endeavouring to educate have been fairly rapidly changing? Have they been receptive?', he gave the answer, 'Very. I think a marvellous feature of the experience we have gained is the receptivity of all the interests concerned with transport.' Maybe he had not quite understood the question, for he went on to say that 90 per cent of the people approached had the greatest desire to meet the Board's requests in every way they could. (The RTB had not found it necessary to use its powers of compulsion!) He may have been a bit uncertain about the long-term effect of his educational efforts. A little later he was asked about the scheme of coordination agreed with the Retail Distributors' Association in London (Harrods, Whiteleys, and so on). Asked whether it would continue after the war, he said that that was 'exceedingly doubtful'. The next question was about earlier individual operations – 'Yet at the same time it is a fearfully wasteful method of getting goods delivered?' Sir Evan's reply was that 'From the purely transport point of view it is exceedingly wasteful, but you would not get these big houses to agree that it was wasteful from their point of view in the way of advertising – that is the point' (Min.3336). When Mr Haslam asked about traders generally, 'You have shown them methods of economy to which they can adjust themselves in future and if they are sensible men they will do so?' the reply was 'I think so. Some of it will undoubtedly stick' (Min.3354). What about big firms like Harrods and Selfridges? 'I do not think they will continue it if they can help it'. (Min.3357). Nobody asked questions about convenience for individual firms and their customers – not even when the Managing Director of Harrods also said that the coordination scheme was unlikely to continue after the war (Min.3631).

In the end the Select Committee which was looking at the general transport picture in the country more or less repeated, in its report, Sir Evan Jones's view that road transport would have a role in particular areas where railway facilities were deficient, and as a feeder to railways and canals. The road transport industry could not be organized like the largescale rail and canal concerns.

One sad footnote to this horrible war – sad, but understandable – was the rabid anti-German feeling which pervaded all classes of people carrying on their work at home. Right from the start of the war any support of any German firm was regarded as disloyal, and the term 'German firm' included many firms operating in Britain which had, or were thought to have had, German shareholders or proprietors. According to *Commercial Motor* several tyre companies, for example the Peter Union Tyre Co. and the Continental Tyre Co. were declared to be enemy property and were wound up in 1916 on official orders, their stock being sold off at about two-thirds of list prices. The magazine reported, too, that in 1914 the Polack Tyre Co. had quickly to elect two English directors in place of two Germans and to ensure that what they sold from then on was of British origin. Given the laws and the attitudes of the time some British tyre companies were able to advertise that *they* were British and were able to name competitors who were not.[41]

Notes

1. *CM*, 9/8/1917, ads p.7.
2. R.H. Beadon, *The Royal Army Service Corps*, Vol. II, p.416 and *CM*, 10/12/1914, p.278.
3. *CM*, 18/9/1913, ads p.24.
4. *CM*, 11/9/1913, p.37.
5. *CM*, 19/10/1916, p.154.
6. *CM*, 29/10/1914.
7. Beadon, *The Royal Army Service Corps*, p.415.
8. *CM*, 22/10/1914, p.134; 29/10/1914, p.168; and 25/3/1915, p.77.
9. *CM*, 3/9/1914, p.3.
10. *CM*, 13/8/1914, p.589.
11. *CM*, 13/8/1914, p.595.
12. *CM*, 8/ 10/1914; 1/4/1915, p.86; 1/7/1915, p.379.
13. *CM*, 17/5/1917, ads p.41.
14. *CM*, 13/8/1914, pp.590–91.
15. *CM*, 17/2/1916, p.488.
16. *CM*, 11/11/1915, p.208.
17. *CM*, 9/3/1916, p.38.
18. *CM*, 21/3/1918, pp.77–8.
19. Road Board – 5th Annual Report (to 31/3/1915) Paras. 16–20.
20. Road Board – 5th Annual Report (to 31/3/1915) Paras. 25.
21. Road Board – 7th Annual Report, 1917.
22. *CM*, 23/12/1915, p.339.
23. *CM*, 20/9/1917, p.77.
24. *CM*, 29/6/1916, p.364.
25. *CM*, 21/2/1918, p.581.
26. *CM*, 16/11/1916, p.248; and 4/1/1917, p.392.
27. *CM*, 10/8/1916, p.481; 31/5/1917; 5/7/1917, p.394a; 1/6/1916; 8/6/1916, p.293.
28. *CM*, 10/8/1916, p.498 and Parl. Debates, Commons 5th Series, Vol. LXXXV Aug. 1916, cols 148/9.
29. *CM*, 1/3/1917.
30. *CM*, 19/7/1917, p.425.
31. *CM*, 21/9/1916, p.77; 19/10/1916, p.152; 2/11/1916, p.198; and 6/9/1917, p.34.
32. *CM*, 22/2/1917, p.563 and 12/4/1917, p.129.
33. *CM*, 4/5/1905.
34. Select Committee on Transport, 1918, Minutes of Evidence – Questions 3564–5; *CM*, 9/8/1917, p.495.
35. *CM*, 3/1/1918, pp.409–10.
36. *CM*, 21/9/1916, ads p.18; 19/7/1917, p.433; 27/9/1917, p.106; 3/1/1918, pp.409–10; 10/1/1918, p.439; 8/7/1919, p.464; and 9/9/1919, p.54.
37. *CM*, 7/2/1918, p.519 and 28/2/1918, p.2.
38. *CM*, 30/5/1918, p.292.
39. *CM*, 29/7/1915, ads p.xii and 11/11/1915, p.211.
40. CM, 5/9/1918, p.26 and 26/9/1918, p.108.
41. *CM*, ads 1/10/1914; 24/9/1914, p.62; 23/3/1916, ads p.13.

CHAPTER SEVEN

Framework of Expansion

The first Great World War ended, perhaps suddenly, in November 1918 and, with the killing and destruction at an end people looked forward eagerly to the new life ahead. Things would never – could never – be the same again. The 'boys' were coming home again – at least those lucky enough to survive the carnage were coming home – and there were great hopes for every aspect of British life. Dawn was breaking on a great new world, it was thought.

Historians of whatever aspect of British life point to the great changes which came over the country because of the war. Transport was one particular area in which substantial change occurred. The next few years would see a transport picture totally different to what had existed up to 1914. Over one hundred railway companies would be 'grouped' into four large companies and the government's attempts at providing a secure basis for their finances would be shattered by a vigorous road haulage industry (as well as by the economic climate). As forty thousand-odd ex-Army vehicles would be added to a similar number already in civil commercial work, fierce competition would take place within that road haulage industry, too, and eventually 'regulation' would come. A giant new ministry would be set up to supervise the transport in Britain and, among other things, to take over the encouragement of road improvement which the Road Board had started. None of the actors in the transport scene would find it easy, for the decades between the wars were to prove economically very harsh, and many would see their hopes, and their capital, perish.

While the fighting was still going on, the government had, in 1917, set up a Ministry of Reconstruction, and its committees galore surveyed every aspect of life. Nothing much came of that. The transport situation of the United Kingdom was examined by a Select Committee of the House of Commons, set up in August 1918,

> for the purpose of considering what steps, if any, it is desirable to take to develop and improve the internal facilities for transport within the United Kingdom, to secure effective supervision and coordination, and to ensure that such developments and improvements shall be adequate and suitable to meet the national requirements.

The main body of the Select Committee's comments and recommendations is in its Second Report published three days after the Armistice – after a very short period of work.[1] What it said about road haulage is in Section C,

Paragraphs 22–28, and that was not very much. The State, we are told, had intervened solely for public safety or convenience or the protection of the roads. It had made no attempt by educational or other methods to influence private owners or users of road transport to combine for the purposes of introducing less extravagant methods. Little had been done except by the railways and other large corporations until the exigencies of war demanded economy in this as in other directions. The Select Committee was obviously impressed by the work being done by the RTB. It is perhaps not surprising that in wartime the members of the Committee should have been concerned about 'wasteful' or 'inefficient' methods and so applauded the efforts of the RTB – as described towards the end of the previous chapter. In the end, however, the Committee did not consider road transport to be capable of being organized to such an extent as railways and canals; but it believed there was much useful work to be done. In particular, when peace was restored the government should endeavour to reap for the community the fruits of the educational work of the RTB by promoting voluntary co-operation between owners and users of road transport. The Select Committee, however, realized that measures suitable for wartime might not be suitable to peacetime conditions; and 'considerations may justify from a trader or agriculturist's point of view what, for the community, appears to be uneconomical use of road transport'.

If the government were to reap any benefits for the community they needed a means of doing it. Their line of thought had, perhaps, already been indicated by the terms of reference of the Select Committee which, among other things, was to point out what steps were necessary 'to secure effective supervision and co-ordination' in transport. There had been much discussion in various circles of the need for a Ministry of Ways and Communications, and the war had been over only about three months when, on 26 February 1919, a bill was introduced in the House of Commons to set up such a Ministry and endow it with appropriate powers. The Home Secretary, Mr E.Shortt, explained that adequate and cheap transport was vital for progress in industry, agriculture and housing. But up to the moment there had been no coordination.

> Speaking practically, in pre-war days our transport depended largely on private effort and private gain, and in a matter so vital as this of transport it is not altogether to the public good that private interest should be the main stimulus of those who control it ... the day for unfettered competition had gone ... [and] the introduction of the motor has prevented road traffic being any longer a merely local question, [The Select Committee has concluded, he went on] that we cannot allow the organization of all the transport agencies of the country to revert to their pre-war circumstances and conditions. ... The government propose, first of all to take control of the railways, light railways, tramways, canals, waterways and inland navigation... Equally with regard to the roads ...up

> to the present under diversified local control. The Road Board has had some control but not really a working or an efficient control. [Furthermore] more and more large items such as boilers go by road [and] have to pass through [an enormous number of local authority areas] ... a matter of that sort requires centralised control,

In addition to all these, the government proposed to take over control of electricity supply on the grounds that 'transport is the greatest and most permanent customer'.[2] The Home Secretary was, no doubt, thinking of tramways, undergrounds, and perhaps of the possibilities of more general railway electrification, though historian A.J.P. Taylor says that 'This was the result of a deal between the Geddes brothers. Aukland Geddes, President of the Board of Trade, offered to surrender either shipping or electricity, but not both. Eric Geddes, Minister [designate], chose electricity.'[3]

Maybe Sir Eric was on unsure ground in choosing electricity, but he was in a much stronger position when he said, during the Second Reading of the Bill, that while people talked of 'foreign policy', 'colonial policy' and so on, he had never heard anyone ask 'What is your transportation policy?' He went on, 'What is our transportation policy and who is responsible for that policy? The answer is that there is no policy and that no-one is responsible.'[4] Hence the need for the Bill. Not surprisingly, W. Joynson-Hicks, a doughty fighter on behalf of road transport interests, both in the courts and in Parliament, was aghast at the extent of the proposed ministry. (Joynson-Hicks was accused of having 'invented a new political Road Party', and of considering himself as 'occupying a specially created post of godfather in regard to roads'.) He argued that 'it will need its minister to be a superman ... a very great man'. It would save time, he said, if a clause were included to the effect that the minister would manage the whole of the affairs of the country. He went on to claim that there was, in Parliament, an unofficial private committee of 280 members 'to promote the use and development of the roads'. These members 'strongly object to the inclusion in one ministry of all these vital essentials to the well-being of the trade and commerce of the country'. The members, too, 'were gravely suspicious of the roads being put under railway control'. He suggested that the roads be hived off into a separate ministry – a revived Road Board – and that the Cabinet itself should coordinate the work of the roads ministry and the railways.[5]

Road interests did not like the proposed ministry one bit. They often referred to the new ministry as the 'Ministry of Railways', no doubt because the railways were far and away bigger than anything else to be included under the ministry. But they were equally concerned about the government's view as expressed by the Home Secretary, about the inappropriateness of 'private interests' and 'unfettered competition'. After all, that had been the basis on which the industry had grown from puling infancy in the early 1900s to vigorous youthfulness in 1919. It was just too much that the private owners who had stuck gamely to the job through wartime impressment of vehicles, and through shortages of labour, vehicles, fuel and spare parts, were now to be subject to 'control' by a powerful ministry in which the railways would be the biggest single element and at the head of which was a railwayman – Sir Eric Geddes, ex-General Manager of the North-Eastern Railway, and ex-Director General of Military Railways.

Sir Eric's experiences in France clearly lay behind the thinking about peacetime needs at home. At the time of the slaughter at the Somme in 1916 military transport was a bit chaotic. One authority was responsible for movement of ships with supplies to France; another for the docks and the off-loading of ships; a third for the railways to move the goods forward; yet another for the lorries; and finally the battalions themselves, for the horse or light-railway transport to the trenches. It was no wonder that Sir Douglas Haig called for a unified control to ensure coordination, and that duly came about.

The Bill to set up the ministry started out as a fairly simple measure, to allow the government to set up the new ministry, to switch to it, from other departments, whatever duties and powers they had in respect of railways, light railways, tramways and 'roads, bridges and ferries and vehicles and traffic thereon'. By the time the Bill had got through two or three committees and the House of Lords, 'Transport' had been substituted for 'Ways and Communications' as the title of the new ministry. A separate section within the ministry, to deal with 'road construction, improvement, maintenance and development', was obligatory, as was a Roads Committee made up of equal numbers of representatives from highway authorities and 'horse and mechanical road transport' – to give advice and assistance to the minister. These latter institutions were the fruits of the road lobby's attempts to get roads and road traffic totally separated into a distinct ministry.

The debate on the Bill was carried on, as might have been expected, in an atmosphere of apprehension – of the monopoly power of railways, of a governmental tendency to control everything, and of a minister to be endowed with very sweeping powers. Oddly, one clause which gave the minister 'power to establish and, either by himself or through any other person, to work transport services by land and water', was not opposed in principle, in the House of Commons, at least, even though Joynson-Hicks made a wry comment that 'My Right Hon. Friend might start a couple of hundred schemes of transport all over the country.' (The Department of Agriculture was said to have 190 schemes for light railways under consideration.)[6] Opposition to this clause was mainly concerned with questions of finance. Naturally enough, there was opposition, too, to the government's attempts to have the work of the Advisory Committee brought under the Official Secrets Act. In the end the Bill became law without the road interests managing to get roads under a different ministry. The government side argued that, because road traffic was going to develop, it had to be included in the Department responsible for coordination. The Bill duly received the Royal Assent at the end of the summer of 1919, but despite Sir Eric Geddes's remarks during the Second Reading, no one was yet any wiser as to what policy the new Ministry of Transport would follow.

Most superficial views of the development of the road haulage industry express the conventional wisdom that the industry started with the release of a large number of vehicles from military service at the end of the First World War. Those large numbers of vehicles had already been doing, for several years, a substantial haulage job in the military field, but it must be emphasized that at least as many were operating in Britain during the war in a commercial capacity, contributing soundly to the transport needs of the nation. One hundred thousand vehicles just did not appear by magic one bright morning in 1919. They had been working before then. Indeed 82,000 goods vehicles were licensed in 1914. No doubt the railways and horse transport were the main means of transport in the country, and no doubt the growth of mechanical road haulage in the next decade would wipe out one of the older forms and severely damage the other, but it must be recognized that at the end of the war in late 1918 mechanical road haulage was an established industry. As we have seen in earlier chapters, there were already quite a number of large fleets operating, both 'own account' by firms such as Lever Brothers and Harrods; and 'for hire or reward' by companies such as Pickford or McNamara; and there were a great many small fleets, too.

Nevertheless, it cannot be gainsaid that the sale of Army surplus vehicles did give a tremendous boost to this young industry. As we saw at the end of Chapter Five, the government declined the British manufacturers' proposals for the handling of the war-surplus vehicles. No reasons were given but it may have been simply that the authorities felt that it was simpler to let one body deal with all the multifarious material of war, not just vehicles, tyres and spares, but other items by the tens of thousands of tons – ships, aircaft, uniforms, boots and belts, factories, huts and whatever else one cares to name.

It is not easy to get precise details of the number and type of lorries sold. A Select Committee on National Expenditure in 1918 reported that 52,130 vehicles were in government hands,[7] but that figure was challenged by the Editor of *Commercial Motor*. Writing in the issue of 28 November 1918, he estimated that 2500 vehicles had been impressed at the start of the war. He went on to estimate that an average of 200 had been built by the manufacturers each week over the 222 weeks the War had lasted. That brought the numbers up to 46,500, he said. The next estimate was 'assumed mortality' of 20,000, leaving the net British figure at 26,500. But the Editor could only ask about the remainder – whether we could have bought so many from the United

States and so on, as to make the number up to over 50, 000. Not much useful can be said eighty-odd years later about the basis or accuracy of these estimates but at least they indicate how an intelligent and knowledgeable man viewed the government figures at the time. Probably at least 20,000 American *vehicles* (that is, including cars) were supplied to the British government. The picture is confused in that some British production was released for civilian use; and AEC, to take just one example, certainly supplied vehicles to the American Forces. Then there were companies such as FWD, manufacturing in both Britain and America and supplying both governments.

Winston Churchill, Secretary of State for War, in reply to a question in the House of Commons a year after the war ended, gave a figure close to that of the Select Committee. He said that the War Department had 51,950 lorries *in their possession* at the date of the Armistice. But he added that up to the date he was speaking, 'the number of lorries reported to the Ministry of Munitions for disposal ... is 33,201'.[8] The various units of the Armed Forces were obliged to notify the MoM what vehicles or other material they had surplus to their requirements. The number for disposal given by Mr Churchill corresponds nicely with that given by the junior Minister of the MOM the following March. Mr Kellaway stated in the House of Commons that up to that momemt 17,806 lorries had been disposed of for £7,239,159, and that there were still 15, 394 in the hands of the MOM – including those under repair at Slough, and at Abbeville and Cologne.[9] It is not clear, however, whether these figures included the 5000 German Army lorries which were to be handed over under the Armistice terms.[10] Further figures to confuse us were provided by Lloyd George, Prime Minister and previously Minister of Munitions. He quoted the following figures 'to illustrate the dimensions of motor transport used by the Army':

	Lorries, heavy and light	Cars, vans and ambulances	Steam wagons	Tractors
Acquired by War Office from every source before 1/9/1916	21,705	9,630	440	936
Supplied by Ministry of Munitions from 1/9/1916 to Dec.1918	37,785	24,170	714	2505
Totals	59, 490	33,800	1154	3441

He explained that the figures did not show how many vehicles were lost through enemy action or otherwise.[11] He might have said, too, that his remarks did not include anything about bus chassis which might later have had lorry bodies fitted. That was done, too, during the war.

A few surplus Army (or rather, Armed Forces) vehicles had been sold as early as the autumn of 1916, and two years later, seven weeks or so before the war ended, *Commercial Motor* could report that 'Sales by private treaty of vehicles for which the services have no further use have, naturally, been taking place for some time.' The Editorial of 26 September 1918 commented on an auction sale to be held the following week in London – 'the first of its kind'. About thirty vehicles were to be sold 'as they stand with all their faults'. By this time the MOM had a disposals organization and an Advisory Council which included, amongst other businessmen, Sir John E. Thornycroft. The policy was to sell vehicles (and everything else) at going market prices as decided by auction.

Sales started off very slowly – at least from the government side – as if the government were waiting to get the Slough repair depot in operation. But as the war ended there was an increased urgency about doing this, and, in the House of Lords, Lord Desborough referred to 'the feverish activity which was displayed after the Armistice was signed'. Contractors were given *carte blanche* to get on with the work with all possible speed and dispatch. 'Work went on by night and by day', and special trains were run from London to convey the workers. If this had only been done earlier, said his Lordship, 'presumably thousands of vehicles would not have been left to rot at Kempton Park'.[12] As the surplus vehicles came back from France immediately after the Armistice they were stored temporarily at Kempton Park. This provoked many letters to newspapers, and questions in Parliament – which usually included phrases like 'their engines red with rust'. The Slough Depot came into operation early in May 1919 – six months after the Armistice. By the time of this debate in the Lords in July 1919 (on the Second Reading of the Bill to set up the Ministry of Transport) Viscount Milner, for the government, was able to say that 'It has already repaired between 1000 and 2000 lorries. It is capable of repairing at the rate of several hundred a week now, and very shortly we shall be able to repair 100 a day.'[13] The organization of the Depot did not appear too efficient, at first, and the government was obliged to call on the services of Mr S.A. Wallace of AEC from 22 May. Under Wallace, AEC had turned out large numbers of good buses for the LGOC and chassis for the Forces, and he now proceeded to put a bit of life into the Slough workshops.

The dilatory progress of sales of surplus vehicles in those early months was not entirely due to the slowness at Slough. To be fair to the government and the Armed Forces, they could not really be certain that the fighting was finally over until a peace treaty was actually signed. Until then they could not say with any confidence how many of their 50,000 vehicles would really be surplus to requirements. But things did begin to happen. The organization for the disposal of surplus war material was tidied up in the spring of 1919 and the new Disposals Board began the issue of a fortnightly catalogue, appropriately called *Surplus,* from the beginning of June. Issue No. 4 of the catalogue on 15 July 1919 said that up to 18 June, 4800 vehicles had been sold for £1.1 million and 'during the last three weeks' another 2738 vehicles had been sold for £651,000. They did not say 'lorries' but, rather, 'vehicles'. Anyway, the process was getting going, and by April 1920 auctions were taking place in London (three days a week) and at about three dozen other points around the United Kingdom.

In an economic boom with the main means of transport of the country badly congested, it was clear that there was going to be a market for the surplus government vehicles. Prices at the auctions, often in response to spirited bidding, were initially good – that is, from the government's point of view. According to *The Times* of 14 August 1919, 'The demand for lorries being sold by the Disposal Board at Olympia continues. On Tuesday Commercar lorries realized from 525 to 700 guineas. A Leyland lorry in need of considerable repair fetched 570 guineas.' Six months earlier (that is, three months after the war had ended) we read in the gossip column of *Commercial Motor*, 'One Hears', 'of auctioned lorries being sold immediately at double their purchase price'. The columnist went on to report the allegation that at one sale a buyer of nine lorries sold four of them before he left the auction room at the price he paid for the nine.[14] The bidders at many of these auction sales were probably not, in the main, individuals buying for their own use. The Yorkshire Motor Car Co. Ltd of Brighouse advertised in September 1919 '1000 motor lorries for immediate disposal'. These included 'Brand New' – AECs for £950, Thornycrofts for £1000, Karriers for £1075 -as well as 'hundreds of second-hand machines'. This firm was not the government's appointed auctioneer, so had obviously bought the vehicles in at an official auction or by private treaty.[15]

Some of the new vehicles they were selling may well have come from manufacturers who were now supplying the civil market again. But it is worth noting that when the fighting stopped there were some new vehicles in the hands of the Army which had not yet seen active service. (The Army had been preparing for a tremendous offensive to take place in 1919.) Although letters went out to the manufacturers immediately on the Armistice giving notice of the ending of contracts, the government was obliged to continue to take new vehicles until the period of notice ran out. The Parliamentary Secretary to the MoM, in answer to a question in the House of Commons in late July 1919, told the questioner that some 500 lorries were still to come under the contracts. He rejected suggestions that they would be left to stand and rust. They could be sold readily.[16]

As well as auctions there were sales by private treaty. The first issues of *Surplus* contained an advertisement for '1500 unused 3 to 4 ton motor lorry chassis with bodies to be disposed of at fixed prices by private treaty'. These included well-known British makes such as AEC, Hallford, Karrier, Lacre, Maudslay, Pagefield, Thornycroft; equally well-known Americans such as Peerless and Pierce-Arrow, and the famous Swiss Saurer.

Some of the sales by private treaty were intriguing. There was a big 'park' of RAF vehicles at St Omer in France, for instance, the sale of which generated questions in Parliament. According to Brigadier-General Croft, speaking in the debate on the MoM Vote on 15 April 1920, a firm had visited the site and counted 1158 Leyland lorries. The authorities, he alleged, did not know how many vehicles there were and had had to accept this figure. At a meeting on 9 December 1919 the firm was told that the MoM reckoned that the vehicles with the large quantity of spares were worth not less than £500,000. The firm pointed out that there were then only 961 lorries at the dump as some had been sent back to England. The authorities then said that in that case the value would be £450,000. The firm offered £375,000. This was declined and the meeting was adjourned. Four days later, on 13 December, the firm having apparently reconsidered the matter, wrote making a firm offer of £450,000. Much to their amazement they got a telegram saying that their offer of £450, 000 was 'unacceptable' but that 'provided unsold, will accept £400,000 cash'. The firm replied, drawing attention to the curious point that their offer of £450,000 had been rejected and a new figure of £400,000 cash suggested instead. If that figure were right, they confirmed that they would buy.

A principal of the firm went to London right away to complete what he thought was an agreed deal. On his arrival there, however, he was met by an employee of his firm who showed him a further telegram dated 15 December from the Disposals Board confirming that the figure should have been £500,000. On a subsequent visit to the Board he was told that a further valuation had been made and that £500,000 was, indeed, the figure.

The apparent offer of £400,000 was, of course, an error, discovered only after the telegram was sent, and it is understandable. But what intrigued Brigadier-General Croft in Parliament was something rather different. After outlining 'the facts' as above, he went on:

> It now appears that, during the whole period of these negotiations, the chief official who was selling these motor lorries in this extraordinary manner happened to be the brother of two directors in another firm. This particular firm were very anxious to obtain these motor lorries, and the extraordinary part of it is that the particular firm purchased these motor lorries at the higher figure of £500,000 when the price had been suddenly raised after the contract had been, as was believed, in fact, accepted.

Two firms wanted the vehicles – Leylands, and Lever Brothers who reportedly wanted the lorries in order to start a fish distribution scheme. Their deal fell through, probably because of the price and the difficulty and cost of getting the lorries shipped back to England. (Despite the innuendos in the quotation from Brigadier General Croft given above there is no reason for doubting that all parties acted perfectly honourably.) The government needed all the shipping space they could get for other things – not the least being railway wagons and locomotives. Leylands had made an offer of £500,000 and were a bit dismayed to find the 'park' subsequently being offered to Lever Brothers for that amount. As it so happened Levers declined and Leylands got the vehicles – just under 700 Leyland lorries, some Crossley tenders, a few Fords, trailers, and a great stock of spares. *They* then had the problem of getting the vehicles back to England. They managed to make a contract with one firm to get the lorries home in small lots at £15 per vehicle. Much later, when shipping space became available, the government offered to bring the lorries home at £30 a time, but in the end settled with Leylands for £16 each.[17] It is to the credit of both firms that they were so quick on the ball – Lever's representatives having visited St Omer within a couple of weeks of the Armistice.

Manufacturers, who had a reputation to protect, were obviously not too happy at seeing their battle-scarred, overworked machines flooding back onto the market (either at home or in the colonies) and they did what they could in buying up and renovating many of them. Albion, for example, who had supplied some 6000 vehicles to the Army, bought many of them back for reconditioning in their depot at Willesden, London. In a written answer in the Commons on 23 March 1920 J.F. Hope, Parliamentary Secretary to the MoM, named Albion, Leylands, Maudslay and a Major H.S. Otto, as each having made contracts of over £150,000 value for the purchase of lorries. Leylands bought a plant at Ham in Surrey to deal with the surplus machines they had bought. Manufacturers tried to help in other ways, too. Thornycrofts included a paragraph in some of their advertisements addressed to anyone who had bought a Thornycroft at a 'Surplus' auction. The firm asked to be advised so that they could note the new owner's name in their records. They offered to inspect the vehicles and advise the owners, free of charge, what needed to be done to put the vehicle in good condition. They offered their services, too, in supplying spares or doing repairs.[18]

As well as manufacturers, other people tried to turn an honest penny by helping purchasers. In the summer of 1919 one firm was advertising its willingness, for a commission of 5 per cent on the price, to advise prospective purchasers on the suitability of particular vehicles for their business, to select chassis, purchase, tune them up and deliver them in running order. They would then advise on maintenance.[19]

Many people were anxious to get into the haulage business and many did not know much about mechanical transport. To try to help readers sort out the good from the bad at the war-surplus auctions, *Commercial Motor* ran an article in the autumn of 1919 describing the markings carried by military vehicles to indicate the work they had been doing. An Ace of Clubs indicated supply column work; an outline of a shell indicated ammunition transport; and so on. If there were none of the various specified marks on the vehicle then it had probably been engaged in road repairs or signals work and would not have been too badly treated. The article warned that a Thornycroft 'J' type would have been subjected to a great deal of hard work simply because it was one of the most successful lorries used in the war.[20]

The sales of surplus vehicles continued for several years and it is not altogether clear when the supply was exhausted. Certainly by the autumn of 1923 supplies were tapering off. The government's own sales were completed in 1923 according to the Final Report of the Disposal and Liquidation Commission (Cmd 2106, 1924). Many of the ex-government vehicles were 'reconditioned' at Slough or by one firm or another before being sold to traders or haulage contractors. It was as late as May 1925 that Slough Lorries and Components Ltd, announced that they had now satisfactorily disposed of most of their material and had therefore decided voluntarily to wind up their business.[21] Leyland ran advertisements in the early 1920s for their famous 'R.A.F. type' 4-tonners (so called because the RAF had used a great many of them), reconditioned at Ham. From February 1923 they were giving a two-year guarantee with the vehicle instead of their earlier six-month guarantee, and six weeks later were advertising proudly that they had sold 1850 of these lorries to date.[22] In July 1924 they said 'there now remain a few hundred only' of the 'thousands re-purchased from Government by the makers'. These famous reconditioned vehicles had, up to then, been going for £590, but because of the rising cost of reconditioning, the chassis would cost £650 from 1 September. That did not seem to put people off and by the middle of that month the advertisements were saying that there were less than 200 left. At the beginning of February 1926 the firm advertised its apology that the supply of reconstructed RAF types was now exhausted.[23] Though Leyland's stock had lasted until 1926, the flood of wartime lorries had become a trickle much earlier. The editor of *Commercial Motor* wrote in November 1923 that:

> The rapid diminution in importance of the ex-service surplus has been particularly marked in recent months ... [whilst] the great age of most of the ex-service vehicles has much reduced their attractiveness created by their low price ... [After] an almost killing period of stagnation in the commercial vehicle industry for some years ... some 40 British, manufacturers have now produced new designs.[24]

It became the practice during 1922 for firms to offer for sale 'reconditioned' vehicles without saying whether or not these were government surplus. Some of the vehicles may well have originated from victims of the depressed economy. Whatever vehicles were left of Britain's wartime fleets, by this time, other surplus lorries were turning up all the time. In 1922 and 1923 we see advertisements under the heading 'Evacuation of Ireland'. (Ireland had been partitioned under an Act of 1921 and British forces had withdrawn from the part of the country which would then be known as the Irish Free State.) The next line of the advertisements reads 'Irish M.T. Surplus Disposals' and they went on to offer 'Splendid 3/4 ton lorries' – Dennis (of 1919 manufacture), AEC and Albions – 'with W.D. bodies, from £150'.[25] Daimler, Maudslay, Peerless, Pagefield, Berna and LGOC (bus) chassis were offered in the 'small ads' as 'Liquidations of Stocks of the British Army' without saying where they came from. Early 1923 saw the evacuation of Allied Forces from the Rhineland, which had been occupied since the end of the war. The following are examples of the classified advertisements which appeared then:

> Harford & Co. Ltd are disposal agents in the United Kingdom for the huge stock of FWD vehicles now released by the evacuation of the Rhine Army of Occupation. Many of these vehicles have not been issued for service, and are still in the depots to which originally consigned [a number of vehicles are listed, e.g.] £400 will purchase an FWD lorry with a general utility body, drop-sides and tailboard ... inclusive of new all-steel 1–5 ton trailer.

(FWD were a company making four-wheel-drive vehicles.) Again, Lane & Co. of London, SE9 advertised that:

> We are offering the whole of the Rhine Army Reserve Thornycrofts – J type 90cwt from £150 in first class condition – a number are to all intents and purposes practically new.[26]

The flood of British Army surplus vehicles on to the market was bad enough news for manufacturers, but worse was the fact that, as a hangover from Britain's free-trade days of the previous century, it allowed surplus American Army vehicles to enter the country free of duty. The Americans had 39,000 surplus vehicles in Europe at the end of the war[27] and did not want to ship them back to America. Many of these vehicles had been built by British or continental manufacturers and these would hardly have been welcomed in America; but the Americans had no hang-ups about free trade and calmly imposed a 90 per cent import tariff on any lorries entering the United States, including vehicles made there and sent overseas. The British-made ones would, in any event, have been admitted to Britain duty-free, but the Safeguarding of Industries Act of 1921, while imposing duties on imported cars, had left untouched road freight vehicles. It is no wonder that the vehicle manufacturers organized petitions early in 1923 and sent a deputation to see sympathetic MPs at the House of Commons in March of that year to put forward the request that 'further importation of war surplus vehicles should be stopped, [and] that new methods be devised for dealing with the stocks on hand'.[28]

There was a suspicion that French war-surplus vehicles had been brought in, too, but none of these appeared in advertisements I have seen, although American Army surplus and plenty of Fiats did. It is hard to say where some of the surplus vehicles came from, for British manufacturers had supplied vehicles to the American Army whilst the British Army had used many

American vehicles. It was bad enough for British manufacturers anyway that new vehicles from France and Germany were said to be at a price advantage of £124 and £200 over British makes because of the relative values of the currencies.[29] (Then a highly valued £ was thought necessary for confidence and to keep inflation under control.)

While manufacturers such as Albion and Leyland had tried to protect themselves by buying up surplus war lorries and feeding them back on to the market over several years, there were other possible strategies. The McCurd Lorry Manufacturing Co. Ltd of Hayes, Middlesex had ceased lorry production altogether around 1920 because, according to *Commercial Motor* 'they foresaw the great slump which must inevitably follow from letting loose on the market the vast accumulation of Government lorries used in the Great War'. But users of McCurd vehicles, it appears, kept pressing for new vehicles, so in the autumn of 1925 the firm came back into production with a 40/50 cwt chassis.[30] If all this was disastrous for British manufacturers and their employees, it made it easy for people to get into transport. Slough Lorries and Components Ltd (about which see below) ran advertisements for quite a long time offering reconditioned (American) Peerless 4-tonners for £195. The firm would accept a deposit of £46 16s. 0d. (£46.80) and the balance by twelve monthly payments of £13, or 52 weekly payments of £3.[31] That was not the cheapest by any means, for one could get an Army surplus lorry in Nottingham for £135.[32] The buyers had to be told why lorries were so cheap. C.H.&L.O. Smith of Nottingham offered in mid-1924 FWD lorries, which originally cost £950, for only £176. 'How can we offer these FWD lorries for £176?' asked their advertisement. They gave the reply to their own question. 'These FWDs were supplied to the American army after the cessation of hostilities. The American government was prevented from taking them back to America by its agreement with the American manufacturers. So the lorries remained on the continent.' If Messrs Smith were making a profit on these, the Americans must have been practically giving them away.[33]

While the Slough Depot under managers like Wallace did a sound job, obviously the term 'reconditioned' was elastic and it is probable that some firms were satisfied with patching up the more obvious defects and giving the lorries 'a lick of paint'. It is hard to know what to make of advertisements claiming that the vehicles were 'practically unused' but at the same time having 'new tyres'. One firm's advertisements claimed that their reconditioned lorries 'ARE RECONDITIONED' – which suggested that maybe some others were not so scrupulous, and Fiat, London, protected their reputation by announcing that any of their vehicles advertised by other companies as reconditioned were definitely not reconditioned by Fiat, either in Britain or Italy, and that their spares were available only for vehicles imported by them.[34]

The firm of Lane & Co. mentioned above were amongst those who did a thoroughly good job. *Commercial Motor* ran an article on 31 July 1923 under the title 'Reconditioning the Rhine Army Lorries' describing the work going on at Lane's Eltham factory where nearly one thousand Thornycrofts were awaiting attention. Reconditioning, we learn, was 'very thorough indeed'. Chassis were stripped down to the last nut. Frames generally were found to need some reriveting. All the springs were dismantled and the leaves reset. Steering bushes were replaced, if necessary. Crankshafts were reground and, if necessary, given new bearings. Considerable wear was often found in the big ends. 'After regrinding the crankpins new phosphor-bronze big-end bushes with white metal linings [were] fitted'; and so on. The engines were 'carefully run in by means of an electric motor'. One firm taking advantage of this work was the Bowden Transport Company of Dartford, whose six Thornycrofts each ran 600 miles a week carrying over 5 tons of paper each trip to *The Daily Telegraph* in London. This was certainly more than their rated capacity, but in giving a repeat order to Lane the transport company expressed their satisfaction with the point that the lorries were doing 7½ miles to the gallon of petrol.[35]

So on to a hungry market came a great supply of lorries in a variety of states. One advertisement on behalf of the Australian Disposals Board said 'Many of these vehicles are in running order'[36] – and *Commercial Motor* complained of the appalling state of many surplus lorries and of firms 'with but a few pounds at the back of them speculating on being able to tinker at them sufficiently in their spare time to enable them to be hawked'.[37]

In the end one has not much choice but to go along with the commonly quoted figures of 40,000 – 50,000 as the number of government surplus lorries that were added to British transport fleets in the years after 1918, and who can say whether the true figure is nearer the upper or the lower limit of this range? People did not get too excited about precise statistics in the early 1920s and one is left feeling in great doubt by information such as that given in the 'Supply' debate in the Commons on 15 April 1920 – that 17,646 lorries had been sold 'during the past few months' and an estimated 15,000 lorries were at Slough. The House was told that of these 15,000, 'a great number [are] seriously crippled' and so might be expected to yield only 10,000 sound vehicles. But there was a probability that more vehicles would be 'thrown up'.

What was being discussed at that moment was the sale of the Slough Depot to a private company headed by Sir Percival Perry and including Lord Inchcape. Mr Wallace, the manager of the depot, was said to have organized the sale after having visited America in connection with the scheme. This raised fears of American capital setting up a manufacturing operation in Britain in competition with established manufacturers, but that did not happen, though there was nothing in the contract to stop it but the fact that the government had not announced its intention to sell, nor had given other firms a chance to submit alternative offers, gave rise to much suspicion.

Under the contract with Sir Percival Perry the works were sold for £3,300,000 – which, the government said, gave them a capital profit of £850,000. The 15,000 lorries and stocks of spares went for another £3,650,000. The contract provided that once the sales by the new owners of the depot reached £5 million the government became entitled to 25 per cent of subsequent sales turnover; after £6 million they were to get 40 per cent and after £7 million, 50 per cent. Since the depot, as well as dealing with surplus war vehicles, had been intended to be a repair depot on a continuing basis for vehicles used by government departments, it is not surprising that a clause was put into the contract to cover this. The company was obliged, in future, to repair vehicles of any government department, if required, at cost plus 10 per cent, though the government was not obliged to send them any such vehicles for repairs.[38] It would appear that the government – despite all the earlier forecasts of great profitability – had had second thoughts about the advisability of keeping a large repair depot just to repair departmental and armed forces vehicles. It is noticeable, too, that the price paid for the 15,000 lorries in the sale of 'Slough' was well below the prices prevailing in the early auctions mentioned in *The Times*. Economic depression and a saturated market for surplus lorries might well have been persuasive on the government's attitude. The group of financiers who bought the Slough Depot were said to have come together originally to buy 15,000 American lorries which were then at Coblenz. They apparently dropped that idea when the Slough Depot came up for sale.[39]

It was not just cheap lorries that came under the heading of war surplus. The purchase price for the Slough Depot included something for spares, as we have seen. There are any number of advertisements, too, in those early postwar years for tyres and all sorts of spare parts. H. Northwood & Sons of London, S.E.1 advertised in *Commercial Motor* of 25 October 1922 that:

> The WHOLE of the ASC MT DUMP at BAUPAUME, Rouen, is now our property. This was the 'spares' depot for the whole of the British Army. Thousands (all kinds, sizes and makes) of SOLID TYRES, MAGNETOS, CARBURRETTERS, RADIATORS, RADIATOR TUBES, JACKS, SPRINGS, WHEELS, ENGINES, CYLINDERS.

The advertisement said that they had over 2000 tons of spares and went on to list some 600 tons in the following manner:

> A few of the many tons of spares we are offering at a very low price.–

COMMER	65 tons	FODEN & SENTINEL	60 tons	KARRIER	30 tons
MAUDSLAY	40 tons	DAIMLER & A.E.C	110 tons	HALLEY	20 tons
BERNA	20 tons	HALLFORD	40 tons		

> These are for sale in one lot or small lots.

(The 'ASC MT' refers to the Army Service Corps, Motor Transport Section.)

As well as the setting up of the new ministry and the bargain bonanza of surplus lorries, the road haulage industry would be affected by another matter – taxation. Up to this time lorry owners had paid their contribution for the use of roads by the few pence per gallon paid on the price of petrol. But this raised all sorts of administrative difficulties. It was difficult to define precisely what should be taxed since there were many users of petroleum-based products other than the internalcombustion-engined vehicle; and there were other substances which could be used for fuel for these vehicles – much of it produced in Britain – gas, benzole, alcohol, and so on. To make matters worse, other users of the roads – traction engines and steam lorries, using coal or coke; electrics, and horse-drawn vehicles – were not caught by the tax on 'motor spirit'. The administration of the scheme was a nuisance, too, for lorry owners paid the full tax when buying their fuel and then had to seek a rebate of half the tax. So a change had to come.

By this time it was being accepted by the local authorities that road transport was going to grow and that the roads would have to be made fit to carry the traffic. There had been dissentient voices, admittedly. The Chairman of the Departmental Committee on Road Locomotives and Heavy Motor Cars, 1918, had summed up the written evidence of the Provost of Hamilton, who represented the Royal Burghs of Scotland, thus:

> You say: It should be regarded as a guiding principle that the roads and highways of the kingdom have been formed for the utility of the people, but are not intended to be exploited by capitalists for gain in competition with the railways by the carriage of goods?
> Yes,
> Does that go as far as to mean that this heavy road traffic should be discouraged?'
> I think it does.
> But there is such evidence from local authorities saying this traffic should not be discouraged?
> I think the general feeling is that the roads are being unfairly used ... for commercial purposes in excess of that may be regarded as legitimate carrying between point and point. In point of fact capitalists are organising both char-a-bancs and bus traffic and also commercial vehicles for the express purpose of competing with the railways and with tramways.
> But what I mean is, are you opposed altogether to competition with railways and tramways? Do you wish to discourage that competition?
> No, not absolutely. Light motor vehicles, I think, are absolutely necessary for the delivery of parcels and for a class of traffic which neither the tramways nor the railways could possibly undertake; that need not be discouraged, but when you get heavy vehicles put upon the road for the express purpose of carrying very heavy material which is not a type of stuff which should be taken by means of roads at all, then that, I say, should be distinctly discouraged. (Minutes 3518–23)

It was obviously a matter of opinion as to what 'type of stuff should be taken by means of roads' but the general view prevailed that roads had to be made fit for the traffic. Road haulage had been there before the railways, anyway. The roads were in a pretty bad shape, though, despite the pre war efforts of the Road Board. Military and other traffic had grown tremendously during the war, and, as we have seen, the activities of the Road Board had been severely curtailed. Sir Eric Geddes, in introducing the Third Reading of the Bill setting up the Ministry of Transport (MOT), had said in July 1919 that Britain's roads were not fitted for heavy traffic or for the traffic that must go on them if the countryside were to be opened up. Indeed the roads were poor, hardly fit for any traffic. In a debate the following spring an MP complained that 'at present owing to the rough state of the roads ... it is almost impossible for a cyclist to keep his rear light burning, on account of the great amount of vibration'. It is not clear which particular roads he was talking about, but certainly even the main roads were unsatisfactory. *The Times* included frequent paragraphs advising readers of the state of particular roads and often suggesting alternative routes. In August 1919 we read that 'On the Oxford Road the surface is rough to Beaconsfield, indifferent only to High Wycombe and then good on to Oxford. Coming out from London motorists are advised to take the road through Staines, Windsor and Slough, rejoining the main Oxford road at Beaconsfield. By doing this the bad stretch is avoided.'[40] Some roads had been dealt with fairly well. In May 1922 we read that the greater part of the Liverpool–Manchester road had been tarmacced in the previous ten years.[41] Many less busy main roads would have had much less than 'the greater part' tarmacced. Clearly the MOT had a task on hand. Initially local authorities made a great deal of use of clauses in the Roads Act 1920 under which they could apply to the Ministry to have specified roads closed to traffic or certain kinds of traffic, but by no means all of their requests were granted. An indication of the state of some roads, even in the capital, was that in March 1921 the Borough of Camberwell in London organized tests of splashguards. Vehicles had to run at speeds of up to 20 m.p.h. between three pairs of boards arranged respectively 12 feet, 16 feet and 20 feet apart. The idea was to see how far up the boards the splash marks reached, given the use of the competitor's chosen 'splashguard'.[42]

A committee which had studied the problem of paying for the roads made recommendations which were implemented by the 1920 Finance Act, to come into operation on 1 January 1921. The chosen means was to impose an annual tax. For goods vehicles the basis would be unladen weight, as follows:

	Unladen Weight Not Exceeding					
	12 cwt	1 ton	2 tons	3 tons	4 tons	Over 4 tons
Tax	£10	£16	£21	£25	£28	£30

Trailers were to be taxed at £2 per annum.

The rates for 'Road Locomotives' were

Not exceeding	8 tons	12 tons	Exceeding 12 tons
	£25	£28	£30

The figures were based on an estimate of the number of vehicles expected to be in use in England and Wales by midsummer, 1920: 210,000 cars, 70,000 hackney vehicles (including buses and charabancs), and 100,000 freight vehicles, plus one-eighth more for Scotland and N. Ireland.[43] Initially the idea was that there would be yearly licences to expire on 31 December and quarterly licenses, as well, to expire 31 March, 30 June and so on. These fixed dates brought a great deal of complaint, particularly from passenger vehicle operators whose 'summer season' might often run into October if the weather kept fine – after which they would lay up their charabancs. They did not much want to have to pay a quarter's tax just for an extra two or three days or weeks. On the freight side, it did not take the operators long to realize where the break-even point was between paying on petrol at 3d. a gallon and paying a lump sum of £25 for a 3-tonner. That £25 would be equivalent to 2000 gallons a year on the old system – perhaps 12,000 miles. Anyone who did less than that mileage would lose out and soon there were vociferous complaints that the new system favored the 'big boys'. People in the small-mileage category – and there were plenty of traders doing only local deliveries, often only on a couple of days a week – were quick to argue that the old tax varied in direct relation to the usage of the roads, but, unfortunately for them, as early as December 1919 the Chancellor had stated that he would not consider any scheme that involved the retention of the petrol tax.

The small users argued, too, that the tax was ill proportioned as between the different sizes of vehicle, in terms of the minimum mileage it assumed. There were complaints, furthermore, and not just from the small firms, that the new system involved a substantial increase in taxation. On commercial vehicles (goods and passenger) the old taxes raised about £800,000 a year, whereas the new figure would be in the order of £3,315,000, even without any growth in traffic.[44] The new system had been designed, however, so that commercial transport would be paying about the same gross amount as private cars, so there was not much room for complaint on that ground. With mechanical transport growing quickly there was an urgent need for action on the state of the roads. The growing number of freight vehicles would provide the wherewithal. The MOT had made available some £10 millions – partly from the balances of the Road Improvement Fund and partly from general government funds. But there were plenty of forecasts of what was needed – £30 million, £40 million, £70 million ... [45]

The Roads Act 1920, together with the new basis of taxation provided for by the Finance Act, reorganized the financing of road maintenance. Among other things the old Road Improvement Fund disappeared and in its place was now substituted the term which is more familiar to later generations – the Road Fund.

Notes

1. Select Committee on Transport 2nd Report 130/136 Nov. 1919.
2. Parl. Debates. Commons. Vol. 112, 26/2/1919, cols 1820–28.
3. A.J.P. Taylor, *English History 1914–45*, p.130, footnote 1.
4. Parl. Debates. Commons. Vol. 113, 17/3/1919, col. 1763.
5. Parl. Debates. Commons. Vol. 112, 26/2/1919, col. 1824.
6. Parl. Debates. Commons. Vol. 117, 1/7/1919, col. 1450.
7. *CM*, 21/11/1918, p.273.
8. *CM*, 11/11/1919, p.275.
9. *CM*, 9/3/1920, p.66.
10. *CM*, 21/11/1918, pp.274 & 276.
11. D. Lloyd George, *War Memoirs*, new ed., p.478.
12. Parl. Debates. Lords. Vol. 35, July 1919, cols 1110–20.
13. Parl Debates. Lords. Vol 35, July 1919, col. 1119.
14. *CM*, 27/2/1919, p.3.
15. *CM*, 23/9/1919, ads p.21.
16. *CM*, 29/7/1919, p.518.
17. Parl. Debates. Commons. Vol. 127 March–April 1920, 15/4/1920; *CM*, 13/1/1920, p.523; 17/8/1920, p.749.
18. *CM*, 3/2/1920, ad on back cover.
19. *CM*, 15/7/1919, p.476.
20. *CM*, 9/9/1919, p.56.
21. *CM*, 5/5/1925, p.361.
22. *CM*, 30/1/1923, ads p.4 and 20/3/1923, ads p.3.
23. *CM*, 8/7/1924, ads pp.2 & 3; 16/9/1924, ads p.38; and 2/2/1926, ads p.2.
24. *CM*, 13/11/1923, pp.371/2.
25. *CM*, 6/2/1923, ads p.26.
26. *CM*, 28/11/1922, ads p.35 and *CM*, 30/1/23.
27. *CM*, 15/6/1920, p.450.
28. *CM*, 13/3/1923, p.87.
29. *CM*, 23/1/1923, p.678.
30. *CM*, 27/10/1925, ads p.36.
31. *CM*, 20/3/1923, ads p.64.
32. *CM*, 13/3/1923, ads p.53.
33. *CM*, 8/7/1924, ads p.49.
34. *CM*, 22/5/1923, ads supplement.
35. *CM*, 31/7/1923, p.770.
36. *CM*, 9/9/1919, ads p.56.
37. *CM*, 7/11/1922, p.352.
38. Parl. Debates. Commons. Vol. 127, March–April 1920, 15/4/1920; *CM*, 13/4/1920, p.195 & p.197; 20/4/1920, p.221.

39. *CM*, 13/4/1920, p.207.
40. Parl. Debates. Commons. Vol. 117, 10/7/1919; Vol. 127, 24/3/1920; and *The Times* 1/8/1919, p.9.
41. *CM*, 23/5/1922, p.424.
42. *CM*, 22/3/1921, pp.134–5.
43. 1st Report MOT Departmental Committee on Taxation and Registration of Road Vehicles, 31/3/1920; *CM*, 27/4/1920, pp.249, 261.
44. *CM*, 18/5/1920, pp.346–7.
45. *CM*, 20/2/1919, pp.562–3.

CHAPTER EIGHT

Brave New World

The war had ended with a considerable pent-up demand for housing and all sorts of goods which had not been available for civilian use during the war. Despite the fact that many overseas markets had been lost forever because of the absence of British suppliers for four years, there was a backlog of orders from overseas, too. This naturally resulted in an economic boom and, equally naturally, a great demand for transport services. The railways were called upon to carry civilian traffic instead of war material. The quantities to be carried were very large in relation to railway resources although civilian industrial output was not yet back to prewar levels. Traders, in a sense, were encouraged to move their goods by rail, since, under government control, the railway rates had been maintained at prewar levels. The government was paying substantial subsidies to the railway companies to ensure that their net income remained at 1913 levels. So with rail rates comparatively low in this boom period, it is not surprising that the most common words in reference to railways for some months after the war were 'congestion' and 'delays'. Worthy Members of Parliament, under pressure from their constituents, raised the matter in the Commons. For example, '26 casks of butter consigned from Manchester on 24th June 1919 to a wholesaler in Nottingham were not yet delivered' (on 9 July).[1] Again, '8 boxes lard invoiced from Liverpool 27th May 1919 were not delivered in Nottingham until 7th July.' In this latter case, the government minister replied that the goods had been 'subject to no unreasonable delay'. They had not been tendered to the railway until 26 June.[2] Was the President of the Board of Trade aware, asked Mr Carter, 'that some pits in Nottingham are on short time because of shortage of wagons?'[3] The Nottingham mines were not the only place where that was happening. On 16 July there were 38 empty railway wagons at Avonmouth whereas 482 were needed for the day's freight.[4] Sir Eric Geddes could only give the usual ministerial reply that 'every possible step is being taken'.

The railways had their problems, undoubtedly. The 8-hour day just implemented had cut working hours by 20 per cent. The railways had, as yet, got back few of the 30,000 wagons that had gone to France during the war. Indeed, counting these with large numbers awaiting repair and the arrears of new construction, they were said to be about 75,000 wagons short[5] – about 10 per cent of what they owned. The harassed officials were obliged to adopt various shifts and devices. To avoid undue shunting and sorting of wagons, the railways began a scheme of 'allocation of traffic'. In London some companies were, for example, refusing traffic for destinations on the lines of other companies with terminals in London. Traders often did not seem to realize that when their traffic was refused at one terminal the intention was that they should offer it to a different railway company. Where several companies served one town the practice was to let the predominant company carry all the traffic to that town. Even when traffic was accepted for some small town it was often carried past that town to a larger depot and the merchants had to pay to have it carted back by road to their premises.

The new Ministry of Transport took one obvious step to try to relieve ports and railway stations. They provided some 600 surplus army lorries to the major ports[6] and about 1300 to the railways[7] to help out. At Christmas 1919 there were said to be 179 lorries at Liverpool Docks (but alas, 36 were 'unserviceable'. Some, it appears, had not been able to travel to Liverpool under their own power.) Whatever the condition of the vehicles they handled over 24,000 tons of freight in the four weeks ended 29 November 1919 – some 9½ tons per lorry per day. However, in that month Sir Eric Geddes was saying that the lorries were of very little assistance. They were very expensive to work. By February 1920 they were being withdrawn as no longer necessary, except from Manchester and Liverpool.[8]

The railway difficulties lasted right through this short economic boom period. In its issue dated 30 December 1919, *Commercial Motor* commented that 'we hear of blast furnaces closing down in the north through the impossibility of maintaining supplies of raw materials ... goods are held up in all directions for as much as six weeks... Hardly a district free from the malady'. The Monmouthshire and South Wales Coal Owners' Association told the magazine that from 1 January 1919 until 30 September they had lost 1548 shifts through want of railway wagons. This amounted to a loss of 523,000 tons of coal. In the issue of 6 February 1920 we read a letter from a manufacturer complaining that 'my firm is down 20% in its schedule of production this month owing to the railway either refusing to accept goods coming forward to us from suppliers or by delays in delivery of such materials as they have been induced to accept'. These difficulties of rail transport certainly had considerable impact, for a group of economists and statisticians would write in 1924 that 'the processes of production were constantly being checked by delays at port, the holdup on the railways, the erratic supply of raw materials, and a series of labour disputes'.[9]

Road transport was only too happy to take some of the burden from the railways, but it, too, had problems. There was the fact that road transport costs had risen, like everything else. A typical 3- or 4-tonner would cost £1000 new in 1919 as compared with half that before the war. Even a fair second-hand 3-tonner would be £500. Wages were now doubled – 30s. (£1.50) above 1913 levels and in mid-1919 transport workers were asking for another 10s. (50p) per week. The employers, having already conceded a 48 hour week as from the end of March 1919, and statutory holidays, declined to give what was asked, but settled eventually for another 5s. (25p).[10] Petrol, though now no longer restricted in supply, was running et around 3s. per gallon, depending on the grade, that is, about three times the 1913 price. There was much discussion on this issue and it attracted the attention of the Central Committee on Profiteering as well as that of a Standing Committee in Parliament. But the petrol companies argued that they had to accept prices as at New York, generated by a very active world market. They were able to show how the price charged in England and Wales had been as high as 4s. at the end of the war and that they had reduced prices. But there were fears of world shortages, and of prices rising to 4s. or 5s. a gallon once government surplus stocks had been used up.[11] The coke used by steam lorries, too, was three times the prewar price, but steamers were still able to compete with petrol lorries.

Commercial Motor published some suggested charges in its issue of 20 March 1919 based on 40 miles per day of 10 hours. These were:

	PETROL VEHICLES					STEAMERS	
						Rubber tyres	steel
	1 ton	2 tons	3 tons	4 tons	5 tons	5 tons	6 tons
	s.d.	s.d.	s.d.	s.d.	s.d.	s.d.	s.d.
Per mile	1.6	2.0	2.6	2.9	3.0	2.9	2.6
Per hour	7.6	9.0	10.0	12.6	14.0	13.0	10.0
Per day	£3.0.0	£4.0.0	£4.10.0	£5.0.0	£6.0.0	£5.10.0	£4.10.0

At these rates road transport would have to fight to get traffic from rail, but speed, lack of breakages and service won the day in a great many cases. Road could compete with rail, certainly, within a 50 mile limit. Indeed, one MP in the course of the Third Reading Debate on the Ministry of Transport Bill, 10 July 1919, said that about 150,000 tons of freight were carried into Manchester annually by rail, from places within 20 miles around, at an overall average rate of 8s. 6d. (42½p). The collection and delivery alone were costing the railways – or the government – more than that rate. He felt that not a single ton of this would pass by rail if the 'cartage' figures were separated out and proper rates charged. 'It would all go where it ought to go', he said, 'onto the roads'.

In talking about the advantages of road haulage, one has to use the word 'speed' with some caution for the old prewar speed limits were still in force. Any vehicle hauling a trailer, for example, was still limited to 5 m.p.h. and even without a trailer the best that could legally be done was 12 m.p.h. Nevertheless, the industry did well enough in this immediate post-war boom period. Perhaps some hauliers, by horse or mechanical transport, did too well for themselves, for the question of road transport rates, too, was referred to the Committee on Profiteering. 'Not guilty', seemed to be the verdict.

The big opportunity for road haulage came in late September and early October 1919, with a railway strike. Wage negotiations had been dragging on through the hot summer without a settlement being reached, and the talks broke down rather suddenly. So the resultant strike from midnight on Saturday 27 September did catch some people unawares. The government, however, perhaps mindful of the effects of the railway strike of August 1911, and perhaps a bit concerned about the events in Russia just a year or two earlier and public worry about red revolution, were not going to be caught. Fortunately for them, they had much of the wartime machinery of control still available – the DORA Regulations, a Ministry of Food with strong powers, a rationing scheme and a divisional organization throughout the country, as well as the Road Transport Board which refused to die; and tens of thousands of army lorries and many trained drivers still in the army. There were even a number of wartime volunteer motor transport corps, not yet disbanded.

The government had been preparing a long time in advance. The RTB, which was supposed to end with the Armistice, was purposely kept in existence. A letter in *The Times* on 4 September 1919 from a former chairman of one of the RTB's area committees said of the Board that it had now risen like a phoenix, and was located with the Ministry of Food. What obviously displeased him was that all the voluntary, unpaid, members of such area committees had been dispensed with and paid officials appointed in their place. The next day brought another complaint to the editor – this time from a vehicle owner who had received a form from the Area Transport Secretary asking what vehicles he had. 'What is the use of this department now?' he asked. Just to show that he meant business, the Food Controller had issued a Road Transport (Requisition) Order under the DORA Regulations on 27 August, and immediately the strike began a Ministry of Food press notice activated the Order by declaring an emergency. The notice stated that horses and road vehicles (whether horse-drawn or mechanically propelled or drawn) in use or capable of being used for the transport of goods by road were to be placed at the disposal of authorized persons. There would be arbitration to determine 'in default of agreement' the compensation to be paid. As *The Times* said on 6 October in an article entitled 'How the Strike was Fought':

> The Ministry of Food has put into immediate use a complete scheme to ensure the feeding of a country deprived of the use of its railway system ... The instrument which saved the situation was the motor lorry. A thousand lorries were brought under instruction to provide London with milk. Every detail of this road transport had been thought out weeks earlier in anticipation of such a crisis ...The maps and plans were ready. By Sunday afternoon Hyde Park – taken over for use as a clearing station – was filled with lorries, each one chalked with its destination and with the number of churns it could carry. In accordance with a timetable, to which they kept closely, the thousand vehicles employed in the service covered 72,000

> miles daily. Farmers took their milk to pre-arranged stops where it was collected by the lorries and brought back to Hyde Park ... When the lorries took back the empty churns to the country they also carried as full a cargo as possible of foodstuffs moved from the docks by horse transport.

The furthest point from which milk was collected was 110 miles from London. On the Wednesday, according to a Ministry of Food notice in *The Times* of 3 October, 153,000 gallons of milk were brought into London and residents received two-thirds of their normal supply. By then, however, some trains were being run, and on the Thursday, when Londoners got three-quarters of their normal supply, half was reported to have been brought in by train and half by motor lorry. (On those figures, something like 85,000-odd gallons were brought in by lorry that Thursday.) One interesting sidelight on the milk supply was a letter from a medical officer to *The Times,* just after the strike, stating his belief that the milk supplied during the strike was actually fresher than was usual in pre-strike days. As part of the Hyde Park operation the Ministry of Food had to set up kitchens to feed some 2000 drivers each day. A part of the Slough repair shops was moved temporarily to Hyde Park, too, to keep the vehicles moving.

While the quotation above refers to London's milk, much the same thing was happening all round the country. Drivers had to be fed in the other fifteen Food Divisions, too. *The Times* carried daily reports from the major cities – Birmingham (3 Oct. 1919) – 'The milk supply of the Midland Area is being maintained by the daily employment of 210 lorries'; Liverpool (2 Oct. 1919) – 'we brought more milk into the city ... by road today than has ever been brought in by railway'. It was not just milk. 'Essential foods which are found outside London will be brought into London by motor convoy and will then be distributed by various centres under the orders of the Road Transport Board', *The Times* predicted on 29 September. Sheffield (30 Sept. 1919) – 'A government road transport office has been opened and within a few hours fifty tons fish were brought into the city'; London (2 Oct. 1919) – 'First consignments of dried milk left London, Tuesday, by motor transport and will be handed over to local authorities from town to town'; Manchester (3 Oct. 1919) – 'The road transport with food supplies is developing rapidly. The amount of imports into the city on Thursday was about six hundred tons.' According to *The Times* on 1 October, over 5000 lorries were now employed in food distribution throughout the country (including those on milk work). By the end of the week, according to the Food Controller, 'fully 25,000 lorries and other motor vehicles were actually working on food transport', though he did not say whether that figure included food traders' own vehicles going about their ordinary work.. It certainly included many vehicles which had been requisitioned from private firms and which were returned to the owners after the strike.

Industry and agriculture had to keep going, too. Nottingham (27 Sept. 1919) – 'the staple trades of hosiery and lace can be kept going by motor transport'; Sheffield (27 Sept. 1919) – 'Manufacturers are arranging to send goods by road motor service' (but, they admitted, inconvenience would be enormous). 'Fortunately, Sheffield is on the verge of great coalfields and fuel can be brought in by road for household purposes and to meet the needs of the smaller works' (but not the thousands of tons needed by big firms). 'The strike will make the manufacturers realize that there is a great need for increased motor facilities.' We read of traction engines each hauling a couple of trailers of potatoes from East Anglia into London. An article in *The Times* of 8 October tells us that at one stage London was almost without hay (remember that there still were thousands of horses pulling vans and drays). 'The matter was immediately taken in hand by the RTB and some thousands of tons were brought in from Berkshire and Hertfordshire, chiefly by means of steam engines which dragged two trailers capable of carrying as much as 18 tons between them.' *The Times* itself quickly resorted to road transport and the paper was 'carried by a powerful fleet of motor lorries and motor cars ... as far North as Lancashire and as far West as Truro'. Other papers followed suit. *The Times* of 13 October reported that McNamara & Co. Ltd delivered papers during the strike to Daventry, Southampton, Ipswich, Marlborough, Salisbury and Portsmouth. Between 8 p.m. on Monday, 29 September, and 8 p.m. on Monday, 6 October, some of their 1½-ton, 2-ton, 2½-ton and 3-ton lorries did 88 trips totalling 14,044 miles. One of the 2½-tonners, in seven consecutive days, ran 1236 miles.

There were mails to be carried, too, and passengers! *The Times* (29 Sept 1919) reported from Portsmouth the recall of naval men on leave.

'Motor lorries are being used to bring the men back. Yesterday, also, motor-lorries took people to London at 10s. [50p] a head'; and from London it reported that 'the lorry-omnibuses carried tremendous loads'. So cars carried newspapers while lorries carried people to work – as indeed lorries had done so frequently in France during the war, though for a rather different kind of work.

While the government agencies concerned themselves largely with food transport, they did help out wherever they could, as we saw above in regard to hay for London's horses. But

> the Ministry of Food advises traders to use their own vehicles or such coastal or railway services as are available … to the fullest extent before making any calls on the special facilities provided by the Government. When it is impossible to arrange transport in any other way application may be made to the Divisional Food Commissioners, who will, if possible, arrange for the use of road transport facilities at their disposal. For this service a charge for carriage will be paid of 6d [2½p] per ton per mile, except in the case of milk, where special charges are in force. (*The Times* 4 Oct. 1919)

Although the government had many army lorries available – a considerable number had to be brought from France – most of the drivers had already been demobilized. So with the Ministry of Food notice on 27 September, declaring the emergency, came another notice – 'The assistance of all persons who are able to drive motor vehicles or steam vehicles is urgently needed. All persons willing to help the Food Controller and drive transport for the Ministry of Food should apply to the Divisional Road Transport Officers or Area Secretaries.' A recruitment office was set up at Grosvenor House, London, where 'several hundred eager volunteers assembled ... before the opening time for registrations ... By far the greatest number [being] discharged non-commissioned officers and soldiers who had served in the transport corps during the war.' Some 2000 applications were received by post, too, on the Saturday before the recruiting office opened *(The Times,* 30 Sept. 1919). A couple of days later the newspaper was able to report that so many offers of assistance had been received from individuals, societies and firms, that it was impossible for Grosvenor House to acknowledge them all. But volunteers were asked to stand by. They would be called upon and possibly at very short notice. They would be contacted by telephone or motor-cycle messengers as soon as their services were required. Applicants were asked to state what kind of vehicle they could drive – heavy lorry, steam lorry, steam tractor, or motor car or light van. They were asked to state, too, what makes of vehicles they had driven and for how many years. (Standardization was not yet universal.)

The strike was settled on Sunday, 5 October, and things quickly reverted to normal, that is, with the railways carrying by far the bigger share of the nation's freight. The inquests began. In its editorial on Monday, 6 October, under the title 'Lessons of the Railway Strike', *The Times* said that:

> if they had known what they know now, the Executive of the Railwaymen's Union would have stayed their hand. They had overlooked another factor which has greatly helped the resistance of the public and is itself a new development of profound and general interest. The strike has proved that neither railwaymen nor railways are so indispensable to the life of the community as they supposed. Other means of locomotion and transport, at first merely supplementary and still so in normal times, have been developed so rapidly in recent years that they are able to replace railways in an emergency. Few people realized the extent of this change. The railwaymen certainly did not.

During the course of the strike *The Times* of 3 October had carried an article entitled 'Motor Convoys v Trains', which also reflected on the theme that the public had known little of the potentialities of the motor vehicle.

> The triumph of the motor lorry, demonstrated so plainly in the prompt collection and distribution of milk and food during the strike, has done more to advertise the possibilities of motor transport to the people of this country than even the much greater success achieved by the motor lorries

> during the war. The road transport system of the British armies in France – employing 88,000 men, operating 60,000 vehicles, carrying food, munitions, guns and other supplies to three million or more men ... proved the value of the motor lorry to the full.

The veil of secrecy over all military operations had concealed this from the public. The article went on:

> It should not be forgotten that for commercial purposes motor transport has had no chance of expanding during the war; practically the whole of the output of commercial vehicles having been required by the Goverment ... Even now, exclusive of the vehicles owned by the Government, there are in use in this country for commercial purposes only about 65,000 petrol and 10,000 steam-driven road transport vehicles

[Those figures, of course, included some passenger vehicles.]

While the enthusiasm of *The Times* for road transport is understandable – it had described the volunteers as 'serving the state and the nation as truly as our soldiers did in the trenches' (29 Sept. 1919) – it must be noticed that the newspaper was talking about what lorries could do in an emergency. There was no way in which road transport could replace the railways, at this stage, as the main carrier. The range of the vehicles was still limited; they could still be expensive to run (in part because most roads were atrocious); and there certainly was not, in late 1919, anything like a national network. There can be hardly any doubt that, had the strike continued for any length of time, industries using very large tonnages of heavy raw materials – such as the iron and steel industry – would have soon ground to a halt.

Commercial Motor was anxious to recognize the efforts of those drivers who had served the nation so admirably and it asked its readers to submit details of any worthy cases they knew of. Subsequently it awarded to driver H. Moon a £5 prize together with a medal and a diploma. Mr Moon, it appears, was travelling from Derby to London on his motor-bicycle to collect a milk lorry. En route his bike skidded and he sustained a broken arm. He pressed on, nevertheless, collected his lorry and, with broken arm, drove all night to get back to Derby. Thus, according to *Commercial Motor*, 'preventing 600 gallons of milk from turning sour on the country'. Another man commended was a volunteer driver who was delivering horse fodder from Somerstown railway goods depot in London. Several such drivers had been attacked and Mr Flint had to get police protection. Although he was in danger and his lorry tampered with, Mr Flint stuck to the job throughout the emergency.[12]

Eager volunteers, taking an attitude that they were protecting their country against the 'red menace', clearly did not owe any allegiance to trade unions, nor did many of the ex-soldiers who were just coming on the scene. The 1000 or so drivers who were still in the army did not have much choice. It would be likely, in any case, that the military men might well feel that they had done their bit for their country and might be none too sympathetic to the strikers. It must be asked, though, about the thousands who were drivers in employment in the ordinary way. The National Union of Vehicle Workers had instructed its members not to touch railway work of any description.[13] It is difficult to see whether this had any real effect. Lorrymen were not highly unionized at the time and, even in a boom with full employment, they may have thought that the risk of losing the job was not worth taking. There were plenty of volunteer replacements.

The strike over, competition with the railways continued. Road hauliers were helped by the long-awaited increases in railway rates which finally came on 15 January 1920. The increases had varied from 25 or 30 per cent for coal, coke and other low-rated traffic, to 60 per cent on general merchandise.[14] By the summer there were discussions going on at the Railway Rates Tribunal about the effects of the increases on railway fortunes. The Transport Committee of the Birmingham Chamber of Commerce submitted a memorandum to the Tribunal stating that there had already been considerable diversion of traffic to road transport. The memorandum argued that as the value of road transport came to be more appreciated the diversion would take on a more rapid character. 'Over vast areas of the country it is possible for firms to deliver either by their own vehicles or hire at cheaper rates' than those of the railways. It was not just short distances. From Birmingham, Liverpool, London, Bristol, Manchester, and so on, for distances of 100 miles and up, it was now possible to deliver by road, more cheaply than rail, goods in classes 2–5 (that is, general merchandise). If there were any further increase in railway rates the only limit on diversion to road would be the absence of an adequate supply of road vehicles. 'The Chamber cannot get away from the conviction that there is something radically wrong with the organisation and management of the railways when it is possible to carry 5 tons of hardware by road from Birmingham to London cheaper than the railways can convey it in 300 ton train loads [and] in quicker time', said the Committee. The Transport Manager of Lipton's told the Tribunal much the same thing on 21 July. It was now possible to make regular weekly deliveries for distances in excess of 100 miles at lower rates than those offered by the railway authorities.[15] The increases, no doubt, eased the lot of many hauliers who were finding it difficult to earn a living in face of the previous low railway rates; but, alas, fate had something worse in store for them – economic collapse.

The boom petered out in mid-1920 for a variety of reasons, and soon the economy was slipping into recession. Whatever economic and financial circumstances, domestic and international, were involved initially, a coal strike in October and November of 1920 helped the decline on its way. The bottom fell out of the iron and steel markets of Great Britain in December

1920 and January 1921 and in three months output fell to less than half its previous level. Worse was to come, however. The dispute in the coal industry would not go away and the mines were closed throughout April, May and June of 1921. Output of iron and steel was almost nil by June and unemployment peaked at just over 23 per cent of trade unionists and remained around 16 per cent until mid-1922.[16] In these circumstances it was obvious that all forms of transport were going to suffer, not least those many hopefuls that had come into road haulage on the strength of cheap war-surplus lorries, army gratuities and the immediate post-war boom. There was quite enough competition amongst all the new hauliers, never mind those who were well established, to gladden the heart of any proponent of the market economy.

Many of the new hauliers had previously been employed in moving ammunition or roadstone or whatever in France and did not have to take account of anything other than the orders of their officers. Certainly there they did not have to worry about the cost of petrol or tyres or of maintenance. The original cost of the vehicle was not of any great interest. Nor, for that matter, were the cost of garaging, or insurance, or the administration which provided their loads. If something fell off the back of the lorry, provided it did not explode, the lorryman would not have to worry about his job. The story was very different in Britain, especially once the comparatively easy period of the boom had ended, but, just as in France, survival would become a way of life. In all probability there would have been a considerable ignorance of costing matters among many of the newcomers. Some things were fairly obvious, such as the cost of petrol for a trip. It was easy enough to see that that, at least, had to be covered by revenue. If one had to meet a hire purchase instalment, too, the need to get something for that was pretty apparent; but if the vehicle had been bought outright with a gratuity then the immediate worry would be simply to get enough to meet the fuel cost and leave a bit over as wages for the weekend. From time to time the cost of a new set of tyres or some repairs or minimal servicing would have to be taken into account. Esoteric words like 'depreciation', however, could be left to people who knew about such things. Admittedly the trade press worked very hard to teach readers how to count their costs and how to charge for their services, but not every haulier read the magazines, and, anyway, one had to live. It is not surprising that there was rate-cutting.

The competitive pressures had been on quite early in 1920 and we find a report in *Commercial Motor* as early as March 1920 that rates were being reduced. Whereas in the past a haulier could get 30s. (£1.50p) per ton for loads from Liverpool to Manchester, now rates were in the order of 17s. to 17s. 6d. (85p–87½p). Indeed, one haulier had been offered a load at 15s. a ton (75p).[17] Not surprisingly, the Liverpool Haulage Contractors' Association issued a scale of recommended rates to its members to be applied as from 29

March. These rates were compiled with an eye on the railway charges for Class I traffic (the lowest classification of general merchandise), but took other things into account as well – for example, competition, the probability of return loads and the nature of the route, hilly or otherwise. The recommended rate to or from Manchester was 22s. 6d. per ton and like all these rates it was for a minimum of 3 tons. To or from Oldham or Rochdale the rate was 30s. These rates were well below what *Commercial Motor* had recommended a year earlier. Hauliers would charge rather more per ton for light, bulky goods such as empty packing cases or furniture.[18]

The Manchester Team Owners' Association issued its list of recommended rates, too, but unlike the Liverpool list did not set a minimum load. It had charges for consignments of less than 1 ton, for 1 ton, 2 tons, for 4 tons and upwards. A 3-ton load between Manchester and Liverpool would cost £4 2s. 6d. (though if it were carried by a member of the Liverpool Association the charge would have been £3 7s. 6d.). From 4 tons upward between the two cities the Manchester Association's rates were marginally cheaper except in the one instance of a 6-ton consignment.[19]

With the recession really hurting, though, recommended rates were all very well, but hauliers would often take what they could get. Towards the end of 1920 the trade press was talking of the concern in the Liverpool area about rate-cutting. A case was quoted in *Commercial Motor* of a consignment of copper from Liverpool to Manchester for which the haulier quoted the recommended 22s. 6d. per ton, but in the end had to settle for 15s. per ton.[20] A couple of months after that *Commercial Motor* of 25 January 1921 was setting out its tables of average costs for various categories of vehicles. These were averages; some owners would do better, some worse, according to working circumstances.[21] It may be worthwhile comparing some of these costs with that of 15s. per ton for a load from Liverpool to Manchester. The tables showed that for a 3-ton petrol lorry on solid rubber tyres the running cost (fuel, tyres, maintenance and depreciation) would average 12.3d. per mile (just over 5p in modern terms). Standing charges (licence, wages, rent and rates, insurance, interest) would come to 1658d. per week (£6.91 in today's currency). The wages would have to be included, even where the owner did not employ a driver, if only to give the owner a minimum return. For a lorry doing 300 miles per week this would work out at 17.83d. per mile (almost 7½p). On a basis of 15s. per ton each way, a round trip between Liverpool and Manchester, loaded both ways, would give him only 90s. to cover the estimated average all-in costs of about 105s. (70 miles). On that basis the return load would be of quite desperate significance. Even the recommended 22s. 6d. per ton would hardly cover running costs in the absence of a return load. The back-load seems to have been assumed, however precarious that would have been.

The revised tables which took into account the abolition of petrol tax, the imposition of the annual licence fee, and the recent wage increase of 5s. per week, showed the following costs. The running costs of a 5-ton petrol lorry on solid rubbers were 16.55d. per mile and, on a basis of 200 miles a week, 25.51d. all in. Steam wagons, not having paid any fuel tax previously, would lose much of their advantage over petrol lorries and would now, if on solid rubber tyres, cost much the same. A 3-ton steamer on solid rubber tyres would average 9.62d. running cost and, on 300 miles per week, total 17.03d. per mile. Similarly a 5-tonner's running cost was 12.3d. and, on 200 miles, a total of 23.59d. If the steam wagon still used the old steel tyres, then in that respect it would be cheaper than its rubber-shod stable-mate. But maintenance, fuel and depreciation would be heavier, and the running cost of a 3-tonner on steel tyres would amount to 9.95d. a mile, and of a 5-tonner, 12.91d. The all-in costs for a 3-tonner (300 miles per week) were 17.36d. and for a 5-tonner doing that mileage, 20.44d. It should be noted that *Commercial Motor* included £2 a week (480d.) as a proportion of a mate's wages in the standing charges for these steamers; and more particularly there is the point that no establishment costs are included – such as office heating and lighting, telephone and clerical wages. The owner of two or three vehicles, particularly if he drove one himself, would certainly have costs of that order. Because of the shift in the basis of taxation to unladen weight the matter of the maximum possible weekly mileage now became important and, more than ever, the question of speed limits began to irk operators.

The question of rate-cutting continued to exercise a malign influence on the industry over years to come as it had done in the past. (A 'Motor Waggon Carrier' had written to the press in 1909 complaining of ratecutting.[22]) Hauliers' organizations strove hard to convince members that the practice was not in their long-term interest. But that seems to have been a bit like trying to convince a horse that if it would but live it would eventually get some grass to eat. In this respect the haulage industry had something of a love–hate relationship with the many Clearing Houses or freight exchanges that sprang up over these years. (The discussions of the time do not distinguish clearly between establishments which simply told the haulier where he could get a load and those that actually handled freight and made up loads.) The year 1920, in particular, saw a considerable expansion of this sort of service and it was claimed toward the end of the year that some three-quarter million tons had been dealt with through their agency in the previous 12 months, of which 350,000 tons were cleared on lorries which would otherwise have returned home light. (The latter figure looks as if someone had simply divided the three quarter million by two and rounded off the result.[23]) On the negative side these bodies were accused of forcing down rates – often, it was hinted, in a sort of Dutch-auction operation – and were frequently castigated for collecting the freight charges quickly from the trader but holding on as long as possible before paying the haulier. This was said to be due to a lack of capital. They were frequently alleged to take more than the recognized commission of 10 per cent.

An editorial in *Commercial Motor* at the beginning of 1921, pointing out that owner-drivers often failed to include their own wages in their standing charges, quoted a case of one who had invested £1000 in his business and was only making £5 per week. 'Such a man is not receiving a fair return' said the editor; but he did not refrain from commenting on the clearing houses. They 'have not helped the haulier – rather they have played into the hands of the producer of merchandise, and particularly of those running their own vehicles'.[24] Later in the year – in September 1921 – a writer in the same magazine said he had never been able to understand how 'the usual type of Clearing House, controlled by people foreign to transport interests, or, at the very least, without any direct concern for the well-being of the haulier, could ever, in the long run, prove to be anything else but a rate-cutting institution'. They would always seek the lowest rates for their trader-customers.[25]

Needless to say, there were many perfectly reputable organizations and they did not take it all lying down. As we saw towards the end of Chapter Six, the Road Transport Board had been engaged in trying to provide return loads, and its efforts were backed up by bodies such as the Manchester Chamber of Commerce. Indeed, Chambers of Commerce, anxious to help their members cope with transport difficulties, were leaders in this field, often setting up transport committees which would establish clearing houses. The Manchester one, set up in 1917 and handed over to a manager, Mr N. Fine, had expanded its activities in mid-1919, and by the autumn was said to be dealing with 1000 tons per week. It had then 600 lorries on its books, based in Manchester and within 50 miles around. The following April it had 500 hauliers with 1500 vehicles at its disposal.[26] By this time Birmingham, Bradford, Bristol, Derby, Leicester, London, Northampton, Nottingham and Sheffield had followed suit and were cooperating with each other.[27]

At Liverpool, Mr J.F. Shaw, while working in the Mersey Docks and Harbours Board, became aware of the need for the efficient organization of road haulage. He worked to get the hauliers to form an association, and with the approval of the Chamber of Commerce, set up the Liverpool Motor Haulage Clearing House at the beginning of November 1919, communicating his intentions to some ninety Chambers of Commerce round the country. (That the first month produced only one thousand tons of freight he attributed to the falling off of imports because of the poor rate of exchange – the pound sterling, alas, was rather weak on the currency markets.) This Liverpool Clearing House charged a commission of only 7½ per cent of the freight charge to members of the Liverpool branches of the CMUA, the Liverpool Cart Owners' Association and the Liverpool Haulage Contractors' Association, but 10 per cent to any others. Mr Shaw became a recognized authority on the organization of freight exchanges, whose views would be sought by the MOT, and he later went on to be Managing Director of National Road Transport Clearing Houses Ltd, which had numerous branches. He was Chairman, too, of a nation-wide organization of clearing houses – The Association of Road Transport Clearing Houses. While still at Liverpool he was a member of the committee which worked out the scale of standard charges mentioned earlier.[28]

Mr Shaw was one of those who defended the many reputable clearing houses and freight exchanges. In response to an Editorial in *Commercial Motor* of 4 January 1921, he wrote a couple of weeks later arguing the case. Members of his Association, he said, had been of considerable help to hauliers. They had diverted large blocks of traffic from the railways to road; many owner-drivers and small concerns had practically depended on clearing houses; the clearing houses had, in many cases, tended to stabilize rates on an economic basis. They recognized that the haulier performed a valuable service and had to be kept on the road, and so the clearing houses always gave preference to haulage contractors in the distribution of loads. (There seems to an implication here that loads were sometimes given to people who were not haulage contractors.) Mr Shaw said that in his experience it was the hauliers themselves, through being in a weak financial position, who would accept practically any rate, whether it paid or not. But in the end it was the economic slump which lay at the bottom of all the troubles.[29]

The question of rate-cutting rumbled on for years, and there were periodic attacks on clearing houses. One director of a clearing house wrote in January of 1923 that there was an increasing tendency for clearing houses to refuse no traffic and to dispose of it at the lowest possible rates. They had little difficulty in so far as there were so many vehicles at a loose end. His firm was 'inundated with lorries'. He alleged that it was *usual* for the rate paid to hauliers to be concealed from the trader.[30] A case was cited ,just at this time of an unspecified clearing house which charged a merchant 75s. per ton for a 4-ton load, that is, £15 in all. They paid the haulier 25s. per ton and from the £5 the 10 per cent commission was deducted, leaving him with £4 10s. 0d. (£4.50). According to the correspondent who supplied this information, it was usual to omit the rate which was charged from the haulier's copy of the consignment note but to show it on the trader's copy. However, the clearing houses were not the only guilty parties. This correspondent alleged that the practice was 'fairly rife in some districts' of hauliers noting the load and the rate that was on offer from a clearing house and then approaching the trader direct with a lower quotation.[31] Obviously the hauliers were under considerable pressure, for another correspondent to *Commercial Motor* revealed one more sad aspect. A Mr H. Roberts wrote that:

> Haulage contractors in a small way of business, such as ourselves ... carry clearing house loads uninsured, because the low road rates brought about

> by some clearing houses, do not allow us to insure the loads and at the same time make the business pay. Loads that we carry direct from traders and not through the clearing houses are insured by us, because the rates quoted by us allow us to do so.

A Mr W. Gammons – MD of a clearing house and haulage business – argued the following week that it was not just small firms that did not insure their loads. 'I know at least one concern with thirty or forty vehicles which effect no insurances and are veritable rate-cutters.'[32]

The difficult position of many hauliers was not improved when the railways cut their rates in May 1923 and took up a more competitive stance. But the 'irresponsible' hauliers and 'illegitimate' clearing houses were still subjected to fierce criticism, even though both of these groups lost many members through bankruptcy. It seems, however, that newcomers sprang up just as quickly. One such aroused a great deal of ire late in 1924. Apparently this new agency circulated hauliers operating out of London to the effect that it was about to establish branch agents in each of the various trade centres and seaside resorts throughout the country. Hauliers could register with them for 1 guinea (£1 1s. 0d. – £1.05). If such hauliers advised the Agency when they would be making the return trip to London the Agency would attempt to get them return loads. According to what the press published of the circular, 'The charge for the return load would be about 60% of the regular one-way rate', and 'you will be required to pay us 12½% of all amounts you receive for return loads which have been secured for you by our agency'. That 60 per cent of the normal rate, minus commission, leaving the haulier with only a little over half the normal rate, caused howls of derision. Readers of the trade press were quick to point out that one man's return load was the outward load of another. Walter Gammons was on the ball again, saying that such agencies were three a penny up and down the country. What was needed was more traffic, not more agencies. 'I cannot see how the proposed idea can succeed where others working on precisely similar lines have failed notoriously, despite ample capital.'[33] Mr Gammons and the agency concerned carried on a battle for a time through the correspondence columns of *Commercial Motor* until the editor called a halt to the exchange. Oddly, or perhaps not, while the agency disclaimed any intention of cutting rates, they were careful subsequently not to mention the proposed 60 per cent of the normal as the rate for return loads. Things probably reached the bottom for hauliers in 1924, but even at the end of that year we find a Mr Roberts – a partner in the hauliers Vigurs & Roberts – writing again to *Commercial Motor*. 'There are some hauliers', he wrote,

> who will travel from London to Birmingham for £7 per 4-ton load and accept £3.10.0 or £4 for a 4-ton load home. They cannot see that the total, say £11, divided by the distance travelled (220 miles), equals 1/- per mile.

> It costs them that sum to run a 4-ton lorry, so they receive no profit for the journeys, and it is small wonder they fail.[34]

Small wonder indeed! But they may well have failed sooner had they not taken that back load.

There were complaints that some traders, delivering their own goods, were only too glad to pick up whatever return loads they could get to contribute a few pounds to offset the expenses of the trip. For them the charge made did not have to match the recommendations of the trade press and the new hauliers' associations which were springing up; nor did the charge have to cover any particular costs, since these costs were being incurred anyway. Any revenue gained was better than nothing. Such firms could easily make use of the proliferating freight exchanges and clearing houses. It is not clear just how much damage was done by the intervention of 'own-account' operators in the haulage markets – probably not very much.

In the midst of such cut-throat competition, people from time to time called for a national association of road hauliers. There were many local bodies, such as those we have seen in action at Liverpool and Manchester; and the CMUA had represented the interests of the operators of commercial vehicles, in the Courts and in negotiations with the government, ever since its inception as the Motor Vehicle and Wagon Users' Association – an offshoot of the Automobile Club – in 1905. But the CMUA included both freight and passenger carriers and it did not concern itself with rates or fares charged by its members. So it was widely felt that a nationwide haulage trade association might be able to do something about rate-cutting.

With the traumatic year of 1921 gone, things appeared a lot brighter for the country in 1922, and traders and transport men alike looked to an economic revival. The railways were trying to work out the solution to the problems presented by the Railways Act, 1921 – the grouping of a large number of small companies into four big companies and a new system of charging and finance. While the attention of a great part of the senior management was devoted to carrying out the intentions of the Act – blending the disparate practices of all the small companies into new, homogeneous working arrangements – they did not forget completely that road transport had grown tremendously. It was now obvious that road carriage could be cheaper than rail transit for much traffic over distances up to, perhaps, one hundred miles or more. Where it was not, the speed (even under the much-ignored existing regulations) and flexibility of lorries, working door to door, with great savings in handling, packing, safety and security of the goods, and general convenience, often won the day. The railways, having suffered years of overwork, wearing out of track, vehicles and locomotive power, with a lack of investment, could not change much on their congested systems, at least in the short term. So they took the obvious course, in the expressive words of the now common saying, 'If you can't beat 'em, join 'em!' That is what some of them now attempted. The companies which comprised what was at that time referred to as the 'L.&N.W. and Midland Group' presented private bills to Parliament in early 1922 to secure for themselves the right to operate lorries. A Major Hamilton had introduced a clause during the passage of the 1921 Railways Bill to allow the railways to run road services, but the Speaker had ruled it out of order in a bill concerned with the grouping of railway companies. Now the railways set about it properly.

From the point of view of the traders and hauliers, the frightening thing was that the railways were not merely seeking to do their collection and delivery work at stations by means of mechanical vehicles – they already had the power to do that. What they were now after was the right to run lorry services to carry goods *which had not been carried or would not be carried by rail.* They wanted to operate a road haulage business completely independently of their railway operations. The road haulage men were just getting over the shock of having an ex-railwayman at the head of the new Ministry of Transport; they had not yet got over the shock of the economic blizzard of 1920–21, and the old hands were still trying to come to terms with the many newcomers (with second-hand lorries) of the last two or three years. This latest news was a further severe blow.

The new large railway companies were giants compared with the pygmies of the road haulage world and had enormous resources at their disposal. They could easily undercut rates, drive the small haulier out of business, and then put the rates up again. They could do what conventional wisdom said they had done with the canals. 'Everybody knew' that the railways had bought up canal companies, deprived them of investment and allowed them to languish, making sure that the best traffic went to the railways. With their great engineering works and great engineering expertise gained in the building of locomotives, carriages and wagons, they could easily turn their hand to the building of lorries. When one considered the powerful railway representation in Parliament the future for road-vehicle manufacturers and road-vehicle operators looked bleak indeed. Not only was there the economic depression but now, too, there was the shadow over investment while operators or potential operators waited to see what would transpire in regard to railway lorries.

The railways, then, had powers to do their collection and delivery work, and although the great bulk of that continued to be done by horse and cart, here and there the railways had turned to mechanically propelled transport. We have seen in a previous chapter how the Midland Railway had used electric vans for this work from 1914 onwards. The threat of more widespread road conveyance by the railway companies was unwelcome news indeed. Some railway companies had obtained such powers early on. The Great Eastern had had powers granted in

1904 and the North-Eastern in 1905. Parliament and public were a bit inconsistent in those years, however, for, having granted those companies (as well as the North Staffordshire and the Great North of Scotland companies) what was asked, they declined or opposed similar applications from the London, Brighton and South Coast (in 1906), the Great Northern (in 1911), and the London and South-Western (in 1913). The position was confused in that, while some companies who had powers to run road services had not bothered to develop freight operations at all vigorously (most companies were more interested in passengers anyway), there were others which operated road services without the necessary statutory authority. A Departmental Committee on Road Conveyance of Goods by Railways, set up in January 1921, reported[35] that the Lancashire and Yorkshire Railway (L&Y) operated some 250 government surplus vehicles plus 200 of their own. These were used partly for C&D work and 'partly for direct road services'. A few paragraphs further on they repeated that the L&Y were running thirteen services without statutory authority, and they listed a number of other services also probably lacking legal authority.[36]

As we have seen, in the shortlived postwar boom the railways had continued to be badly congested and there was a general shortage of wagons. A great part of the problem was that so many wagons were sitting loaded in sidings awaiting delivery of the goods by the slow horse-and-cart method. But the railways, obviously doing what they thought best in the public interest, used some lorries to carry goods directly between consignor and consignee without touching rail at all. They may well have realized that there was something to be said for road haulage after all.

The rub came in 1920 when boom had turned to slump and traders everywhere were trying to be more efficient and cut costs. New and old haulage operators were fighting for their lives and there was that epidemic of rate-cutting. In 1921, according to a memorandum which the North-Western and Midland group of companies issued in February 1922[37] to justify their Parliamentary Bill, an estimated 6 million tons of traffic had been diverted from rail to road (that is, to road hauliers). This, they said, was mainly of the more valuable classes. (Remember that the railways charged on a basis of classifying goods according to the value of the commodity, so that a ton of fine linen would pay much more than a ton of iron ore. The argument was that since 'cost' could not be established objectively, the next best thing was to charge 'what the traffic would bear'. So higher-valued goods could stand a higher transport cost than low-valued commodities.) According to the memorandum,

> A considerable proportion of the traffic so diverted passes between places within a radius of fifty miles, but the competition by road motors is being very largely extended for longer distances, such as London and Birmingham,111 miles; Liverpool and Birmingham, 88 miles; and Manchester and Birmingham, 84 miles.

Naturally enough, recession-hit traders, having lived for years with congested and not very 'user-friendly' railways, were aghast at the possibility that the railways, by using their might in unfair competition, would be able to destroy the new form of transport which had already brought relief to many and the probability of better service to many more – a system which, in the words of the railways' memorandum, 'has opened up a new vista of transportation'. So a great number of protests were addressed to Government and Parliament – from 33 municipal corporations, 18 county councils, 4 district councils, and 7 transport trade associations, among others.[38] Admittedly, many of these referred to the possibility of new bus services being operated by the railways, but the Association of Municipal Corporations viewed the Bill 'with serious apprehension and are of the opinion that grave injury would be inflicted upon the trading community' if the powers were granted. The interests of the country required competition and the policy of the railways had been to stifle competition; even among themselves competition was almost at an end through 'private arrangements' and the effects of the 1921 Act. The Association saw no need for the granting of these powers. All the road transport necessary could be provided by private enterprise. Road competition, 'daily becoming more effective', would be jeopardized. The best thing for the railways was to confine their attention to the improvement and cheapening of the railway service. (Maybe the Association's real worry was in the fears they expressed in their final paragraph – about the effect on the roads of more heavy traffic. They were having a job keeping up with road maintenance.[39])

The Departmental Committee on Road Conveyance of Goods, known, as is the normal practice, by the Chairman's name – the Balfour-Browne Committee – was not a great help to the legislators. A minority of the Committee (the chairman and two railway members) recommended that road operating powers be given to the railways, subject to various statutory restrictions which the railways would have had to obey; publication of rates, no unreasonable preference to one customer over another, the obligation to provide reasonable facilities, and so on. The remainder (the majority) of the committee were opposed to giving the railways new powers. The railways had taken traffic in the past from the old wagon hauliers and the canals. Now they, themselves, were suffering the same fate. In no sense did traffic 'belong' to the railways. 'In our view only those are entitled to traffic who can carry it in the best and cheapest way.' This section of the committee, not surprisingly, included two representatives from road transport, but more importantly, also included the representatives of the Federation of British Industries and of the Association of British Chambers of Commerce respectively.

When the Bill came to its Second Reading in the House of Commons on 10 April 1922 the junior minister, Mr Arthur Neal, gave the views of the MOT. He mentioned that some people thought that the Balfour-Browne Committee had not made a full investigation of the problem. If the Bill were given a Second Reading, that would allow a fuller examination of the matter. But unless some machinery could be devised to prevent the evils which were feared, they would be well advised to reject the Bill on the Third Reading. This was not very helpful but, in the end, the Bill was given a Second Reading by the slim majority of 146 to 141, which indicates that only about half the members of the House had voted.

The promoters of the Bill had been working hard to achieve that success. They had dropped completely their original intention of including bus operation in the powers they sought – thus removing many local authorities from the list of objectors – and they had quietly negotiated an agreement with the SMMT to the effect that, for five years, they, the railways, would not manufacture any vehicles and would limit their purchases of second-hand lorries,[40] thus silencing the manufacturers. In their memorandum published in *Commercial Motor*, 21 February 1922 the railway companies had set out their arguments. A trade revival would bring renewed congestion on the railways, they threatened; and that could be relieved only by large capital expenditure, which would be difficult for them in view of their prevailing financial problems. The use of lorries could save traders from that threat. They discounted the idea that their use of lorries would lead to the killing off of the small road carrier. Indeed, the killing off was actually happening, not by the railways, but, they alleged, 'as a result of the concentration of road transport business in the hands of the large and wealthy associations, which, by means of coordination and amalgamations, are gradually building up the very kind of monopoly which they themselves say will result from railway competition'. Their Bill, they pointed out, provided for the imposition on railway-owned road services of all the statutory controls to which rail services were subject. This would prevent such road services from cutting rates or withdrawing services after having destroyed the competitors. The Bill, too, had provision for the accounts of these road services to be separate from the normal railway accounts – just to show that road services would not be running at a loss. The document pointed out that 'The railway companies desire to use road transport for the conveyance of merchandise *in any district to which their system affords access'*. This would be done, they said, 'in the interests of the railway companies with due regard to economical working, and with proper safeguards to the trading public and competing road carriers'. Many people believed that the interests of the railways were scarcely compatible with safeguards to competing road carriers. Many such carriers were concerned.

There was more in the memorandum, for example about the rates to be charged, but the railways had to come back again with another memorandum four weeks later.[41] In the introduction to it the railways said that because of criticisms in the press and elsewhere about the proposed safeguards 'the railway companies ... desire to make it perfectly clear that they are willing and anxious to meet such criticisms not only by definite assurances but, where necessary, by amendments to the Bill designed to make those safeguards more explicit'. The opposition kept up the fight, however, still worried about a railway monopoly.

The Bill next went to a committee of the House of Commons, which heard evidence from a number of interested parties.[42] A Mr Abady, for the London County Council, reminded the Committee that Parliament did not usually give powers to undertakings to carry on the work of their competitors. Gas companies were not given powers to provide electricity. Mr Macmillan, K.C., for the promoters, however, surprised the Committee by telling them that the railways had been given powers, in 1864, despite similar arguments, to operate coastwise shipping. That certainly swayed the Committee, and railways and road hauliers alike began to see the probability that the Bill would go through. There was to be a surprise ending to the drama, though.

When a Mr Cash of the Chartered Accountants, as a witness for the railways, failed to convince the Committee about the accounts that could be drawn up, the chairman took the view that the MOT would need to prescribe the form of the accounts. A witness was called from the Ministry. This witness, Sir George Beharrel, however, talked about more than accounts. He went on to talk about rates to be charged for (railway) road transport. The railways proposed to charge their standard railway rates as authorized by the Railways Act,1921, subject to certain exclusions, for example charges for the use of terminals. They would take advantage of their right to offer 'exceptional rates', too, which could be as much as 40 per cent below the standard rates. Sir George thought it an unsound principle to start from a basis of railway rates to charge for road operations. But worse was to come. The railways had imported into their Bill a section from the 1921 Act by which the reasonableness of a rate would be decided by the Railway Rates Tribunal. Most people had accepted that as a fair way to deal with rates. But Sir George pointed out that the tribunal was charged with the duty of ensuring the maximum development and extension in the public interest of carriage by rail. That would be an odd way to decide on the reasonableness of rates for road haulage; and it would not be possible to alter the wording in the Bill to refer to carriage by road, for that would impose conflicting duties on the tribunal. The railways, who may already have been negotiating with some traders for road haulage on the basis of their railway rates, saw no immediate way forward. Given the views expressed generally by the MOT officials, the railways felt that they had no choice but to drop the Bill. That was that. Road haulage breathed only a very short sigh of relief, for immediately rumours started to circulate that the railways were going to set up subsidiary companies to run road haulage operations.

Notes

1. Parl. Debates. Commons. Vol. 117, col. 1848, 9/7/1919.
2. Ibid., Vol. 118, col. 897 & 898.
3. Ibid., Vol. 117, col. 1848, 9/7/1919.
4. Ibid., Vol. 118, col. 1353/4, 23/7/1919.
5. Ibid., Vol. 117, col. 2075, 10/7/1919.
6. Ibid., Vol. 122, col. 18, 1/12/1919.
7. Conference on Road Transport. Sir E. Geddes and members of Parl. Cmd.493 10/12/1919.
8. *CM*, 23/12/1919, p.451.
9. J.J. Astor, A.L. Bowley et al., *Is Unemployment Inevitable?* p.13.
10. *CM*, 22/7/1919, p.496.
11. *CM*, 9/3/1920, p.76.
12. *CM*, 2/12/1919, p.372.
13. *The Times*, 4/10/1919, p.9.
14. *CM*, 6/1/1920, p.504.
15. *CM*, 10/8/1920, pp.714/715.
16. J.J. Astor, A.L. Bowley et al., *Is Unemployment Inevitable?* pp.20, 21.
17. *CM*, 23/3/1920, p.119.
18. *CM*, 6/4/1920, p.183.
19. *CM*, 20/4/1920, p.236.
20. *CM*, 23/11/20, p.504.
21. *CM*, 11/1/21, pp.729/30.
22. *CM*, 2/12/1909, p.267.
23. *CM*, 2/11/20, p.412.
24. *CM*, 4/1/21, p.675.
25. *CM*, 20/9/21, p.142.
26. *CM*, 16/9/1919, p.87 and 27/4/1920, p.259.
27. *CM*, 25/5/1920, p.380.
28. *CM*, 4/11/1919, p.251 and 13/4/1920, p.199.
29. *CM*, 18/1/1921, p.764.
30. *CM*, 23/1/1923, p.705.
31. *CM*, 2/1/1923, pp.597/98.
32. *CM*, 21/11/1922, p.433 and 28/11/22, p.461.
33. *CM*, 11/11/1924, p.389 and 2/12/1924, p.493.
34. *CM*, 16/12/1924, p.553.
35. Report of Departmental Committee on Road Conveyance of Goods by Railway Companies (Balfour Browne Committee), Cmd 1228, 1921.
36. Ibid.
37. *CM*, 21/2/22, pp.9 and 10.
38. *CM*, 21/2/1922, p.4.
39. *CM*, 11/4/22, p.223.
40. *CM*, 21/3/22, p.144.
41. *CM*, 21/3/1922, pp.127 &128.
42. *CM*, 23/5/1922, p.425; 6/6/1922, p.509; 20/6/1922, p.557; 27/6/1922, pp.581/2.

CHAPTER NINE

The Roaring Twenties

With the deluge of ex-War Department 3- and 4-tonners on to the market the need for vehicles of that size was easily met. The Ford 1-tonner, too, met the requirements of many people, but as motor transport became more and more popular there arose a demand for vehicles both below the 3-ton size and above 4-ton. In particular the taxing of steam wagons by the 1920 Act substantially reduced their advantage in the 5- and 6-ton range and operators were finding that petrol vehicles could be started up quickly in the mornings and did not present problems of disposal of ash and of soot from the smoke-box. Steam wagons and traction engines used up fuel even when standing waiting; and there was always that problem of water supply to contend with. However, they were robust and could stand a great deal of rough treatment over poor roads, and could cope with the 5- to 10-ton loads fairly readily (with a trailer if necessary), so they did not disappear from the scene just yet.

One area where steam did not have any competition at all was in really heavy loads. We can read any number of accounts similar to that in *Commercial Motor* in mid-1925 which told of the haulage of a 90-ton 'stator' from Manchester to Liverpool by a couple of Fowler rubber-tyred traction engines belonging to N.E. Box & Co. of Manchester. This piece of heavy engineering for a power station at Liverpool was hauled on a specially built 8-wheeled truck, itself weighing some 16 tons. The total load hauled, therefore, was in the order of 106 tons and the overnight journey took 15 hours. The modern spectator at weekend steam rallies may believe that traction engines were used only for ploughing and for hauling fairground machinery from town to town. They did both these things but also much more.[1]

Box & Co., in particular, were specialists in dealing with awkward loads of exceptional size or weight. In the early 1920s they undertook the 80-mile haulage from Sheffield of a 24-foot-wide rudder-frame for H.M.S. Rodney. It is not at all obvious that the engineers who built such things really gave much thought to their transportation. The hauliers then had to do a route survey. In those pre-motorway days the route often had very narrow stretches, low or narrow bridges (there was one on the Great North Road only 14' 3" wide), tight corners and every imaginable kind of obstruction. In the case of this rudder-frame Box & Co. had to arrange for the removal and subsequent restoration of scores of lamp-posts and telegraph poles and the demolition and later rebuilding of walls. They had sometimes to provide special trailers, too.

H.M.S. Rodney's rudder-frame was hauled on a special high trailer which permitted motors to pass under the projecting load! It was all in the day's work to the firm, and they found plenty to keep their 15 Fowler steam traction engines busy.[2]

Traction engines were still subject to the very low speed limits imposed in the last century, so outsize loads hauled on trailers could take a little while to get to their destination. *Commercial Motor*'s issue of 14 October 1924 described the moving of a 65-ton load from Birmingham to London. This was another electric stator – 12' x 12' x 11' 2" – made by GEC for an electricity station run by the St Marylebone Corporation. The railways had politely declined the load, so road haulage – in the shape of a firm called Bentley & Co. – did the job. They used a specially designed low-loader trailer hauled by two traction engines. A third engine came along, too, hauling a caravan for the crew and a coal wagon. This engine was called upon, at times, to give assistance on hills. Given the dangers of road subsidence or damage to pipes or whatever below the surface, the hauliers had to bring along and lay out in places large steel plates to protect the road and the 'works' underneath. It is hardly surprising that on one particular day only 220 yards' progress was made. That, perhaps, was exceptional, for the 118-mile trip was done in 11 days. Amongst the goings-on described, we learn that 'Over the narrow road from Watford through Radlett into London it was often necessary to divert other traffic.'[3] It is as well to remember that even the main roads in those days usually had room for only one lane in each direction.

Although by the end of 1925 steam road locomotives were about to begin a slow decline, they were, nevertheless, still doing a useful and economical job. Their first cousins, the steam wagons, too, were still competitive despite taxation. While admitting their disadvantages – a lack of cleanliness and a mechanism which called for a skilled driver – the editor of *Commercial Motor* could still be enthusiastic about them. 'There is a belief in certain transport circles', he wrote in February 1926, 'that the steam wagon will gradually be ousted by the petrol type. In our opinion, this will never be the case, providing that the manufacturers of this type of vehicle continue to improve it.' There had been considerable improvements, he wrote, in the previous two or three years – as great as in the preceding ten years or more – and progress was continuing. He referred, first, to the heavy type which could cope with bad roads and building sites, and he went on to enthuse about the modern high-speed, long-distance steam wagon, with or without trailer, which ran 'at an extraordinarily low cost per ton mile ... Recent tests have shown that railway rates can, in some instances, be halved, and this with door to door delivery', concluded the editor.[4] Indeed, they did go on for a few years yet. I have vivid memories of my childhood astonishment at seeing one charging down a street at night with sparks and smoke flying to the sky, and the light from the firebox lighting the driver's grimy face – for all the world like something that Dante ought to have written about.

A test run in July 1926 of a new 6-ton steam wagon built by the Yorkshire Patent Steam Wagon Co. illustrates some of the pros and cons of this form of freight transport. A magazine article tells us that the fire was lit at 8.30 a.m. and after 19 minutes the pressure gauge was showing 5 lb of steam (which would not have taken the wagon anywhere). After 53 minutes 'the engine was moved to free the bearings' and by 63 minutes an adequate working supply of 160 lb of steam was available. (It should be pointed out, of course, that that did not happen every morning. A fire could be kept 'in' and the working steam pressure raised quite rapidly.) During the run of 66 miles the fire was stoked on average every 2½ miles, though we are told that that was only because considerable attention was being given to ensure economy. Ordinarily stoking would have taken place about every five miles. On instructions the driver kept the speed to 13 m.p.h. during the first hour but in the next couple of hours an average of 15.5 m.p.h. was attained. The water tank of the wagon – 180 gallons' capacity – was exhausted after 45 miles and the driver then resorted to a reserve tank which was being carried. The trip from Leeds to Tadcaster, Knaresborough, Harrogate and back home was completed in an actual running time of 4 hours and 50 minutes – an average speed of 13.65 m.p.h. The average net load was 6 tons 2 cwt and the average gross weight was 13 tons 7 cwt 2 qrs 21 lb. The fuel cost was only 1.1d. per mile (that is, less than ½p in present-day currency). As part of the test the wagon was stopped on the 1 in 6 gradient of Pool Bank, held on its brakes. It then started up the hill again quite easily. For this was one of the features of steam – the ability to move very considerable loads from a stop.[5]

But petrol was competing strongly. The manufacturers, after a shaky few years when the market for new vehicles was so stifled by army surplus, were able to put the lessons of war to use and they steadily improved the petrol lorry. These not only got better, but they got bigger. Leylands were advertising 6- and 8-tonners in September 1921 and a good many similar vehicles came into use. May 1925 saw, for example, a Maudslay 7- to 8-ton petrol platform lorry being brought into service by Midland Dairy Farmers Ltd to carry 48 x 17 gallon and 20 x 12 gallon churns of milk from the farms around.[6] A few weeks earlier the magazine published a photograph of, in the words of the caption-writer, 'what is believed to be the biggest load ever tackled by a petrol vehicle in this country'. The load in question, on a vehicle of E.W. Rudd's, was a petrol tank measuring 23 feet by 16 feet by 11 feet high, and weighing 15 tons.[7]

The vehicle concerned was what was then described as a 'tractor-lorry' but more recently as an 'artic'. The arrival of these on the scene may well have discouraged the trend in the direction of bigger rigids. As we saw in an earlier chapter, Thornycroft had tried, and abandoned, an articulated vehicle right at the beginning of the motor saga. De Dion, the French manufacturers, tried too, somewhat later. Then among the imports from America in the early part of the Great War came the Knox tractor-lorry in 1915. Although there were a number of these Knox tractors around by the end of the war, they could hardly be termed a tremendous success. When talk got around to the possibilities of tractor-lorries people would raise questions about problems generally with the turntable connection between tractor and semi-trailer, about uncertain tracking, about difficulties with braking; and drivers would complain of the problem of manoeuvring in reverse. One of the arguments in favour of such vehicles was that they could lift the contents of a railway wagon at one go. But 10-ton loads could be handled easily enough by a steam wagon and trailer using home-produced coal which was not prey to the submarine menace nor to the Chancellor's hand outstretched to receive the petrol tax. The postwar boom, however, changed the situation. The furore about road damage and the calls to have weight spread over more wheels would have encouraged the development of the tractor-lorry.

On the road from February 1920, and sitting cheek by jowl with Caledon, Leyland and Maudslay 6-tonners at the Commercial Vehicle Show at Olympia in October that year, was what was to be the first real success story -a Scammel articulated 8-tonner (unladen 4 tons 10 cwt), with a 16-foot platform and a price label reading £1350.[8] Within 18 months the firm was advertising that there were already about 100 of these on the road. By then – March 1922 – there were four models with capacities ranging, from the original 8, up to 15 tons; and they were all claimed to be able to haul a 5-ton trailer. Those in use in 1921 included a 2000-gallon tanker by Shell-Mex, with a massive pressed channel-section steel frame with depth of 12 inches; and a pantechnicon for furniture with a body 27½ feet long x 7½ wide x 7 high, able to carry two or three times the normal load.[9]

Right at the beginning it looked as if the articulated vehicle was to suffer its own legislative millstone as bad as any 'Red Flag' Act. The Heavy Motor Car Order of 1904 was still in force and the legislators of 1904 had decreed that any vehicle hauling a trailer could not safely (and legally) proceed at more than 5 m.p.h. At a time when words such as 'Leviathan' were applied to 5- and 6-tonners, many people argued, in face of these new monsters and out of concern for road damage, that the semi-trailer was a trailer, and so was caught by the 5 m. p. h. limit. At first the MOT said nothing, and policemen, uncertain of the law, generally looked the other way. Eventually, though, the Heavy Motor Car (Amendment) Order, 1922, legalized the large artic. Provided that the axle load on the trailer was no more than 6½ tons and the combined axle load on the three axles was no more than 22 tons, the artic could run at the legal maximum of other lorries – 12 m.p.h. This opened the way, and in the next year or so artics came on the market from a number of other firms, with tractors both in the steam and the petrol varieties. Trailer-builders such as Carrosserie Latymer or Carrimore came up with their contributions. The latter firm advertised the advantages of the artic in dealing with an 8-ton consignment from Birmingham to London. According to their figures the traditional way would have been to use two 4-ton lorries. Two drivers for a day totalled £1 6s. 8d. and petrol for two lorries x 113 miles @ 6 m.p.g. cost £3 16s. 0d. Add in 6s. for lubricating oil and the total they arrived at was £5 8s. 8d. (£5.43½ in decimal terms). On the other hand, the Carrimore semi-trailer on a modified Leyland lorry needed only one driver (13s. 4d), and used petrol at a rate of 5½ m.p.g. (113 miles cost £2 1s. 0d.). Lubricating oil at 3s. brought the total to £2 17s. 4d. (£2.86½p), a really substantial saving.[10]

One of the main problems was eased when AEC, in the autumn of 1923, put a couple of models on the market with Westinghouse air brakes.[11] So, just as in other types of mechanical transport, improvements went ahead. In mid-1924 the latest Shell-Mex Scammell was an articulated 3000-gallon tanker, the tank itself forming the frame of the trailer, thus saving about 15 cwt in weight.[12]

While the articulated vehicle was achieving moderate success in the first half of the 1920s, leading magazines like *Commercial Motor* campaigned steadily for multi-wheeled rigids. The idea was not new. Fodens had drawings for a 6-wheeled steamer in 1903.[13] The argument for them was not that bigger loads could be carried – there were already the means to do that – but rather that by spreading the load over more wheels the damage to the roads would be reduced, as would 'wheel-spin'. The editor of *Commercial Motor* was well aware that opponents of road haulage (and of road passenger operations) harped constantly on the theme of road damage and the enormous cost of road maintenance and improvement. There was a large and sympathetic audience (in the shape of the rate-payers) for anyone who urged restrictions or heavier taxation on mechanical road vehicles. One ironical aspect of the whole thing was that 6-wheelers were taken much more seriously on the Continent and in America than in Britain. The reason for that, argued *Commercial Motor*, was that the roads in those places were so much worse than in Britain. Six wheels at least were necessary on the appalling roads abroad, if vehicles were not to shake themselves to pieces. In late 1924 *Commercial Motor* said that there was sufficient interest and investment in the United States 'to warrant the assertion that the rigid 6-wheeler has passed the experimental stage in that country'. They were talking of a model to be manufactured by Peerless in which the four rear wheels would all be driven and all be braked.[14] Within a month of that, however, came the news that the Scottish company, Caledon, had supplied a 6-wheeled rigid to W. Parks & Co. a haulage contractor in

Gloucester, for 10-ton loads.[15] As was usually the case, however, it was in passenger work that such advances were taken up most rapidly.

Whatever the demand for the heavyweights, there can be no ignoring the demand for lighter machines. As we have seen, Ford had made the running with a 1-ton van and an even smaller version. This had proved very popular and a great many tradesmen, seeking to be modern and replace their horses, looked for something of that capacity. The war had not been over long before the technical press was asking 'Where is the British 1-ton van?' There were firms like Lacre who had produced 25 cwt vans prewar for Shoolbreds and Harrods and the like, but experience had shown that a 2-tonner, at that time, could carry 25 cwt just as economically as a 25 cwt capacity van. Lacre, then, concentrated on the 2–2½-tonners.[16] So there was no immediate answer to the question, possibly also because manufacturers were happy enough to cater for the considerable demand for private cars. The disposal of army surplus provided cars as well as lorries but not in anything like the same numbers. Towards the middle of the decade, though, as the flood of army surplus dried up, more and more manufacturers came in to supply 1-ton and 30 cwt vans. There is no reason to think that a fleet described at the end of 1924 was in any way exceptional. This belonged to haulage contractors Hall, Lewis & Co. of Cardiff. Their smaller vehicles on parcels work were 2 x 7 cwt Fords, 3 x 1-ton Fords, 3 x 1-ton Chevrolets and 2 x 30 cwt Fiats. At the same time Pullars of Perth, dyers and cleaners, were using 22 x 15 cwt Dodge vans.[17]

Once the vehicle manufacturing industry had got over the assault of surplus army vehicles, it was able to settle down and increase production. This meant that manufacturing costs of new vehicles did not rise so rapidly as the cost of living generally. In other words, lorries tended to be relatively cheap in the middle and late twenties. According to data published by the Society of Motor Manufacturers and Traders (SMMT), the prices of commercial vehicles at the end of 1926 were only about 2.8 per cent above those of 1914 whereas the cost of living index at the mid-year had reached 69 per cent above 1914.[18] There were plenty of price reductions, too. A Scammell advertisement in June 1924, for example, had announced the reduction in the price of their 12-ton 6-wheeler from £1400 to £1255 and 'other models proportionately'. There was still more to come after 1926, too. Dennis reduced the price of their 30 cwt chassis from £350 to £315 in October 1927 and a year later to £298. The advertisement for the latter listed four other models with substantial price reductions. Even optional extras came down – a self-starter for the 30 cwt chassis was reduced from £14 to £9.[19] Furthermore, the vehicle of end-1926 was a very different animal from that of 1914. With five times as many lorries on the road, all doing a greater mileage than their 1914 counterparts, there was a wealth of practical commercial operating experience to supplement the experience gained in wartime. (As mentioned previously, there was also the fruits of the booming road passenger industry available.) So the 1926 lorry was much more efficient and capable of much longer runs. It became ever more reliable, the incidence of mechanical breakdowns decreasing steadily; it had a life generally of about 160,000 miles.

The relative cheapness of the new lorry was achieved despite the British user's propensity to ask the manufacturer to make little alterations or additions to the standard model, and the manufacturer's willingness to meet such requests. Indeed the manufacturers themselves had their own desire for individuality and were not at all anxious to buy in engines, gear boxes, back-axles, or whatever from specialist suppliers who might have been able to achieve considerable economies of scale. Although the total market was growing, too, production was essentially small-scale. In mid-1925 there were some forty-odd British manufacturers supplying petrol vans and lorries to the home market, not to mention nearly thirty foreign firms. Between them these two groups offered some 274 models from 5 cwt to 12 tons' capacity. Admittedly the differences within a firm's range were often in such factors as length of wheelbase or type of tyres. But the picture remains one of a great number of smallish-scale vehicle builders nearly all offering a wide choice. It was the same story in steam wagon production, with sixteen builders (all British) offering a total of 47 versions, and in electrics where ten manufacturers produced 40 different models. Whatever the needs of the individual haulier or ancillary user, there was sure to be something in this list to meet those needs. A great part of those needs was for small-capacity vehicles.

By the end of 1925, when *Commercial Motor* published specifications of vehicles available on the market in Britain, we find no less then 81 British petrol-driven goods models on offer in the range under 3 tons (out of a total of 149 models). There were eighty-odd foreign models under 3 tons as well, and a couple of dozen electrics in the same range.[20] Small vans and vehicles were clearly popular at the time, the Post Office, for example, having a reported total of 928 small vans in the summer of 1925.[21] These were predominantly Fords (none over 1-ton capacity), indeed predominantly British Fords, for in its postwar expansion Ford had first set up a plant in Cork and followed that with Trafford Park, Manchester, and, in 1924 they bought the Dagenham site.

Evidence of the popularity of the small-capacity vehicle is found, too, in the Ministry of Transport's first *Census of Mechanicallly Propelled Road Vehicles,* showing the numbers of vehicles with current licences in the Quarter to 30 September 1926. This shows the following 'goods vehicles' registered in Great Britain:

	Internal combustion	Steam	Electricity
Unladen Weight			
Not exceeding 12 cwt	1,270	–	
Exceeding 12 cwt but not exceeding 1 ton	128,870	–	N.E 25 cwt 156
Exc. 1T but not 2T	48,118	5	25 cwt – 2T 75
Exc. 2T but not 3T	19,144	20	105
Exc. 3T but not 4T	26,349	110	150
Exc. 4T but not 5T	21,969	5270	101
Exc. 5T but not 6T	947	976	7
Exc. 6T	432	2755	3
Exc. 4T but exact weight not specified	285	50	6
Totals	247,384	9186	603
These included –			
6-wheelers	363	44	–
4-wheelers used for drawing trailers	4,421	4509	23

Of just short of a quarter of a million petrol-engined goods vehicles, then, over half did not exceed 1 ton unladen. Something like 80 per cent of the petrol vehicles were in classes up to 3 tons unladen whereas in the steam wagons we see only 25 registered in those categories. The bulk of the steam wagons were what would then have been considered big vehicles – 4 tons and upward.

Mention of the Post Office reminds us that, of course, contractors still figured largely in postal work – firms like J. Blake & Co. of Liverpool which discarded their 65 horse-hauled vans at the beginning of July 1925 and added 32 new motor-vans to their existing 23 to make a total of 55, all on mails. With this the mail services in Liverpool were entirely motorized. Not surprisingly, the additional 32 motor vans included 20 Fords as well as six 30 cwt Garfords and six Beans.[22] That year Blake had completed twenty years of motor mail services, having instituted a daily service to Stoke-on-Trent in 1905.

There had been much campaigning in favour of multi-wheel rigids. When they were developed in any number the great majority of the bigger chassis were in passenger work. On the freight side we see what to us looks a trifle odd – again the small vehicle of 2 or 3 tons – on six wheels. Perhaps the important factor here was what the Army wanted and was prepared to subsidize to the extent of £40 a year for three years. They had, as we have seen, gone in for 3- and 4-tonners during the war, but in the 1920s they were clearly having second thoughts about that. The army authorities played a leading role in the development, between 1924 and 1926, of 6-wheeled 2½-

tonners. The two rear axles were both drivers and the idea was clearly that these vehicles could surmount the most difficult of terrain where the absence of roads would not be too much of a hindrance. The trade press of the time shows plenty of photographs of these 2½-tonners with the rear four wheels in all sorts of weird contortions over holes and hummocks. The Army preferred the wheeled vehicle as being faster over rough country with a useful load than the caterpillar-tracked machine. Where there were roads, the caterpillar-tracked vehicle was not much faster than over rough country, and its running and maintenance costs were higher than those of the 6-wheeler. So 6-wheelers became a feature of the War Department's subsidy scheme and literature extolling their virtues made much of their usefulness to farmers and in the trackless territories of the then British colonies. By late 1926 nine manufacturers were building them and a year later that number had doubled.[23]

Perhaps the oddest case of the tiny 6-wheeler was one in 1928 based on an Austin 7 chassis. This small car in its commercial form carried a load of 2½ cwt. Mr W.D. Gairdner of Andover devised a frame extension which made the Austin into a 6-wheeler capable of carrying 8 cwt. He did not wish to undertake production of his frame-extender himself but sought manufacturers who might be interested.[24] (I am not aware whether he had any success.) Despite the popularity of small multi-wheelers the bigger ones came, too, and early 1928 saw the first 8-wheeled rigids.

Motor vehicles were clearly catching on with haulage contractors and ancillary users, and the horse would steadily diminish in numbers. But the user in the mid-1920s had still to face problems. While the efficiency of the engine was improving year by year, the owner or driver had to work with a vehicle which was a long way short of what is known to us today. There was the job of getting it started, for example. Electric starters were usually fitted to light vans before the middle of the decade but they were not all that effective and cold engines could still present problems. For the big vehicles (the 3- or 4-tonners or over) there was nothing for it but to swing the starting handle. That back-breaking task was enough, sometimes, to make strong men weep, or at least to get tired before the day's driving had really begun. Here and there progressive owners used 'a fairly powerful [and portable] electric motor with a reducing gear and a suitable claw by which it could be connected to the starting handle'. That was fine, if infrequent, for fleet garages. The remedy of getting one vehicle started and using it to tow the rest was still advocated. The one-vehicle man normally had to rely on sheer muscle power, however, and the suggestion that the larger engine should have a reduction gear fitted so that the engine could be freed before normal cranking was not taken up. As ten years earlier, there was much discussion of clever ideas for getting the engine to fire – priming the engine with ether; warming the petrol one way or another; playing a blowlamp over the relevant pipes and on the magneto; even channels where a little burning petrol could flow gently along to warm the engine. There was the suggestion that for easier starting the mixture strength could be improved. Simply 'fit an air-strangler to the air inlet port'. In May 1927 the editor of *Commercial Motor* could still complain of the absence of 'impulse starters' on the magnetos of commercial vehicles. These devices, we learn, had been used on private cars for a long time and could provide a good spark even when the starting handle was turned quite gently. The driver's lot was not a happy one in cold weather, and starting a big engine 'is often a difficult task for two, and sometime even three men'. One might use miners' Davey lamps for keeping the garage warm at night, or straw, pillows and blankets to keep the engine cosy.[25]

The chemists had not yet devised a satisfactory anti-freeze and the possibility of a cracked block or burst radiator had still to be kept in mind. As late as January 1928 *Commercial Motor* ran an article by a barrister discussing liability for such damage where the insurance policy covered damage by 'accident'. He thought that this was a risk 'that would, in the majority of cases, be covered by such a policy', unless of course the policy excluded liability for the negligence of one's 'servants'. In the case of a snowbound vehicle, the driver would obviously have the opportunity of draining the radiator before he abandoned the vehicle. So the block should not be cracked.[26]

The engine could be started, eventually, but even then, we read, 'It does not seem to be commercially, or even scientifically, practicable to eliminate vibration in the 4-cylinder petrol engine', so 'in order to prevent damage to the transmission and engine bearers, designers have been in the habit of stiffening the crankcase and securing it very rigidly to the frame'. But no attempt was made to prevent the transmission of vibration from engine to the frame, it was alleged in 1924.[27] Then there was the sad letter in 1926 asking about ascertaining the oil level in the engine. On one well-known make 'the only means of telling the oil level is by the two taps on the back of the crankcase. This we find rather extravagant. To be on the safe side our drivers like to see the oil running out of the top tap.' On another well-known make 'the only means of telling how much oil is in the sump is by looking through the filler cap, which makes it more or less guesswork'. The writer asked, 'Is there a device such as a tube, similar to a water gauge, or a dip rod, to tell us how far the oil is above the level of the bottom tap on the crank case?'[28]

What if it rained when one was driving? The year 1924 saw a little news item about a windscreen wiper, held in place by spring pressure. According to the description, it could easily be drawn across the windscreen by hand.[29] Perhaps more than any other topic, the magazines of the time were concerned with brakes. In an article at the beginning of 1925, enumerating design changes that were necessary, *Commercial Motor* asserted categorically that all lorries should be fitted with brakes which should be powerful enough to hold the vehicle, when fully loaded, on the steepest hill. The writer was generous enough to the designers to admit that it was easy enough to say this but not so easy to design brakes which would perform this duty. He stressed that brake connections needed to work regardless of the load. 'Even today', he wrote, 'there are commercial motors in which the brakes will act well enough when the vehicle is unloaded, but will lose much of their power when the springs are depressed by a full load. It is quite possible to design brakes so that they are absolutely unaffected by the compression of the springs'.[30] Warnings were voiced to tell drivers that the way to adjust brakes was not simply to thump the rods with a hammer or kick them so as to put a bit of a kink in them; and manufacturers were implored to put some sort of an adjusting device in an easily accessible place.

By the mid-1920s the expanding haulage scene was including more and more night running. We read in March 1925 of a steady stream of vehicles northward during the night on the London–Dunstable–Coventry–Birmingham route. 'The coffee hut has, indeed, become quite a feature of the Birmingham Road, each one having a line of half-a-dozen leviathans.' Leviathans they were, 'mainly of the heavy type capable of taking a load of at least four tons'. There was a fair sprinkling of tractor-lorries taking up to 12 tons and a few lorries towing 4-wheeled trailers.[31] One important aspect of night work was the vehicle's lights. 'Invariably oil lamps are employed at each side and the tail, but a more efficient headlamp of some type or other is nearly always used in addition.' That more efficient headlamp would usually use acetylene, a gas which burned to give a steady white light. In many cases, we learn, two headlamps would be mounted in front, often fitted so that one of them cast a beam down to the road edge. Electricity was coming in, though, and the same *Commercial Motor* article tells us that 'McNamara have fitted their Scammells on the Birmingham express service with electric headlamps in addition to oil sidelights. They say they have found the electrical system pefectly satisfactory and reliable'.[32] Only a month later the editor would state bluntly that 'the use of such makeshifts as hurricane lanterns attached with string or wire to any convenient projection is unjustifiable, except in case of emergency. The cost of dynamo sets is probably prohibitive for many small hauliers and carriers ... but other satisfactory systems are in existence.'[33] While electric head- and tail-lights were coming into use for haulage vehicles, they were already well established for the private car. The problem of dazzle caused by the blinding headlamps of oncoming cars was an ever-recurrent theme in these years, and the best course of action for drivers was widely discussed. Dire remedies like pulling straight in front of the offending vehicle were frowned upon as being dangerous, as was switching off one's own headlamps; but the debate went on. One could paint the upper half of the headlamp glass so that no beam was cast upward. There were dipping devices which tilted the headlamp when a lever was pulled. When the CMUA voted £100 in April 1925 for anti-dazzle tests there had already been some attempts to develop suitable headlamps and the RAC had organized tests of some forty-odd devices.[34]

Another aspect of night driving, and indeed of all commercial driving, was the matter of the driver's time at the wheel. The article mentioned above pointed out that a run from London to Birmingham generally took about twelve hours. The driver might be called upon to operate his vehicle for the best part of 24 hours. While the drivers had to be 'picked' men (for their intelligence and physique), nevertheless, there was a serious risk from fatigue. There were reports of accidents having been caused by drivers falling asleep; and while these were probably very exceptional cases, there were still many incidents arising from fatigue. The problem was not overcome by speed, for until October 1928 lorries generally were limited to 12 m.p.h. or, if they had trailers, 5 mp.h. The talk in the transport 'caffs' often turned to police speedtraps and how employers would often expect the driver to pay the fine. One hardly knows how to judge letters to the press, for it is easy to fall into the trap of thinking that one swallow really does make a summer. A letter from 'North Country Owner-Driver' in *Commercial Motor* on 23 March 1925 makes interesting reading, if nothing else. 'I know of cases', he writes,

> where one man is regularly in charge of a four-ton lorry for 40 hours or more, without any provision being made for him to get any rest. He leaves a town in the North, nearly 150 miles from London, at 5 p.m. and arrives in London the next morning; he is engaged all day delivering his load and picking up another one, and then starts straight away for home again.[35]

This can be read in a context of a rapidly expanding industry where, in a rather depressed economy, people had to fight hard to make a living; where rate-cutting was prevalent; where a few shillings one way or the other could make the difference between success and failure. The attitude of the MOT is noteworthy. When MPs raised the matter in Parliament, the minister would point out that this was a matter of conditions of work to be sorted out between employer and employee. It was not the ministry's concern.

Apart from that particular reasoning, the letter must be read too, like most of the preceding comment about brakes, speed and lights, in a context of the strange paralysis of British law-makers. As has been seen in earlier chapters the industry really began to take shape only from the time of the Motor Car Act, 1903 and the Heavy Motor Car Order,1904, which laid down the first sketchy 'construction and use' rules and speed limits. Thereafter very little happened, so that until the late twenties hauliers and merchants had to operate their vehicles at maximum speeds laid down more than twenty years earlier, during which time there had been enormous technical progress and roads had improved considerably. The proportion of Class I roads in England and Wales with the old 'water-bound' macadam, that is, untarred, fell from 38 per cent in 1922 to 12 per cent in 1925. In this time pneumatic tyres had become fairly general, and protection of drivers from wind and weather had been greatly improved. It was not just in the obvious areas of speed limits and axle loads that new regulations were needed, for people were confused about other topics, such as what to do at road junctions. Ideas such as giving way to traffic on the right, or having notices saying which of two roads had priority, were debated endlessly.

The MOT published a draft Road Traffic Bill in October 1927 based largely on some reports of a couple of departmental committees in 1922 and 1925. The draft Bill was really a consultative document, setting out alternative possibilities for regulation; but although motoring and trade organizations gave their views on the draft, no general legislation was forthcoming. There ,just never seemed to be enough parliamentary time to deal with road transport except for a couple of urgent matters. These were, first, the Road Transport Lighting Act,1927. This embodied a part of the ministry's draft Bill and came into operation on 22 April 1928. It required most vehicles to carry two white lights in front and a red one on the tail, agricultural vehicles getting away with one white light in front. Second, a new Order, effective 1 October 1928, allowed heavy motor cars – that is, those above 2 tons unladen – to travel at 20 m.p.h. if on pneumatic tyres. These two measures did not really satisfy either MPs or those members of the House of Lords who (impatient and worried about a rising death toll on the roads) tried introducing their own private members' bills, without much success. A general overhaul of the law was postponed repeatedly. Parliamentary time was needed for bills to give road operating powers to the railways and then, in the end, there was the appointment, in 1928, of a Royal Commission to look at all aspects of transport and road traffic. The Commission started off by taking evidence on traffic regulation and made its first report on that aspect, in 1930 – *The Control of Traffic on Roads* – but more of that later.

As is well known, the year 1926 saw the General Strike, when miners, railwaymen, dockers and other workers tried jointly to maintain miners' wages at the then existing levels. The story, as generally told, is that since the Chancellor had taken Britain back onto the Gold Standard at a level of the pound which was too high, British exports – of coal in particular – suffered, and the only way out appeared to be a reduction of wages to maintain Britain's competitiveness. Whatever the merits of the argument on either side, governments generally take the view that they have a responsibility to the populace for the maintenance of essential food and other supplies. They regard it as their job, too, to keep law and order and to prevent any catastrophic disruption of the life of the nation. To this end successive governments had kept at hand, since the war, provisional arrangements for Civil Commissioners to act on behalf of the government in each of the several regions of the country should the central government not be able to maintain effective rule throughout. It is said that even the Labour Government of 1924, under Ramsey MacDonald, had twice thought of bringing these arrangements into effect.[36]

Relations between the mine-owners and the mine-workers had been very poor for a long time and things came to a head with a threatened strike in August 1925. The government, with only an outline organization, were certainly not ready for a showdown at that moment so they gave the mines a temporary subsidy and took refuge in that good old standby of the politician – a commission to enquire into the matter. They then quickly took action. They had several advantages which they did not have, or had had in a lesser degree, during the 1919 rail strike. The MOT was now well established and had a sound knowledge of the transport situation in the country. Second, there were now almost a quarter of a million commercial freight vehicles in use in the country, albeit many of them small, compared with only one-fifth or one-sixth of that number in 1919. Third, and importantly too, was the fact that these quarter million vehicles were owned by people who were rapidly acquiring considerable commercial transport expertise. The 1919 men, no less astute, had had their operations circumscribed by the needs of the wartime economy, or had had experience limited to the conveyance of military supplies to the fighting men at the various fronts. And the Home Secretary, Joynson-Hicks, was a man with considerable personal knowledge of the road haulage industry, gained as a lawyer in many courtroom battles in defence of hauliers. True, he was variously described as one of the government's intransigents[37] and as one of those 'spoiling for a fight',[38] but knowledge of road haulage he had. On the other hand, the surplus army lorries and redundant army drivers were no longer available to the government, and the Defence of the Realm Act had gone, though regulations could still be made once a State of Emergency was declared.

England and Wales were promptly marked out into ten divisions and Scotland into five. The Civil Commissioners for these divisions were appointed in September 1925 and they included a 'Roads Commissioner' in each division. The ten Roads Commissioners in England and Wales were, in fact, nine engineers from the MOT and one county surveyor, and under them, Road Officers were appointed for each of 150 areas of England and Wales. The master stroke in the organization, however, was the setting up in each area of a haulage committee whose members were prominent figures in the local transport scene. Their job was to ensure that transport was diverted from all non-essential operations to essential work.[39] In London, for example, the London Haulage Committee included H. Gaunt of J. Lyons, Cadby Hall, the well-known caterers with their own organization for the distribution of foodstuffs; James Paterson of Carter Paterson; Cecil Rickett for the coal distributors; E.W. Rudd, a well-known meat and general haulier; W. Wolseley of Thomas Tilling; J.H. Turner of London Haulage & Contractors' Association; and Lt-Col. Sir Maxwell Hicks (brother of the Home Secretary and for a time Chairman of McNamara) for the newspaper industry. These men worked under the chairmanship of a 'giant' of the time, Sir Henry Maybury, Director General of Roads at the MOT. It must be repeated that an essential feature of the Haulage Committee was the expert knowledge, contacts and influence which the members had in local transport activity. Another member of the London Haulage Committee, Major E.G. Monroe, for example, was chairman of a Covent Garden committee which constituted the central machinery for the transport of fruit and vegetables. In the event, branch markets reported their transport requirements to the Covent Garden committee, which coordinated the requests. Monroe would have a good picture of what was needed before he went to the Haulage Committee's meeting each morning at 10.30.[40]

This organization for dealing with a national emergency was in place by the end of November 1925 and letters went out to the local authorities telling them of the plans. During December conferences of Road Officers and Haulage Committee chairmen took place in each division. In January 1926 further conferences discussed matters such as the protection of lorries and drivers in the event of strikers taking militant action. The decision was taken that convoys of vehicles would present rather easy targets whereas single lorries would be a more difficult problem for anyone inclined to attack them. In January and February 1926 detailed instructions went out to the chairmen of the Haulage Committees and conferences were held in March to discuss them. So the preparations went on – maps were drawn up, routes marked out, and the local Police Liaison Committees advised. It became more and more probable that the Samuel Commission would recommend the withdrawal of the subsidy and that the miners' strike or lockout (readers must choose their own word) would begin on 1 May. Road Officers and Haulage Committee chairmen were told to keep their diaries clear to allow meetings to be held on 27 and 28 April for the polishing of final details. These meetings were duly held.[41] A 'State of Emergency' was proclaimed on 30 April. The next day the MOT issued Emergency Regulations which empowered the ministry, amongst other things,

> to regulate, restrict, or give directions; take possession of horses, vehicles ... either absolutely or by way of hire; prohibit or restrict the carriage of goods by road or prescribe the radius in which goods might be carried by road; give directions with respect to the carriage of goods on any particular vehicle or by any particular clearing house or depot; regulate

> priorities in which goods might be carried or vehicles used; and prescribe conditions or rates for the carriage of goods by road.[42]

The term 'General Strike' is a misnomer since it was never the intention to call out all workers when the seemingly inevitable dispute eventually came to a head; but the strike leaders did want to allow foodstuffs to be distributed whilst halting other vital services. The TUC meeting on Saturday 1 May, therefore, decided that 'railways, sea and road transport, and all dock, wharf, harbour and canal services' would be stopped. Ernest Bevin for the TGWU announced that, if no settlement had been reached by then, those called out must not go to work after the Monday night shift.[43] It is difficult to decide how far road transport services were affected, for news reporting during this major strike tended to be propagandist, and, anyway, strikers were often replaced by 'volunteers'. About one thousand employees in despatch and transport work for J. Lyons & Co., Cadby Hall, were called out on strike on Thursday 6 May, for example, and duly obeyed the call. But their places were immediately taken by 'volunteers'.[44] According to *The Times* of Tuesday 11 May, these thousand employees went back to work again early in the next week, the availability of 'volunteers', no doubt, influencing their decision. The same issue of the newspaper tells us that

> at the request of the Aerated Bread Co. sixty volunteer lorry drivers were supplied from the Ministry pool ... last night to replace men who had been called out by the Unions. When the volunteers came out with the ABC lorries a number of the strikers returned to work, with the result that the ABC will hold only forty of the volunteers in reserve against any eventuality.

It seems hardly likely that the firm would have kept as many as forty volunteers unless a somewhat similar number of their regular staff were on strike or threatening it. The situation, undoubtedly, was patchy across the country. At the beginning of the week the Smithfield (Market) Emergency Committee called for volunteers to load and unload meat at Smithfield. 'Trucks of 3 tons and upwards with or without drivers are wanted' *(The Times,* 11 May 1926). But the next day the paper reported that there had been a 'good' response to the Smithfield call and no more volunteers were wanted. It did not mention lorries.

By the Tuesday when the strike really began, apart from the railwaymen, some 400,000 'transport' men had been called out, but these would have included dockers and bus drivers as well as lorrymen. Certainly most of the dockers came out. On that day *The Times* reported from Manchester that 'The millers state that when they send motor vehicles to the dock area for wheat, strikers stop the lorries and permits to enter the docks are refused.' Who drove the lorries? Volunteers? Was that why Union permits to allow food to be moved were rejected? Certainly the Liverpool & District Motormen's Union, after a meeting with the TGWU, had decided that on and after 3 May any heavy motor vehicle not adequately staffed – that is, not having the requisite two men – would not be loaded or unloaded in the districts of Liverpool, Manchester and Preston. The intention was, too, that the men on such vehicles would be union members. Employers had been grousing for some time that conditions in Liverpool were strict but that outsiders (and Manchester was often mentioned) had not always adhered to the Union rules. The employers would try to get over these difficulties. Wagons from outside Liverpool would often take on a hired man on arrival at Liverpool just for loading and unloading.[45]

Volunteers there were in plenty, at least in the London area. *The Times* of 4 May, not very impartially, reported a 'Splendid response in London'. Volunteers were being interviewed at the rate of 400 per hour at temporary buildings in the Foreign Office Quadrangle. They were volunteering for all sorts of work, not just lorry-driving. No such reports from other parts of the country appeared in *The Times* and there may well have been shortages of drivers here and there. Leeds saw increasing unemployment towards the end of the week in which the strike started. 'Many works are finding it impossible to continue full time owing to the lack of raw materials and transport facilities.' Two clothing factories were closing 'tomorrow'.[46] Similarly, in the Paisley area 30,000 people were affected – 'Many factories and works in Scotland are having to close down owing to the impossibility of moving their products away.'[47] Not only textile factories suffered a shortage of essential transport. 'Sheffield is threatened with a beer famine.'[48]

Some lessons had been learnt from the 1919 rail strike and in 1926 again the 'milk pool' was organized at Hyde Park, with milk being collected by road from 100 miles around London. A total of 500 lorries were on the job on the first day of the strike. This number quickly grew to 1200 but as more and more trains were run, lorries were released for other work and by the last day of the strike no lorries at all were on the 'milk run'. One of the other jobs done by lorries got a good deal of publicity – the task of moving flour from the London Docks. Ever since the first day, said *The Times*, the strikers had concentrated their efforts on preventing access to the docks. But on Sunday afternoon

> a convoy of 158 motor-cars [i,e. lorries], each of them heavily laden with bags of flour, drew up in Hyde Park. Armoured cars provided an escort at the head of the column and at the rear, and two or three men of the Welsh Guards, steel-helmeted and wearing their active-service uniform and equipment, perched high on each lorry.

With 105 lorries on the Saturday and the largest convoy of 220 lorries on the Monday, this operation moved altogether 483 loads of flour 'without casualties or incidents of any kind'.[49]

It may well be that the hearts of the railwaymen and road transport workers had never been in it from the start. Loyalty to fellow workers in the mines was probably the main motivating force, and with that being subjected to strain for various reasons, with growing uncertainty about the effectiveness of their action, and with the presence of so many willing volunteers, strikers began drifting back to work. At mid-day on Thursday 13 May, after nine days, the strike was called off (at least by the transport men, for the miners struggled on for several weary months thereafter), thus, it must be said, putting at least one nail in the coffin of the steam wagon. The road transport men and the dockers, said *The Times*, quoting an official of the TUC, 'in many parts of the country ... had resumed work on the old conditions with the old agreements recognized by the employers. There had been numerous difficulties but many of these had been overcome.' Ernest Bevin, Secretary of the TGWU, gave a version which did not mention 'numerous difficulties'. According to him, 'Road transport workers all over the country had, with one or two exceptions, returned on the old conditions.'[50]

The Times of the 22 May 1926 reflected on the strike.

> The two main factors which contributed to the success of the emergency transport organization during the general strike were the efficiency of the volunteers and the good condition of the roads. The maintenance of the transport of essential supplies was a notable achievement and credit is due to the Minister of Transport and his staff, for the success which attended their efforts, There was no lack of volunteers to undertake the task of driving motor lorries and the position was further simplified by the excellent state of the roads. There could be no better justification for the policy of the Ministry of Transport in getting the main roads into first-class condition than the experience of the strike period during which long distance road haulage was of paramount importance.

The article went on to talk of the 400 lorries which were distributing food from Hull in the first few days, of the 'milk pool' at Hyde Park, of the transport organization worked out in detail beforehand, and of the 150 Road Officers and volunteer Haulage Committees, 'each Committee with a Chairman who was a well-known haulage contractor and who had entire knowledge of the transport work of the district and knew the vehicle owners in his area'.

A columnist claimed that Marxist theory had been undermined by the discovery that a flapper could drive a lorry, and indeed there were pictures in the papers of girls – complete with cloche hats – driving lorries, the bonnets of which were bedecked with barbed wire, and with a policeman in the cab beside the lady driver. But there were other opinions about the efficiency of some of the volunteers. One writer held that Haulage Committees had to keep a close eye on the volunteers, some of whom got lost. 'Volunteer drivers would damage engines, or drive into ditches. Some of them, having brought their transport to a standstill ... would wander about looking for a garage, and on returning would find their cargo gone.'[51]

The Haulage Committees clearly did a sterling job, even if there were moments of near farce. It has been alleged that the idea of full back loads could become a mania with some committees. The example of a Manchester vehicle was given to substantiate this. The vehicle went with a full load to Liverpool, then was given one to Barrow-in-Furness. From there it took a full load for HMSO to Edinburgh. Then it went to Glasgow; then to Paisley; then with flour to Carlisle; and then with biscuits from Carlisle to London. 'That lorry passed completely out of the control of the Manchester organization and was never heard of again until the owner began worrying about it.'[52] Clearly one owner/organization was not in charge throughout. One wonders, too, whether the regular driver was in charge, or a student just enjoying a break from his studies.

The same writer, however, probably hit the nail on the head in offering a view about the success (from the government's point of view) of the road haulage industry. Apart from those differences between 1919 and 1926 already mentioned, there were other – more significant – differences. Whereas in 1919 the road haulage industry was small, by 1926 it had grown to be a quite vigorous industry; and, here is the point, whereas in 1919 there had been substantial requisitioning of vehicles, very little of this was done in 1926. The industry ran virtually completely on a commercial basis through the nine days of the General Strike, subject only to a certain amount of direction from the industry's own representatives in the Haulage Committees, and given the temporary dispensation of legally setting aside normal haulage contracts when required to carry foodstuffs. The Minister of Transport certainly had taken powers to requisition, but

> by foresight which proved to be as tactically expedient as it vas psychologically wise, the Minister made hardly any use of these Emergency Powers. By deciding, for instance, not to requisition vehicles, he avoided serious dislocation in the haulage trade, and equally, avoided serious provocation of the striking trade unionists.[53]

Perhaps the last word on the subject of the General Strike should go to Lloyd George, one-time prime minister, who, whatever his sympathies, would tend to see the situation from the point of view of one who had to cope with a similar one in 1919. In a Foreword to George Glasgow's book *General Strikes and Road Transport* he wrote about 'the decisive efficacy of road transport for the purposes of feeding the nation in a sudden emergency' and he added that 'few of us were prepared for so complete an illustration of its power'.

From the point of view of the history of the road haulage industry it should be noted how limited a role these words allowed to road haulage. The ex-premier certainly did not say that motor transport could cope with all the nation's transport needs, and he clearly limited the time scale of its ability to carry food to 'sudden emergencies'; and to further chasten the vigorous young industry, one must notice how often in news reports and official documents motor transport came second in the wording behind horse transport – as in the Emergency Regulations mentioned above.

A letter in *The Times* on 24 May 1926 referred to 'the deep debt of gratitude which the country owes ... to the smaller road transport firms and individual hauliers' for carrying on the country's transport so well during the General Strike. Certainly the nation was grateful, for a few days at least; but the letter-writer, a Mr R.W. Sewell, said of those small transport firms and hauliers that he feared they 'will be put out of business by the increased taxation in the present Budget'. Many of them had told him how they had struggled through years of bad trade, hoping for better times. 'With competition most intense between all forms of transport it will not be possible for them to raise their prices, and the result will be extinction.' But let us go back a little.

The motoring interests claimed that, during the consultative stages before the passing of the Roads Act, 1920, they had extracted a promise from the government that the proceeds of motor taxation – the licence duties -would go into the Road Fund and would be used for road maintenance and improvement. That was the idea behind the 1910 Act which had imposed petrol taxation. Private motorists and commercial firms alike wanted better roads for there was much to be done after years of neglect. It has been said, for instance, that of Nottingham's 408 miles of main road, only 40 miles had been tarmacked by 1918 though another 167 miles had had the centre of the road done.[54] There was still much to be done, although as we have seen earlier in this chapter the extent of the old water-bound macadam on Class I roads had been reduced to only 12 per cent by 1925. Better roads would mean lower running costs – particularly lower fuel, tyre, repair and maintenance costs, and, indeed, lower depreciation. Mechanical transport owners, then, were willing enough – as willing as any taxpayer can be – to pay a tax if that was the only way to get good roads. Willing though they might have been to pay tax, the motor users were determined to get value for money and they kept a jealous eye on where the money was going and groused vehemently if things were not to their liking. One particular niggle was in regard to the choice of roads for improvement. Governments favoured schemes in districts where the work would relieve heavy unemployment but motoring interests frequently alleged that these were not the ones most needed by motor transport users. Questions were asked in Parliament about how many unemployed people had been taken on to road improvement schemes. The answers did not necessarily provide evidence of misused funds, for the government would point out that some of the schemes were financed by the Unemployment Grants Committee and others by the Road Fund – as in the case of 603 schemes employing 25,000 men in September 1927. When an arterial road was being constructed in the Liverpool area the accusation was made that Liverpool was going in for estate development to gain ground rents rather than building roads purely for traffic purposes.[55]

A certain amount of apoplexy was generated in the mid-1920s by the allocation of £750,000 from the Road Fund to improve rural (that is, unclassified) roads. Since little mechanical transport used these roads the MOT and the government were accused roundly of keeping the rural gentry sweet by subsidizing their rates bills. A good deal of debate continued on and off as to what might legitimately be funded from the Road Fund. Footpaths were necessary to keep pedestrians off the roads, so that appeared reasonable enough. Could the same be said for tracks for horsemen, along the verges? Policemen on traffic control duty were clearly there as a result of the growth of motor traffic, but when farmers started claiming that weeds in their fields originated from uncut verges along the roads the motor-taxation payers did not look too kindly on claims for recompense from the Road Fund.[56] It was not simply a case of 'We pay tax; you build roads for us.'

The whole thing boiled up merrily in 1925 when rumours started to circulate that the Chancellor, Mr Churchill, had designs on the Road Fund. There were allegations subsequently by Col. Moore Brabazon, that the Treasury had always resented the fact that this Fund was not under its control. There were more allegations that it was really the railway directors who were behind it all. Lord Montagu certainly started something when he told the country what was bothering him in mid-1925. The Editor of *Commercial Motor* could hardly believe what he had heard. This is how he reacted:

> Owners of motor vehicles should not take too seriously the prospect of a realization of Lord Montagu's apprehensions as to a raid on the Road Fund by the Chancellor ... If such a proposal ever got beyond the stage of inclusion in some officially prepared minutes of items to be surveyed by the Chancellor ...there would be such a public outcry that the project would be strangled at birth. The proceeds of the Road Fund were strictly ear-marked for road improvements and development, whilst the Ministry of Transport is committed to a programme which will absorb all the revenue for several years. It is fairly certain that the Chancellor of the Exchequer is quite well aware that the country would not tolerate any restrictions or tinkering with the great policy which is now beginning to transform the conditions of road transport in this country. He would certainly have little support from Members of Parliament.[57]

But many people took it seriously, particularly the highway authorities, who had visions of a smaller contribution from the Road Fund towards road works. They sent a deputation to see the Chancellor in January 1926 to seek assurance. Mr Churchill, who had earlier said that what he was considering did not involve any permanent diversion from the Road Fund, had now hardened his attitude. Regarding previous governments' commitment to devote the revenue from vehicle taxation to road works, he stated categorically that chancellors and governments had the right to review any arrangement from time to time. The government was not barred in perpetuity from reviewing road expenditure. He then went on the attack and talked about the damage caused to roads by heavy vehicles. The whole system was unfair, he said, in that ratepayers were subsidizing certain users of road transport and this was in competition with, and at the expense of, the railways which were themselves amongst the largest ratepayers in the country. He thought it necessary to consider whether an undue proportion of Britain's national resources were not being devoted to road construction.[58]

It is understandable that a hard-pressed Chancellor should look at the growing balance in the Road Fund. It is clear that the government and mechanical transport people who had struck the deal in 1920 had not foreseen the enormous growth, over the next few years, in the number of vehicles licensed; and although the expenditure on roads went up, so too did the balance in the account. From about £9 million in 1920 the balance had doubled to £18.7 million in 1926. The road interests argued that this was not a surplus since so much work had to be done and, because of the lengthy process between MOT and highway authorities in agreeing projects, much of the balance would soon be committed, anyway. There were even dark hints that the Treasury was blocking road expenditure in some cases so as to build up the balances. C.T. Brunner, certainly no opponent of road transport, writing in 1929, did an interesting exercise. By taking prewar road expenditure and scaling it up for the rises in materials and wages costs, he arrived at an estimate of the cost, in the late 1920s, of maintaining roads at pre-motor standards. The excess of actual expenditure over his 'pre-motor' estimate he attributed to the growth of motor traffic and he added in the cost of policemen on traffic control duties to get the 'cost of motor transport' as £27 million per annum. He then compared this 'cost of motor transport' with the revenue from motor taxation. He concluded that motor transport was not paying its full share of road costs currently, there being a deficit of £12.7 million in 1925–26. But just to complicate the picture he argued that there had been a considerable neglect of roads during the Great War (to the extent of £80 million at 1925 prices). Much of current expenditure was to make that good, and the wartime shortfall was certainly more than the total deficit in motor cost minus motor taxation up to 1928. However, the increased vehicle taxes since 1927 had helped to ease the growing total 'motor' deficit.[59]

The Treasury and the Chancellor had already arrived at the conclusion that motor taxes did not pay the cost of roads, so the 1926 Budget increased vehicle taxation. As from 1 January 1927 the following licence fees were payable on goods vehicles:

Unladen weight					
under 1 ton	1–2 tons	2–3 tons	3 tons +	4 tons +	5 tons upward
£16	£26	£40	£48	£54	£60

In addition to the tax increases, the Chancellor also made his famous 'raid' on the Road Fund, transferring £7 million to general government funds. He 'capped' the balance on the Road Fund, too, stating his intention of transferring out of it in future years whatever amount was necessary to keep the balance at the 1926 level. This 'raid' (Mr Churchill thought the term 'rather vulgar') caused a great deal of argument both in Parliament and outside. With a politician's usual confidence, the Secretary to the Treasury said that shortly after the Armistice the Exchequer had given £8 million to the Road Fund and the worst that could now be said was that it was now taking back seven-eighths of its gift. He forgot to mention the money diverted from motor taxation to the Treasury during the war. Outside of Parliament, the National Farmers' Union wrote to *The Times* that the Union, representing over 100,000 ratepayers 'views with dismay the Exchequer's decision' and it added that 'such confidence [in the State] as remained among them will be finally shattered if Mr. Churchill's proposal be sanctioned by Parliament'.[60]

Those who study the British democratic system will not be surprised that when a government puts forward such a proposal, MPs – in the words of W.S. Gilbert's sentry – 'if they've a brain and cerebellum too, they've got to leave that brain outside and vote just as their leaders tell 'em to'. So the Finance Act was duly passed, the 'raid' and increased vehicle taxes were carried into effect. Even before the passing of the Finance Act it had not embarrassed the Secretary to the Treasury, when asked about the number of resolutions sent in by local authorities regarding the proposed 'raid', to say that there had been 'a considerable number' but no records were kept. So the road transport industry had no choice but to accept the idea that taxes on vehicles could no longer be considered as purely for road works. Mr Churchill reinforced the point again the next year by moving what he regarded as surplus balances from the Road Fund to general government funds. 'The coffers of the Road Fund are continually overflowing', he said in his Budget speech in April 1927, 'increasing by more than £3 millions a year'.

There was obviously a great deal of noise from motor vehicle interests about the increased licence fees. The smaller firms, the operators of one or two vehicles, were already arguing that the flat-rate tax bore harder on them, because of their low mileage, than on the big firms. They argued, logically enough, that flat-rate licence fees were in no way related to the usage of, and damage to, the roads. Big firms, with lorries doing big mileages, were getting away lightly. So there was continued moaning about the iniquity of licence fees and continued calls for a reversion to the system of tax per gallon of petrol. Unfortunately chancellors are always looking for ways to raise revenue and it does not do to offer them suggestions. It is true that the petition asking for a return to the petrol tax, signed by 920,000 people, which Col. Howard-Bury presented to the House of Commons a few days before the 1928 Budget, may have had little bearing on the outcome of the Budget, but the Chancellor undoubtedly had heard of it much earlier. So that 1928 Budget brought the imposition of 4d. (about 1½p) on a gallon of petrol, the Chancellor pointing out that petrol prices, at one time in the order of 2s. (10p) per gallon, had fallen to about half that. Since the beginning of 1927 the price of No.1 spirit in London had fallen by 5d. (and then, as now, chancellors believed that the public have no God-given right to benefit from such windfalls). Lorry operators were not mollified by knowing that the price of petrol had fallen.

Indeed, this imposition brought forth howls of rage because of the reason for the Chancellor's action. The government had concocted a great scheme to help the struggling basic industries and agriculture through the Depression. The Balfour Committee on Industry and Trade had argued that railway rates were bearing hardly on the world competitive position of British heavy industry (Cmd. 3282). The government's idea was that the railways be given, in effect, a subsidy by a reduction of their local authority rate bills by 75 per cent. But they were not themselves to benefit. They had to give a rebate on the freight rates for specified traffic forwarded by the hard-pressed basic industries and agriculture. (Agriculture was relieved totally of local rates.) Local authorities, of course, had to be compensated for the loss of rates revenue – to the extent of £24 million, and that was where the need for the extra petrol tax came in. It would yield £17.8 million in the first full year and thereafter increase by £1.25 million per annum. Private cars and buses would be paying the greater part of that. Road haulage did not have to meet it all.

The road haulage people, naturally enough, took the view that they were having, indirectly, to pay a subsidy to the railways. Even though the scheme was intended to ease the lot of basic industry, the effect of it was to secure the specified traffic to the railways. An industrial firm was likely to think twice before offering its freight to road if it was receiving rebates on rail freight charges. The traffic on which rebates of 10 per cent were given included goods such as coal, coke, pit props, and raw materials for iron and steel plants. Road haulage did not carry much of this traffic anyway, though they had been trying to win from railways bulk manures, cattle foods, potatoes, milk and livestock, also entitled to a 10 per cent rebate. If they had a case in respect of the latter agricultural traffic it is doubtful whether, overall, the claims of the road operators that it was all a plot to get road haulage to subsidize the railways were really justified. Road transport operators had a better case in complaining that, though the petrol tax amounted to no more than ½d. (one-fifth of 1p) per lorry-mile, they were not making much profit and so the additional fuel cost would have to be passed on to customers.

Partly to off-set this petrol tax, and partly to reduce road damage, the Chancellor modified slightly the licence duties for smaller vehicles and generally reduced the licence cost by 20 per cent for vehicles on pneumatic tyres. This meant that a 5-tonner on pneumatics, for example, would pay £48 for its yearly licence instead of £60 from 1 January 1929. This was fine for some vehicles, but it was not necessarily easy to switch from solid tyres to pneumatics, for the design of the vehicle around the wheel arches and adjacent frame might not leave room for pneumatics. In any case if the vehicle had fairly new solids it would not be worthwhile replacing them immediately – for the cost of a new set of pneumatics would far outweigh the gain from the reduced licence fee. There would, clearly, be gains from the lower maintenance costs generally for a vehicle on pneumatics.

So the possible rebate on the licence certainly did not quieten the many voices raised in anger or anguish against the petrol tax. Mr Churchill's remarks at the time of his 1928 Budget confirmed people in their belief that the government were definitely pro railways and against road transport. He pointed out that £50,000,000 a year was being spent on the roads – already the best in the world. It was not in the public interest to spend, in the next few years, several hundred additional millions if the result was to render artificially and prematurely obsolete the splendid railway system. This system represented a thousand million pounds of British capital and gave employment to 700,000 men. He may well have known that the road transport industry and related manufacturing were already bigger than the railways in terms of employment, directly and indirectly. But he did, first, say nice things about road transport.

> The immense expansion of road transport by motor vehicles is an economic advantage of measureless consequence to the whole industrial life of the nation. Its influence in enriching that internal trade, which so greatly exceeds our external trade, is of incalculable advantage, and nothing must be allowed to restrict this development, so long as it proceeds on a sound economic basis.

There was a sting in that tail, and he went on a little later to say that Britain had seen in recent years

> road transport increasingly taking many forms of traffic from the railways. If the road vehicles which carry these forms of traffic, inflict far more injury on the roads than they pay for, the competition ceases to be fair … It is the duty of the state to hold the balance even between road and rail, and to let the best form of transport win on its merits. No-one can say that the balance is even at the present time.[61]

There was no end to the misery heaped on road freight transport in the late twenties. Annual licence fees and petrol tax were bad enough, but now came to life again the railway companies' desire to be able to operate road vehicles freely, regardless of whether the passengers or freight had seen, or would ever see, a railway station. The railways were, by this time, aware of the economies of mechanical road vehicles as compared with horse wagons and vans for collection and delivery services at stations. They did not move particularly energetically, however, to substitute motor for horse collection and delivery, which was alleged to be losing them £3.5 million per annum in the late 1920s. The railways owned just under 2000 motor freight vehicles at the end of 1922 when they had last sought road operating powers. They added about 100 lorries a year for the next three years and then, after 1925, they increased the rate. At the end of 1927 they already had some 2800 motor goods vehicles in service. The London Midland and Scottish Company, with 1592 motor vehicles, accounted for rather more than half of the total and the Great Western came next with 719. The other two big companies – the London and North-Eastern and the Southern had just over 500 between them. It is likely that these latter figures reflect the nature of the markets open to them in their respective territories – industrial freight or passengers – rather than any difference in policies.[62] It must be noted that these figures were quite trivial in relation to the 280,000-odd motor goods vehicles in operation in 1927 – the railways owned just about 1 per cent of the goods vehicles on the road. The number of mechanical road vehicles owned by the railways was small, too, in comparison with the number of horse-drawn vehicles they had. At the beginning of 1928 the railways had some 35,000 road vehicles of which only those 2800 were motor vehicles.

Road operators, then, were more worried by what might be in the future than by what the railways already had at the time they promoted their new bills in Parliament. Time and time again we hear reference to the size of the railway companies, their enormous resources, and to how easy it would be for them to drive out of business the hordes of small road freight firms. Major-General Sydney Long, Managing Director of Lever Brothers and Chairman of the Transport Committee of the Federation of British Industries, speaking for the Mansion House Association, told the Parliamentary Joint Committee of his thoughts. The Parliamentary Joint Committee was a normal feature when private bills were before Parliament. Such bills were given the usual Second Readings which, in essence, approved the principle, but the case would be argued in detail before the Joint Committee, which would call for interested parties to come forward and present their arguments for or against the bills. General Long thought that there would be a 'war of extermination between road and rail'. He did not apparently mind that part if it involved the cutting of railway rates. That war would exterminate the long-distance road haulers, who, he thought, were not of any great advantage to the country. There would be a railway monopoly in ten years' time, with the bulk of road traffic in railway hands. What did concern him, however, was the thought that 'one vast union of transport workers could bring the country to a standstill.[63] He was wrong, as subsequent history would show; but he was simply expressing the commonly held idea that the great power of the railways could destroy road transport.

The road transport interests were afraid of that danger. The railways, they knew, had always had powers to do collection and delivery work, and Sec. 49(1) of the Railways Act of 1921 had confirmed their full and unrestricted powers to carry goods by road to and from rail. Collection and delivery of goods had always been considered a legitimate ancillary part of railway transport. This C&D work had been done mainly by horse transport, which, as mentioned above, was still their mainstay. That the railways were now promoting bills before Parliament to obtain general powers to run mechanized road transport certainly gave the impression that they had something more in mind than just collection and delivery, and something more than the 'country' services they were running from a number of centres. So when the bills were deposited by the railways at the beginning of 1928 the road interests were quick to attack. The bills, said Mr E. Shrapnell-Smith of the CMUA, to a meeting of the Institute of Transport in Leeds in mid-January, 'are noteworthy for the wide scope of the powers sought therein and the absence of either limits or safeguards. They place no limit whatsoever upon that which the companies may do by road.' He feared the strengthening grip of the railway unions (just as much as did Major-General Long). He feared the flooding of the highways by excess vehicles. There was plenty of existing road transport to meet railway needs. Trade and industry demanded a non-railway alternative. Only mechanized road transport could stimulate the railway monopoly. Without a non-railway mechanized road transport traders would lose the benefit of 'exceptional rates' for what they did send by rail. Anyway, had not the Balfour-Browne majority in 1921 considered it undesirable to give the railways such powers?[64]

There was little to be gained by a reference to the earlier investigating committee. The *Commercial Motor*'s parliamentary correspondent reported a month later that the government was going to let the bills take their ordinary course in Parliament. It had certainly no intention of setting up a commission to investigate the issues involved, directly or indirectly.[65] So the bills got their Second Reading towards the end of February, after a good speech by the Minister of Transport. The main argument of the railways, he said, was equality of treatment.[66] So the vote was taken, with 357 in favour and only 42 against. The division was not on party lines. The number of votes in favour of the bills' being given the Second Reading was just a few less than the number of petitions (368) objecting to the grant of road powers, which came flooding in, from county and town councils, from chambers of commerce, from tram and bus companies, and, obviously, from road transport associations.[67]

Apart from the fear of the power of the rail unions and of the strength of the railways, there was uneasiness in other respects. If the railways continued to run their road services at a loss, or worse, cut road rates to compete with established road firms and thus, probably, make a bigger loss, what would be the consequence? Since the loss would reduce their total profit, would the Railway Rates Tribunal then allow a general increase in rates to ensure that the companies would earn the 'Standard Revenue'? This was the one thing that bothered the Association of Chambers of Commerce and which they discussed with the railway companies. The railways wrote to the Association on 9 February 1928 to assure them that 'the deficiency shall not be made good by an increase of railway rates and that the loss will fall upon the shareholders'. Other old questions kept cropping up, and in the same letter the railway companies assured the Association that it was not their intention to manufacture road vehicles if the requested powers were granted.[68]

The Joint Committee of the two Houses of Parliament set to work on the Bills at the end of April with a battery of barristers arguing the pros and cons. H.P. Macmillan, KC for the railways, argued that, in seeking powers to provide road services 'in any district to which they had access', they were not asking for anything unusual. The activities of the railways were not confined to the rails. Their scope had gradually been enlarged. They had started C&D services a long time back without parliamentary sanction. They provided sea transport too.[69]

Much of the argument before the Joint Committee centred on the parlous position of the railways and on road competition, and anticipated the arguments presented to the Royal Commission on Transport over the next couple of years. Much of the evidence, not unexpectedly, was partisan. Mr Shrapnel-Smith, for example, told the Committee that the £1.6 million paid annually as local rates by the railways towards the upkeep of roads, was 'a very small sum for the use they made of the roads'. He pointed to the £40 million paid by motor users, but he did not relate these amounts to the respective numbers of vehicles or the mileages run.[70] Mr Gosselin's line was that road haulage was in just as difficult a position as the railways. He had found that certain haulage firms with combined capital of over £186,000 had made a net profit of £3680 in 1925 – a return of only 1.9 per cent.[71]

Mr E. Charteris, KC, for the County Councils Association, contended that the railways' objective was not to serve the public need but rather to improve their revenue by recapturing traffic. The authorities he represented had submitted a clause for insertion in the bill, requiring that a railway company, before running a road service, should contribute towards the cost of adapting the road to the traffic it was proposed to carry.[72] That sounds as if some county councillors had long memories stretching back to the time when they could put a penalty charge on 'extraordinary traffic'.

So the arguments continued, and at the end of June 1928 the Joint

Committee announced that it found the preamble of the six Bills proven. According to H.P. Macmillan, KC, the railway case had emerged unscathed after 24 speeches and 16,700 questions,[73] though Stafford Cripps, KC, for the Federation of British Industries complained that the railways had put forward no details of what services they would run; of what classification of goods they would use; of what rates they would charge or of what capital expenditure they would undertake.[74]

The matter was practically finished on 12 July when the bills passed the Third Reading. Clause 3 was intact. 'The company may provide, own, work and use road vehicles, drawn or moved by animals, electrical or mechanical power in any district to which access is afforded by the system of the company.'[75] It was not many years after the weeks of work by those barristers that people were wondering what it was all about. For the railways really did very little in the road haulage field. Perhaps, for them, it was all worthwhile on the passenger side. It must certainly have been worthwhile to the several worthy King's Counsellors who argued their clients' cases so stubbornly.

Notes

1. *CM*, 30/6/1925, p.604, and 21/7/1925, p.707.
2. *CM*, 19/1/1926, pp.782–3.
3. *CM*, 14/10/1924, pp.254–5.
4. *CM*, 2/2/1926, p.827.
5. *CM*, 6/7/1926, p.637.
6. *CM*, 12/5/1925, p.394.
7. *CM*, 23/6/1925, p.574.
8. *CM*, 17/2/1920, p.682 and 19/10/1920.
9. *CM*, 30/8/1921, p.41 and 28/3/1922, ads p.25.
10. *CM*, 28/2/1922, p.37 and 14/3/1922, ads p.10.
11. *CM*, 9/10/1923, pp.222–3.
12. *CM*, 3/6/1924, p.497.
13. *CM*, 10/7/1928, p.704.
14. *CM*, 21/10/1924, p.285.
15. *CM*, 4/11/1924, p.337.
16. *CM*, 1/7/1924, p.628.
17. *CM*, 25/11/1924, p.439 and 23/12/1924, pp.578–9.
18. *CM*, 9/11/1926, pp.344–5.
19. *CM*, 3/6/1924, ads p.29; 18/10/1927, ads p.36; 6/11/1928, (back cover).
20. *CM*, 27/10/1925, pp.363–74.
21. *CM*, 14/7/1925, p.680.
22. *CM*, 7/7/1925, pp.657–8.
23. *CM*, 12/10/1926, p.210; 19/10/1926, p.239; and 1/11/1927, p.304.
24. *CM*, 11/12/1928, pp.549/560/561.
25. *CM*, 8/1/1924, p.700; 20/1/1925, p.697; 1/12/1925, p.554; 31/5/1927, p.484; and 1/5/1928, p.376.

26. *CM*, 24/1/1928, p.799.
27. *CM*, 12/2/1924, p.848.
28. *CM*, 20/4/1926, p.334.
29. *CM*, 29/4/1924, p.330.
30. *CM*, 20/1/1925, p.686.
31. *CM*, 3/3/1925, pp.79–81.
32. Ibid.
33. *CM*, 7/4/1925, p.236.
34. *CM*, 3/3/1925, pp.71–2; 21/4/1925, p.295; and 13/3/1928, p.98.
35. *CM*, 31/3/1925, p.232.
36. Geo. Glasgow, *General Strikes and Road Transport*, 1926 pp.22–3.
37. H. Pelling, *A History of British Trade Unionism*, p.177.
38. Cole and Postgate, *The Common People*, p.579.
39. Glasgow, *General Strikes*, p.32.
40. Ibid., pp.34–9.
41. Ibid., pp.55–9.
42. Ibid., p.115.
43. *The Times*, 3/5/1926, p.14.
44. *The Times*, 8/5/1926, p.2.
45. *CM*, 4/5/1926, p.375.
46. *The Times*, 8/5/1926, p.4.
47. *The Times*, 10/5/1926, p.2.
48. Ibid., p.4.
49. *The Times*, 10/5/1926, p.3 and 11/5/1926, p.3.
50. *The Times*, 15/5/1926, p.3 and 18/5/1926, p.8.
51. Glasgow, *General Strikes.*
52. Ibid., pp.85–6.
53. Ibid., p.115.
54. P.S. Bagwell, *The Transport Revolution*, p.208.
55. *CM*, 17/8/1926, p.820.
56. *CM*, 31/8/1926, p.39.
57. *CM*, 4/8/1925, p.766.
58. *CM*, 2/2/1926, p.826.
59. C.T. Brunner, *Road Versus Rail*, 1929, p.57.
60. *The Times*, 3/5/1926, p.10.
61. Parl. Debates. Commons. Vol. 216, Cols 855 et seq.
62. *CM*, 23/10/1928.
63. *CM*, 3/7/1928, pp.674/5.
64. *CM*, 17/1/1928, pp.772/3.
65. *CM*, 14/2/1928, p.917 and p.923
66. *CM*, 6/3/1928, p.65.
67. *CM*, 21/2/1928, p.9.
68. *CM*, 17/4/1928, p.309.
69. *CM*, 1/5/1928, p.373.
70. *CM*, 26/6/1928, p.647.
71. Ibid.
72. Ibid.
73. *CM*, 3/7/1928, pp.674–5.
74. Ibid.
75. *CM*, 24/7/1928, p.778.

CHAPTER TEN

The Coming of the Diesel

By the end of the 1920s the road haulage industry was well established.

Early in 1931 the *Roadways Goods Transport Guide* published lists of hundreds of haulage firms throughout the United Kingdom, mostly with some information about their fleets. There is no way of knowing just how complete it was. No doubt there were many small proprietors whose reading did not include the trade press and who, therefore, did not know of the impending publication. Many of these would probably have been included in the editions of subsequent years as they became aware of the publicity value of the *Guide.* Whatever the deficiencies of the first edition, the *Guide* does provide a useful picture of the road haulage industry in 1930, after a decade of rapid development and before subsequent legislation would put severe restriction on the industry's expansion.

Obviously it is not easy to summarize nearly 800 pages of detailed listings of firms and their advertisements into a page or two of text or tables. For one thing, many firms having branches or depots in different cities appear more than once in the list, sometimes with the same details of fleets and their work shown against each entry. On other occasions slightly different fleet details would appear, so that it is difficult to decide whether the intention was to give details of the fleets normally based in each city. Sometimes fleet details are shown but as an agency. A number of firms did not give any details whatever of their fleets. Carter Paterson's entry merely stated that the firm had 1600-odd vehicles of 'various' types and that they dealt with express parcels deliveries and luggage, but there is no information as to capacity. Pickford simply said that they had a 'very large fleet' with capacities from 1 to 100 tons. The entry for McNamara is a little more informative. They claimed to have had 50 plus vehicles from 1 to 10 tons capacity and 70 plus 6-wheelers from 13 to 30 tons. Sutton & Co. had 100 vehicles from 1 to 10 tons' capacity while Hayes Wharf had 'a very large fleet'. The tables in Appendix I attempt to summarize the data for the major cities, so far as the information given in the listings allows. The 875 London firms which gave details showed a total of 9386 vehicles with a total capacity of 43,994 tons, which puts the average vehicle capacity between 4 and 5 tons. But there were 55 firms (including big ones like Pickford, mentioned earlier) which did not give sufficient information for statistical calculation. That 43,994 tons, however, was not the total capacity – even allowing for Pickford and others. A great many firms had trailers, but unfortunately the listings generally do not say how many trailers nor what capacity; so trailers are not counted in the capacity statistics here.

One firm included in these tables and calculations was Coulson, which listed 3 heavy traction engines, 2 heavy tractors (steam), 2 light tractors (steam), 1 x 20 ton steam wagon, 1 x 5 ton steam wagon, 1 x 100 ton trailer, 1 x 60, 1 x 50, 1 x 25 and 12 x 5–10 ton trailers. Apart from their couple of steam wagons their capacity was all in trailers, and these have been excluded for reasons mentioned above. This firm is one of the few that mention steam specifically. Apart from this one, only 29 others in London's 930 firms mentioned steam wagons and only four showed steam wagons as forming more than half their fleet. (And three of the four had only a total of eight vehicles of all kinds). These 29 other firms had a total of 524 petrol vehicles and 139 steam wagons. The steam wagons were as follows:

Capacity (tons)	5	6	7	8	10	12	15	20	unspecified
Number of vehicles	7	9	1	9	84	4	10	1	14

The steamers were clearly in the 'heavy' category in comparison with the general average of 4–5 tons but the fact that there were only 141 (that is, 139 plus Coulson's 2) in a total of over 9000 vehicles in London points to the fact that steam was already in a proportionately minor position before the events which are usually quoted as the cause of their decline – the advent of diesels, speed limits in the 1930 Act, the recommendation of the Royal Commission that they ought to be banned, or the punitive taxation from 1933.

Most firms listed their business as 'General traffic' or 'General and Furniture'. Parcels, heavy machinery and perishables also are well represented, with a major part of the firms offering to work in several or all of these categories. There was not much complete specialization, except in 'Furniture'. Of London's 900-odd firms, 77 listed only 'Furniture' as their traffic. A couple would carry 'Pianos' and three more 'Pianos and Furniture'. Nine firms would carry 'meat' – and those mainly within the London area . Four firms specialized in carrying 'Films' and one mentioned only 'Horses' (it had ten horse-boxes). Only one firm, with 8 tons' capacity, stated its business as 'period contracts'. There were, undoubtedly, many more doing this, as Shrapnell-Smith had told the Royal Commission. 'Some of the big firms who have their own fleets additionally give 100% work to contractors' fleets, which are not doing general haulage' (Minutes of Evidence. Minute No.4726 – see next chapter).

As to where they would go, almost exactly 500 of London's firms said they would go 'anywhere' (and this included several small firms with, say, a couple of 1-tonners). The remaining 400-odd generally put limits on their sphere of operations – The Docks, London only, Home Counties, London plus 50 miles, South Coast, Midlands, and so on. A few were quite specific –

'Southampton' said one firm with 16 big vehicles. 'Birmingham' said another with its 111 tons of capacity spread over 22 vehicles. Of course, it may well be that these firms, in stating their geographical limitations and traffic carried, were simply stating what they normally did. In a severely competitive market firms were hardly likely to turn away a paying load if it was outside the scope of their normal operations. One further feature of the time was that regular services had been well established but surprisingly few mentioned the fact. One firm with 150 x 30 cwt (vans?) ran twice daily with express parcels to London suburbs. One firm offering to carry 'General, Heavy Machinery, Bulk Liquids, Perishables specified 'Bi-weekly' to 'Midlands and South'; another carrying 'Furniture and Pianos' ran daily to destinations within 50 miles of its London depot and weekly up to 200 miles distant. Probably the majority regarded the matter of regularity as so obvious as not to require statement.

The road haulage industry was about to undergo significant changes at the hands of inventors and of legislators.

The petrol engine had, by now, had a life story stretching over some fifty years and had been improved beyond the wildest dreams of the pioneers. From the early struggles to make the 'horseless carriages' go, the engine had now been developed to such a stage that it could propel very much more certainly the big vehicles of 10 or 12 tons or more. But while Lenoir and Otto and others had wrestled to develop an effective engine, there were different ideas as to how that might be accomplished. In particular, Rudolph Diesel had put forward in 1890 the idea that an engine might work through the simple expedient of compressing air in a cylinder until it became very hot, and then injecting heavy oil into the hot air. The heat of the compressed air would ignite the oil and the resultant explosion would move the piston. There were problems with this idea, certainly. In the petrol engine the fuel was sucked in by the vacuum created by one of the four strokes – the induction stroke – of the cycle. But that would not work with Dr Diesel's system given that, at the time the fuel had to go in, the cylinder would already be full of highly compressed air. So the fuel had to be injected either by an air blast or a mechanical pump of some kind. Diesel, a German, though born in Paris, patented his idea in 1892 and had an engine working by 1897 and from then on it was a question of development and refinement.

It should be pointed out here that although today we know 'heavy oil', or 'compression-ignition', engines as 'diesels', there are disputes as to who really invented the system and who produced the first working model. As in the case of many other inventions the idea seems to have been around a long time. It was said of compression-ignition, in particular, that it 'had been known and used for centuries before by the Asiatics in connection with their fire producers'.[1] The Asiatics, whoever they were, had not turned their knowledge towards the making of an engine. That was left to Western people.

E.L. Cornwell said of the first working engine that there were many conflicting claims but the balance of available evidence appeared to show that 'the first practicable compression-ignition engine in the world was developed and built in England by Herbert Akroyd Stuart in 1890 following naturally the Priestman Brothers' work of a few years earlier'. He went on to say that the Stuart engine was put into production by Richard Hornsby & Son as the Hornsby–Akroyd in 1892.[2] Some of the dispute seems to centre, in part at least, on the method of getting the fuel into the cylinder – how and when. Diesel, it seems, had originally been working with coal-dust as a fuel and had tried an air-blast to inject it. Failing with coal-dust he turned to oil as the fuel but continued with his air-blast equipment which he had to hand. So where others used mechanical pumps instead, they could say their engine was not a diesel. But Diesel did not mention air-blasts in his patent application,[3] and the Hornsby–Akroyd patent pumped in the fuel at a different point in the cycle, using a lamp to heat the combustion chamber. This latter certainly worked though it had its critics.[4]

Initially the compression-ignition engine was quite heavy – much heavier than a petrol engine – because a fairly robust structure was needed to cope with the high compression, and because moving parts like crankshafts and connecting rods were heavier than for petrol engines. There were difficulties, too, in getting it to run at different speeds because of the problem of varying the minute amounts of fuel that had to be injected into the cylinder. So the engine was used initially in applications where considerable weight and problems of engine speed would not be so disadvantageous as in road transport. Marine work could cope with these disadvantages, as could the usage in stationary engines, and it was in these applications that the engine had a fair amount of success up to the First World War. Temple Press, the proprietors of *Commercial Motor* installed a diesel engine in their premises just before the war started, to provide for their power and lighting needs and so that journal thereafter campaigned indefatigably for the adaptation of the engine to road transport purposes.[5] Diesel himself had tried to produce a suitable engine for road transport right up until his death in 1913, when he was lost overboard from a cross-channel steamer. Mr Cornwell tells us that Diesel and Saurer, the Swiss manufacturer, combined to produce an engine design which was built by another Swiss firm in 1908–09 and that MAN 'exhibited a road-vehicle diesel engine' at Turin in 1911 and Berlin in 1912.[6]

Early work had centred, as we saw, around the problems of how to get a controlled amount of fuel into the cylinder, whether by Diesel's air-blast method or some form of mechanical pump; of the design of the combustion chamber; and of whether an ante-chamber (pre-combustion chamber) should be used. The British commercial-vehicle press was, perhaps, too excited about the rapidly improving petrol engine – for example in London buses – to give much thought to the heavy oil engine; and the World War turned inventive talent in other directions from August 1914 until the end of 1918. Once the dust had settled and some semblance of normal life had returned, the developers could get to work again to try to produce an engine suitable for road transport vehicles – that is, a lightweight engine whose speed could be varied at will. Alas, this was not in Britain, although it seems that some work was done (for airship engines?) at the Royal Aircraft Establishment at Farnborough in the early 1920s.

Little was heard on the topic for the first three or four years of the decade. In its issue of 29 April 1924 *Commercial Motor* cautiously announced that 'We believe that a distinct forward step has been taken by a concern with a world-wide reputation.' Just what the step was, or what was the name of the firm, they did not reveal; but they went on to describe the basic details of what compression-ignition was all about.[7] A few months later, near the end of the year, they tantalized readers a little bit more by saying that they hoped soon to be able to release details of a diesel engine by a reputable manufacturer. This engine would be suitable for commercial vehicles. 'The makers of the engine we have in mind have aimed at the production of a power unit that can start on these heavy fuels from dead cold, and in this, we believe, they have succeeded.' Again, the journal was secretive about names.[8]

When the press did get around to mentioning actual names they were German – MAN, Benz, Daimler (whose technical director was one Dr Porsche); and the hope of *Commercial Motor* mentioned in the previous paragraph had 'not been fulfilled'.[9] At the end of 1925 came the news that Benz were putting on the market a 2-cylinder engine for lorry or tractor. This was said to produce 30 h.p. at 800 r.p.m. The Berlin Motor Show just then, however, did not show much evidence that the very considerable amount of experimentation by several firms was producing much in the way of actual workable results. There was only one chassis displayed with a diesel engine. This was a MAN chassis with a 45–50 h.p. engine.[10] The German firms kept at the problem, for there was clearly a great harvest to be reaped. At that time it seemed that virtually any kind of heavy oil could be used and the oil was cheap; the engine worked at a much better thermal efficiency than petrol engines, and even at a fairly low rate of revolutions per minute the engine could develop great torque. Even before a petrol tax was applied to petrol in Britain, people were being regaled with promises of fuel costs per mile being only a quarter of those for petrol – with the additional merit of an engine which could start easily on cold mornings and lift a load at low speed. Any hopes that British manufacturers would be getting involved were unfounded at this stage. Indeed, when in late 1926 the question was raised at a meeting of the Institute of Automobile Engineers as to what Britain was doing about diesels, no reply was forthcoming.[11]

If British manufacturers were waiting to see, the French were now taking steps. One firm near Paris, which made oil engines for motor-boats to the design of an Italian called Bagnulo was happy enough to do just that, but Bagnulo, himself was working on one for lorries. *Commercial Motor*, having examined it, were 'favourably impressed'. Peugeot, too, were trying; and late in 1926 we heard of an engine described as a 'Peugeot–Tartrais, which has actually been employed for some time on a Paris bus'. There was also a 'Montazet' engine whose rights were bought by Germany.[12] The Swiss Saurer firm was hard at work, too. The following summer (1927) saw the editor of *Commercial Motor* complaining that while Britain was usually quick enough to take up a new idea

> We seem, however, to pay altogether too little regard to the claims of the diesel. ... Motor manufacturers are content to regard the petrol-consuming engine as sufficiently satisfactory for the moment whilst commercial motor users are, again for the moment, content with the price of the fuel they are using ... [but, and here was the point of the article] We know of no British commercial motor manufacturer who has done more than to establish in his research department a file of published information on the matter.[13]

That accusation was levelled only three months after plans had been announced in America for a 24-hour race for oil-engined cars. Obviously progress was being made in America as well as on the Continent.[14] The grouse by the editor of this road transport magazine is understandable, for only a month earlier the news pages of the journal reported that even Belgium was achieving success with the 'Held' engine. This had been tested on a Citroen chassis which did roughly 23 m.p.g., averaged nearly 30 m.p.h., and 'approaches more closely to the true diesel than anything of the kind which we have yet seen'.[15]

It all came to a head with the Olympia show in November 1927 where a 5-ton Mercedes–Benz was displayed with a 6-cylinder diesel engine. The advertisements at the time modestly claimed that it was 'revolutionary', that it would save 50 per cent in fuel costs.[16] According to the 1929 edition of the *Transport Managers' Year Book*, this first ever diesel-engined lorry, that is, as 'a production job', arrived in London on 30 April 1928. By the time it was written up in the *Year Book* it had already done 15,000 miles, always with a full 5-ton load. It averaged 14 m.p.g. and 24 m.p.h. though its top speed on the level was 38 m.p.h. It took less than a minute to get it started on the coldest of days and only 30 seconds in spring and summer. This, said Capt. Goddard, the writer of the article, was 'undoubtedly the most reliable and economical machine ever put on the road'. Furthermore, 'it will run on diesel oil, gas oil, solar oil, tar oil, ordinary fuel oil, and even simple lubricating oil if necessary'. The article goes on to say that the first one supplied to a customer for ordinary regular service – a 1500-gallon tanker – was put into commission on 1 January 1929. That there was only one in commercial service at this time was put down to two factors – the price, which included transport costs from Germany and a heavy import duty, and inherent conservatism. Despite the high capital cost, 'so much above the ruling price for a petrol lorry', there were big savings to be made. A contractor with four wagons doing a total of 200,000 miles per year would, it was claimed, save £530 on fuel alone and another £400 on maintenance and tyres, practically the cost, on one year's work, of a new petrol 5-tonner.[17] Maybe; but a Mercedes–Benz 10-tonner would have cost £1775, which was big money in mid-1929.

Commercial Motor, a long-time advocate of diesel for road transport, had been equally enthusiastic when their staff had an opportunity to witness tests back in the summer of 1928. (Some of the *Year Book* information may have come from the same tests.) The magazine had commented on the variety of possible fuels, and on the quick starting. There was no question of warming up in the ordinary sense. The engine was started from cold in 28 seconds and the vehicle was immediately driven off, displaying remarkable acceleration. There was no carburettor, no magneto, which was just as well, for 'statistics show that 33⅓% of breakdowns on vehicles are caused by ignition and carburation'. The vehicle could take a trailer, too, and with 15 tons' payload could still do 8 m.p.g. So the editor concluded that 'We consider this type of power unit presents unbounded possibilities ... We expect to see very rapid progress with the heavy oil engine. It has arrived at a propitious time and may easily mark a new era in transport development.'[18] In its 'Outlook' issue on 1 January 1929 the editor summed up: 'The situation regarding the diesel engine is somewhat obscure. Many designers appear to be sitting on the fence, but we know that important makers are alive to its possibilities. Actual engines are under test.' He went on, 'As it stands at present it would appear that the diesel engine possesses great possibilities for use in connection with goods vehicles.' He thought it would be some considerable time before it would be quiet enough for passenger use.

The RAC tested one of the Mercedes–Benz diesel lorries further between 10 and 15 September 1928. The first day was devoted to checking the facility of starting the engine, and the fuel consumption. The heating element was used for the first couple of starts. The first, time from cold it was used for 30 seconds and the next time 22 seconds with the engine starting 9 seconds later. None of the remaining sixteen starts took longer than two seconds. A trailer was attached that day for the 51½ mile test run from Cricklewood. The total payload was 12 tons 5½ cwt and the gross 19 tons 15½ cwt. The average running speed of this outfit was 7.9 m.p.h. and the fuel consumption of 6.58 m.p.g. worked out as 80.8 net ton-miles per gallon. On the subsequent days starting time was checked again. Ten starts were made from cold, the longest taking 48 seconds and the shortest 19 seconds but none of the other 48 (warm) starts took longer than 4 seconds. No trailer was used on these days and the vehicle ran with a payload of 6 tons 5¾ cwt. The 691¾ miles showed 13.48 miles to the gallon, which was equal to 84.7 net ton-miles to the gallon. The exhaust was checked, too, for there had been a great deal of talk about smell, and in Germany, earlier on, there had been bother with the police in regard to the emissions. But the RAC found no noticeable smoke during steady running and only a slight emission of 'odorous smoke' when the gears and engine speed were being changed.[19] It would appear that these tests demonstrated that at last a real competitor to the petrol engine had arrived; and very soon after the 1928 summer test the LGOC began serious work. In retrospect it seems odd that the first attempts had been made virtually at the same time as the first petrol cars were getting going, yet it was forty years before the diesel could compete seriously. The First World War can account for only a small part of that period. Maybe it was just easier to improve the petrol engine than to struggle with the difficulties of compression-ignition, notwithstanding the constant cries of the impending exhaustion of petrol supplies.

That 'first-ever' diesel vehicle in commercial service mentioned by the *Year Book,* the 1500-gallon petrol tanker, was at the Sunderland depot of Major & Co. Ltd. A transport press mention on 8 January 1929 of its coming into service provoked a letter from Saurer to say that 'a 5AD-type Saurer (which is our 6-ton model) with diesel engine fitted was actually in service with one of our largest users in October last, and has been in service ever since'. Captain Goddard, however, replied saying that the vehicle was not on the market generally. It was evidently an experimental machine on test.[20] Several years later the managing director of Saurer would say, in an article, that deliveries of Saurer oil-engined lorries were made to prominent customers in England in October 1928. He added that the customers were to record working results for the guidance of the manufacturers and that Saurers would meet any maintenance costs beyond the level experienced for petrol lorries.[21] Though Monsieur Saurer used the plural 'lorries', his remarks seem to bear out Goddard's contention that these were, indeed, experimental vehicles.

Anyway, diesels were now beginning to be talked about and things did eventually happen. They could have happened sooner, according to William Beardmore & Co. That firm, for long engaged in the manufacture of diesels for railcars and other purposes, was stung by allegations of lethargy of British manufacturers. According to an article written in the summer of 1928 Beardmore had pointed out that the firm had been perfectly willing during the previous two or three years to supply engines which could have been put into immediate service in road vehicles, and with guaranteed performance. They had received very little encouragement in Britain. They had offered small railcar engines to British lorry manufacturers but, in the words of the article, 'without the negotiations coming to fruition'.[22] In November 1928 Richard Garrett, better known in relation to steam traction, installed unspecified oil engines in a couple of test vehicles – a 4-wheeler and a 6-wheeler – for Barford & Perkins of Peterborough.[23] In the Spring of 1929 Kerr Stuart & Co. of Stoke started trials with a 7-ton chassis (later, stated to be the first British diesel lorry), using a 4cylinder engine built by J.&H. McLaren. When that engine was displayed at Olympia later in the year it was described as a McLaren–Benz.[24]

Another attack on British manufacturers came in a letter from E.W. Goslett, for Mercedes–Benz, to *Commercial Motor*, published on 14 January 1930. The topic was smoke emissions from diesels, but Mr Goslett complained, in his letter, that the RAC had dropped, at the request of one or two English manufacturers, road trials proposed the previous year. He went on, 'The small amount of organized scientific research carried out in many of the English works, as compared with what is done abroad, is appalling.' Whatever the big manufacturers were doing, we find Frank H. Dutson (Leeds) Ltd displaying several diesel-engined vehicles at the Great Yorkshire Show at Hull in the summer of 1930. Mr Dutson and his chief engineer, T.H. Parkinson, had installed Gardner engines in an RAF Leyland, a Saurer 8-tonner and a Berna 8-tonner. The Leyland had been road-tested first – chassis only – showing, for its 4 tons odd, a respectable 17.3 miles per gallon. This enterprising firm then tried out the complete vehicle over a 48-mile route to the north of Leeds which included gradients of 1 in 6 and 1 in 8. With a payload of 4 tons 10 cwt and a gross weight of 8 tons 13 cwt the vehicle completed the run on 3 gallons, that is, 16 m.p.g., which works out at 72 net ton-miles per gallon. It was claimed that on this basis a 4½-ton load from Leeds to London would have incurred only 5s. (25p) for fuel. Dutson did not leave it at that but made more tests, including the climb over Shap in Cumbria with a 6½-ton load, with satisfactory results.[25] As usual it was passenger vehicles that made the news. At the same time as Dutson was trying out his freight vehicles, Sheffield Corporation were bringing into use a Mercedes–Benz bus, Barton Brothers were using Gardner and Blackstone engines in four 32-seater buses, and the LGOC had an AEC bus in service.[26]

The publicised action was mostly on the part of users – some small at that. An intriguing 'small ad' appeared in October 1930:

> Several 4–5 ton lorries with new bodies, new 38" x 7" tyres, new 50 h.p. diesel engines, with a consumption of 14–16 miles per gallon (4½d gal.) chassis in first class order, with electric lighting set, complete and ready for the road, £595, running 600 miles per week the year's fuel bill will not exceed £40; this is the most reliable and the cheapest transport ever produced. Box No . ...

It looks as if small engineering firms were getting in on the act. Three months later one such firm, Gurney & Ewer of Ruislip, were running small advertisements to the effect that 'the Blackstone all-British heavy-oil engine may now be fitted to any make of lorry with remarkable reduction in the cost of fuel'.[27] Vehicle manufacturers, whatever the allegations, were doing something, even if not making the headlines. Sir John Thornycroft told the company's AGM in November 1930 that the company had been running experimental vehicles for some time.[28]

That November of 1930, too, AEC had 'heavy-oil' engines optionally available for six of their eight chassis, including a Mammoth 6-ton Tipper at £1437 and a 7/8-tonner for £1467. *Commercial Motor* reported on 25 November 1930 its road test of an AEC Majestic 6-tonner. The 6-cylinder engine could be started from cold in 14 to 20 seconds and instantly if warm. The test was carried out with the chassis weighing 4 tons 3 cwt, a body of 1 ton 0 cwt 3 qrs, a payload of 6 tons and the driver and two observers 3 cwt 3 qrs. This all came to a gross of 11 tons 7 cwt 2 qrs and with this the vehicle was able to accelerate from rest to 26.1 m.p.h. in 36 seconds, using second, third and top gears and from 8.7 m.p.h. to 26.1 in 30 seconds using top gear. In top gear the lorry ran at various speeds from 6.09 m.p.h. to 39.15 m.p.h. (though a policeman stopped one on a demonstration run on the Great West Road out of London when it was alleged to be doing 45 m.p.h.). Fuel consumption worked out at 9.45 m.p.g. of gas oil for the test run of just under 40 miles, giving just over 107 gross, and 56.7 net, ton-miles per gallon. Compare this performance with that of a well-known make of petrol vehicle which was tested a couple of weeks earlier. The petrol 5-tonner, which grossed 9 tons 13 cwt 1 qr for the test averaged 6.95 m.p.g. which equals 67.13 gross and 34.75 net, ton miles per gallon.[29] As always, enthusiasts fastened on any evidence available to highlight the wonders of the new engine. In September 1929 *Commercial Motor* took evident pleasure in reporting from Yorkshire that a Mercedes–Benz 6-tonner diesel carrying 1600 gallons of petrol had been called upon to tow a broken-down petrol lorry, itself laden with 1100 gallons of petrol. The report emphasized that the gross load hauled for 100 miles was 21 tons and pointed to the diesel's 'enormous reserve of power'.[30]

So the diesel had arrived. It had a better rate of fuel consumption per mile than an equivalent petrol engine and, for the moment, the diesel fuel was cheaper in itself than petrol and free of tax. But the capital cost of such a vehicle was high and there was a considerable element of the unknown. Indeed, as late as the autumn of 1931, a regular writer in *Commercial Motor*, faced with direct questions from readers, could only advise the smaller firms with one or two lorries to go cautiously and leave it to the larger firms to try out the new engine. If you had only one vehicle and that was a diesel which went wrong, then you were in trouble. But someone with twenty or thirty vehicles could probably weather the storm if one of those proved unsatisfactory. 'I believe', said the writer mentioned, 'that the oil-engined chassis is rapidly reaching a stage at which it may be said to be as reliable and as useful ... as the average petrol chassis'. There was no knowing, however, when fuel suppliers would push up the price of heavy oil. There was no knowing when (it would be 'when' rather than 'if') the Chancellor, ever hungry for revenue, would tax heavy oil fuel. There were technical points, too. Cylinders wore rather more rapidly than in the case of petrol engines, as rings were adapted to try to stop fuel escaping, under high compression ratios, into the lubricating oil. The consumption of lubricating oil was said to be twice that of a petrol engine. The fuel-injection pump mechanism required as much attention as a carburettor, though there was less need for decarbonizing and valve-grinding. These technical pros and cons about balanced each other but there was always the fact that depreciation and interest on first cost were based on that initially high capital cost; and as for the additional weight, that might call for heavier tyres and might just push the chassis over the line into a higher taxation class.[31]

These points in themselves would make adoption by the haulage industry rather slow, but there were other factors. The article writer did not need to remind his readers of the cut-throat competition within the haulage industry, nor that the railways were now fighting back to recover traffic. Some of the readers, too, might have known that industrial production was sagging, with the index of production dropping 8 per cent between 1929 and 1930. Hauliers were in a dilemma. They saw the prospect of greatly reduced running costs something they badly needed in their battle for survival (for too many of them fuel cost was the main criterion for judging success); and on the other hand was the known heavy capital cost and the fears of the unknown prospects for the economy in general and the diesel engine in particular.

It may well be that it was not just the hauliers who were affected by the uncertainty surrounding possible fuel prices and possible taxation on diesel fuel in the late 1920s. For manufacturers, too, their markets must have been uncertain, and they may have deemed it wise to hasten slowly in developing diesels. There was the Sword of Damocles of a Road Traffic Act that never seemed to materialize with who knows what new Construction and Use Regulations to come. The recently appointed Royal Commission would have views on that, but no one knew what sort of recommendations would come from it about control or limitation of road traffic. It was not a propitious time to launch revolutionary but high-cost products. Despite having reasonable cause for hastening slowly, several manufacturers decided to risk it. When the Tenth (biennial) International Commercial Motor Exhibition was held at Olympia in November 1931 there were fourteen manufacturers with heavy-oil engines in their exhibits; and only two of the manufacturers were foreign (that is, if Armstrong–Saurer is counted as British). But at the previous show in 1929 there had been only three manufacturers with such engines, and those were all foreign firms. In 1931 all the well-known names were there – AEC, Crossley, Foden, Guy, Leyland, Pagefield, Thornycroft, and Tilling–Stevens (TS Ltd), as well as one or two less well known such as Hardy and Gilford. It is noteworthy that some of the fourteen firms were famous in the making of steam wagons, for example Fowler and Garrett. One who had clearly seen the writing on the wall as far as steam was concerned (for the number of steam wagons on the road had been dropping slowly but surely), was Mr E.R. Foden, who resigned from the Board of the steam-wagon manufacturers when they announced that 'we honestly feel that we should be better keeping to steam'. He set up his own business, under the name ERF, in the same town to produce diesels using standard parts – Gardner engine, David Brown gearbox and so on, and his first production models rolled out in September 1933.[32]

Of the fourteen manufacturers exhibiting diesel-engined vehicles, some were offering passenger vehicles, as might be expected (AEC, Gilford, Guy) but the majority of the diesel exhibits were freight vehicles and mostly in the bigger capacities. True, Mercedes, Pagefield, and TS Ltd had 4-tonners on display, but most were 6-tonners. Even bigger was the Hardy, a 6-wheeled 8-tonner (with an AEC engine). One of the Armstrong–Saurers was a 6-cylinder, for a 6-wheeled lorry of 11–12 tons' capacity; and the Leyland Rhino on show was a 12½-tonner. Mercedes, too, had a 12-tonner.[33] No doubt the bigger vehicles were better able to cope with a heavy engine and the heavier moving parts. With such a display of confidence by the makers, road haulage operators could not but be impressed, and slowly but surely the diesel, or heavy-oil, or compression-ignition, engine would forge ahead. It would take years, but the petrol engine would inevitably be displaced.

Notes

1. *CM*, 28/10/1930, p.375.
2. E.L. Cornwell, *Commercial Road Vehicles*, p.105.
3. *CM*, 11/11/1930, pp.446–7.
4. *CM*, 13/12/1927, p.619.
5. *CM*, 22/11/1927, p.448.
6. Cornwell, *Commercial Road Vehicles*, pp.107–8.
7. *CM*, 29/4/1924, p.324.
8. *CM*, 9/12/1924, p.498.
9. *CM*, 6/1/1925, p.620; and 8/9/1925, pp.94–5.
10. *CM*, 1/12/1925, p.559 and 8/12/1925, p.593.
11. *CM*, 23/11/1926, p.451.
12. *CM*, 26/1/1926, pp.806–7 and 9/11/1926, p.353.

13. *CM*, 2/8/1927, p.771.
14. *CM*, 3/5/1927, p.342.
15. *CM*, 5/7/1927, pp.650–51.
16. *CM*, 8/11/1927, ads p.68; and 22/11/1927, pp.447–8 and ads p.96.
17. *Transport Manager's Year Book*, 1929, p.43.
18. *CM*, 12/6/1928, pp.580–1.
19. *CM*, 2/10/1928, p.213.
20. *CM*, 8/1/1929, p.689; 12/2/1929, p.878; and 26/2/1929, p.89.
21. *CM*, 10/11/1931, pp.438/9.
22. *CM*, 3/7/1928, p.684.
23. *CM*, 3/12/1929, p.630.
24. *CM*, 22/10/1929, p.314–5, and 19/11/1929, p.544.
25. *CM*, 22/7/1930, pp.808, 817.
26. Ibid.
27. *CM*, 21/10/1930, ads p.57; and 17/2/1931, ads p.68.
28. *CM*, 25/11/1930, p.496.
29. *CM*, 4/11/1930, pp.388–9 and 25/11/1930, pp.508–9.
30. *CM*, 3/9/1929, p.66.
31. *CM*, 1/9/1931, pp.90–1.
32. TV. Broadcast, *Classic Trucks*, Channel 4, 17/1/1995.
33. *CM*, 10/11/1931, pp.450 et seq.

CHAPTER ELEVEN

What to Do About it All

A major event of the late 1920s was the appointment of a Royal Commission to look into the whole problem of transport. The number of vehicles on the roads had grown enormously – private cars and commercial vehicles, passenger and goods. The cost of road improvements and maintenance had increased considerably and, despite tax rises on road vehicles, ratepayers were feeling the pinch. Nobody likes rate increases, especially when someone else appears to be getting the benefit. The accident rate was growing. People were becoming alarmed at the carnage, and road safety became a regular topic of discussion in the press and elsewhere. Road transport was, in some respects, an evil. Lurid tales were told of competing buses racing each other recklessly to get to the next group of passengers. Railways were suffering a loss of traffic, not only because of economic depression, but also because of these buses and lorries; they were crying 'Foul!' Public opinion echoed Churchill's views about Britain's wonderful railways, regarding them with a veneration approaching that bestowed on the Monarchy, the Church and Motherhood. They could not be allowed to perish.

No doubt the competition, both within the industry and against the railways, was cut-throat and it was a question of survival of the fittest in a dangerous jungle. There were a great many sound and reputable firms in that jungle, but there were many, too, who ran poorly maintained, even dangerous, vehicles; overloading them, paying poor wages, cutting freight rates to an uneconomic level and generally making life difficult for everyone. Apart from anything else the regulations under which road transport had to operate were certainly badly out of date – the improvements in the mechanical efficiency of vehicles, of the quality of pneumatic tyres, and of the roads they ran on, having left the legislators far behind. A couple of Departmental Committee Reports in the early 1920s had been pigeon-holed. Manufacturers were uneasy, not knowing when, or what, new regulations would be coming. So from all quarters the cry went up to successive governments for some action, and at last, after much procrastination, a Royal Commission was appointed in July 1928. It may well be that the appointment was simply to postpone decision-making as cynics allege; there was that endlessly postponed Road Traffic Bill, for example. (Sadly, between 1921, when Sir Eric Geddes resigned, and 1931, when Herbert Morrison came in, the Minister of Transport did not have a seat in the Cabinet.) There were complex problems for the Commission to struggle with. Governments had never before had to cope with such numbers of vehicles; with the problem of competition between two major carriers; with the technical problems of vehicle speed and fitness inherent in the question of the safety of the public on the roads; nor with the problem of providing fit roads at a reasonable cost for those hordes of vehicles.

The terms of reference given to the Royal Commission were:

> to take into consideration the problems arising out of the growth of road traffic and with a view to securing the employment of the available means ... to the greatest public advantage, to consider and report what measures, if any, should be adopted for their better regulation and control, and so far as is desirable in the public interest to consider their co-ordinated working and development.

There are echoes here of the 1918 Road Transport Board and the inclusion of a reference to 'co-ordinated working' met the wishes of many who saw road transport as merely an appendage of the railways, feeding passengers and freight to the nearest railway-station or delivering these from the stations to their final destination. Road interests were not directly represented in the membership, though Sir Arthur Griffith-Boscawen, the Chairman, had been a former President of the National Association of Traction Engine Owners and Users, and a member, for a number of years, of the Standing Joint Committee of Mechanical Road Transport Associations. Mr Lobjoit, too, had had connections with road transport. The Royal Commission was appointed in July 1928 but did not get to work until late in the year.

Much of the evidence offered to the Royal Commission was disappointing. The bulk of it was already known to anyone who took an interest in the transport scene and read newspapers regularly. It would not surprise anyone, for example, that trade unions would argue for control and/or nationalization; or that railway unions would call for wages and conditions of service in road haulage to be brought up to the levels prevailing on the railways. The way some railwaymen, at least, were thinking was shown by the straightforward statement by Mr C.T. Cramp of the National Union of Railwaymen on Day 7. Mr Cramp was quite clear. He thought that the number of vehicles on the roads should be definitely kept down unless it could be shown that they were absolutely needed in the interests of industry and trade. He was referring to public carriers (Minutes of Evidence – Minutes 2207 and 2208). He wanted the Minister of Transport to be given power to decide whether particular goods ought to go by road or by rail (whatever the owners of the goods might wish) (Minute 2211).

Unfortunately, too, a great deal of the evidence was unsubstantiated opinion or merely anecdotal. There was not a great deal of solid statistical or accounting information. Indeed, the chairman of the Royal Commission commented on the inadequacy of evidence when Sir Josiah Stamp (Chairman of L.M.S. Railway) was answering questions on the memorandum which the railways had placed before the Royal Commission. 'I have read this Memorandum', said the Chairman,

> which I think I may say is largely a matter of opinion. It may be perfectly accurate opinion, but you have not, as a schoolboy, done the working. You say that the railways have suffered, by reason of the road traffic, disabilities, and so on. That may be admitted, but you have not shown to us to what extent they have suffered, what parts of the railway, what parts of the traffic, what sections of the line. (Minutes of Evidence, Day 4. 19 Dec. 1928, Minute No.1636)

To be fair to Sir Josiah and the railways, the Chairman of the Commissioners might have said much the same to many more of the witnesses. But that was quite early on in the proceedings, before the Chairman had had time to get used to the kind of evidence which would be laid before him.

The railways, through the memorandum they submitted and through their witnesses, made a number of points:

1. That road traffic was not bearing its fair share of road costs. It was being subsidized by the ratepayers. Whereas the railways had had to provide their own track and signalling system from their own capital, road traffic had had theirs provided by the ratepayers amongst whom the railways were included.
2. The railways were handicapped. They carried heavy industrial traffic which contributed little above the cost of haulage. But the higher rated traffic which they also carried, which did contribute, was subject to road competition. Sir Josiah referred to 'a competitor who can dart in and out and sting like a gnat, and take the things that appeal to him' (Minute 1053).
3. The railways were handicapped, too, by a series of obligations imposed by Parliament when the railways had a monopoly of public transport – publication of their rates, obligation to provide reasonable facilities, and prohibition of undue preference toward any particular customer.

They suffered, too, by restriction, under the 1921 Act, of their freedom to quote rates (H.L. Thornhill, L.M.S. Railway, Minutes 1121–42). But Sir Josiah would say, next day, that they were merely pointing out differences between rail and road, not listing railway disadvantages (Minute 1347).

So what was to be done about it all? When first called, Stamp had said that all the railways asked was, 'first of all, that the road traffic should be made, as far as possible, to bear its own costs, and then and then only we should have the best possible means for co-ordinating the interests of the country'(Minute 1055). In particular, the Road Fund should bear a much larger proportion of the cost of all road maintenance and the vehicles should make a more substantial contribution to the real working cost of the roads (Minute 1080). After further questioning he suggested additional ways of tackling road haulage:

> We have in mind regulations on undue preference, or on speed, or on tonnage, or on the trailers that may be used and the methods of using them, tyres and the like, conditions of service, such as hours of duty and personnel, standards of construction, maintenance of the vehicles, and obligation for third party risks (Minute 1091).

The reference to tonnage and trailers probably meant limitations on individual vehicles rather than any general capacity restriction on the industry, but nobody queried his remark. Regarding all the obligations heaped on railways, he suggested that some would have to remain while others should be compensated for by analogous burdens which should be put upon road transport (Minute 1347). He did not say which; nor did anyone ask him.

Up to the time of the Royal Commission conventional wisdom held the view that the railways were losing their higher-rated traffic (that is, general merchandise) to road competition. Stamp implied as much in his remark about the competitor who took whatever appealed to him. However, Sir Josiah himself raised a very real question about this conventional idea. In answering questions on the topic, he said that it was impossible to say what percentage of freight traffic was lost because of road competition. There were increases in traffic in some districts, decreases in others, but even with the whole, it was impossible to say what would have been carried in the absence of road competition. There were very large decreases in freight tonnage, but 'we can account for a decrease of more than that tonnage in three or four heavy industries such as branches of the iron and steel trades and the like, showing that in the other classes of goods we have increased our tonnage' (Minutes 1471 and 1472). It is a pity that he had not been a bit more specific, but it was enough to challenge received opinion.

Regarding the complicated rates structure and limitations imposed by the 1921 Act, which were already looking a bit unsatisfactory even though they had been operative only for a few months – since the beginning of 1928 – Stamp was reminded that the road transport industry already existed when the Act was going through Parliament. He dismissed the idea of road competition at the time. Then 'there was nothing like the number of vehicles on the roads ... the problem was present, but like the baby, it was only a little one' (Minute 1504). This seems a clear enough admission that railway management were either oblivious of the potential of road transport as revealed in the war or in the Railway Strike of 1919 or (more likely) thought that the 1921 Act would enable them to meet the competition.

If that particular railwayman thought little of road competition around 1920 or 1921, other railwaymen, possibly with a little help from hindsight, thought differently. The memorandum submitted by the Railway Clerks' Association (Memorandum No.7, Day 7, 17 Jan. 1929) was a bit scathing about top management. Paragraph 11 of that memorandum gave the example of management's alleged inaction when wartime surplus lorries were being sold off cheaply. 'It had already been abundantly demonstrated that road motor transport was a paying proposition.' The railway directors stood by while vehicles were sold off to new competitors, and the couple of railway companies which sought road-operating powers in 1922 'abandoned it (that is, the Bill) in a very half-hearted way'. The Chairman of the Commissioners regarded some of the paragraphs in the memorandum as 'a very formidable indictment of present railway directors'.

Mr George Walkden, speaking for the Railway Clerks, elaborated on this. He called on his own experience when canvassing for traffic 25 years earlier in Nottingham, to say that road competition already existed even then – if only in its babyhood. But this means of transport was developed fully during the war. Then came the disposal of surplus vehicles.

> The railway directors did not appreciate the position,. They did not appreciate that motor transport had proved itself, had won through ... This new form of transport that helped to win the war was there, and the railway directors did not make up their minds about it ... It was not until 1928, after these road vehicles had been operating in opposition to the railways and had brought them to the beginnings of an economic breakdown ... that anything was done. I say you cannot have a better case of the ineptitude of the directors. (Minute 2312, Day 8)

Asked 'Your belief is that the reason the railways did not take up the question of road transport earlier was because they did not realize the potentialities of it?', he replied 'Although it was staring them in the face' (Minute 2313).

It may be natural enough for lower ranks to criticize the top brass but the railway generals had to take criticism from other quarters, too. Lord Monkswell, a writer and speaker on railway matters, submitted a memorandum attacking the easy-going ways of the railways (Memorandum No. 8). In paragraph 13 he said 'With regard to goods traffic, high rates are largely due to the very small consignments in which all kinds of goods pass. The railways often complain ... but do little or nothing to put pressure on the traders to remedy this state of affairs.' Even the introduction of containers was due, not to railway initiative, but to pressure put upon them by certain trades. The question was then put to him, 'I take it, in your view, the present difficulties of the railways and the great difficulty they have had, for example, in meeting motor competition, is due to inefficiency. In your view, the railway service might be much better than it is?' His reply to that was 'Much; that is very largely the trouble. In fact I regard the whole business of road transport as something in the nature of a "red herring". I do not believe road transport is going to affect the railways very seriously one way or the other. It may be a matter of 5% of their receipts' (Minute 2452). His crystal ball was not any clearer than that of the railway directors of 1920–21.

On the other side some of the road interests might well be accused of a degree of naïvety. A Conference of Motor Organizations (22 of them, including the AA, the RAC, the SMMT, the CMUA, Mansion House, and the Furniture Warehousemen & Removers' Association) had submitted its memorandum (No. 9) arguing that 'There is no just warranty for placing any portion of the cost of the roads on the road users, or on any section of the road users, except as a temporary expedient.' This was because the community benefited economically, as a whole, far more than the users of motor vehicles themselves, by the increased fluidity of road transport introduced by the motor vehicle (Para. 4). Furthermore, 'mechanical road transport is at present differentiated for taxation from other road transport and is taxed excessively. This should be reduced forthwith and in due course abolished, having regard to the fact that it is a tax upon the plant, tools and raw materials of industry' (Para. 6).

It was not that the road interests were presenting a united front against the railway arguments. Far from it. Mr J. Smith, Secretary of the Scottish RAC, speaking on this memorandum, argued that commercial vehicles did not bear their fair share of road costs. Smith sought 'an equitable adjustment between the different classes of cars' (that is, vehicles) even though that would be passed on to trade and industry as increased costs (Minutes 3095–98, Day 10, 31 Jan. 1929). That was what the railways wanted to hear.

Naturally enough the CMUA argued the opposite in their memorandum (No. 16, Day 14, 15 Feb. 1929). The tax on petrol-driven commercial motors was equivalent to between £2 and £4 per horsepower as compared to only 13s. 4d. (66½p) for private cars. In large cities like Liverpool, too, commercial motor transport 'suffers acutely from the absence of any comparable taxation on horse vehicles, e.g. 5-tonners used on dock work which pay £60 per annum despite the fact that they never leave the city. This tax of 23/1 per week [£1.15] has proved to throw a number of motor vehicles out of use' (Para. 14).

The CMUA memorandum tells us something about the Association at that time. It claimed some 5000–6000 members owning upwards of 100,000 vehicles (Para. 3). Motor coach proprietors formed 10 per cent of the members, road transport contractors 25 per cent, and ancillary users 65 per cent, though it was not claimed that vehicle numbers were in similar proportion (Para. 4). But Mr E. Shrapnell-Smith, Secretary of the CMUA, said of the 25 per cent of members who were public hauliers 'we reckon that about 1000 own three vehicles or less and that the remaining 500 will average perhaps 25 vehicles each' (Minute 4991). Paragraph 9 of the memorandum pointed out that no comprehensive records existed of road-borne goods nor of what proportion of goods, then passing by road, had at some time previously been carried by rail. The CMUA estimated that of all goods passing by road 80 per cent (by weight and volume) were being carried either in traders' own vehicles or vehicles working solely for them. The other 20 per cent were carried by road hauliers generally. A little bit of history leading up to that situation was given: 'There has been a steady diminution of profitable working in goods haulage by road, other than where a haulage undertaker is linked with a special trade, since the year 1921, and large numbers of haulage contractors who were apparently flourishing in 1921 have gone out of business.' The raising of railway rates in September 1920 had given a great, but artificial, stimulus to road haulage. Then the market was flooded with surplus army vehicles.

> This sudden accession of very large numbers of low priced vehicles in the hands of owner-drivers, who did not possess much business training, caused grave upset to the stable portion of the road transport industry. This state of affairs was no more satisfactory to the better organised elements in road transport than it was to the railway companies, and some of the consequences still retain, as, for example, the difficulty of re-establishing economic rates for services rendered. From this 'welter' of excessive services at unduly low charges there has been a survival, as small owner, of many of the best types of ex-servicemen, more particularly those who were in the RASC(MT) and RAOC. (Para. 8)

The CMUA was very confident that road transport now bore at least a fair proportion of highway costs – whatever may have been the case in earlier years (Para. 14). They pointed out, furthermore (Para. 10), that the term 'highway expenditure' covered a great deal more than just road expenditure – gulleys, drains, tree-planting, sea-walls, ferries, streetcleansing; and that highway rates were not paid solely for the benefit of motor traffic. Road and street users included all subjects of the King – cyclists, naval and military, livestock droves, railway vehicles. Then there was the point that services to property made use of the roads – sewers, gas, water, Post Office, police and fire services (Para. 10). Shrapnell-Smith pushed the point. 'The State and the Exchequer', he said, 'should recognize the road system as a national service' (Minute 4736). He did not see why motor traffic and ratepayers should finance totally such a national service -'The State escapes scot-free in relation to roads in this country whereas in America the State bears 11½% – out of the Federal Exchequer' (Minute 4736).

Mr Shrapnell-Smith went on to argue in great detail the point that commercial vehicles paid at least a fair share of road costs. On the basis of average loading and average mileage in 1927, vehicle licence duties worked out at an average of 0.18d. per gross ton-mile (and that was before the 4d. extra petrol tax in the 1928 Budget). The Ministry of Transport's Traffic Census of August 1925 showed that on Class I roads an average of 2130 gross tons per day passed each of the 4000-odd Census points. Even 2000 tons per day @ 0.18d. yielded £540 per annum compared with the ministry's cost figure of £544 per mile (in 1927–28) (Minute 4804). The members of the

Royal Commission were, perhaps, bemused by Mr Shrapnell-Smith's argument and the supporting tables he submitted, for they did not raise any questions. But some of them may have realized that they were being 'blinded with science' when he claimed both that on average the licence duties just about paid for road costs; and that because some busy stretches of road carried 9000 tons gross per day, the yield of commercial vehicle licences was away beyond the ministry's cost figure. A rebate was justified. Mr Shrapnell-Smith had a less good argument in regard to Class II roads. He was able to show only that licence duties contributed less than half of the annual cost (Minute 4805).

Whatever the arguments about road costs, The Royal Commission had to deal with other things. Included in their terms of reference was a mention of that popular theme of the time – coordination – which was seen as the great cure for all the evils of 'cut-throat competition'. Few people took the trouble to define it and road haulage people were afraid that it would be construed so as to make road transport a mere feeder system for the railways. The CMUA memorandum rightly said that it was difficult to reduce the matter from the abstract to the concrete. In Paragraph 13 they attempted a definition, anyway: 'Two or more systems, whether in the same or separate ownership, working together efficiently under an agreement mutually agreed and conditioned by the public interest.'

'Working together efficiently' and 'conditioned by the public interest' seem about as abstract as the original 'coordination' and do not get us very far. But the CMUA was quite clear that it was premature to lay down arbitrary rulings of any kind. The extent to which it was practicable for the movement of goods traffic to be coordinated would be determined over the next five or seven years if its working out were left to voluntary arrangements between railway and road companies, they argued (Para. 13).

The CMUA was strongly of the opinion that control, other than in respect of fitness of the vehicle, hours of work, wages, and insurance, was not the way to achieve coordination or ease the railways' burdens. Road goods vehicles, they argued in Paragraph 12, should be allowed to continue to be worked on such jobbing, hiring and contract terms as might be negotiated between the owners and their customers. They should not be restricted. 'The choice in these matters rests with and is exercised by the producing and trading communities ... and not by the owners of the vehicles.' When asked whether he agreed, Shrapnell-Smith answered 'I do, Sir. I think there should be a free market in respect of them. I think if restrictions are put on they should be from the operating point of view ... and not from the point of view of the work they do' (Minute 4769). So the CMUA had no proposals for control, he said. 'We, as an Association, do not make any submission, and we do not see how it can be done without grave interference with the ordinary industrial requirements of the country' (Minute 4787). He knew subsequent witnesses were going to 'formulate' a scheme of licensing and restrictive control of commercial haulage, but the Association was not a party to it (Minute 4940). He agreed with a commissioner's question that it was very important to preserve the liberty of choice of the offerer of transport work. 'Very important', he said. 'The choice rests with the man who gives the load. The suggestion is that the road haulier picks and chooses ... but the picking and choosing is done by the man who gives the load'. (Minute 5038). One can understand the reluctance of the CMUA to suggest the imposition of controls on capacity since the bulk of their members carried only their own goods, and it was generally hoped and expected that no restrictions would be put on them.

Before passing on from the CMUA's evidence, we must note another attempt by the Commissioners to get hard evidence. Had Mr Shrapnell-Smith any figures to back up the CMUA's claim (in their Para. 8) that profitability in road haulage had been declining since 1921? 'Only the figures of former members who have become bankrupt', he replied, without offering any further detail. Were these mainly small contractors? 'No', he said. 'A good many were among men owning quite a large number of vehicles.' They had come in after the war, when railway problems were abnormal and when railway rates had been raised. They had been able to make a living then, but not subsequently (Minutes 4992 and 4993). So once again no precise quantitative information was available to the Commission.

The sixteenth day (1 March 1929) saw Mr P.R. Turner giving evidence on behalf of the National Road Transport Employers' Federation. Their memorandum (No. 18) explained that they were a confederation of associations in England and Wales (these were probably mostly local groups) and that they represented about 3000 firms owning some 80,000 horse-drawn vehicles and 50,000 motor vehicles. These latter figures show that even after the tremendous increase in the number of lorries over the previous ten years the horse was by no means a minor part of the goods transport scene – at least for local transport. Turner argued that whereas a year or two earlier the horse was competitive with motor transport in cities and dock areas up to a distance of three miles, increased taxation on motor transport had stopped its expansion and brought back the horse in Liverpool and probably London for distances up to four miles (Minutes 5717–26).

The Federation's big worry was about wages, a problem raised, too, by the National Union of Railwaymen, and one which would arise frequently over the next few years. There was a great disparity in wages throughout the country and wage agreements had no legal force. 'Contractors in most large centres find themselves subjected to grossly unfair competition. Some owners severely undercut prices, and are able to do so owing to the fact that they do not pay anything like the same rate of wages and recognise no restrictions as to working hours.' Mr Turner went on to say that a Joint Industrial Council had been set up during the war (actually June 1919) but the machinery broke down and ceased to function because of the lack of 'statutory effect'. Lack of machinery had led to many local strikes. The Federation called for enforceability of voluntary agreements. A Private Member's Bill to give such force had had a Second Reading in the House of Commons on 30 May 1924 but got no further because of the dissolution of the Labour Government. The TUC had resolved, in September 1925, to urge on the government the desirability of giving national voluntary agreements the same validity as awards under the Trade Boards Acts,1909 and 1918 (Paras 4 and 5). Mr Turner added that, following the 1921 slump, some employers, particularly in outlying districts, broke away from the agreements 'although in the chief ports we have managed to maintain a wage standard and recognized conditions of working' (Minutes 5729–30). He quoted 72s. (£3.60) for a motor driver's 48-hour week in London (as compared with 60s. on the railways). Motor drivers earned 70s. in Liverpool, 65s. in Manchester and 60s. (£3.00) in England away from the big towns. But outside these Trade Union agreements for organized labour some people 'are paying anything ... We have heard of rates as low as 40s.' (£2) (Minutes 5865 and 5872).

The Federation was strongly critical of the increased taxation on motor transport which they could not recover from their customers. They offered figures to support their case:

	5-tonner			12-ton artic	
1925 licence		£30.0.0			£34.0.0
1928 licence	£54. 0.0			£60.0.0	
Petrol tax 4¼d to users* – 24,000 m.p.a. @ 6 m.p.g.	70.16.8		24, 000 m.p.a. @ 4 m.p.g	106.5.0	
Total		124.16.8			166.5.0
Increase		94.16.8			132.5.0
Total tax per vehicle per week		£2.10.0			£3.0.0

*(The government had imposed a tax of 4d per gallon but the petrol companies charged 4¼d to cover their extra administrative costs.)

On the overall picture the Federation argued that the extra burden of taxation on motor users (including private cars) was £8.76 million per annum. They had arrived at this like Mr Brunner (mentioned in Chapter Nine) by scaling up 'pre-motor' road expense for increased costs as at 1928. This gave a hypothetical cost ('in the absence of motors') for that year of £27 million. But the MOT gave current actual cost as £56 million. So road traffic was costing an extra £29 million per annum.

Adding £2 million for the cost of traffic control by the police brought the cost of motors up to £31 million. In 1928–29 licence revenue was £26.16 million and the 4d petrol tax yielded £13.6 million, a total of £39.75 million (Para. 7).

The remedy they proposed for the ills of transport was the setting up of Area Transport Authorities with representatives of transport (employers and employees), traders and the MOT. These authorities should be given power to control 'in order that wasteful competition may ultimately be eliminated'. Coordination was desirable, but the unrestricted competition of the time was 'conducive to waste and not in the public interest' (Paras 12 and 13). Mr Turner amplified this by proposing that the number of vehicles licensed in an area should be adapted to the needs of the area. Traders running their own lorries should not be allowed to take a load from other firms. Only licensed hauliers might do that (Minutes 5791, 5803–13). *Bona fide* carriers at the outset should receive licences as of right (Minute 6062). 'I think we should have to put up with interference in the conduct of our business if it could be reasonably shown that it was for the public good' (Minute 5893).

The SMMT submitted a memorandum (No. 22) with appendices giving road costs over 35 years, tax rates on 4-tonners in England and other countries, tables of other tax rates, and so on. They argued that road costs had been rising steadily even before the advent of motor traffic and that present receipts from motor taxation equalled the increase in road costs since motors came on the scene (Para. 11). They lambasted the government who had adopted 'the vicious and uneconomic principle of raising general revenue by taxation of road transport ... Such a policy must tend to raise the general level of prices and reduce the competitive efficiency of our industry in world markets' (Paras 20 and 21). On the general question of competition between the major carriers they offered the opinion that 'The dominant public interest in the long run is not in the protecton of any one means of transport against the inevitable effect of economic forces, but the progressive development of the most economic and efficient system of national transportation.' Coordination would be effected by the normal interplay of economic and commercial forces (Paras 22 and 23).

The TGWU's submission (Memorandum No. 24, Day 20, 20 March 1929) called for licensing of hauliers by District Transport Authorities who would consider 'the requirements and needs of the district'. The licence would be subject to the operator maintaining the vehicle in an efficient and satisfactory condition, observing ministry regulations about hours of duty and rest periods, and taking out third party insurance. The Authority would be entitled to refuse a licence on the grounds of 'the needs of the district'. All existing contractors would undoubtedly have a good claim to a licence as otherwise hardship might be involved (Paras 10 and 37–40). Mr John Cliff, the Assistant

General Secretary of the TGWU, argued that since such a scheme would give a monopoly to existing carriers they ought to accept some obligations, for example common carrier status, or a Rates Tribunal. (Minutes 7130–32).

Evidence offered by other bodies throws some light on the road transport scene of early 1929. The SMMT memorandum, for example, claimed that some 4000 million net ton-miles were being hauled by road transport at the time as compared with 19,000 million by rail. The 4000 million was not all traffic competitive with rail. Indeed, it included railway C&D traffic and general deliveries to consumers (Para. 15). This time someone did ask about the statistics. The net ton-mileage by road had been calculated, said Sir George Beharrell (formerly of the N. E. Railway and the Ministry of Transport), by taking the 306,000 vehicles on the road, an average 15,000 miles per annum ('very conservative' he said), assuming half of the mileage was empty (though probably 60 to 70 per cent loaded would be nearer the truth, he said) and assuming an average 2-ton load. This gave 4590 million which had been rounded down to 4000 to be on the safe side (Minute 6570). Sir George, too, supported the argument that taxation on motors had led to a revival of horse transport (Minute 6815). Major G.W. Allen, speaking for the Traction Engine Owners' and Users' Association, told the Commissioners that of the 1300-odd traction engines owned by the Association's members, 'approximately 387 are used for road haulage only' (Minute 6156). This clearly indicated the impending demise of steam. The representative of the Furniture Warehousemen and Removers' Association, Mr A.G.Coombes, said that members had some steam vehicles – 'I think it is chiefly a question of wearing them out … they are not looked upon as economical or altogether suitable today' (Minute 6434). The Association estimated that their 800 members had about 6000 motor vehicles and the same number of horse-drawn vehicles (Minute 6429). Eighty per cent of their vehicles were still on solid tyres (Minute 6373) and none of the motors had brakes on all four wheels (Minute 6432).

More interestingly, their members were putting a considerable volume of traffic on rail and finding it advantageous. It was not economic to send a motor van more than 100 miles.

> Since the war the railway companies have rather complained that they have lost practically all our traffic. That was accounted for by the number of vehicles that were flooded on to the roads ... But during the last year or two we have been getting back to rail traffic ... During the last two or three years the railway companies have gone out of their way and done everything, or at any rate, most things that we think are practicable to help and encourage our traffic. They want our traffic. (Minutes 6419–24)

Were the railway rates satisfactory?, he was asked. 'Yes. When a person has to move he has to move. We charge the customer.' But not what you like?

'Unfortunately there are too many of us in the business.' [But, in any case] the railways had cut their rates to get the traffic back (Minute 6425–27).

There were the horror stories, naturally. Capt. J.W. Moore, speaking on the Chief Constables' Association memorandum (No.32, 18 April 1929), had a cutting taken from the *Leeds Mercury*. This described a case where a man had been regularly starting at 4.00 a.m. from Morecambe to Huddersfield and finishing at 2.00 a.m. (Nobody asked how the driver concerned whiled away the other two hours between 2.00 and 4.00 a.m.). The officer also referred to a driver he had prosecuted who had been on the road continuously from 3.00 a.m. until an accident occurred at 10.38 p.m. (Minutes 8874 and 8878). The drivers of the late 1920s were undoubtedly hardy types.

Even the academic world, as represented by Dr K.G. Fenelon, Lecturer in Economics at Edinburgh University and writer on transport subjects, did not contribute anything startlingly new to the argument. He pointed out that each form of transport had advantages for particular traffic but that there was a great deal of overlapping. Furthermore it was difficult to specify the area of advantage of a particular mode because of (continuing) developments. (Minutes 14756–64). Maybe this seemingly crashingly obvious point had to be made since so many of the witnesses seemed to assume that hard-and-fast distinctions could be made between rail and road, based perhaps on length of haul and/or type of traffic.

What did Dr Fenelon think of the licensing scheme proposed by the TGWU? 'The difficulty is, from my point of view', he replied,

> that we do not want regulations brought in which would be too restrictive of the road transport industry. It is a young and new industry. The history of the railways has shown the difficulties and the harm done by undue restriction. At the same time, some regulation does seem necessary in the public interest ... [If a scheme were brought in] I think the regulations should be fairly elastic, (Minute 14781)

He did not make any direct reference to the TGWU's proposals, nor elaborate on his phrases such as 'too restrictive' or 'fairly elastic'.

The turn of the MOT came on 14 May 1930 (Day 42). Their memorandum (No.54) sought to reply to those who had argued that motor transport was already paying a fair share, or too great a share, of highway costs. Paragraph 3 set out total expenditure on highways in Great Britain during 1927–28 as £58,816,937, only a little less than the previous year. It gave total licensing revenue for 1929–30 as £26.8 million and then deducted the one-third of private motor-car and motor-cycle licence revenue which did not go into the Road Fund but to the Exchequer as a luxury tax. This left a mere £22,150,000 for roads. Even in regard to the 4d. petrol tax which the government had put towards derating of industry, the ministry's memorandum pointed out that it did not all arise from motor transport. They then deducted £1 million-odd to show that only £14 million came from motors in 1929–30.

Mr H.H. Piggott, speaking for the ministry, was asked whether the cost of £61 million (that is, including £2 million for police costs) less licensing and petrol tax left £25 million for the ratepayer to meet. He answered 'That is so. That is, assuming that those two sums could properly be set down as revenue derived from taxation of users of motor vehicles towards the cost of highways, *which is not the case'* (italics added). Clearly the government had accepted Mr Churchill's view that a Chancellor might legitimately apply revenue from motor taxation to any purpose he chose. Paragraphs 6 and 7 went on to criticize the figures presented by Mr E. Shrapnell-Smith (for CMUA) and Sir G. Beharrell (for SMMT). In particular, said the ministry, 'Motor transport has had the good fortune to inherit this valuable network of roads'. So the calculation of road costs ought to include interest on the capital sum, say £1.6–£2 million per annum.

Mr Piggott claimed to have difficulty in understanding a point when Major Crawford asked whether the inherited roads were exactly what motorists wanted. He thought they would want dead straight roads. 'So they pay because they inherit what they do not want, and pay to alter it?' was the Major's next query, but Mr Piggott replied 'I'm afraid that is beyond me' (Minute 14338). When asked whether certain traffic was not paying its way, his reply was to refer to the memorandum and to admit that when all was said and done it was a matter of opinion (Minute 14398). Earlier he had said that it was almost impossible to form any estimate as to the proportion of the cost of the upkeep of the highway system that should be reckoned to the charge of the community as a whole or the motor users in particular – or indeed how costs should be shared over different classes of motor (Minutes 14181–2).

Not surprisingly, the ministry memorandum did not address the general question of controlling the numbers of vehicles on the roads, but confined itself to matters of highway costs and taxation revenue. The ministry in particular and the government in general were expecting the Royal Commission to come up with ideas for solving the problem of road traffic. Any view expressed by a government department would, perhaps, have been taken as an instruction. It is a pity it is not the practice of governments to give to Royal Commissions some summary of the pros and cons of an argument as they see it; but perhaps people would be so busy looking between the lines for government policy that they would not see what was actually written.

On Day 44, 25 June 1930, the Long Distance Road Haulage Committee of Enquiry submitted its memorandum (No.58). This committee had been set up a little while before by some long-distance operators, specifically to sort out what points ought to be made to the Royal Commission on behalf of long-distance hauliers. Originally only five or six hauliers had been involved, but since then 'some 25 or 30 of the others amongst the biggest of the firms in this section have definitely signified their approval of the investigation' (Sir

Maxwell Hicks, Minute 14969). Mr.Lobjoit, a commissioner, tried to find out if there really were a long-distance haulage industry, but there seemed to he some confusion between him and the witness as to what was being asked. Mr. Lobjoit then went on, 'Is not long distance the basis of the business of almost every considerable transport company?' Sir Maxwell replied:

> In my experience, no. For instance, I should not say the biggest transport companies, all who ply for hire – Carter Paterson and Pickfords – do any long distance haulage to any extent, except with specialized work; but they are not taking goods for profit to towns 100 miles apart day by day and night by night. They do a little, but we should not reckon them, roughly speaking, as in the long distance section.
> (Was it not possible to select and segregate certain firms who were long distance hauliers only?) I beg your pardon; I should say that of the 40 firms who approve the objects of this committee, 30 would be primarily, if not entirely, long distance hauliers.(Minutes 11979–80)

Sir Maxwell had earlier been asked, 'You cannot give any very exact figures as to the mileage operated, but you think that each year many million tons are carried by road, an average of 100 miles?' His reply was that there was no question that that was so (Minute 14884). He had used 100 miles, too, as the meaning of 'long distance' when speaking about the two major firms. But, in fact, 30 miles was the figure normally used as the definition, both by witnesses and commissioners. No doubt Sir Maxwell accepted that definition though there were some quibbles about it.

The Long Distance Hauliers' Committee of Enquiry was concerned about the small man who cut rates and so made it difficult for the rest of the industry to be remunerative. Regarding the parlous state of the industry generally, Sir Maxwell Hicks said that in his view it was in very considerable jeopardy (Minute 14878). He contrasted 'the small man' with the organized companies which had their own premises at several points in London, Birmingham, Bristol, Liverpool, and so on, often including their own warehouses. They were definitely organized to carry long-distance goods under the best possible conditions, he explained, working in close touch with trade unions, 'employing sound labour at a good wage ... essential to make it worthwhile to attract a sound class of driver, the men who drive big lorries through the night for 100 miles must be ... necessarily sound men, men of good character and of good experience' (Minute 14884). Sir Maxwell was not very happy about industrial firms which operated lorries on their own account looking for back loads – to the detriment of the hauliers. Some of these, of course, were reputable firms, charging reasonable rates. On the other hand, he knew cases where fleet users who, on going light, would take almost anything. He had one case in mind where the total amount for a run of about eighty miles was 25s. (£1.25) for the whole load (Minute 14896). He stressed the point that a trader, having got a load carried one day at a cut rate, would want that rate on subsequent days even with different hauliers (Minute 14901).

Not only was the competition of the 'small man' and own-account operators a problem, but there was railway competition, too, and that was not always very fair. Where the railways had constructed bridges in the early days to carry roads over the railway lines, they were obliged only to maintain any given bridge to carry the amount of traffic that was passing at the time of the construction of the bridge. Furthermore, the railway companies were entitled to place notices at a bridge specifying the maximum load that the bridge could carry. Anyone who put a greater load on the bridge would be liable for any damage that might occur. The Long Distance Road Hauliers' complaint (as indeed that of the Traction Engine Owners over many years) was that the railways often deliberately understated the load a bridge could carry in order to obstruct road transport. Sir Maxwell had no hesitation in saying that there was a practice which had grown in the previous few years to a great extent, and which was done admittedly as a deliberate piece of tactics by the railway and canal companies, to force road traffic to go a longer way round. 'There are many bridges, particularly in the Midlands, posted for 3 tons and 5 tons, where habitually 8 tons or 10 tons or 12 tons go over them.' He referred to one bridge 'posted at 5 tons' over which four loads of 117 tons had passed. (Nobody asked him whether he thought the hauliers concerned were foolhardy, reckless or just knowledgeable!) 'We are bringing this forward as deliberate tactics on the part of the railway companies, which is unfair competition' (Minutes 14908–17). Since he was so free with reference to bridges carrying much more than the loads stipulated in notices, he might well have been questioned as to just how far those notices really did hinder road transport; but the matter was allowed to pass. It should be noted, however, that road transport people over many years had argued that these bridges ought to be taken over by the highway authorities and maintained at a standard to carry modern traffic.

The Long Distance Hauliers' memorandum (Paras 24–9) had called for the extension of the system of Traffic Commissioners to cover the licensing of hauliers – all hauliers, as Sir Maxwell explained. The Chairman of the Commissioners pointed out that Traffic Commissioners had to 'take stock (so to speak) of the traffic requirements of the district and license just a sufficient number of vehicles to give the public a good service, but to eliminate unnecessary competition'. Did Sir Maxwell suggest anything of that sort? Were the Traffic Commissioners to say 'we have already licensed so many lorries in this district. We do not think it necessary to have any more?' It seems surprising that the Long Distance Hauliers' memorandum should have asked for the system of Traffic Commissioners without mentioning this crucial point. The Bill which would become the Road Traffic Act 1930 had now almost completed its parliamentary journey and it is hard to imagine that the freight men did not know what was going to happen in the passenger field. Sir Maxwell, however, replied 'No ... We are not seeking here a route value or monopoly by licensing the vehicle; we are simply asking for the efficiency of the vehicle to be certified from the point of view of the interests of the road users and the public.' Asked more specifically about the applicability of a restrictive scheme for goods vehicles similar to that soon to apply to passenger vehicles, he replied 'That does not apply in regard to goods at present; it may apply in five years time, but it is a very difficult point' (Minutes 14908–35). It certainly does not appear that the Long Distance Road Haulage Committee of Enquiry had given much concentrated attention to the topic of restriction of total capacity of road haulage fleets, even though that topic had been discussed quite frequently in the press in the recent years.

One of the Commissioners asked Sir Maxwell Hicks about coordination. 'In the very last line or two of your memorandum you make reference to a word which appears in our terms of reference – co-ordination; that blessed word – but you do not throw any light on your views in regard to it. Have you abstained purposely, for some particular reason?' Here again the Long Distance Committee had obviously had difficulty. 'My Committee ... felt that they had quite enough to submit to you without entering into the controversial subject of co-ordination', replied Sir Maxwell lamely (Minute 15045). There followed some exchanges on cooperation between road and rail. Sir Maxwell explained that a year earlier he had conferred with the general managers of the railways on this subject and that he had submitted a memorandum to the GMs but he did not think the suggestions they had discussed were bearing any fruit (Minutes 15087–8).

What about clearing houses, then? The companies Sir Maxwell represented did not find it necessary to have any dealings with such bodies, as, generally, they had their own branches. There were good and bad clearing houses. He agreed that the objectionable ones had no warehouses but were merely agencies for bringing the owner of the goods in touch with the transporter. He talked of one of the best known of a few years earlier -the National Road Transport Clearing House Ltd which, he said, had come out with a very good scheme in principle.

> I happened to be in control of that clearing house in its later days, but I very shortly buried it definitely because I formed the opinion that with the competition that was springing up it was impossible to conduct that clearing house at a profit with satisfaction to its customers or with satisfaction to the contractors.

He thought the ideal clearing house was one controlled by the hauliers and by the traders, or by the local chamber of commerce, with a vote and not working for profit, so that there was no incentive to sweat the haulier or to cut unduly.

The one in Nottingham was a good example, but it was in a unique position with little competition. 'They have support in a town like Nottingham, which is very clannish, from the traders generally; [and] they have a strong personality in Mr Donaldson Wright, who is in charge of it' (Minutes 15119–22). Towards the end of his long session of evidence Sir Maxwell Hicks expressed the view that to get complete coordination there had to be nationalization (Minute 15135).

All good things must come to an end, and so eventually did the process of taking evidence. The last few of the 1000 or so double-columned foolscap pages contain a couple more interesting submissions. The railways came up with a memorandum (No.59) to counter some criticisms of their Classification of Goods made by the London Chamber of Commerce (LCC). The classification system, they said, was of long standing, had been reviewed many times and re-enacted; the Traders' Co-ordinating Committee favoured it and traders generally asked for 'as little change as possible'. As for the LCC's request that rating should be on a cost basis for truck loads there were many anomalies in the classification due precisely to that. A large proportion of the country's trade was in small lots and the classification was suitable for that. Anyway, traders could always get exceptional rates and despite complaints of delay in quoting rates, 95 per cent of the requests had the rates quoted on the same or the following day. (One of the complaints had been regarding reductions outside the range 5 to 40 per cent below the Standard Rates which had to be authorized by the Railway Rates Tribunal (RRT). The railway memorandum here seemed to consider it a sufficient answer to say that the RRT did not meet every day.)

The other interesting document at the end of the proceedings was a second memorandum from the CMUA (No. 62). This memorandum set out in Paragraph 3 what it claimed were 'some of the achievements of road motor transport, accomplished under direct competition with other forms of transport'. These included:

a) to establish a form of alternative service to existing transport services,
b) to reduce materially the time and cost of transporting goods,
c) to improve and develop the road vehicle propelled by steam, petrol, and heavy oil,
d) to re-establish the road system of the country on national lines,
e) to increase considerably the rateable value to frontages created by the construction of motor roads,
f) to create a new industry of enormous potentiality, as well in its direct employment and production as in the immense number of industries which it fertilizes,
g) to evolve a new agency of transportation which has come more intimately into the lives of the public probably than any other form of transportation the world has ever known.

There could hardly be much argument about that. Paragraph 4 argued that some of the effects on other forms of transport have been:

a) That the railways have been stimulated to give better and cheaper facilities to the public and increased facilities for travel at reduced fares,

b) a material reduction of rates on competitive routes and easement of conditions, the introduction of containers and other labour-saving devices to meet competition,

c) the conclusive effect of road transport on the general transport system of the country has been beneficial,

Well, the railways, particularly, might have argued about some of that. The memorandum went on with pleas to the Commission. Motor transport had not yet passed through the development stage, said Paragraph 5. 'So far as possible it should be left free and untrammelled ... Cheap road transport is essential to the nation, and is only possible by the full and unhampered development of motor traction. It affects costs through innumerable phases of industry as well as throughout the whole process of distribution of foodstuffs and materials.' Paragraph 6 said that one of the most powerful benefits of motor transport was mobility (did they mean flexibility?) and the CMUA strongly urged the Commission not to recommend regulations or restrictions which would reduce this. Paragraph 8 argued that the regulation of hours, speed limits, and the compulsory insurance of the new Road Traffic Act would be sufficient regulation of the industry.

Paragraph 9 made the further point that surplus vehicles in road transport paralleled surplus facilities in trade and industry generally, due to the prolonged trade depression. Economists of the time did not pay as much attention as do their latter-day descendants to questions of 'slack' in the economy and its consequences for growth rates and inflation, so the point may have passed unnoticed. Just in case they were thinking of recommending capacity restriction, Paragraph 11 reminded the Commissioners of Sir Henry Maybury's evidence. He had pointed out that in America the licensing system had broken down, the restriction simply forcing traders and industrial firms to provide their own lorries. There were other points but the memorandum concluded with Paragraph 25 calling for a reduction of taxation. Such calls generally have about the same result whether they are placed first, last, or somewhere in between. Chancellors develop thick skin and hard hearts when in office.

CHAPTER TWELVE

The Reports and the Consequences

The Commission eventually issued three reports in all. The first, which covered the whole matter of hours, speed limits and the construction and use of vehicles, was very much a matter of regulation and control which the terms of reference had asked about. It was right and proper that this area should have been the subject of the First Report since, as we have seen, successive governments had shied away from bringing in an up-to-date Road Traffic Bill and because road safety was very topical. The Second Report was concerned with passenger road transport and does not concern us here except to notice that it was partly a response to the terms of reference which sought coordination. There was already a substantial degree of coordination in the passenger industry in so far as there had been a good deal of merging of companies and the railways had taken shares in many of them. To finish the job neatly, the method chosen was to set up Area Traffic Commissioners whose job it was, after hearing applicants and objectors, to issue licences to allow road passenger services to be run, or, as was often the case, to refuse to permit those services. Some in the road goods haulage sector were painfully aware that this way of dealing with competition might well be applied to freight, too, particularly as there had been very little combination of freight companies. Admittedly the railways had taken shares in some of the bigger companies, but in general the industry was considered as not 'organized'. There was the further worry that the First and Second Reports had been quickly followed by the Road Traffic Act of 1930 which had accepted the main recommendations of the Royal Commission. Many hauliers waited in trepidation, therefore, for the coming of the Third Report which would affect the road goods transport industry. They expected that it, too, would swiftly be given legislative effect.

The new Road Traffic Act, following the first two Reports, and the subsequent Construction and Use Regulations, in part, did affect hauliers and merchants delivering their own goods. There was that legislation about drivers' hours, for example – the maxima of 5½ hours continuous and of 11 hours on duty in 24 hours had shaken some of them – and those figures were rather better than the 5 and 10 hours originally proposed. Only very vigorous opposition by the CMUA and many others had achieved that improvement. Even the final version, which included some exceptions, caused complaints. At a joint meeting of CMUA and the Long Distance Road Haulage

Association on 10 November 1930 Mr E. Marston of the Liverpool firm whose business was abnormal loads asserted that it was impossible to work the restricted hours with abnormal loads. These loads just could not be left in the middle of the road when the driver's 5½ or 11 hours had expired. Mr A.C. Norman of a Brighton firm said that total transport costs would rise by 15 per cent.[1] The Worcester County Surveyor announced in February 1931 that the county would buy no more steam wagons. They were just not economic in view of the hours restrictions. For instance, the time spent by the driver in raising steam at the beginning of the day would be counted as part of the 5½ hours.[2] It would, presumably, have been too expensive to employ men for the sole purpose of raising steam at the start of the day. Then there was the introduction of third party insurance, which had been debated for years.

The bigger and better-financed firms were reasonably happy to go along with this part of the Act in that they felt that it would help to put paid to many of the small operators who lived a hand-to-mouth existence, running dangerous and poorly maintained vehicles, cutting rates and generally being a nuisance. But what really came as a nasty surprise was the new law about speed limits. In the years preceding the Act, police and everyone else had recognized that the earlier speed limits were totally out of date, given better vehicles, better braking, better tyres, better roads and so on. So in practice speed limits were non-existent. Nobody bothered to enforce them and operators ran their vehicles at whatever speed, within reason, they found convenient.

The Act, however, set out new limits – limits which would be enforced. For goods vehicles they were:

Motor cars (i.e. including vans) on pneumatic tyres	30 m.p.h.
Motor cars on 'soft or elastic'	20 m.p.h.
Heavy motor cars (i.e. over 2½ tons unladen):	
on pneumatics	20 m.p.h.
on 'soft or elastic'	16 m.p.h.
with trailer all on pneumatics	16 m.p.h.
with trailer all on 'soft or elastic'	8 m.p.h.
Otherwise	5 m.p.h.

For a modern 'heavy' vehicle of the time, on pneumatic tyres, to be limited to 20 m.p.h. was a disaster, and the road transport interests certainly had reason to consider that they had been treated unjustly. Such a limit would mean that, in practice, journeys of any distance would be run on average at about 15 or 16 m.p.h., whereas previously they had been done at twice that speed. Taken with the maximum 11 hours' driving, this speed limit meant that a 5-tonner, say, would be limited to about 180 miles in the day, so that London to

Liverpool or Manchester would be out of the question. With a trailer the average could not be more than perhaps 12 m.p.h. and for the many vehicles and trailers still on solid tyres the 8 m.p.h. limit was unsatisfactory. Possibly new engines in time would allow the average to get a little nearer the legal maxima, but for the time being, averages were likely to be too low to suit haulage interests. Long-distance operators had certainly received an economic blow of the first order. Not surprisingly, accusing fingers were again pointed at railway influence. Even the short-distance deliveries by van had had a knock, too, in the limit of 30 m.p.h. when such vehicles were capable of doing 50 m.p.h.

There were other things to worry the industry. The Construction and Use Regulations of 1931 provided, amongst other things, that for a 4-wheeler the maximum gross weight permissible would be 12 tons. The editor of *Commercial Motor* fulminated that this gross 'has remained the same for many years, but in the past has proved so ridiculous that it has been honoured more in the breach than in the observance'. The police would now become more active, 'with the result that a somewhat desperate situation has arisen, for considerably over half of the heavy classes of vehicle in use cannot be loaded to their full capacity and yet remain within the 12 ton limit'. Steam wagons had been particularly hard hit and there was not even a period of grace when they could work out their useful lives. The editor called for the limit to be raised to 14 tons, preferably as a general rule, but at least in respect of vehicles registered before 1 January 1932. (The Departmental Committee reporting in 1922 had recommended 14 tons gross on two axles.[3]) Eventually the MOT relented as far as the steamers were concerned and settled for 13 tons if the wagon were registered after 1 January 1932 and had pneumatics fitted all round.[4] Those 1931 Regulations were certainly restrictive, for, they reduced the maximum legal overall length of an artic from 36 to 33 feet; and all motor cars (that is, up to 2½ tons unladen) and heavy motor cars registered after 1 January 1933 would have to be fitted with pneumatics. All such vehicles and their trailers would have to have pneumatic tyres by 1 January 1940. Nor did traction engines and tractors escape rules about tyres.

So the industry waited to see what the Commissioners would say about competition for freight, coordination and related topics. The Final Report, dated December 1930, was published at the beginning of 1931 and was found not really to have said very much. So far as the roads were concerned, the Commission thought 'our roads are the best in the world [but] much more remains to be done' (Para. 184). The highway system as a whole was not congested and afforded adequate facilities. It was only in the vicinity of towns and in urban areas that there were any difficulties (Para. 185). They were 'strongly opposed' to the building of motorways by private capital. If such roads were successful, the highway authorities might neglect their roads in the vicinity. If the motorways were unsuccessful the owners might simply abandon them and there might be pressure on the highway authorities to take them over (Para. 223). The Commission, however, strongly recommended a programme of the complete reconstruction of many existing roads, widening, improvement of junctions and lines of sight, construction of by-passes, strengthening of weak bridges, freeing of roads and bridges from tolls, and progressive reconstruction in built-up areas (Para. 191). The private ownership of bridges carrying public highways should be abolished and the ex-owners should pay for being relieved of the burden (Para. 202).

On the vexed question of the relationship between highway expenditure and the taxation of motor vehicles, the Commission could only say, lamely, 'we confess that, in spite of the great amount of thought we have given it, we have been unable to reach a conclusion which we could confidently put forward as demonstratively and mathematically sound' (Para. 224). They had asked the MOT for additional evidence on the question, but the ministry had replied that

> data do not exist for forming any accurate estimate of the proportion … which should be properly borne by the users of motor vehicles [and] it is a far more difficult matter to attempt to strike a balance between the value of the highway system to motor users as a class, and its value to the community as a whole … or to decide how to apportion taxes to different classes of vehicles in proportion to which they use the roads.

The ministry memorandum stuck to the government line that it was always open to Parliament to impose tax for general revenue purposes (Para. 236).

The Royal Commission took a dim view of the raids by the chancellor on the Road Fund. It was

> 'deeply concerned' … that two very large sums of money, collected for a certain purpose and definitely hypothecated for that purpose, should have been diverted to other purposes. (Para. 245) These raids present no redeeming feature; they are bad finance since the ever-present fear of a recurrence makes it quite impossible for any Minister of Transport to formulate with any degree of confidence a firm policy to be followed. (Para. 246)

The next thing was a carefully non-committal remark about the level of motor-vehicle taxation. The Commission were satisfied that the users of mechanically propelled vehicles were not, as a class, paying too much taxation. Nor did they think in a general way users were paying too little. But ratepayers were bearing too great a proportion and the burden was becoming intolerable (Para. 248). So the Commission recommended that motor vehicles should pay two-thirds and ratepayers one-third of highway expenditure. There need be no increase in taxation if all licence and petrol duties went to the roads (Paras 249–50).

If lorry owners had breathed a sigh of relief on reading that, some of them might have sighed too soon. A few paragraphs later we read that expert opinion supported the conclusion the Commission had reached, that the class of vehicle responsible for by far the greater part of the wear and tear on the highway was the heavy commercial lorry. This was particularly so when the lorry was travelling, as it frequently did, at speeds in excess of the legal maximum. The combination of weight and speed was disastrous, and witnesses were quoted to the effect that vehicles were travelling at anything up to 40 m.p.h. when their legal limit was 12 m.p.h. The witnesses said also that weights carried were much in excess of the legal maximum (Para. 259). The Commissioners had no doubt what was to be done. No heavy motor car ought to exceed 10 tons unladen. Maximum laden weights should not be increased. The maximum weight on any *wheel* should not exceed 4 tons. There should be increased duty on vehicles over 4 tons, and more steps should be put into the tax scales beyond 5 tons, at intervals of 1 ton. The Commission did not recommend any particular rates but they saw no reason why 9–10-tonners should not pay as much as £120. (The current rate was £60 for a rigid of 5 tons or more, unladen, less 20 per cent if the vehicle were on pneumatic tyres.) In general, though, the whole question of how tax on mechanically propelled vehicles was to be raised was a very technical matter, outside their province. They recommended the setting up of an expert committee to sort it out (Recommendation LIV p.160). They added that the use of lighter vehicles, say under 4 tons unladen, ought to be encouraged (Paras 264–6).

The next paragraph brought great cheer to the hearts of railwaymen and to their supporters amongst the general public. The Commission had been thinking about the railways as well as about road damage, they said, when making these recommendations. They were very definitely of the opinion that it was not in the national interest to encourage further diversion of heavy goods traffic from the railways to the roads. Such diversion would add to the expenditure on roads and make the railways unremunerative without any commensurate advantage (Para. 267). It is not at all clear just what they were thinking of in their mention of heavy traffic. There had not really been much diversion of heavy traffic like iron and steel, nor of coal and minerals. Was there, perhaps, some confusion between heavy traffic and heavy vehicles? Certainly the public would read the recommendation as being against the use of heavy lorries.

The Commission tossed in a few more recommendations for good measure. Every mechanical vehicle (including steam wagons but not locomotives) should be on pneumatics, and steel tyres should be abolished (Paras 271 and 273). They were not in favour of national roads, that is, roads maintained and controlled by some central authority. Centralization could be carried too far. They thought that their recommendation that road transport should bear two-thirds of the cost and ratepayers one-third should be sufficient. On one major point the Commission hedged – the matter of limitation of the capacity of the road haulage industry. Specifically they said they did not propose to make any recommendations about control and regulation of traders' own vehicles [which probably accounted for the greater part of the diversion of traffic from the railways].

As for hauliers, there had been 'almost complete chaos' following the flood of wartime surplus vehicles and only recently had there been relative stability. Supply had reached a more reasonable proportion in relation to demand (Paras 298–300). With this talk of relative stability, supply matching demand, it would appear that the Commission believed that their previous recommendations regarding hours of drivers, speed limits, third party insurance and so on, and their present ones about taxation, ought to be sufficient to deal with both the cost of road maintenance and road competition with railways; and that no control of capacity was called for. Admittedly, they did point out that it was abundantly clear that very unsatisfactory conditions still existed (Para. 300), but they did not suggest any remedy such as they had recommended for passenger transport. They believed that it would be greatly to the advantage of the haulage industry if it were placed on an organized basis. That was an essential precedent to any attempt at general coordination with other forms of transport (Recommendation LX). So hauliers should be licensed, though not those 'contracting to carry for one employer only and not offering vehicles for hire to the public generally', nor firms carrying their own goods. In licensing, the Traffic Commissioners would be concerned only with the fitness of the vehicle and the wages and conditions of service of employees. The 'Fair Wages Clause' should be applied to hauliers (Recommendations LXI, LXV, LXVI).

The important question was clearly the one about coordination. Paragraph 500 of the Report makes interesting reading, coming, as it did, from a group of people who had spent many weary months in grilling knowledgeable witnesses and reading many long memoranda. Ideally, said the Commission, if every ounce of goods were consigned by the most economical route and form of transport, many of our transport difficulties would disappear; overlapping and unnecessary services would be eliminated. The rail, the road and so on, would convey just those passengers and goods for which each was best adapted. But as things were, was such a state of affairs, or even any approach to it, practicable? Who was to decide, for example, what rail services were desirable, or what goods should, in the national interest, be sent by rail, road, canal or ship? The next paragraph noted some of the difficulties – most goods by road were carried in trading firms' own vehicles. In the United States licensing of hauliers had brought a switch to firms' own vehicles. Lorries were not confined to fixed routes, but were analogous to tramp shipping. Paragraph 502 went on:

> we have given the most serious and anxious thought to the whole question, taking into account not merely the roads but all the other means of transport. We confess that for the present we can see no positive solution. Under existing circumstances, any such attempt at compulsion or coercion would, we believe, be a great mistake and would be strongly objected to, not only by the transport agencies but also by the traders, and any such attempt would probably prove to be quite ineffective in practice ... We think, however, that the measures we have recommended for the improvement of the various forms of transport will go far to make their co-ordinated working more easy to accomplish in the future.

Because of changing circumstances the Royal Commission thought that governments would always be in need of help and advice; so they recommended that there should be a permanent Advisory Council on Transport, which Council 'by means of suggestion and persuasion ... might be able to bring about a co-ordination of transport facilities which might not otherwise be possible' (Recommendations CXIV and CXVI).

The Final Report of the Royal Commission had left the whole subject of road and rail coordination largely unresolved. Even the minister, when he spoke at the Institute of Transport dinner in March 1932, took the view that the question of the relationship which should prevail between road and rail had baffled the Royal Commission.[5] Baffled or not, the Commission had apparently not said what the government wanted to hear and the publication in April 1932 of a little booklet summarizing the responses of a number of bodies to the Final Report did not add anything that would help the minister to formulate a policy. It consisted mainly of reiteration of evidence given at the Commission hearings or expressions of approval or disapproval of the Commission's recommendations. The Railway Companies' Association, for example, did not want the ownership of bridges carrying roads over the railways to be handed over to highway authorities (on the grounds that maintenance of these interfered with railway working). They were happy enough that highway authorities should be responsible for the roads over the bridges. Predictably they wanted road haulage firms to be licensed and regulated. Without that, they argued, there could be no proper co-ordination. Naturally enough, too, the National Road Transport Employers' Federation rejected the Commission's view that it was not in the national interest to encourage further diversion of heavy goods traffic from rail to road. The Federation asserted that traffic should be allowed to develop 'through natural channels'.

The Long Distance Road Haulage Association backed the recommendations for improving the road system. They approved, too, the recommendation that road hauliers be licensed. But they were adamant that the only points to be considered in licensing should be wages and conditions of service, fitness of the vehicles, and the suitability of the applicant. The

Employers' Federation had said the same but, in addition, wanted wage agreements to have statutory force.

The CMUA opposed the recommendation that vehicles over 4 tons unladen should be discouraged. They opposed the licensing of hauliers. They opposed the setting up of a permanent transport advisory council, even though most respondents liked that particular proposal. They wanted to retain existing practice whereby ministers consulted organizations from time to time. But they did support the proposals for the strengthening of weak bridges.[6]

So the argument continued apace, with the railways sending a statement to the MOT, and the motor organizations sending their counter-arguments. The railways demanded further regulation and taxation of road traffic. In particular they again called for road traffic to pay interest on the £1600 millions of capital value of the roads they had 'inherited'. The reply from the Conference of Motor Organizations was to the effect that they were not the only users of the roads. The track the railways used was a private one under the complete control of the railways. The roads, however, were public and the road transport concerns were subjected to all the effects of sharing the roads with the public.

The press, too, saw a great number of 'letters to the editor' from readers anxious to argue one point or another. Even the Chairman of the Royal Commission, Sir Arthur Griffith Boscawen, felt impelled to put in his word, in *The Times* of 25 July 1932, reiterating some of the points made in the Final Report. But, as with the government's little booklet summarizing the observations of various bodies on the Final Report, there was little new. It had all been said before half a dozen times over.

The minister, however, in a dilemma after the Royal Commission's Report, did the only possible thing, though there were plenty to argue that he was being pushed by the railways. He had already decided to call a conference of the opposing parties to tell them to sort out the problem amongst themselves and let him know what they wanted done. Even that was not as easy as it sounds for, immediately on the appointing of the Pybus Committee, as it was first called, there were arguments about the membership, about whether all varieties of road freight transport were properly represented. The minister had called a preliminary meeting to discuss membership of the new committee and decide on its terms of reference. According to Mr E.C. Marston, President of the LDRHA, speaking at a meeting of that body in Liverpool on 2 April 1932, although the LDRHA had three representatives at this preliminary meeting and the four railway representatives supported their case for inclusion, the representatives of the Standing Joint Committee outvoted them.[7] Admittedly the LDRHA was not as big an organization as it subsequently became, so it may be that the Standing Joint Committee representatives felt that as a body it was not representative of hauliers generally or even of long-distance hauliers. But the editor of *Commercial Motor*, bewailing the exclusion of the LDRHA, complained that some of the constituent bodies of the Standing Joint Committee itself were small, of little importance, and not vitally concerned with road haulage.

So the Pybus Committee (then called the Road and Rail Committee and finally known as the Salter Conference) came into being in March 1932 under the chairmanship of Sir Arthur Salter, KCB. The other members were the chairmen of the four main-line railway companies, plus the road freight transport representatives – Messrs C. le M. Gosselin MIAE, of H. Viney & Co. of Preston (and Past President of the CMUA), W.H. Gaunt, OBE, Distribution Manager of J. Lyons & Co., E. Graham Guest, JP, President of the Scottish CMUA, and P.R. Turner of Thos. Allen Ltd, Vice-President of the National Road Transport Employers' Federation and President of the London Haulage Contractors' Association. Owing to illness, Mr Turner was replaced from 10 June 1932 by Mr W.Edwards, President of the Employers' Federation.[8] Apart from Messrs Turner and Edwards, whose Federation consisted of a wide range of owners, the road transport representation seems to have been biased towards the 'own-account' operators who formed the bulk of the membership of the CMUA which inexplicably had two representatives.

The Committee got to work, then, to tackle the problem that had defeated the Royal Commission. On one aspect, alas, the minister gave them a strong hint when he told Parliament that he did not suppose that the conference would keep any detailed record of its proceedings, nor did he think it desirable that it should be fettered by any understanding that the proceedings would be made public. Committees are alleged to design camels when horses are required. No doubt that process is easier if no one is ever to know who drew the hump.[9] One cannot help wondering why the secrecy, after the publication of all the Royal Commission evidence, of three Reports, and of a booklet containing people's observations on the Final Report. While secrecy may have helped the Conference to arrive at a conclusion which had escaped the Royal Commission, it did, subsequently, provide ammunition for those who alleged that it had all been 'fixed'.

The LDRHA (or, as it had now become, the Road Haulage Association – RHA), as we saw, unfortunately did not have a representative at the Road and Rail Conference, but it was able, like other bodies, to submit a memorandum of its views which, subsequently, the Conference Report would describe as 'of especial value'. The 22-page memorandum handed in by the RHA on 7 July 1932, shortly before the Conference reported, expressed fears of the entire collapse of the transport system of the country if the prevailing conditions were allowed to continue. The industry was overcrowded, a feature made worse by the ease of obtaining vehicles on hire purchase. The easy entry into the industry attracted individuals having no knowledge of it and who could obtain work only by cutting rates. All this led to unbridled competition, to the detriment of both the railways and existing road transport operators.

The RHA's memorandum reiterated the point made to the Royal Commission that there should be a system of licensing of hauliers and clearing houses but not of the ancillary users carrying their own goods. The emphasis in the system would be on the fitness of the person, the conditions of service of his employees, and the fitness of his vehicles. Lorries would require an annually renewable certificate of fitness. The RHA did not want a licensing system which would in any way restrict a haulier to particular routes or would require him to prove public need for his service. Such a licensing scheme would have the effect of restricting entry to the industry and so make life more tolerable for those already in. One can imagine the RHA people agonizing over their document, trying to ensure that the licensing system would not result in a monopoly for existing hauliers – they had been grousing long enough about railway monopoly – but would, at least, allow the entry of 'responsible' firms while, at the same time, making it difficult for 'cowboys' (in modern parlance) to get in on the act.

Should a 'cowboy' manage to get in, the RHA had other proposals to deal with one of the worst features of such irresponsible fellows – rate-cutting. There would be a Rates Tribunal to lay down minimum standard rates for road or for rail. The Rates Tribunal would consist of representatives of the road transport contractors' associations, of the railways and of industry, and there would be an independent chairman. The RHA was of the opinion that the basis which the railways had used for rate-making in their monopoly days – 'charging what the traffic would bear' – was economically unsound. The proposed Rates Tribunal would 'probably' have regard to the class of traffic, its value, its bulk in relation to weight, the route, the density of traffic on the route, and the cost of cartage to and from stations and road transport depots. The memorandum believed that such a Rates Tribunal, working with, or superior to, the Railway Rates Tribunal, would enable coordination between road and rail to develop.

The sore subject of taxation of road vehicles received attention, too, along with many other topics. The remedy now proposed was the establishment of an impartial tax-assessment committee which would decide what proportion of road maintenance costs would be fairly attributable to road users and which should be divided equitably among the different classes of users – including horse-drawn vehicles. Writers of such memoranda have a touching faith in the wonders that may be wrought if only a few sensible men can put their heads together. In this case the hope was that motor taxation would be reduced. In particular, too, the method of petrol tax was advocated as the one which would reflect the load on the vehicle and the extent of road usage.

The deliberations of the Conference did not take nearly as long as those of the Royal Commission. To use Dr Mawhinney's phrase, there was no 'paralysis of analysis'. The members signed the Report on 29 July 1932 and it was immediately published. It set out at the beginning the questions which had been considered – the incidence of highway costs and the contributions of the different classes of vehicles. It was 'obvious', the Report said, that the newer means of transport did not pay a fair share of road costs. Second, they considered the nature and extent of the regulations which should be applied to goods transport by road and rail. This reads, not *whether* further regulation ought to be enacted, but *how* it was to be done. The matter of additional regulation seems to have been taken for granted. The third question considered by the conference was what measures might assist the two forms of transport to carry out their functions under equitable conditions. The whole object of the work of the conference, said the Report, was to secure a fair basis of competition. The Report warned against extravagant expectations of the effect of their proposals for increased taxation and regulation of road vehicles in forcing traffic back to the railways. Some railway services, essential in the previous century, were no longer indispensable and it would be undesirable to force the traffic to use them by extra taxation beyond what represented a fair share of road costs, and so deprive trade and industry of the convenience of the new form of transport. Anyway, part of the railways' problem was due to the economic depression and there was no remedy except from general recovery.

Regarding the allocation of highway costs, all was sweetness and light among the members of the Conference. All the railway people asked was that road transport should pay its fair share (rather less than what their memorandum to the minister in January had asked for); and the road transport people did not ask that they should pay less than their fair share. But the Conference as a whole saw their tax proposals only as an alleviation of the situation. They were by no means convinced that, when the unfairness had been corrected, it would be possible to keep the two systems, charging on different bases, in perfect equilibrium. Some industries had been built up on the basis of the railways' charging 'what the traffic would bear'. To switch now to charging them the full cost of the service would affect them adversely.

The Conference looked at several possible bases for allocating road costs. They weighed up the arguments about the inheriting by road transport of a track worth £1600 million capital, but a track used by all and sundry. They decided that community use and the 'legacy of the past' would just cancel each other out. That was convenient for them! They then proceeded to the calculations. First they did their sums on the basis of 'speed tonnage', multiplying the tonnage of the vehicle by its normal speed. That was rejected. Then petrol consumption was tried. That was no good, either, because clever engineers had succeeded in getting more work from heavier vehicles in relation to their petrol consumption. Next they looked at ton-mileage. This, they decided, was important but not, in itself, sufficient. It would need adjustment for speed, for differences in character of road use, wear and tear on the roads, and the effect of pneumatic tyres and multi-axles. It was clear that heavier vehicles would have to be punished for the MOT had told them that if there were no vehicles of over four tons unladen on the roads, annual road expenditure might be cut by 2 or 3 per cent. The Conference had no hesitation in applying this logic to each successively heavier class of vehicle.

Finally, the Conference concluded that ton-mileage and petrol consumption ('or equivalent for non-petrol vehicles') equally should be their foundation for allocating highway costs. There had to be, however, adjustment for heavier vehicles, on the one hand because of extra wear and tear on the roads, and on the other hand because of the speed of the lighter vehicles. This worked out as requiring £23.5 million per annum from commercial freight vehicles and the remainder of the £60 million annual highway cost from all other mechanically propelled vehicles. The £23.5 million was £2.5 million more than the then yield of petrol tax and licences on goods vehicles, so taxation had to be increased. In addition, there were anomalies in the existing taxation in that steam, electric and 'oil-engined' vehicles enjoyed a concealed subsidy in not having to pay petrol tax. Worse, the scale of licence duties stopped at five tons unladen so that a 10-tonner was paying the same as the 5-tonner.

The first element in allocation per vehicle was to decide what it should pay on the basis of the average ton-mileage of the (weight) class (that is, assuming the £20.5 million of the cost was being recovered on a flat ton-mile basis). Then the calculation was repeated as if the £20.5 million were to be recovered by petrol duty or equivalent. The mean of these was taken and then a flat £8.45 was added in the case of every vehicle for its 'franchise' of the roads. This £8.45 flat addition would produce the remaining £3 millions of the total £23.5 million. As an example of the calculation we take a steamer in the 6–7 ton category:

Number of licences	Average ton-miles per vehicle	Amount @ 0.389092517d. per ton-mile	Average petrol consumption*	Amount @ 12.61783514d. per gallon	Mean	Total incl £8.45
2592	113,848	£181.726	2297	£120.763	£151.245	£159.695

*or equivalent

This basic £160 was then adjusted to give a recommended taxation of £170 for a vehicle on solid and £136 for one on pneumatic tyres. The net result of these computations was a proposal for steep increases in licence fees, particularly for the heavier vehicles and those not paying petrol tax. A 1–1½ ton unladen petrol vehicle would pay just the same as before, £20, whether it was on pneumatics or solids, but a 5–6 ton unladen would jump from £48 (pneumatics) or £60 (solids) to a proposed £108 or £135 respectively. But the effect was more substantial the higher up one went on the weight scale. A 9–10 ton unladen petrol vehicle, formerly at the limit of the scale (5 tons and over) also paying £48 or £60, would henceforth be called upon to pay £226 or £282, and beyond that an extra £32 or £40 would be payable for each additional ton. A diesel in the 9–10 tons unladen category would merit an annual licence fee of £332 or £388, and the addition for each additional ton would be £54 or £60. The fact that a steam wagon did not accomplish as many ton-miles in the year as petrol or diesel vehicles was reflected in the smaller duty for a 9-10 tons unladen wagon – £170 or £212 with £32 or £40 per additional ton. Trailer duties would go up from the prevailing £6 to £16, whatever the tyres. Where a vehicle of 4 tons plus, unladen, worked exclusively within an immediate port area (to be defined by the minister), there would be a rebate of 25 per cent of the duties, for it was better that in these congested areas loads should be carried in bigger lots. The proposals assumed the continuance of the current petrol tax of 8d. per gallon and the Conference felt that no review would be needed for the next five years.

The Conference made its recommendations on regulation of the industry, too. It all started off very gently in the Report. All owners of goods motor vehicles would require a licence, but it would not cost them anything beyond the annual revenue tax already mentioned. The licence would be conditional upon the payment of reasonable wages, the observance of proper conditions of service and the maintenance of the vehicle in a proper condition of fitness. It would not be necessary to have a prior check of the vehicle annually. So far so good, but the punch line was to come. The licensing authority would have to grant the licence requested by the haulier except where that would be against the public interest on consideration of the following factors – any excess of existing facilities suitable to meet the public requirements, and any actual or prospective congestion or overloading of the roads. The licensing authority would be entitled to take into consideration, too, any convictions of the applicant in the previous year in respect of his vehicles or bankruptcy. As if that were not enough, the Conference recommended that the minister obtain powers to prohibit the transfer from rail to road of classes of traffic which 'having regard both to the character of the commodity and the distance, are unsuitable for road haulage'. Such negative action, thought the Conference, would be used only to a relatively limited extent. Then they must have had second thoughts about this knotty question of suitability of traffic for one or other form of transport. They added an observation that there was room for 'scientific enquiry' as to the most economical form of transport for each class of goods – up to what distance in each case road was the more economical, and up to what point, the railway. There still seemed to be that lingering idea that black and white cases could easily be distinguished.

The Report was received warmly by *The Times* and other leading papers, which found it all very wise. They were all impressed by the fact that the findings of the Conference were unanimous. Had it been happening fifty or sixty years later they would, no doubt, have labelled it 'a victory for common-sense'. The same could not be said for the road transport industry or its customers who read the recommendations with heat rather than warmth. There is no part of the human anatomy so tender as the wallet, and pencils were immediately sharpened to calculate the additional costs per ton-mile which would be imposed by Salter's taxation proposals. There can be no argument that the proposals were pretty drastic, bearing in mind that bigger vehicles would have their annual tax increased three- or four-fold, but some people took comfort in the view that such a nightmare could never become reality.

The Report was attacked from all directions – by the RHA, the CMUA, the Furniture Removers, The SMMT, by other motoring organizations, by individuals, by the Federation of British Industries (FBI), and by a conference of 66 national firms in industry and commerce. Here and there, there were some points with which people agreed but most of the comment was critical. The idea of charging the whole road cost of £60 million per annum to motoring was attacked. After all, the Royal Commission had recommended that ratepayers bear one-third of it. The £60 millions itself was attacked as being too high, for recent figures had been lower than that and the total was diminishing year by year. The calculations were attacked – the estimates of ton-mileage and so on were wrong and the whole arithmetic was school-boy stuff. The Conference members were attacked as being incompetent to make such involved calculations in such a short time. The lack of representation of the rapidly growing RHA was attacked. Those members from road organizations were attacked. How could they ever have agreed unanimously to such recommendations? It was beyond belief! There must have been considerable pressure on them from the railway side. The Conference members generally kept their heads down and made no attempt to justify the Report, though they did write to the minister on 17 December 1932 to point out the misconceptions in their critics' arguments. Oddly enough, not a great deal was said about the proposals for regulation by licensing. One wonders whether hauliers just happily assumed that the bit about 'any excess of existing facilities' would simply get rid of the irresponsible types and leave the sound men untouched. It can hardly be denied that many well-established and reputable hauliers believed that some regulation was needed to deal with the 'cowboys', but they did not appear to follow the argument through to a conclusion.

By the beginning of February 1933, when the various sides had pursued their arguments *ad nauseam,* a statement issued by the British Road Federation (BRF) raised another point which had only had a little airing up to that time. The Salter Conference was supposed to be about road *and* rail. It had produced any number of recommendations for road transport. But what about rail? The BRF anticipated Dr Beeching by asking questions like, Were all the railways (lines?) essential to a national transport system? Were not some branch lines being worked at a loss? Was there not much that was obsolete about the railways, which, if pruned out would relieve them of a burden of expense? If the railways were, for certain purposes, obsolete, why should they not suffer the penalty, as the cotton industry had suffered because of the rise of the artificial-silk industry? Until all this was defined, was the case that the railways needed protection proven? The BRF document had no doubt that here was a case of a vested interest which, by propaganda and political pressure, by every resource in its power, was seeking special terms and peculiar treatment for itself, so long as it escaped the economic consequences of its past and of the Depression.[10]

It would appear that there was substance in these points. Journalists had pointed out that railway stations were generally only two or three miles apart – suitable for times when there was no mechanical road transport and people had to rely on horses or their own leg muscles to get themselves and their packages to and from the stations. A good deal of rationalization was possible given the availability of motor transport. Indeed a speaker at the British Association meeting at Leicester in the summer of 1933 was reported to have forecast that half of the 20,000 miles of railway line would soon be abandoned through the need to write down capital.[11] The railways had certainly made some attempts to use motors to avoid having to stop trains at country stations. An LMS brochure in the late summer of 1933 claimed to have 'country services' operating at 140 centres. Their 1000 lorries on these services each covered a 10-mile radius from the centre.[12] About the same time the GWR were ordering just over 100 Thornycroft 2-tonners as well as other vehicles and trailers for use at 135 centres.[13] That was the time, too, that negotiations were going on between the four main-line railway companies and the two big road firms, Carter Paterson and Pickford. Despite this activity by the railway companies in road freight transport, most writers in pointing to enterprise by the railways generally refer to passenger traffic – particularly to the taking of shares in road passenger concerns – and suggest that really very little was done in the road freight field. The railways, though, certainly never really did tackle the enormous expense of transhipment and of shunting and remarshalling freight trains every few miles. No doubt the railways were in a difficult position. The fact that they had had to cut freight rates to counter road competition left them with very little spare cash to undertake any substantial reorganization. They did cut rates and whenever hauliers got around to talking about rate-cutting a few stones were generally cast at the railways for their efforts in that way. Perhaps the railways, then, could only rely on getting their competitors bound hand and foot. The BRF's accusation of a 'vested interest' using its powers seems to be borne out by Professor Derek Aldcroft's comment in his *British Railways in Transition* that 'the government acceded to the railways' demands by passing legislation in 1930 and 1933 to regulate their competitors'. The railways did have a great backing of national affection, and the Salter Report, which led to the legislation of the latter date, certainly seems to have met the criterion of what we today call 'political correctness'.

Notes

1. *CM*, 17/11/31, p.533.
2. *CM*, 17/2/31, p.7.
3. *CM*, 10/3/31, p.103.
4. *CM*, 2/6/31, p.533.
5. *CM*, 15/3/32, p.158.
6. *CM*, 26/4/32, p.369.
7. *CM*, 12/4/32, p.288.
8. *CM*, 29/3/32, p.219 and 22/8/32, p.40.
9. *CM*, 19/4/32, p.322.
10. *CM*, 3/3/33, p.860.
11. *CM*, 22/9/33, p.155.
12. *CM*, 8/9/33, p.102.
13. *CM*, 11/8/33, p.908.

CHAPTER THIRTEEN

Binding Legislation

Those who looked at the Salter recommendations on taxation with confidence that it would never happen did so more in blind faith than in judgement. In a sense they were proved right, for although taxation was increased substantially in the Budget of April 1933 (to operate from 1 January 1934) it did not approach the levels recommended by Salter. But when Neville Chamberlain, the Chancellor, came to propose the increases, he was reported to have made it fairly clear that the increases were solely in the interests of raising revenue and that their effect on the transport organization of the country was not one of the essential considerations involved.[1] Given the anxiety to produce a balanced budget at the time it is quite probable that the effect on an industry might well have been ignored though, no doubt, the Chancellor could have gone closer to the Salter proposals without alarming the general public. A few examples will illustrate the situation regarding taxation:

Type of vehicle	Licence duties pre-Salter		Recommended by Salter		Imposed by 1933 Budget			
Petrol engines								
Tyres	pneu.	solid	pneu.	solid	pneu.	solid		
	£	£	£	£	£	£	s.	d.
2–2½ tons unladen	28	35	33	41	30	40		
5–6 tons unladen	48	60	108	135	90	120		
9–10 tons unladen	48	60	226	282	170	226	13	4
for each additional 1 ton beyond 10 tons	–	–	32	40	20	26	13	4
Oil engines								
2–2½ tons unladen	28	35	64	72	35	46	13	4
5–6 tons unladen	48	60	188	215	120	160		
9–10 tons unladen	48	60	332	388	225	300		
For each additional ton	–	–	54	60	25	33	6	8
Steamers								
2–2½ tons unladen	28	35	58	72	30	40		
5–6 tons unladen	48	60	121	151	90	120		
9–10 tons unladen	48	60	170	212	150	200		
For each additional ton	–	–	32	40	15	20		

As can be seen, vehicles on solid tyres were severely dealt with. In regard to steamers it may well be that, as well as the ton-mileage factor, the proposed and imposed figures were influenced by pressure either from or on behalf of the coal-mining industry which had been having a rough time in the Depression. The Coal Utilization Council, for example, had arranged a demonstration of steam wagons in London in early April 1933 to call public attention to the merits of the steamer and to their annual consumption of one million tons of coal.[2]

While new taxes are always unpleasant, these particular ones came at a time when there were distinct signs of revival in the economy. Unemployment had peaked in the autumn of 1932 and was declining. Exports were picking up. Because of house-building schemes the demand for bricks was outpacing supply – and every three-bedroom house built needed conveyance of some 140 tons of materials.[3] It has to be said, though, that large consignments of bricks were nearly always moved by rail, not road. The Ministry of Health had just announced a big slum-clearance programme but it had not yet started. The MOT had, in the summer, authorized work to begin on a few road projects which had been deferred.[4] Railway goods traffic was up almost 10 per cent in the four weeks ending 9 September 1933 as compared with the same period in the previous year.[5] New freight vehicle registrations in September and October 1933 showed heartening increases over the previous year in all weight categories up to 4 tons unladen though it must be admitted that some of that could have been due to a shift to smaller vehicles in face of the impending severe taxation of the higher weights. But people were still buying some of the larger vehicles despite the taxes. Fifty-six vehicles of over 5 tons were licensed for the first time in September 1933 as compared with 72 in the previous September.[6] The Minister of Transport at an Institute of Traffic Administration meeting in October was optimistic that there could be enough traffic for both forms of transport. Despite improved results from the railways, road freight was doing better too, and he pointed to an increase of 4 per cent in the total number of vehicles licensed.[7] One not inconsiderable factor, also, was the reduction of 2½d. per gallon (about lp) in the price of petrol in May 1933.[8] One cannot help wondering why this came when life was returning to the economy. Did the petrol companies fear that the budget licence duties would harm their business?

The other main ingredient of the Salter medicine came in the form of the Road and Rail Traffic Bill, which got its formal First Reading on 7 April 1933 – a bill 'to make provision for regulating the carriage of goods on roads by motor vehicles and for controlling the use of vehicles on certain roads ... to amend the law relating to railways and to make provision for constituting a council to advise on questions in connection with the means of, and facilities for, transport', and so on. By this time Mr P.J. Pybus had resigned his position as Minister of Transport and had taken up a job with the Phoenix Assurance Co. Ltd (which did not seem to bother anyone in 1933).

It fell, then, to Mr Oliver Stanley, the new minister, to explain the Bill on 3 May 1933 on its Second Reading, just after the Budget. According to him, the new taxes would deal with any concealed element of public subsidy which might prejudice the choice of the individual as between different forms of transport. Then there was the question of whether the State was putting greater restrictions than necessary on one competitor and lesser than necessary on the other. The third factor, in his mind the most important and by far the most difficult to deal with, was what he called the factor of 'regularity'. He drew a picture of one competitor providing regular services and making facilities available at all times. Here the cost of the service taken up by a customer could not be the basis of charging. The railways charged rates intended to give a proper return on capital. The public '[had] got used to paying at a flat rate so that the facilities for whatever it wants to do will always be available for it'. (The factor of 'regularity' could well have applied to some of the bigger, well-established hauliers, too.) On the other hand there was the competitor who came along, charging cost on the one specific job he undertook but not always being available for other services. The minister thought that in the future, as road transport became more and more organized, more and more people would be prepared to provide regularity of service (Parl. Debates, Commons, 5th Series, vol.277, cols 853–4). He talked of what had led up to the Bill – the Royal Commission and the Salter Conference. No-one pretended 'that the four distinguished gentlemen who attended [the Salter Committee] on behalf of the roads had any intention or had any authority to bind by their recommendations the providers of road transport in general'. But their recommendations could not be ignored (col. 855). The present Bill would enable the ministry to enforce the safety conditions [of the 1930 Act and subsequent regulations] in a way in which it had not been able to enforce them up till then. It would, he believed, provide within the road industry some protection for the man who was prepared to offer a regular service against the pirate who only came to skim the cream, and would prevent some of the overcrowding in the road traffic industry. It was in no sense based on a desire simply to find the least that the railways would accept and the most that the road industry was prepared to tolerate.

After describing the system of A, B and C Licences in the Bill he reiterated the point about regularity:

> So I have attached – I do not disguise it – provisions to this Bill to give some advantage to the regular providers, to give the man who is prepared to offer continuous and not sporadic facilities, some advantage over the provider who just 'blows in' on the chance of picking up what traffic he can at the expense, and very likely to the detriment, of the man who is prepared to provide regular facilities,

He did not think the system would be too onerous on road transport. There was more danger that it would not achieve its objective (col. 863). 'I do not believe', said Mr Stanley,

> that to bring order out of chaos is in the long run going to do any harm to the road industry. I do not believe that the present position of unbridled competition is really good for it. Nor do I believe that it is really good for industry in general, or that the cheapness available during a war of cutting rates is a cheapness which in the long run is good for the industries of this country. (col. 878)

The minister was not too bothered about the 'little man'. The 'little man' had chosen, he said, to come into a job which involved certain dangers to the security of the public. He had to be able to meet the obligations as well as to take the advantages which the industry offered (col. 870).

As for the railways the minister did not agree that there was 'a whole mass of unnecessary regulations' stifling their enterprise. So the only thing the Bill would do would be to allow ' a new rate, an agreed rate, which may be agreed between the railways and the traders on any basis, apart entirely from the basis of the ton-mile'. Such a rate would require the approval of the Railway Rates Tribunal, but the law of undue preference would not apply to it. The safeguard for other traders lay in the fact that the railways had lost their monopoly (col. 873). As an example of what the minister had in mind, there could be agreement simply to take the tonnage which a firm had forwarded by rail (in a year, say) in whatever consignment sizes, for whatever distances; to average that out as *x* amount per ton, and to charge that as a flat rate per ton for all future consignments of whatever size to whatever destination. Such an agreed flat rate would hold considerable attraction for traders, both in administration and in cost accounting. For those consignments travelling the longer distances, too, it would be highly competitive with road haulage charges. The concept of an 'agreed charge' was not quite as new as the minister thought. The GWR had brought in exactly such a scheme for a firm of oil and cake merchants (Messrs Robinsons of Bristol) in December 1931 though subsequently (September 1932), lacking statutory authority, it failed to get the approval of the Railway Rates Tribunal.[9] Finally the Bill provided for a Transport Advisory Committee to replace the old Roads Advisory Committee.

So the minister introduced legislation which would bind road haulage for the next thirty-odd years. Whatever the lorrymen thought about it, it was not of world-shattering importance to the elected representatives. For, when the Opposition followed the minister's introductory speech with an amendment to reject the Bill because it did not unify transport services under national ownership and control, the members present had to be counted to ensure that there was the obligatory quorum of forty members.

There was much discussion of detail both inside and outside Parliament.

Public hauliers for hire or reward would get their first A Licence, and traders operating their own vehicles but doing some public haulage, their first B Licence, as of right for whatever tonnage they owned and used in the year from 1 April 1932 to 31 March 1933. But this was at the depth of the Depression, people argued, when many vehicles were laid up. Then again those operators who ran old, heavy vehicles in that year would be in a position of advantage, for they could get a licence for that tonnage and could then replace the heavy vehicles by lighter modern machines. Why did the Licensing Authority need to know from the applicant what rates were going to be charged for a service if that was not to be considered in deciding on the application? Hauliers could become redundant through no fault of their own. Would they be compensated? (An amendment to give such compensation was rejected by the Lords.) Only a small section of the industry was competing with the railways, yet the whole industry was to be taxed and restricted. Why, asked the railways, was there no provision for the publication of rates for road transport? The small man, said others, would be handicapped by having to leave his work and go off to hearings of the Licensing Authority or see either his own or an objector's solicitor.

The Bill went through the legislative procedure without any serious amendment and received the Royal Assent on 17 November 1933. So the great restrictive legislation came into force, together with its provision for heavy goods vehicle (HGV) licences, the keeping of records, and for vehicle examiners to check on the mechanical fitness of vehicles. In due course the dates were announced for its coming into operation. Those who were making applications for 'claimed' tonnage (that is, what they had 'owned and used' in 1932–33) must apply before 1 April 1934 and the HGV licence system (that is, for drivers of lorries over 2½ tons unladen or of artics) operated from the same day. The system of checks by vehicle examiners would start on 1 May 1934. C licences (for those operators carrying only their own goods) would be needed as from 1 July (the date originally envisaged) and A and B licences from 1 October (three months later than originally provided). Mr E.C. Marston, President of the RHA, in an article in *Commercial Motor* on 3 November 1933, referred to a series of meetings he had had with haulage contractors all over the country in the previous few months. This series of meetings, he said, had convinced him that haulage contractors as a body were rapidly gaining the impression that the Road and Rail Traffic Bill would ultimately have a beneficial effect on their industry, provided that it could adjust itself to the provisions of the Bill. He went on to argue, though, that there ought to have been machinery in the Bill to bring offences to the notice of the Licensing Authorities. It should have been open to hauliers to oppose renewal of a rate-cutter's licence.[10]

To try to judge the effects of the Act, one turns naturally to the *Annual*

Reports of the dozen licensing authorities. These reports, which appeared from the end of the first year of operation onward, contain a mass of statistics about the number of applications for licences, numbers rejected and pending and the total number of vehicles currently licensed. They tell us about the number of HGV drivers who got licences as of right through being able to show that they had been driving before 1 April 1934; about the number of tests, passes and failures of those who could not satisfy the authorities about their experience.

Whatever impression Mr Marston obtained from the members of the RHA it seems that not everyone welcomed, or perhaps even knew of, the legislation. The *First Annual Report* of the Northern Licensing Authority (for the period from 1 January 1934 until 30 September 1935) tells us that those owners taking up Road Fund licences in the early months of 1934 were given notice, by the Local Taxation Officers, of the new Act, but many of these vehicle owners 'showed disinclination to take any steps to acquaint themselves with their obligations'. Vehicle examiners, as far as available, then made personal calls, but applications, due by 1 April 1934, still came in only slowly. Chief constables were then asked to help and there followed an avalanche of applications. Saturday 30 March saw no less than 223 owners visiting the offices of the Licensing Authority (LA) in Newcastle-upon-Tyne. The Report adds that of the applications for A and B licences received by post, at least 70 per cent had to be returned for amendment or amplification. During the year this LA held 88 public inquiries regarding A and B licence applications, but found that:

> the work of conducting Public Inquiries has been made somewhat difficult by failure of many carriers (the small carriers particularly) to appreciate the full significance of the proceedings for them, and their omission to produce adequate evidence in support of their applications. No less than 381 applications had to be adjourned either for production of additional evidence or through the failure of the applicants to attend,

Perhaps all that might have been expected on the introduction of a new system but laggard owners were soon to find that the Authority intended to take the legislation seriously. By 30 September 1935 the Northern Area LA had issued licences for 19,741 vehicles and the *Report* (p.14) tells us that 5390 vehicles were examined of which 3694 were found to be defective in one way or another. This resulted in immediate prohibitions in 174 cases and delayed prohibitions in 633 cases. It is not known whether the vehicles examined were randomly chosen or simply looked as if they might be defective. That would make a difference for if the former applied there would be a good case for arguing that almost two-thirds of all vehicles would be defective. It is far more likely that the obvious 'baddies' were picked out. The LA added, incidentally, that it was now known that approximately 400 vehicles had been replaced as a direct result of the first examination. The 807 vehicles prohibited by the Northern Area Authority's examiners showed the following:

	% of vehicles defective	Total no. of defects
Brakes	45	623
Steering and front axles	40	1329
Springs and shackles	35	555
Frames and fittings	19	166
Rear axle	15	136
Engine, gear box, prop. shaft	12	140
Road wheels, studs and nuts	20	236
Exhaust and petrol system	6	61
Body, wings, etc.	33	418
Tyres	33	500

About the 5390 examinations (and 3446 re-examinations) made in that first year, the LA commented that the inspections revealed that the standard of maintenance was generally low. The majority of small owners had little knowledge of the machines they operated and made no serious effort to maintain them in roadworthy condition. When vehicles were run until something went wrong and were then put back on the road after tinkered repairs they were bound to deteriorate and become ultimately a menace on the highway. Those operators carrying only their own goods came in for some harsh words. The C licence operators 'generally appear to have little regard for their vehicles and expect the driver to be responsible for maintenance'. The drivers, however, were not inclined after a hard day's work, and in many cases did not have the necessary knowledge, to maintain the vehicles. This comment is pertinent since it had always appeared from the press and from hauliers' talk that the villain of the piece was the small man carrying for hire or reward. But whilst there were prohibitions there were no suspensions of the licences. Loss of one's licence would undoubtedly have been a sanction to be feared.

There were plenty of prosecutions in the courts, some brought by the police and some by the Licensing Authorities. Some LAs gave statistics of prosecutions by each body but the *First Report* from the Northern LA simply records 'prosecutions against 255 companies or persons, 413 charges':

	No.of charges	Convictions	Dismissed	Outstanding
Using vehicle without carrier's licence*	127	117	2	8
Driving hours	126	95	7	24
Failing to keep/carry records	137	128	2	7

Operating vehicles under prohibition	13	13		
Violating conditions of licence	1	1		
Failing to display identification	6	6		
Inefficient brakes/excessive noise	3	3		
Totals	413	363	11	39

* including 24 motor-cycle combinations

It would appear that charges for drivers' hours were a little bit harder to prove than the other cases.

It is not that the Northern Authority Area was any different from the rest of the country. The Metropolitan Area with 117,000-odd vehicles licensed as at 30 September 1935 reported 33,000 inspections (including second and third re-examinations). These resulted in 3358 prohibitions (approximately 10 per cent of all examinations), of which 814 were immediate and 2544 which were allowed up to ten days before the prohibition took effect.

It is not easy to deduce from the *Reports* what effect these prohibitions had on the operators. Certainly those who received prohibition notices had to take some action, and there were many replacements of old vehicles, as we saw. But what about those who had escaped inspection? Did they carry on as before, waiting for the Sword of Damocles to fall? LA *Reports* of later years suggest that that was indeed the case. The Northern Area *Report* three years later (1936–37) records 6485 vehicles examined. Of these, 2135 were prohibited, which is a higher proportion than in the first year. It is likely that the examiners were applying more rigorous tests than they had done at the beginning, and several of the *Reports* for 1936–37 claimed that there had been an improvement in the standard of maintenance. The East Midlands Authority was one of those which said so, recording that in 1934–35 prohibitions were 10.4 per cent of the vehicles inspected, in 1935–36 9.2 per cent and in 1936-37 only 6 per cent. Steering and brakes continued to be the chief problems. While the Western Authority said much the same, it added a comment to the effect that in some cases maintenance was now worse – the increase in trade had reduced time available for maintenance.

The Western Authority's 1936–37 *Report,* too, pinpointed the failures of C licence holders. 'With few exceptions maintenance was found to be very much neglected', it said of them. This was particularly so of shops where the driver was only part-time behind the wheel. The North-Western LA in a way, supported this by indicating that vehicles under 2½ tons unladen showed a lower standard, possibly due to overloading. The Northern Report for that year, also, said that it was

> particularly noticeable that long-distance vehicles of the heavy type are generally well maintained. The long-distance of the lighter type, i.e. those below 2½ tons unladen take second place. Those operated locally have a lower standard of maintenance, and, of these, the C class vehicles are generally maintained in an unsatisfactory condition,

The Northern Area, Scotland, Authority had something to say about overloading. There was a tendency for major operators to dispense with the heavier types and substitute the 'under 2½ tons unladen' which could do 30 m.p.h. 'The result is a consequent tendency to overloading and many of the vehicles concerned have been found to suffer from defects due thereto ... for example, the main chassis members, spring brackets and rear axle casings are regularly found to have been bent or displaced through overloading.'

That, no doubt, had been a problem for a long time. The Yorkshire LA, in its *First Report,* 1934–35, had said 'The question of overloading of goods vehicles is one which, in my view, requires to be dealt with further by regulation ... There were many instances of lorries designed to carry 2-ton payloads which were laden with 5, 6, 7, and even 9 tons of goods.' Some of these vehicles had had stronger springs, tyres, and so on fitted. 'There seems to be no doubt that a high percentage of steering and brake faults ... in light goods vehicles is due to the carriage of excessive loads.' The fitting of an additional (trailing) axle appeared to give many operators an exaggerated conception of the additional load which could be safely carried, it added. The comment of the South-Eastern LA on this matter in 1936–37 was that the type most usually prohibited was the open lorry of under 2½ tons unladen. These vehicles were not robust enough for the strenuous work which they were often called upon to perform. It continued, saying that the increasing tendency on the part of the chassis manufacturers to push up the advertised payload capacity had, in the opinion of the certifying officer, resulted in reducing the safety factor of vital components to an unwise degree. In fairness to manufacturers, however, no other LA made that point, and at least one, commenting on the improving situation, referred to the scrapping of vehicles of older design and the substitution of more modern designs. Given the high hopes raised by the 1933 Act, it is sad to note that thirty years on from the coming into operation of the 1933 Act the Geddes Committee reported that special checks showed some 10 per cent of vehicles in an unroadworthy condition.

One little nugget of information about the maintenance question appeared in the Yorkshire *Report* for 1936–37. The survey of A licensed vehicles in the area had been completed during that year. There were 2305 holders of A Licences, with 6087 vehicles (1431 under 2½ tons unladen). The maintenance facilities were:

838 holders	had their own maintenance and repair staffs
784 holders	relied solely on outside garages
591 holders	had maintenance staff but relied to some extent on outside garages
92 holders	had no regular system of maintenance.

The LA summed up the vehicles of these 2305 licence holders as: 50 per cent with 'good' vehicles, 42 per cent with 'fair' vehicles, and 8 per cent with 'bad' vehicles.

Noting the small proportion who were without maintenance facilities we read the views of the West Midlands Authority in its 1935–36 *Report,* a comment which also, in some respects, bears out what a colleague had to say. Before the beginning of regular inspections,

> few carriers had adopted a systematic method of vehicle maintenance. The standard adopted by the private carrier was, in general, even lower than that of the public or limited carrier. ... Some of the large business houses controlling their own transport have shown a lesser degree of efficiency in the maintenance of vehicles than is evident in other sections of their business. Neglect has been most apparent among retailers ... due, in some instances, to the location of the vehicles at a distance from the company's main base ... upkeep being left to the discretion of the van-men,

A necessary part of the concept of public safety was the hours drivers worked. Received wisdom at the time held that many of these poor fellows were so tired at times that they would lose control of their vehicles. The hours of work as prescribed in the 1930 Act and now enshrined in the Road and Rail Traffic Act, 1933, as a condition of every carrier's licence, could be, and would be, enforced either by the police acting on their own or by the LA. Most of the *Annual Reports* contain tables of prosecutions under various headings but unfortunately there was no agreed format for the statistics. Some Authorities showed only convictions whilst others showed prosecutions as well. One can, however, pick out from ten of the *Reports* a total of 2782 *convictions* for 'hours' offences in 1935–36 (that is, the second year of operation of the Act) and for the other two Authorities (South Wales and the Metropolitan) a total of 1631 *prosecutions.* At a guess, then, we might say that around 4000 convictions were obtained in that year, which is not really a very significant figure considering that at 30 September 1935 there were just under 460,000 freight vehicles licensed. Considering, too, that the iniquitous, ubiquitous, piratical 'small man' was often alleged to work, or work his driver(s), scandalous hours, there was surprisingly little comment from the LAs on this topic. The 'statutory requirements have been widely and persistently disregarded', said the South Eastern LA about no particular class (1934–35), 'a great deal of deliberate evasion'. The Metropolitan LA that year listed all the commonly quoted attributes of the 'irresponsible operators' and included 'working drivers for excessive hours'. But it is not at all clear whether it was simply expressing conventional wisdom or was speaking from experience of the first year's operations. For, the next year, we find the North Western LA saying that proscutions for excess hours were not confined to any particular type of haulier, but adding that 'It is manifest there existed an impression in the minds of a large proportion of traders operating vehicles under C Licences that 11 hours per day should be regarded as the normal working day for the drivers of goods vehicles'.

More worrying was the comment by the East Midlands LA in its 1935–36 Report. He had had complaints from both drivers and drivers' wives that the former were being compelled to work excessive hours. They had either to disobey the law or be dismissed. Unfortunately it did not say whether the LA had tackled the difficult task of investigating such allegations. It is not altogether clear whether the South Eastern LA was sympathizing with operators and drivers when, in its *First Report,* it commented 'The conveying of soft fruit and market garden produce from certain parts of Kent and Hampshire to the London Markets (particularly to Covent Garden) has, perhaps, provided the most flagrant examples in my Area of excessive hours of driving and of work'. It went on to say that the notorious conditions of unloading and loading at Covent Garden made it difficult or impossible for the same driver to bring produce to the market night after night from any distance without exceeding the maximum of 11 hours. The LA in Yorkshire would not appear so sympathetic, for its view was that 'the number of hours a driver is required to work is an essential part of the conditions of service which should be the basis of fair competition' (1936–37 *Report*).

It was the hope of the legislators that offences such as overloading, speeding, and the working of excessive hours would all be revealed in the records of their work which drivers were required to keep. Alas, it would seem that many operators and/or their drivers were not too anxious to fulfill the politicians' hopes. Again we find that the tables of prosecutions in the *Reports* include a great many for offences for failure of drivers to keep records or failure of their employers to 'produce or preserve' records. Ten of the Authorities report a total of 8508 *convictions* in 1936–37 while the remaining two (in this case East Midlands and South Wales) record 1974 *prosecutions.* Of the perhaps 10,000 convictions a great many resulted from the police acting on their own, but the LAs did their bit too. We can read in the *Reports,* of LA staff standing by the roadside, recording the time lorries passed by, and subsequently comparing that with what the driver had recorded. But some LAs had to confess that roadside checks, for whatever purpose (records or condition of vehicle), could be carried on only for a limited period of time. The news soon got around – to anything up to 50 miles from the checkpoint – and drivers took avoiding action.

So far as records were concerned, the Authorities commented regularly on what was happening. The North of Scotland LA in 1935–36 said that duplicate records were common, and the next year several other LAs joined in. 'Falsification of records' (North West), 'still too large a number of operators and drivers who ignore limits on hours, speed, weight, and who falsify records to disguise this' (West Midlands). From the neighbouring East Midlands came the comment that the practice of checking records had led to 'faking', but there was now a preference for taking a chance with no records or false ones rather than to have accurate ones which showed irregularities of hours. The next year, 1937–38, the North Western LA reported a decrease in prosecutions for 'drivers' hours'. It was of the opinion that this decrease was not to any great extent due to a better general observance of the law. The principal reason for the decrease was an increase in the falsification of drivers' records, so that the detection of offences became more difficult. So it had instituted road-side checks which showed 'conclusively the wide extent to which the falsification of records is practised'. How wide an extent? According to the *Report,* when one road check was done 'it was subsequently found that 90% of the drivers' records concerned were false in so far as they purported to show the movements of the vehicle concerned'.

It seems a sad fact of life that when legislators pit their wits against those they regard as wrongdoers, the latter, in turn, pit their wits against the legislators. Before leaving the topic we note that the drivers were frequently pitting their wits against their employers also. The South Scotland LA recorded in 1937–38 that 'one driver spent an afternoon at the Empire Exhibition at Glasgow and then drove on through the night without taking his proper rest'. One can only smile at some of the activities that led drivers into such criminal falsification of records in those far-off days. The West Midlands LA reported the same year that 'some drivers, intent upon concealing their activities from their employers, maintain inaccurate records for trivial purposes e.g. concealing time spent upon journeys whilst gathering mushrooms or picking blackberries'. How easy life is today when we can simply go to the supermarket for our mushrooms. How difficult was life in those days for employers who had to pay for the time the drivers spent on these frolics of their own. (Yes, tachographs had been invented.)

It must be doubted whether the prosecutions had the desired effect. There is more than one comment from LAs about trivial fines. The Western Authority in its 1935–36 *Report* talked about the considerable variation in fines imposed. It mentions that in cases brought, 328 had resulted in fines between 2s. 6d. (12½p) and 5s. (25p); 18 had resulted in fines between 1s. 6d. (7½p) and 2s. 6d. (12½p); and 78 of 1s. (5p) only. The nature of the cases is not explicit, so one cannot say whether a fine of five times the smallest fine was in any way remarkable. A fine of one shilling in those days would have deprived the culprit of a packet of twenty cigarettes. In some cases employers would pay the fine, particularly if the driver's offence was to the employer's advantage. But the North of Scotland LA railed against this in 1935–36. The payment by the employer of fines for speeding, it said, was a pernicious practice which went a long way to defeat the ends of justice. In case it should be thought that all fines were extremely light it should be mentioned that there were other possibilities. The South-Eastern LA recorded, in its 1935–36 *Report,* that in one particularly bad case a retailer, holding a C licence, was convicted on 233 counts for causing or permitting his drivers to work excessive hours. This retailer was fined £3 + a half guinea costs, on each count, making a total of £821 6s. 6d. (£821.32½). That was enough to bring a small business to its knees in those days. In case, too, it should be thought, from our references to all these thousands of prosecutions, that lorry owners and drivers were generally a bad lot, note must be taken of a remark by the West Midland LA in the 1936–37 *Report.* 'Although breaches of the law are so numerous', it said, 'I would not have it inferred that commercial vehicle owners are, as a rule, more prone to lawlessness than other classes of the community; on the contrary it is evident that the majority appreciate the statutes by which they are governed.'

The *Annual Reports* of the LAs give a mass of statistical information about the number of applications they received, granted, refused or left pending; about prosecutions under a number of headings concerned with the maintenance and use of vehicles; about HGV tests and licenses granted, and so on. In one major respect, though, they are singularly disappointing. The Road and Rail Traffic Act, 1933, under which the LAs operated in respect of goods vehicles, had as a major feature, the control *by capacity* of goods vehicles operating for hire or reward. But whilst we can get information in the actual *Reports* about the number of vehicles operating under each type of licence, nothing is said about the capacity of the vehicles concerned. When one reads of increased number of vehicles under C licences (operated by a business for its own goods), a great desire arises to know just what sort of total capacity was involved. It can hardly be assumed that the tonnage increased absolutely *pro rata* with the number of vehicles. We get references, for example, to the common rule that when replacing horses it was usually one vehicle to a horse-and-a-half but we are left to guess what size of vehicle it would be. Similarly, when the East Midland LA reported in 1936–37 that 253 A licence holders had surrendered their licences, it added that 140 of these had given up because their vehicles had been either scrapped or taken back by the finance companies; but we are left without information about the capacity of the vehicles concerned. There is surprisingly little comment in the *Reports* about how the LAs saw their function in respect of capacity.

The Metropolitan Authority's *First Report* points out that the Appeal

Tribunal had ruled, in the case of E.&H. Ridgewell, that 'during the first currency period of licences the principle to be applied under the Act ... is to maintain the status quo, and not to make any radical changes as to the extent of the facilities which the industry offers to the public'. No doubt that ruling would have been followed then and later by other authorities, certainly in the direction of not allowing increases. The Metropolitan LA, though, seemed to be prepared to wait and see. It thought that 'it was then too early to state what might be possible in overcoming the various difficulties ... to which both road and rail transport might be subject, or what form of transport might ultimately be most in accord with the interests of industry for carriage of particular goods'. Such questions, it said, could not be answered until the then existing condition of strain in the industry had been removed, and more economic conditions for all forms of transport had resulted. If all forms of transport were able to develop fully the advantages which they could respectively offer, it went on, it was manifest that controlled competition would confer very important benefits on British industries. There was a clear indication in this, that this Authority, at least, was prepared to be flexible. One wonders whether the LA at West Midlands took the same view. While the current 'in' phrase referred to 'cut-throat' or 'wasteful' competition, the LA of West Midlands introduced a nice new concept in the reference, in the 1935–36 *Report*, to 'the evils of *wrongful* competition'.

That year Mr Gleeson Robinson, representing the Metropolitan Authority, commented on suggestions that industry was already suffering inconvenience and loss through a shortage of road transport resulting from licensing control and it may be worth quoting him at some length. 'Such suggestions are without any present justification', he argued, and he went on to say that

> When the licensing procedure was introduced, there was an immense reserve of transport available in excess of public need, and under the licensing procedure great elasticity exists. There is abundant evidence that a very large amount of claimed tonnage has never been taken up, because the licencees have been unable, notwithstanding the improvement in trade, to find work for it. In addition to claimed tonnage not taken up, large numbers of vehicles specified in licences have not been used, and it is no infrequent experience to find that vehicles forming a considerable percentage of large and of small fleets have not been taxed for months or years. This does not mean that all licence holders have been short of work; far from it. There has, throughout the road transport industry, been a great improvement in trade, and very many licence holders have found that they were unable to meet their customers' needs with the vehicles they had in 1934, when licensing control commenced. Many of them have increased the capacity of their fleets, both large and small, by substituting new and more efficient vehicles for old and obsolete vehicles. Many new vehicles have been put on the road under the provisions of Section 7 (I) of the Road and Rail Traffic Act, 1933, as contract licence vehicles. The greater part

> of any need which has existed for additional transport facilities, has, however, been met in the normal manner contemplated by the Act, namely by licence holders making application for additional vehicles and supporting their applications by evidence. ... Any real need can be, and is being, met.

But some kinds of evidence were insufficient, and here he mentioned that provided by letters

> from traders who are willing, as customers, to support an applicant merely in the same way as they would give a testimonial to any employee, actuated by the feeling that it is the proper thing to do, or the evidence of those who desire to have as much transport as possible available at all times, so that they can pick and choose, regardless of whether vehicles can be properly supported if licensed, or who desire to employ a particular haulier because he charges lower rates than his competitors. (pp.99,100)

Those letters produced in evidence clearly were a problem, for the East Midlands LA mentioned them, too, in 1935–36. Some traders readily gave letters to hauliers saying they would give traffic if the licence were granted. 'so many such letters ... that they may well have been produced by a copying machine'. This LA, too, had suspicions that the firms in question simply wished to get as many vehicles as possible on the roads to get more competition and lower rates.

There were objections to the applications, as might be expected. The railways, at a conference with the Metropolitan LA and various road transport associations on 19 February 1934 to discuss procedures under the new legislation, had stated their policy. They would not oppose any application for an A licence made before 1 April 1934 in respect of tonnage which the applicant owned or had under a hire-purchase agreement at the date of the application, provided that the applicant also applied for claimed tonnage. But they would oppose any other application, as they would for additional vehicles in subsequent licensing periods. They would give no such assurance in regard to B licences, and they held themselves free to act as they saw fit in future.[11]

Oppose they did. In subsequent years the LAs' *Reports* contain frequent references to the fact that the railways were the main objectors, and often statistics are quoted showing the proportion of applications to which the railways objected. The Northern LA in its *First Report,* for example, stated that there had been 1858 objections to A and B applications during the period covered by the *Report,* of which the railways accounted for 1408. There are a number of mentions, too, of the point that other hauliers did not usually object, unless they were owned by the railways or unless the applicant was in direct competition. In rural areas, with fewer vehicles around, any expansion would be quickly felt, and so most of the applications would be opposed. The objections were often pressed with considerable vigour, leading one LA representative to say rather tetchily, in the 1935–36 *Report,* that 'objections have been maintained in instances where I have fully explored the position previously, and I have felt constrained to make observations upon waste of public time as well as on the unnecessary inconvenience suffered by the applicant to whom it may mean at least the loss of a day's work'. On the other hand the South Wales Report of 1935–36 could not say of the railways, which had opposed practically every application for additional vehicles on existing A licences, that 'their attitude at the Public Enquiries has been in any way unreasonable, and in those cases in which the applicant has made out anything like a case they have not pressed their objections unduly'.

The Yorkshire LA's *Report* for 1936–37 contains a summary of the cases made by some A licence applicants (long-distance operators) for additional tonnage and the responses by the railway objectors. The applicants based their request on:

i) the difficulties in undertaking C&D work;
ii) the need to have a reserve to allow overhaul and repair;
iii) the fact that work was being refused and it was not possible to hire vehicles within a reasonable distance;
iv) the increase in applicants' business and that of some of their customers who detailed the inconveniences.

The case made by the railways concentrated on:

i) attempting to show by statistics that the railways had not fully shared in the national prosperity;
ii) showing under-utilization of the railways, their ability to carry extra traffic – in particular the applicants' traffic which was mainly, if not wholly, commercially suitable for the railways;
iii) giving particulars of the improvements effected in rail facilities, for example wagon and locomotive stock, mechanical appliances, new lines, extended times for collection, warehousing, quicker transit;
iv) producing the results of tests demonstrating the efficiency of their services;
v) showing that as common carriers they should be safeguarded against hauliers carrying the higher and more remunerative grades of traffic as otherwise basic industries might suffer;
vi) suggesting that the LA should divide the applicants' trunk route traffic between 'commercially suitable for rail-borne' and 'special for road' and then reduce applicants' fleets to a size necessary to carry the latter;
vii) endeavouring to prove that the applicants had abstracted traffic from them;

viii) showing that applicants' rates were, generally speaking, below the rail rates for similar traffic.

Counsel for the railways argued generally that, in so far as the objectors provided suitable facilities, any grant of further facilities would involve an excess over requirements, which meant wasteful competition, which was not in the public interest. The LA commented particularly on the proposition of item (vi).

> This was, in my opinion, tantamount to saying that my discretion ended at the point when I had determined, if it were possible to determine, the tonnage necessary to carry on trunk services the goods which ought not under the foregoing contention to go by rail. It seemed, however, that my duty was to take into consideration anything and everything which the objectors rightfully put before me but that my discretion was unfettered other than by what is specifically laid down in Section 6 (2) of the Act and decisions of the Appeal Tribunal.

The LA then went on to point out that nowadays (1936–37) traders no longer held large stocks of goods and that they required more urgent and frequent deliveries over longer distances. The fact that the road hauliers had suited their services to the traders' requirements was one of the chief reasons which had acted in their favour in the past and which had caused the railway companies to improve their services. But the evidence made it clear that road transport was frequently the only form of transport which could supply suitable facilities. Regard had to be had to the public interest, and this change in conditions could not be overlooked, nor could a definite public demand for speedy long-distance traffic by road be disregarded.

These remarks of the LA representative, taken with what he went on to say, might well have been used as the basis of an advertising campaign by the RHA. The march of progress in the road transport industry ought not to be retarded. The construction of heavy types of motor vehicles for trunk road work should not be discouraged. To follow the railways' request generally would result in some thousands of trunk-route vehicles ceasing to run. Such a heavy loss of mobility would be extremely serious in the event of a national emergency. In the particular cases he was considering the applicants provided later collections and earlier deliveries than the railways, even on long-distance trips like York to London. He then gave half a dozen reasons why the applicants' customers preferred the applicants' road services to rail, reasons which, over the years, have been quoted in countless college textbooks – personal attention to customers' requirements, road transport faster and more dependable, more flexible as to running time. Less packing was necessary, less handling, less damage occurred.

Perhaps to counter the scary notion of thousands of vehicles ceasing to run, the LA representative then undertook a brief discussion to show that

'Some redundancy (did he mean 'surplus'?) of railway wagons and road transport vehicles seemed to be inevitable under any competitive transport system, as provision has to be made for peak periods of traffic.'

In the cases which the Yorkshire Authority had been discussing, the requests by the A licence applicants for additional tonnage were granted, in whole or in part. If the railways vigorously opposed many of the long-distance A licence applications they were equally concerned to limit the activities of B licence holders. These were ordinary businesses – coal merchants, furniture dealers, dairymen or whatever – operating lorries or vans for their own goods but being allowed to carry some goods of the general public for hire or reward. The coal merchant delivering coal to a farm might pick up a back load of sugar-beet to take to the refinery, or he might do a small furniture removal job en route to the colliery to get his supplies of coal. The coal merchant's trade, of course, was often slack during the summer and so he liked to have some other work for his lorry. It was not just small firms like the local builder or coal merchant who tried to do a bit of public haulage as a sideline. The statistics as at June 1938 show 44 operators holding B licences, each with 25 or more vehicles. But that has to be considered in the light of a total of 34,120 B licence holders. Such operators were probably disliked as much by many A licence holders as by the railways. The big difference from the A licence was that restrictions could be, and were, imposed on the B licence; restrictions on the distance, restrictions on the goods, limitation to particular customers, particular districts, and so on; 'and such other conditions as the Authority may think fit to impose in the public interest and with a view to preventing uneconomic competition'. But no conditions could be imposed in regard to the rates charged. The objectors did their utmost to hamstring these operators with as tight restrictions as possible.

The LAs were well aware that in some areas, particularly rural areas, B Licence operators provided a useful service. The South Wales LA, in its 1934–35 *Report*, for example, noting that in its area there were twice as many B as A licence holders, said that the public were obviously depending on the services of B licence holders, so that it could not deprive the public of facilities they were used to. The Eastern LA in the 1936–37 *Report* sets out a little table showing that in the 324 'centres' in the County of Norfolk (excluding the County Boroughs of Norwich and Great Yarmouth), 172 had only one operator and in 110 of those that operator held a B licence only. In 72 more fortunate small towns and villages each with two operators it records that in 31 of the centres the operators held only B Licences; while in 28 centres there were A and B licensees. But while not depriving the public of the occasional transport services of the local coal merchant the LAs were not going to allow them *carte blanche* to do all the haulage work they wanted in competition with A licensed hauliers and the railways.

There are ample references in the *Reports* to the restrictions imposed. The volumes of *Reports* each include a couple of foolscap pages listing a great many types of goods where restrictions had been imposed – from general goods (the biggest category) through 'fish, ice, poultry and game,' and 'fishermen's gear and requisites', to 'Theatrical scenery and equipment' and 'Wool and woollen goods (other than clothing and drapery)'. These are divided up among 'Goods not limited to Specified Persons'; 'Goods for Specified Persons'; 'Goods to Specified Destination'; 'Goods in one direction only'; 'Goods lifted within a specified District'; and 'Special limiting conditions not in previous categories'. There could be more than one restriction on any given licence. The figures given in the tables appear to refer to the numbers of restrictions, since the totals are a long way different from the number of B licences and from the numbers of vehicles. The following data of restrictions applied to B licences are abstracted from the summary table for 30 June 1938:

	Goods not limited to specified persons						
	Not exceeding 10 miles	10–20 miles	20–30 miles	30–50 miles	50–100 miles	>100 miles	Overall totals
General goods	2969	6437	3856	2009	687	315	17,402
Bldrs' material: sand, ballast, gravel, etc.	2012	3548	2234	1351	373	182	11,273
Coal, coke, & patent fuel	3737	982	322	184	45	43	6445
Furniture & household effects	1694	2073	1847	2319	941	1686	12,367
Totals	14,167	17,611	12,092	9497	3611	3562	77,463

Since the total number of B licences in operation at that date was 34,767, we have an average of rather more than two restrictions per licence. The figures for furniture are interesting in that such a high proportion of them fall into 'long-distance' categories. It is not surprising that the Furniture Removers' Association should have been mentioned specifically by one LA as opposing strongly certain applications. The railways not only put forward their protests at the public hearings of the LAs but did whatever else they could. The East Midlands LA noted in its 1934–35 *Report* that coal merchants brought coal for sale when going to collect sugar-beet under their B licences. This was having 'a serious effect on the haulage of coal by rail'. So the railway companies 'have sought to protect themselves by making agreements with colliery companies by which the latter will refuse to supply coal for delivery by road over a greater distance than, in most cases, 7 miles'.

It is clear that in one respect, at least, the 1933 Act had the consequences desired by the legislators. The number of firms and vehicles engaged in public haulage work ceased to increase dramatically as it had been doing before the 1933 Act. The *Reports* of the LAs show, for A Licences, other than railways:

	Operators	No. of vehicles
1936	25,616	76,292
1937	23,718	74,011
1938	22,967	73,604

and we read in many of the later *Reports* words like 'stabilization'. The figures for B licences also show a marked tailing off of growth:

	Operators	No. of vehicles
1936	34,100	52,809
1937	34,061	53,775
1938	34,120	54,906

It must be said that the decrease in the growth rate could not all be attributed to the licensing procedure. From the trough of 1932 the economy had been growing slowly, but right through these years there were large numbers of business failures, both in trade and industry generally and in the haulage sector, and the slight recession from 1937 did not help matters at all. There are many references in the *Reports* to the collapse of businesses and it is difficult to judge how much influence that had on the figures. As an illustration of the difficulty of interpretation the Southern Scotland LA referred in 1936–37 to a licence holder with 40 vehicles who had gone out of business. 'It is significant', it commented, 'that there were no applications for additional vehicles from other licence holders in the district to balance this loss of facilities-, although it was referred to as a contributory cause in 2 or 3 cases.' Probably in most cases where a firm surrendered a licence on going out of business, however, it would be replaced by either newcomers or by the existing hauliers adding vehicles to their fleets.

It is more than likely that the stabilization in the number of A and B licensed vehicles (whatever size they may have been) did not add a great deal to the fortunes of the railways. We recollect that the Salter Conference members were hesitant to suggest that the railways might gain much from the restrictions on the number of road vehicles. Perhaps what Sir Henry Maybury had told the Royal Commission about the process in America had happened in Britain too. Traders finding it difficult to get road transport facilities, and preferring road to rail, would go over in great numbers to running their own road vehicles. The numbers of C licences and vehicles expanded rapidly:

Date	No. of licences	No. of vehicles
30 April 1936	161,221	316,714
30 June 1937	186,481	362,380
30 June 1938	178,586	365,025

Here again the figures cannot be taken absolutely at face value, particularly the big jump from 1936 to 1937, because as from 1 October 1936 C licensed vehicles were required to display an identity disc. There was then an influx of people who had not bothered to take out a licence previously. Furthermore, there were some indications that in the later years B licence holders, faced with high insurance premiums for public haulage work (and possibly, too, the effects of the recession) were reverting simply to C licences. There was, too, the ever-present movement to motor vehicles away from horses. The drop in numbers between June 1937 and June 1938 is likely to be mainly due to an overstatement of numbers in 1937. A great many businesses had gone to the wall without ever advising the LA that they were no longer running vehicles. It would only be when the licences were due for renewal that the Authority would be aware of their demise. The North-Western Authority, for example, subsequently deducted 4094 C licences (4659 vehicles) from its 1937 figures because of non-renewal.

Another possibility relating to the levelling off in the numbers in the A and B categories was the increasing use of A (contract) licences. Where a haulier could not expand as he wished with an A licence, he could show that he had a contract with a trader, for a period of at least a year, to carry that trader's goods. He could then get the A (contract) licence as a matter of course, just as a trader could have got a C licence. The figures for such licences were:

	No. of licences	No. of vehicles
30 April 1936	2844	5156
30 June 1937	4417	7475
30 June 1938	5430	9467

It should be noted that the figures quoted here and above are of vehicles 'in possession' and do not include those (comparatively few) which the haulier or trader might hire (and which required licences too).

There were silly things in the system. An operator seeking to replace an older vehicle by a new one had to take care. At first, if the new one was no more than 5 cwt (560 lb) greater than the old one in tare weight then he was likely to have no problems, but if the extra weight of the new vehicle were more than that – say 10 cwt – then he would have to go through the procedure of applying for a variation of his licence because of 'additional tonnage', and being subjected to the objections of his competitors. The 5cwt margin was eventually changed to 10 cwt when the LAs realized the silliness of the earlier figure. One wonders, too, about the period of validity of the licences. Initially A, B and C licences were valid for two years, one year and three years respectively. Did the legislators really consider the risk that an A licensee, for example, would be taking, in buying a new vehicle with a five- to ten-year life-span, knowing with certainty only that his licence would allow him to operate it for two years? After that he was in the hands of the LA. An 'Order' was issued in March 1938, however, extending the period of validity of an A licence to five years (or three for newcomers) and to two years for a B licence.

The commercial vehicle press looked for anything in the new system which would show how the life of practical men was bedevilled by politicians and others. *Commercial Motor* did not appear too unhappy at having to report cases where the railway objections appeared frivolous, e.g. against an application for a B licence for a 7½ cwt van, on the grounds that their grain trade had suffered since the van had been put into service; or their objection to the substitution of two vehicles for one of the same total unladen weight, on the grounds that two vehicles could cover a larger geographical area than one.[12]

Notes

1. *CM,* 9/6/33, p.588.
2. *CM,* 14/4/33, p.310 and 20/10/33, pp.296/7.
3. *CM,* 5/5/33, pp.414–416 and 16/6/33, p.651.
4. *CM,* 5/5/33, p.400 and 21/7/33, p.804.
5. *CM,* 1/12/33, p.595.
6. *CM,* 17/11/33, p.534.
7. *CM,* 6/10/33, p.217.
8. *CM,* 26/5/33, p.525.
9. G. Walker, *Road and Rail,* pp.76–80.
10. *CM,* 3/11/33, p.414.
11. *CM,* 23/2/34, p.49.
12. *CM,* 28/12/34, p.675.

CHAPTER FOURTEEN

Wages and Charges

Two important aspects of the haulage industry remain to be discussed. Ever since the industry had got going at all, there had been argument about the rates charged; and as competition became ever more vicious through the twenties and into the thirties the problem of the cutting of rates became almost an obsession – not surprising when people were fighting for their livelihood; not surprising when so many operators knew with any certainty only their marginal costs for the immediate job – the cost of their fuel in particular; not surprising considering the ever-present problem of obtaining a back load; and not surprising considering the need of many to get immediate cash to meet looming hire-purchase payments.

Tied up with this was the question of the wage levels paid. Given severe competition and a severe economic slump with heavy unemployment, wages could be, and were, forced down. The bigger firms, looking to the long term and appreciating the benefits of a reasonably contented workforce, might well have paid fair wages, but for many others, facing extinction, the proverbial peanuts may well have been the only solution.

As we have seen in Chapter Eleven, a Joint Industrial Council (JIC) was set up at the end of the war but faded away by 1920 through lack of enforceability of the recommended wage rates. The famous Ernest Bevin was leader of the workers' side on that council. There was that attempt, too, in Parliament in 1924 to attach legal force to agreements in the industry -an attempt without success. So through the twenties and thirties wages remained an outstanding problem – outstanding in the sense of remaining unsolved and outstanding through being of major significance. There were a number of attempts by local associations to agree wages for their areas. In Liverpool we saw attempts to lay down haulage rates. That city was prominent, too, in trying to establish wage rates. In May 1924, for example, an agreement was reached between the employers and the Liverpool Carters' and Motormen's Union for wage rates for a six-day week of 48 hours.[1] These rates were linked to the Cost of Living Index (a forerunner of the Retail Prices Index and based on 1914 prices) which stood at 78 on 1 March 1924 and 85 at the time of the agreement. For each five points of movement in the index an adjustment of 1s. (5p) would be made in the wage rates. Overtime payments were provided for. From 5.30 until 6.30 p.m. overtime would be paid at the hourly rate; the second and third hours of overtime would be paid at time plus a quarter; and thereafter at time plus a half. The agreed rates of pay were:

	Permanent employees	Casual (daily) Weekdays		Casual (daily) Saturdays	
	s.	s.	d.	s.	d.
Drivers, 6-wheelers	78 (£3.90)	14	11¼	7	4
Second man	71	13	8	6	8
Drivers, Steam	72	13	10	6	8¾
Second man	65	12	6¾	6	2
Drivers, petrol					
Vehicles 2 tons and over	72	13	10½	6	8¾
Under 2 tons	65	12	6¾	6	2
Second man, petrol					
Vehicles 4 tons and over	65	12	6¾	6	2
Under 4 tons	64	12	4¾	6	0½
Trailermen	59	11	5¾	5	7

By the end of the year the parties had agreed further that for new entrants there would be a rate of 59s. per week for drivers of vehicles up to 1 ton capacity. All the agreed rates would stand until 31 May 1925.[2]

Four years later we find the parties locked in negotiation on the employers' (Merseyside Road Transport Employers) proposal to reduce the top rates by 4s. per week and others by 2s. The rates being discussed were apparently those that had been originally agreed. When the discussions reached stalemate the employers suggested going to arbitration but the Liverpool Carters' and Motormen's Union refused, and proposed, instead, reductions of 2s. per week and 1s. The argument seems to have been, not about the point reached by the Cost of Living Index, but about the assertion that Liverpool rates were higher then those of the rest of the country.[3] In the event, at the beginning of October 1928, the employers accepted the Union's proposal, to operate from weekending 6 October 1928.[4] As the economic situation got worse, however, the parties had to come back to the negotiating table and at the beginning of 1933 they agreed a further reduction of 3s. per week, bringing the pay of a steam-wagon driver, and that of a driver of a petrol wagon over 2 tons, down to 67s. per week (£3.35).[5] It was said in October 1932 that the negotiations had been going on for 18 months. The same sort of thing was happening elsewhere. When a new agreement between the TGWU and the Swansea and District Road Transport (Owners') Association was reported that October, it was said that because rate-cutters did not pay the earlier scales of wages, those owners who did pay the right wages had been unable to get work.[6]

The 1930 Act, by Section 93, gave the unions in the passenger industry the right to appeal to an industrial court where wages did not match up to what would have been required by the 'fair wages' clause of government contracts. The Salter Conference had recommended that the proposed Licensing Authorities should collect and publish information as a guide to the local standards of wages and that reasonable wages would be a condition of every licence. In due course Section 32 of the 1933 Act applied to the goods transport industry the same requirements as the 1930 Act had done to the passenger industry – at least for that part of the industry made up of public hauliers (the A and B licence holders). Since the firms operating lorries on their own account (C licence holders) were in all sorts of different industries and trades, many of which had their own agreements, it was not feasible to apply Section 32 to them. From a comment on Salter's recommendation that ancillary users should also be required to pay reasonable wages, we learn that 'The T.&G.W.U. already has wages agreements with such large trade groups as the millers, brewers, furniture removers, launderers, drapers and others.'[7] The basic idea of Section 32 was that wages would be judged against current awards by conciliation boards, JICs and similar bodies, and agreeements made by employers and workers' organizations. The effect of Section 8 (2) of the 1933 Act was that it became a condition of every A and B licence that fair wages would be paid, though the LA could not fix wage rates. But we note an application before the East Midland LA at Skegness on 7 June 1934. When the Boston applicant admitted that he was paying only 35s. (£1.75) per week the LA said it had not yet passed a licence at that wage, and was not going to start in Skegness. The applicant was prepared to pay £2 per week and got his licence subject to his promise to pay that amount.[8] Whether £2 was a fair wage is difficult to say, for some other applicants had been paying only 35s.

A few months before Mr J.H. Stirk had dealt with that case, a National Joint Conciliation Board (NJCB) had been set up under the Conciliation Act,1896, with 15 employer representatives and 15 worker representatives (again including Mr E. Bevin). This was the kind of body to whose 'determination', according to Section 32 of the 1933 Act, an industrial court would have to pay regard; so there were hopes in some quarters that perhaps now some measure of consistency could be introduced into the wages paid in the industry. The LA would be the enforcing body, via the Conciliation Officers of the Ministry of Labour, which could lead to the industrial court.

Together with the national body there were similar (and subordinate) area JCBs mostly coinciding with the areas of the LAs. The National Board laid down rates for London and for long-distance services but for other than those the system operated in a strange way. It was not for the Area Boards to negotiate specific rates for their area, taking into account whatever was regarded as a fair wage in the locality; but rather that the National Board laid down wage rates for various grades and the Area Boards would negotiate regarding the grades to be applied in their areas. Admittedly the National Board did discuss matters with the Area Boards and, by the time it published its proposals to operate from 1 January 1935, the Area Boards knew what was coming. They had already done much of the spadework regarding the local application of the proposals. The rates laid down as the minima covered, first of all, long-distance and trunk services for England and Wales. These ranged from 60s. (£3.00) per week for drivers of vehicles under 2 tons' capacity, to 70s. (£3.50) for drivers of vehicles over 12 tons' gross laden weight and up to 22 tons' gross laden. Then there were the London rates, initially ranging from 54s. (£2.70) for drivers of vehicles under 1 ton capacity, to 72s. and 73s. for drivers of vehicles over 5 tons capacity, though these were still subject to negotiation at the time the scheme was to start. When these had been finalized there were no less than five schedules covering the Metropolitan area ranging from 45s. (£2.25) to 75s. per week, including slightly lower figures for new entrants.

Outside London, and other than trunk and long-distance services, there was the following scheme of grading:

	Grade 1	Grade 2	Grade 3
	s. d.	s. d.	s. d.
Drivers of vehicles of			
Under 30 cwt capacity	52 6	49	45
30 cwt but not over 2 tons	57 6	54	50
Over 2 and up to 3½ tons	62 6	58 6	54 6
Over 3½ and up to 12 tons gross	65	61	57
Over 12 tons gross laden	70	66	62

Grade 1 covered important industrial centres and the principal ports; Grade 2 was for 'other industrial areas' and Grade 3 the rural areas. All these rates were for a guaranteed 48-hour week and there was a great deal more detail about the rates for mates, attendants and youths. As usual, there were rates for overtime and minimum payments when reporting for duty as well as rates for daily men. Where a man had been in continuous service for a year and had not been absent for more than seven days without reasonable cause he was entitled to a week's holiday with pay.

Examples of the grading in a couple of the less difficult areas are:

West Midlands (temporary agreement): Grade 2 within radius of 16 miles of Town Hall, Wednesbury; 8 miles of Post Office, Milton; and 5 miles of Broadgate, Coventry; Grade 3 remainder of area. Trunk and long-distance services rates apply over 65 miles.

South Eastern (temporary agreement): Grade 2 in Southampton, Portsmouth and Poole; Grade 3 remainder of area. Trunk and long-distance service 70 miles or more.[9]

The temporary agreements were supposed to expire on 30 June 1935 but it was not easy to reach permanent agreements and sparks often flew at Area Board meetings. The National Board (which had set up an appeals committee) had the final say and this did not always please. In Devon and Cornwall an agreement had been made in November 1934 but the National Board rejected it. Eventually the national body recognized the Devon and Cornwall rates in so far as the drivers were 'internal' to those counties; but for traffic over their borders the Area Board had to bow to the National Board. In Yorkshire the position was worse. In a summary published in May 1935 the simple word 'undecided' appears against the Yorkshire area and a textual note added that the position was most complicated and no final settlement had been reached.[10] Indeed the position *was* most complicated. A meeting of nearly 1000 A and B licence holders organized by the Yorkshire Stage Carriage Operators' Association was held in Leeds one Sunday in February 1935. The meeting was told that counter-proposals to most of the NJCB proposals would be submitted to the Yorkshire Board. The meeting passed unanimously a long resolution including 'disapproval of the restrictions imposed by the operation and administration of the 1933 Act. It also expresses its deep dissatisfaction with the unrepresentative composition, as well as the unjust recommendations of the National Joint Conciliation Board'. The resolution concluded with a request that representations be made to the Minister of Transport and members of the House of Commons to have the JCBs abolished. The counter-proposals included one that required the rates to be for a 53-hour week; pay rates from £2 13s. 0d. for a vehicle of up to 2½ tons capacity; £3 1s. 0d. from that up to 12 tons gross laden; and £3.6.0 beyond that. There would be no special rates for long-distance and trunk services, no payment for holidays, and overtime would be paid for at normal hourly rates except on Sundays.[11]

When these were put to the next meeting of the Area Board in Leeds in March, the meeting was described as 'stormy' and no agreement was reached.[12] When the employers' side met in Dewsbury at the beginning of April there was only a small majority in favour of reaffirming the previous offer, but worse still, the Yorkshire Stage Carriage Operators' Association began considering withdrawal from the Area JCB.[13] When, in May, both sides finally accepted the National Board's interim award to operate from the first pay-day in June, there was still confusion, with the employers' side assuming that the award did not include the original conditions of service, and the employees' side assuming that it did. The Operators' Association forthwith circularized its members telling them to pay the weekly wage rates as set out in the award but on the basis of a non-guaranteed 53-hour week![14] The saga rumbled on. Elsewhere there were difficulties, too, and in April the RHA had to set up a small committee to investigate and report on the situation in each traffic area. In London the National Board had to ask the municipal authorities to put a clause in contracts requiring the haulier to observe wages and conditions as laid down by the Metropolitan JCB.[15]

Some LAs began commenting that not everyone was paying the wages as required by the JCB's decisions; and to deal with this several of the Area Boards set up Observance Committees. Then it all came to a head in the East Midlands Area where there had been only provisional agreement. In December 1935 the Appeals Committee of the National Board laid down gradings for the Area and these included Grade 2 for Oxfordshire. Soon after this, the TGWU complained that an Oxford haulier was paying only Grade 3. The Chief Conciliation Officer of the Ministry of Labour was unable to get agreement between the parties and the matter went to the industrial court in London. The ruling there sounded a death knell of the whole scheme. On 16 September 1936 the court ruled that since the Conciliation Board rates had never become operative in Oxford, and since the firm was, in fact, paying the level of wages commonly paid by road haulage employers in Oxfordshire, the firm could not be said to be contravening the statutory requirements for fair wages.

By this time, though, a Committee had been set up (on 21 July 1936) under the chairmanship of Sir James B. Baillie, OBE, to 'examine the present position in regard to the regulation of wages and conditions of service'. The evidence to the Baillie Committee was again much as might have been expected. Mr Holdsworth, chairman of the Employers' Panel of the Yorkshire Area Board, talked of the difficulties of working with the unions. A sub-committee of the Area Board had concluded that Grade 2 should apply in the Area. Both sides accepted this and were on the point of ratifying it when the TGWU members received a telephone call from London and they then said they could not ratify. 'In the whole of our deliberations', said Mr Holdsworth, 'we seemed to be weighed down by what happened in London' (Minutes of Evidence, third day, 13 Oct. 1936). Others were very unhappy about the administration of the scheme. The S. E. Area Employers' Panel thought that each Area Board should be represented on the National Board. In their memorandum to the Baillie Committee (7 Nov. 1936) they said:

> We suggest that we should pause, get machinery for automatic enforcement and general observance, arrange for better liaison between the Areas and the National Board, clear up the obscure and ill defined points ... generally overhaul the machinery now set up ... We are told that this cannot be, not because *the* employees want or need better wages, but because 'final' grading is necessary by some set date. [But] It is admitted by both sides that there is no such thing as final grading ... Why the set date? Merely that the National Board can report that it has 'finished' the task set by the Ministries! A ridiculous position which shows that they do not appreciate the nature and magnitude of their work. Neither they nor me will ever 'finish' our task.

There were a number of comments to the effect that the National Board did not listen to anyone. An appendix to the above memorandum said 'We tried in conjunction with employers from other areas to make constructive criticisms of the Report of the Sub-committee of the NJCB before it was adopted by the NJCB but were rebuffed and our suggestions completely ignored.' Mr O.S. Moore added on behalf of the S.E. Employers' Panel regarding suggestions to the National body that 'We were immediately faced ... with the fact that they were not prepared to discuss anything that deviated from the National Report.' The Sub-committee referred to was the one charged with investigating prevailing wage agreements and levels in the road haulage industry of the country. Its findings were adopted by the National Board and were the basis of the National Board's decision about rates to be paid. According to the S.E. Area Employers' Panel memorandum 'the members of the NJCB (and their Sub-committee) when considering wages and conditions, did not ascertain the average wages paid by good employers in the S.E. Area'. But according to Ernest Bevin, a member, when the NJCB fixed the wages rates, it had before it and examined 'Co-operative Agreements, Railway Agreements, agreements such as Bristol, Liverpool, Sheffield, London, actually operated in the district and a number of agreements with firms, and out of all the welter of those we produced what you see in the Report' (Minutes of Evidence, Q201–3).

The NJCB itself submitted a memorandum to Baillie, which, among other things, pointed out that about 80,000 men came within the 'fair wages' Section of the 1933 Act, and these were organized mainly by the TGWU, the Liverpool and District Carters' and Motormen's Union, the United Road Transport Workers' Association, and the National Union of General and Municipal Workers. These bodies acted jointly on the Boards. The employers were organized in the Associated Road Operators (that is, the RHA), the Motor Transport Employers' Federation, and the National Road Transport Employers' Federation. Their members owned about 120,000 vehicles out of the 459,626 licensed as at 30 September 1935. The memorandum went on to review the wages situation over the years up to the appointment of the JCBs and their work to date. It noted three difficulties: the reluctance to accept awards of the Appeals Committee and the chairman; the failure of Section 32 to gain universal observance; and the exclusion of C licensees. In regard to the second of these the memorandum talked of the difficulty of getting evidence (operators did not need to keep records of wage rates paid) and the fact that the machinery for 'dealing with delinquents' was defective. It protested strongly about the exclusion of C licensees and stressed their impact on the public hauliers.

The Report of the Baillie Committee (Cmd.5440) was dated 24 April 1937. At the time of the passing of the 1933 Act, said the Report (p.4), there was 'an almost negligible degree of effective voluntary collective wage regulation'.

Wages, for the most part, were the subject of arrangements between individual workers and their employers. It went on to explain the history of the JCBs in the road transport industry and referred (p.12) to the 'generally agreed dissatisfaction with the results of the operations of the National Joint Conciliation Board' and of the desirability of establishing 'some more effective means'. The difficulties had brought the Board members in deputation to the Ministry of Labour on 24 March 1936 and this was followed by the setting up of the Baillie Committee. The Committee noted some of the problems under the JCBs. The wages fixed had all the appearance of being imposed from outside rather than being truly representative of the industry. Though the National Board had tried to recognize existing agreements it did not adequately consider them all. Area Boards had not been 'consulted' but had had to accept the scales handed down. 'It cannot but be considered unfortunate that the hasty procedure of the National Board should have been a means of creating discord from the first.' Their procedure aroused opposition and induced some employers' organizations to go their own way in fixing rates. Anyway, the rates fixed by the NJCB were too high, being based on London and Liverpool rates. The 'fair wages' concept was too vague and there was no guidance from the government (Paras 27–29). Then there was that Oxford case. The industrial court had decided that it had only to 'have regard' to the Board's determinations; it did not have to adopt them. So it was still possible for employers to set up an entirely different district rate of wages (p.13).

But it was not all a disaster, according to Baillie. The National Board had 'done a valuable service to the industry' – the formation of voluntary local joint boards, and the formal recognition of the need for establishing and enforcing standard wages. Its decisions had been substantially observed by a considerable proportion of organized employers, in spite of opposition. 'These are important achievements.'

The Report commented that there was a quite separate Conciliation Board for Scotland set up in December 1934 but that that Board and the National one for England and Wales proceeded independently and there was no machinery for coordinating their work. From Scotland, too, came complaints that the decreed wage levels were too high, and evidence that there was widespread disregard of the JCB decisions. From the north of England there were complaints that haulage firms were suffering competition from Scottish operators who paid lower wages. In recommending a new Central Wages Board, the Baillie Committee wanted one that would cover the whole of Britain.

So the Committee recommended that a Central Board be set up to determine standard wages, hours of work, and conditions of service for drivers of A and B licensed vehicles. The minister would confirm these by Order. There would be local or area boards, too, to do full justice to local feeling and these area boards would be represented on the Central Board. The Central Board would have representatives of employers and labour, but, in addition, there would be three independent and impartial members who would have no personal or professional connection with the industry (Paras 45, 46, 52).

The Report described the position in regard to the drivers of some 9000 railway lorries. These men were organized by the National Union of Railwaymen and came within the ambit of comprehensive machinery for the negotiation of railway wages. However, there were many differences between the railwaymen's wage structure and the wages ordained by the NJCB, and 'comparison between them is not capable of being effected with strict accuracy. Nevertheless, taking the terms of employment as a whole, we are satisfied that there is substantial equivalence.' Baillie, then, saw no need to alter the machinery for the railways' road employees.

Owner-drivers, some 15 per cent of A licensees, were another body of drivers considered by the Committee. Since these drivers were not affected by any wage-regulating schemes, 'we think it desirable that they should be controlled in some other way'. The obvious way was to control rates and charges but that was outside the Committee's scope. Anyway, fair wages were essential, for charges should depend on wages and not vice versa. This would apply to B licensees, too. One thing that did concern the Committee very much was the exclusion of C licensees (ancillary operators) from the NJCB scheme. Salter had been well aware of the threat posed by the exclusion of these operators and had wanted them brought into the fair wages scheme, but the 1933 Act had not included them in its provision for fair wages. 'We cannot view without grave misgiving the continuation of an exemption which from its inception has created new and serious difficulties for the motor industry', said the Baillie Report (p.84). That exemption seemed to have been based on two assumptions: (a) that C licensees were so diverse that no single wages scheme could be applied, and (b) that there was only one method of determining fair wages. Neither assumption was correct. Baillie distinguished C licensed drivers doing work directly comparable and competing with A and B licensed hauliers, and, on the other hand, those engaged in retail distribution who did not compete and whose work was not comparable, with the A and B men. It was not necessary that the method of determining fair wages for the latter should be used also for drivers of C licensed vehicles. The Committee recommended that for those doing work like the A and B vehicle drivers, it should be made a condition of the licence that 'fair and proper wages' be paid and 'fair conditions' prevail. Those drivers doing retail distribution should come under a Trade Board (Paras 106–108). The C licensees had opposed this idea, arguing, among other things, that drivers were employed for part of their time on duties unconnected with transport; that complications would arise if drivers' wages were not in a proper relationship with those of other staff; and, they said, state regulation of wages would be 'an endless source of industrial friction'.

The Committee claimed to be fully aware of these arguments but 'we are clearly of the opinion that some regulation of C Licence drivers' wages and conditions is desirable and necessary' (Para. 101). Their view was that:

> The very diversity of rates of wages paid for similar classes of work demands some uniformity of method of fixing rates for C Licence drivers. ... We cannot regard it as satisfactory that numerically the largest class of drivers should be left indiscriminately to accept such rates of wages as they can obtain. If a rate of wages is held to be a means of ensuring fitness for driving in the case of the minority of drivers (those of A and B licensed vehicles) it cannot be desirable to ignore the whole question of wages in the case of C Licence drivers who constitute the majority. (Para. 97)

The Committee were right in saying that 'fair wages' had been considered by press and public to be a way of getting the right men to drive vehicles safely, but perhaps more important was their view that charges should depend on wages and not vice versa. Certainly most of the talk within the industry was about the need for fair wages for A and B drivers to ensure that the operator would be less able to cut his freight rates.

The outcome of all this was the Road Haulage Wages Act, 1938 which did largely what Baillie had recommended. Part I, Section 1, set up the Road Haulage Central Wages Board and Area Wages Boards. The Central Board would have 3–5 independent members, 12–18 members representing equally employers and workers, and 2 representatives from each Area Board in England and Wales. Scotland would constitute an Area and would have 4 members on the Central Board. This Central Board, according to Section 2, had powers to submit to the minister proposals for fixing the pay of A and B licence drivers (excluding railway employees), and to make such recommendations as it might think fit to any government department for these A and B drivers, regarding safety on roads, the health and comfort of the workers, and any other matter affecting the efficiency of, and conditions of work in, road transport. It would also have to consider any matter referred to it by the minister. The Central Board would first send its draft proposals to the Area Boards for consideration and it would also consider objections in writing from any persons affected. The Central Board would then submit the proposals to the minister who might refer them back or might make an Order confirming them.

Part II of this short Act provided for the C licence drivers. Where workers in this section, or a representative trade union, considered remuneration 'unfair' they could make an application to the minister. Section 4(3), following Paragraph 108 of 'Baillie', set out what was *not* unfair.

A worker's wage rate was deemed not unfair if it was:

(a) equivalent to the wage paid to A and B drivers under an Order;
(b) in accordance with an agreement between a Trade Union and an employer or employers' organization regulating wages in the same trade or industry as the worker;
(c) equivalent to that paid to similar workers by other employers in the district in the same trade or industry under an agreement between an employers' body and a Trade Union;
(d) or under a decision of a Joint Industrial Council conciliation board or similar;
(e) or under an Industrial Court decision regarding wages to be paid by another employer in the same district and trade or industry.

The minister would refer any complaints to an Industrial Court and, under Section 5, if that Court found the prevailing wage unfair it would fix a fair wage, specifying exactly what hours of work it applied to. Such a ruling would fix the rate for three years [apparently regardless of any changes in the cost of living].

Part III of the Act provided for a fine of up to £20 for contravention and the worker would have to be paid the difference back for the previous two years. This part also confirmed that the LA's power under Section 13 of the 1933 Act to revoke or suspend a licence could be exercised for such contraventions. Finally, the Third Schedule to the Act carefully defined a 'road haulage worker' to include not only a driver and person assisting in the driving or control of the vehicle, but also anyone loading the goods to be carried, attending to them while in transit, and unloading or delivering them after they had been so carried. The definition also included anyone acting as an attendant to the vehicle who was required to travel on or accompany the vehicle for this duty.

So after twenty inter war years of 'every man for himself' with a couple of feeble attempts by the State to do something, and a great many attempts by employers and unions to sort things out for themselves, the State finally did something concrete. But it did it on the eve of the Second World War during which the haulage industry, like most industries, would encounter a general and serious inflation of costs.

The other great problem was the rates to be charged for haulage services. We have seen in Chapter Eight that when the haulage industry got going again after the First World War, competition quickly brought about rate-cutting. In places such as Liverpool and Manchester local associations attempted to introduce standard rates but they were very difficult to maintain. The problem would not have been made any easier by the flood of surplus vehicles being sold by the government. This brought hordes of new hauliers into the market and a great many of them knew little, if anything, about the commercial aspects of vehicle operating. So they became the villains of the piece, right through to the late 1920s, (when the Royal Commission was told of their irresponsible ways) and beyond.

As the Depression worsened from 1929 until 1931 the railways, losing traffic one way or another, were fighting back. As we have seen, the 'interventionist' mentality of British legislators had provided an all-pervading structure of standard rates and standard revenue for them. The grouping of many small companies into a few large ones under the 1921 Railways Act may have helped the railways to secure some economies, but the new rates scheme ordained by that Act, and operating from 1928, did not achieve what had been hoped. It was supposed, by setting out a wider classification with more classes and more rate variations for different quantities, to bring most traffic within the system of standard rates and so dispense with the need for exceptional rates. But the exceptional rates continued, and indeed were used even more as road competition encroached and the economic depression worsened. According to Gilbert Walker's estimate, exceptional rates accounted for over 83 per cent of tonnage and over 68 per cent of gross freight receipts of the railways in 1935.[16] It is difficult to know how much of this was due to pressures of traders in the face of the Depression and how much to road competition. But road competition must often have been a factor.

A big problem with the cutting of rates by one party to retain or recover traffic is that the competitor is quite likely to respond in the same manner. Walter Gammons, a well-known figure in haulage and clearing-house work of the time, wrote to the editor of *Commercial Motor* in mid-1932 with a list of road rates to some 600 destinations which, he said, were then 50 per cent below the original figures. He attributed these cuts to the fact that they were necessary to retain traffic to road in the face of railway rate-cutting. The net result of it all, he said, was the loss of many thousands of pounds to the hauliers and no gain to the railways. (He did not comment on the loss to the railways when traffic went over to road originally.) In his letter Mr Gammons cited a case where a rail rate to Birmingham had been 60s. per ton. The traffic was won to road transport and the railways retaliated. However, even when the road rate had been cut to 35s. (£1.75) per ton the railways made further cuts and the road operators had to reduce their rate further to 29s. (£1.45).[17] The fault, if any, with that sort of thing must have lain in the system of charging used by the railways. Charging what the traffic would bear originally would inevitably give way in the face of road haulage firms charging at cost – and a more readily ascertainable cost at that. Furthermore, the 1933 Road and Rail Traffic Act had given the railways a considerable weapon in the shape of 'agreed rates' which would not be tied to the 'standard rates' and which therefore would be more of a threat to road hauliers, especially on longer-distance traffic.

None of this was to save the railways and many of their supporters felt that things would be easier if only road haulage had a similar structure of universal standard rates. It was not only the railway supporters who sought such a rates structure for road haulage. A great many substantial hauliers felt that obligatory standard rates would eliminate many problems. Clearing houses were often accused of forcing down rates, and here the country's economic position, no doubt, had an influence. A letter from a haulier to *Commercial Motor* in the summer of 1932 complained that he had been offered a load from Hull to Liverpool by a new clearing house that had opened in Hull. For the distance of over 150 miles he was offered a rate of 14s. (70p), that is, a little over 1d. per mile. When he declined he was told that hauliers with oil-engined vehicles would do it, and this apparently turned out to be the case.[18]

Certainly clearing houses were in a strong position to manipulate those hauliers who had cut rates to the limit for an outward run and badly needed a return load if they were to make any profit at all on the trip. Some, alleged a *Commercial Motor* article in 1933, 'select as their haulier clients those whom they well know to be so circumstanced as to be almost compelled to accept any load at any price'.[19] Clearing houses did other things too, like sub contracting to other clearing houses. The article just mentioned went on to quote the case of a haulier who, having no vehicle available to deal with a load, offered the load to a clearing house at 48s. (£2.40) per ton. Next day he was offered the same load by another clearing house at 27s. (£1.35). The article alleged that the job concerned had been through the hands of half a dozen other clearing houses before reaching the one which had offered it to the original haulier. As one aggrieved reader complained, it was easy for the clearing houses to cut rates as they stood to lose only 10 per cent of the reduction. (Their commission was usually 10 per cent of the rate charged to the trader.)

Even traders operating vehicles on their own account were vilified generally because, now and then, one would pick up a return load for a fee which otherwise would have gone to a recognized haulier. Most often, though, the 'big boys' complained of the irritating and unsettling competition of the irresponsible 'small men' who cut rates with such reckless abandon. Attempts to shackle such people through compulsory third-party insurance, limitation of driving hours, and a tightening up on repair and maintenance had not had the success that people had hoped for in keeping up rates and keeping down cut-throat competition. It has to be acknowledged that traders, fighting for survival in a grim economic situation, sometimes did not scruple in playing off one haulier against another.

There were not many with unblemished records in this area, and attempts to blame or apportion blame may be a fruitless exercise. The editor of *Commercial Motor*, in the issue of 18 August 1933, lambasted some of the bigger firms. The assumption that practically all rate-cutting was done by small hauliers 'is not a true statement of the case. There is almost, if not quite, as much rate cutting by large haulage contractors as by small ones.' When vehicles were idle it was a case of having to 'accept traffic at rates which little more than cover the bare running costs – not even the operating costs – of their vehicles'. The large firms readily took the view that any contribution to overheads (that is, anything above direct running costs) was better than nothing. 'Which, would we ask, is the more culpable, he who cuts rates in ignorance and often in dire straits, or the concern who does it deliberately and with full knowledge of the harm which is being done?' wrote the editor.[20]

Whether it was done by the small man or the large company, the practice of charging in difficult economic circumstances with a view to maximizing the contribution to overheads by getting what one can above marginal cost might, arguably, have been a realistic strategy – provided that one is considering running costs, not just fuel costs. Clearly, however, one needed to be careful. A letter to *Commercial Motor* in September 1931 from a haulier in Bedlington, Northumberland, told how he used his 30 cwt vehicles to convey 600 bricks a time when no other work was available. He quoted, as one of his examples, a rate of 20s. (£1) per 1000 bricks to deliver them to Hexham, 36 miles away. The periodical's writer on rates pointed out that the haulier would still be losing money at twice the quoted rates. The Hexham one equalled 12s. (that is, 144 old pence) for a round trip of 72 miles or 2d. (somewhat less than lp) per mile which hardly paid for petrol and oil. Incidentally, apart from the question of 600 bricks (2 tons?) on a 30 cwt vehicle, one cannot help wondering what the local brickyard did when this haulier was otherwise occupied. Did they have to pay higher rates to someone else?[21]

A similar question of undercharging arose in April of that year, when a group of sand and ballast merchants and hauliers met at Hounslow to form a new association. The resolution passed unanimously mentioned 'the specific object of dealing with haulage rates and protecting the interests of its members generally'. The meeting was told that present rates did not allow adequate provision for depreciation so there was difficulty in providing modern rolling stock.[22] While some hauliers did go out of business, others survived in a way that puzzled many. Mr W.R. Jackson of Warpool Transport Company suggested some possibilities in a contribution to *Commercial Motor* in late 1931. After asking why the rate-cutters did not go out of business in one or two years, he answered that manufacturers 'will frequently make absurd allowances for old machines thus enabling a haulier to capitalize what would have been a loss and start again with renewed hopes, that by lower running costs and freedom from repair of a new vehicle, he may still be able to sell for 18s. (90p) at a profit work worth £1'. The manufacturers, too, would sometimes provide free repairs and replacements and 'those who make the most noise receive the most attention'. He had pointed out to a manufacturer one man who ran three 8-tonners, covering 800 miles a week. That man had been in business for two years with each lorry continuously overloaded. The manufacturer gave free repairs, in effect subsidizing one contractor at the expense of others. The same sort of remarks applied to tyres, insurance and accessories. These points, taken with low wages and long hours allowed the rate-cutters to remain in business.[23] [One may be willing to accept that manufacturers, in a depression, may have had to do what hauliers did, cut rates or give generous allowances, but it is difficult to imagine that they lay behind the fairly general problem of rate-cutting.]

Local Authorities also were criticized. They were accused of always accepting the lowest tender for contracts and so of encouraging hopeful owners to trim their quotations to the lowest possible figure. A Mr Butterwick complained at a meeting of the West Riding Branch of the RHA in June 1933 that the rate for certain work for Leeds Corporation had dropped from 5s. (25p) per ton to 1s. 7d. (8p) per ton over the years. He may have been accusing the Corporation but he might as well have accused the Depression and severe competition – which, clearly, was not confined to haulage.[24] The following February the editor of *Commercial Motor* was saying that 'In the municipal sphere, for instance, contract rates are often ridiculous, resulting in poor maintenance of the vehicle and semi-starvation of the personnel and their families.'[25] To prove the point further an article soon afterwards in that journal pointed out that it was 'notorious that most municipal haulage rates are uneconomic'. The usual rate for a 3-ton tipper with driver was 4s. (20p) per hour, whereas the magazine's cost tables showed a cost of 3s.8d. per hour and the magazine argued that 6s. (30p) per hour would be a reasonable charge.[26] Another month on, an article claimed that

> There can be no doubt whatever that one reason why so many haulage contractors are able to quote the absurd rates for municipal haulage is that they underpay their drivers. I have plenty of proof that this is the case. In all those instances [quoted in the article] it is true to claim that the municipality ... cannot escape the blame.[27]

Arguments might well be raised of the 'chicken and the egg' type. But there can be no doubt that customers of road haulage, generally, had become accustomed to beating down rates and setting one haulier against another.

Few people in the haulage industry wanted this sort of thing to continue. So by the end of 1933 we find the RHA setting up machinery to maintain economic rates. Each branch would have a Rates Committee and the rates proposed would be submitted to open meetings of members, convened for the purpose. If agreed by the majority the proposals would then be submitted to the National Standing Rates Committee, sitting in London. When approved by this body, the rates would then be deemed to be the agreed rates and circulated. If subsequently any member of the RHA had a complaint regarding rates charged by another haulier (member or not), he was first to point this out in writing to the offender. If no amicable settlement were reached the complainant would then put the matter to the Area Rates Committee, where both parties would be invited to state their cases. If the Area Committee felt that the matter justified further consideration, it would refer it to the National Standing Rates Committee. This body might refer further to a permanent committee of three people not directly concerned with a transport undertaking, whose report would go to the Council of the RHA. The Council, if the case were proven, would advise the offender that his next licence application would be opposed.[28] In pursuing its objective of rate maintenance, the RHA, about the same time, began to issue lists of 'approved' clearing houses, with which members were encouraged to deal.[29]

From this time onward there was an increase in the number of attempts to fix and stabilize rates (perhaps encouraged somewhat by improving trade in 1934), whether by the RHA's rates committees or by other groups of hauliers and/or traders setting up their own voluntary schemes. We find in the summer of 1934, in one place in Scotland, for example, a Joint Haulage Committee set up by the Milk Marketing Board, local distributors, and hauliers. This Committee produced its rates for the conveyance of milk at so much per gallon according to distance, and, after criticism, revising its scales so that for up to ten miles milk was carried at ½d. per gallon (about one-fifth of 1p) and for distances over 40 miles at 1½d. per gallon. The railways came into the act by undercutting the latter rate by charging 1.34d. (rather more than ½p) for collecting milk in Dumfries and carrying it to Edinburgh.[30]

Nevertheless, the course of true transport never did run smoothly, and complaints of rate-cutting continued. A letter from Millichamp Bros, Bolton, in *Commercial Motor*'s issue of 17 August 1934 complained that

> We are having the experience of being cut by some of the largest haulage contractors in the country and, incidentally, these concerns have only recently started to operate in this area. We can only suppose that this is their usual way of opening up new fields.

[The newcomers had modern machines and ran their businesses efficiently] 'yet they do cut rates, and what is more, they continue to run at these rates'.

It is, perhaps, difficult to chastize hauliers who may have been able offer low rates because of their efficiency and, perhaps also, economies of scale.

The letter went on to cite an example. One of their jobs was taken from Millichamps when the newcomer cut the rate by 25 per cent. 'When we dropped to retain it they then cut still lower, and are now doing the job.'[31]

Then there were the railway road services. The CMUA and the RHA both opposed the LMS Railway's application to the Yorkshire LA in the summer of 1934, on the grounds of rate-cutting. Whereas hauliers generally charged 12s.

6d. ($62\frac{1}{2}$p) per ton for carrying wool from Bradford to Leeds, railway lorries were taking it at 8s. 4d. ($41\frac{1}{2}$p); and other examples were given – and denied.[32] The picture was obviously patchy, for a 'rates tribunal' formed in 1933 in Bradford was credited a year later with having 'obtained a certain measure of success ... They had certainly stabilized the rates for the transport of a number of commodities between the ports and the Bradford district.'[33] By the end of 1934 it was being said that over 750 rates had been stabilized in the Bradford area.[34] By this time there were half a dozen 'rates tribunals' in Yorkshire, one of the newer ones, at Brighouse, having 35 haulier members.[35] In January 1935, the Yorkshire Area Committee of the RHA resolved to set up an Advisory Rates Committee to include representatives of all the rate-stabilization organizations in the county and the RHA headquarters were planning to convene a national conference on the problem[36] – as indeed was the CMUA.

The idea of rate stabilization was certainly gaining ground. In the autumn of 1934, Mr E.O. Gray, Secretary of the East Midlands Section of the RHA, told a branch meeting in Northampton that

> the Traffic Authority in this area has made special reference quite recently to local rates schedules put forward by responsible bodies of haulage contractors and he is determined – if those bodies be representative enough – to make every contractor in the Area conform with them. He has said he will brook interference from nobody in that regard.[37]

In May 1935 *Commercial Motor* ran a feature under the title 'Is the Time Ripe for Rate Stabilization?' and the general view expressed there by a number of contributors was that the time was indeed ripe. But stabilization was clearly a hope rather than a fact. Mr E.B. Hutchinson pointed out that 'the foolish orgy of uncertainty and constantly reduced prices' was not doing anyone any good. But others pointed to the atomization of the industry and the need for 'organization' or 'association'. Still others argued the need for wages to be settled first. If the wage rates then being considered by the National Conciliation Board were enforced a good many hauliers would be out of business, they contended. Haulage rates would need to go up by 25 per cent.[38]

Clearly, all was still not well at that time. A few weeks after the article mentioned, *Commercial Motor* was having to say that 'The Leeds Road Transport Rates Tribunal ... established with a view to the voluntary stabilization of haulage rates ... is, we learn, to all intents and purposes, dead ... Rate cutting is still rampant in Leeds and other parts of Yorkshire ... on average haulage rates in Leeds are now lower than twelve months ago.' This article also said that rate stabilization was impeded by the delay in settling wages.[39] Wages, businessmen setting one haulier against another, local authorities forcing down rates, clearing houses seeking out financially weak hauliers, the railways, 'small men' ignorant of their costs and having to find hire purchase payments, not to mention an overcrowded industry and a bleak economic situation – there were many 'culprits' .

Another one was singled out in April 1935 by the firm of Dick, Jackson & Co. Ltd. This firm had run its first loads from London to the North-east in November 1930 – 20 tons per week – but by the spring of 1935 was doing 450 tons per week in one or other direction between London and the North-east, on behalf of 150 customers. This haulier issued a circular (4 April) alleging that a coastal shipping company had cut the rate to 30s. (£1.50) per ton, that is, 5s. (25p) below the road rate. The haulier claimed that the coastal company had told him that they would persist in price cutting to gain traffic, whatever the economic consequences. They recommended that the haulier withdraw his long-distance services. The circular alleged that their competitors would restore the original rate of 41s. 8d. per ton (£2.08) when road competition was eliminated. Dick, Jackson & Co. then responded with new rates for butter, cheese, bacon and lard – 29s. per ton up to 10 tons (no minimum) and 28s. per ton above 10 tons.[40]

So the story went on. Earnest bodies striving to stabilize rates were defeated time and time again by the realities of the situation. In August 1935, when both the RHA and the London Chamber of Commerce had committees studying the problem, proposals were being circulated by the CMUA to hauliers and chambers of commerce. The proposals suggested, amongst other things, that fair rates ought to be made a condition of A and B licences. Rates Committees (each consisting of four hauliers and two users) would receive rates proposals from public hauliers. An average would be struck -'or some other suitable formula adopted' and these would be regarded as 'fair rates'. The Committees would review the rates annually.[41] There were objections – about the constitution of the committees and about the basis of the rates. There were plenty of people willing to suggest 'some other suitable formula'. Rates should be based on railway rates. Rates should be based on cost. The RHA should determine rates. Hauliers, like most mortals, ran on roads paved with good intentions.

If the problem of rate-cutting persisted through the middle thirties it must be said that it was not all disaster. It is worth bearing in mind points made to the Transport Advisory Council (TAC) by the British Road Federation (BRF). The Federation, representing (if indirectly) the majority of A and B licence holders, submitted a memorandum to the TAC in March 1937, in which it pointed out that

1. the intensity of competition between hauliers meant that the economies in operating costs were rapidly and automatically passed on to the consumer.[42] Economies there were, as road vehicles became relatively cheaper and ever more efficient.

2. Road haulage had no special advantage as against the ancillary user. Most purchasers of transport services, provided they had a sufficient volume of traffic, could have provided the service for themselves. So it was 'usually necessary for a public haulier to quote rates to a trader showing some substantial savings against his [that is, the trader's] own costs'. This was possible only by the haulier's obtaining greater use from his vehicles and so reducing the cost of overheads per mile; or if he could obtain a better loading factor; or particularly if he could secure return loads.[43]

So, whatever the misery to the haulage industry, there can be no doubt that industry and commerce in general were helped through difficult years by the existence of the haulage industry, albeit a haulage industry competing savagely within. In the absence of motor transport it would have been highly likely that many more industrial and commercial firms would have succumbed to the harsh economic climate of the times. There were further benefits brought to commerce by road vehicles beyond those of their cost economies. The railways had virtually to abandon the system of standard rates (based on the theory of 'charging what the traffic would bear', and appropriate only in a monopoly situation). The railways were obliged to grant more and more exceptional rates, based, like road transport rates, on size and regularity of consignments, total traffic and ease of handling. (However, Gilbert Walker maintained that rate reductions per ton-mile for general merchandise – averaging 2 per cent per annum, 1928–37 – were not much greater than those for low-rated traffic not subject to road competition, 1.6 per cent per annum over the same decade.[44])

The BRF, in putting to the TAC in March 1937 its thoughts on rates, found itself handicapped by the very unfortunate absence of data about the haulage industry, or for that matter, ancillary road transport. The habit of collecting statistics about anything and everything had not yet come to be a feature of British national life. There was no information about traffic flows or tonnages carried. There does not seem to have existed even estimates of these essentials. A second problem was that the licensing system and the new taxation had barely had time to take effect and so it was far from clear how the industry would develop. The whole question of wages, too, still had to be resolved and this was serious, for wages comprised as much as 40 per cent of a haulier's total costs. The BRF did not make a great deal of noise about the point that the TAC had required that the road transport industry's 'proposals should be so formulated as to be capable of inclusion, at a later date, in a comprehensive scheme directed towards the closer co-relation of the various forms of transport'. The BRF did, however, say, that 'The dangers of attempting to force the road haulage industry, without the full agreement of the industry, into a system of planned "co-ordination" cannot be too strongly emphasized.' It is fascinating to reflect that it was the road haulage industry which was being required to put its house in order and to find a way to allow coordination with other forms of transport. Those few rash souls who had dared suggest over the years that other forms of transport could do with some self-help were simply ignored. The atmosphere of the time was a very long way from the now fashionable certainty that 'The market rules, O.K.!' The buzz-word continued to be 'coordination', although like most buzz-words it continued to lack adequate definition.

While the BRF went on to make proposals, it had to avoid 'any attempt at the present stage to grapple with detail'. But it had to start by mentioning things that needed to be done or put right before anything else could be done. Information would need to be collected about traffic and rates, so a standard consignment note might be introduced. Then there were the matters of fair wages, better observance of driving hours, better observance of speed limits and safe loading. The BRF was concerned, too, about a number of features of the licensing procedure: public enquiries where traders giving evidence were treated as hostile witnesses by objectors; where information about traffic had to be revealed to the benefit of competitors; where the attitude of the LA was that in a period of declining trade any reduction in services must of necessity apply to road haulage only; and, again, the short life of A and B licences. The BRF did query why rates needed to be controlled at all. After all, prices in commerce generally were not controlled. But they found easy enough answers to that. The limitation of entry to road haulage gave a monopoly to existing hauliers, so traders needed to be protected by having maximum rates determined. On the other hand, other providers of transport needed to be protected against rate-cutting, so minimum rates were necessary.

Once information had been collected about current rates, the next thing would be the establishment of a Road Rates Tribunal (the BRF actually said that consideration might be given to this). The Tribunal would take responsibility for fixing and for altering road haulage rates and would act as a court of appeal. It would decentralize much of its work to Area Rates Commissioners. Hauliers' representatives would form Area Rates Advisory Committees to work closely with the Rates Commissioners, and, naturally, there would be a National Rates Advisory Committee as well. The enforcement mechanism would be through the LAs, for observance of the official rates would be a condition of A and B licences. As to the rates themselves, it was not really feasible to base them on 'costs' since costs varied widely according to the type of journey, the type of vehicle, mileage per annum, load factors, and so on. The only thing to do 'in the first place' was to base the official rates on the 'actual rates charged by reputable operators'. Some services such as furniture or heavy machinery, would have to be outside such a scheme. The rates system would have to be 'flexible' and the BRF foresaw the possibility that hauliers might just decide to boycott particular traffic if the rate did not attract them. The BRF assumed that there would be some hauliers who would take the traffic [and they would not, of course, be rate-cutting] if they only had the vehicles – so the LA could grant them licences for additional wagons. No wonder the BRF did not want to get into detail! All this would take time but the BRF thought there was a tendency to over estimate the urgency of some of the problems. The conclusions of the BRF overall were that

> The best results are likely to come from an ultimate co-ordination based on each agent of transport being able to speak as a co-ordinated unit, and having every incentive to improve its efficiency and increase its traffic, with some form of Supreme Tribunal to co-ordinate rates and adjudicate upon disputes. ... A solution on these lines can only be treated as a goal for the distant future.[45] [Quite so!]

The Transport Advisory Council published its *Report on Service and Rates* in October 1937, but it did not suggest any world-shattering changes. It recommended that a road rate structure should be built; that it should be the product of the industry itself; that the rates should be arrived at in relation solely to factors affecting road transport rather than by attempting to consider rates prevailing in other forms of transport. These rates should not discriminate as between one customer and another and the rates should be published. The assumption all the way through this report was that once this recommendation was implemented coordination would take place automatically and voluntarily. The railways, in particular, were unhappy that the report offered them so little comfort and they set about preparing their 'Square Deal' campaign. The road interests began work, whether, as Mr C.Dunbar is reported to have suggested at a meeting of the Institute of Transport in October 1967, 'under the threat of the Square Deal campaign', or, more likely, that they realized that a system of road rates had to be sorted out. The various organizations which had been represented by the BRF in submitting its memorandum to the TAC now came together again, under the auspices of the BRF, as a Liaison Committee. A deputation from this committee to the MOT on 23 February 1938 was told that the government intended to bring in a bill for statutory control of road rates, but the industry was expected itself to work out the rate structure. So work was begun on standard conditions of carriage. It would appear, however, that there was some duplication of effort in that other bodies were working on the same lines (for example, the parcels carriers).

The railways now put forward to the MOT (23 Nov. 1938) proposals for a relaxation of the controls on their rates and there was a considerable amount of discussion between the railways and various trade associations. The railways talked, too, with the Liaison Committee on Road Transport Rates, though the discussions probably merit the label of 'horse-trading' where no one would concede anything without a *quid pro quo* from the other side; but a certain degree of agreement was reached. Road interests agreed to the relaxation of control on railway rates. The railways, in turn, and in order to give the road operators an opportunity to negotiate voluntary agreements amongst themselves, would not, for a period of two years after they got their rates freedom, object to a renewal without change of existing A or B licences. The Liaison Committee and the railways set out their positions in a Joint Memorandum which was published as Appendix VI of the TAC *Report on the Railway Proposals* in 1939. According to Paragraph 45, page 25, of that report,

> the fundamental basis of the agreement lies in the arrangements to be made between the railway companies and the road haulage interests for consultation on matters affecting both parties, including the free discussion of difficulties and the consideration of constructive measures. To this end a Central Consultative Committee ... is to be set up for the purpose, inter alia, of formulating the principles on which voluntary agreements can be entered into in regard to the charges to be made for the carriage of merchandise traffic by road and rail.

The report recommended that the railway system of standard charges, plus the whole structure of exceptional and agreed rates together with standard revenue should all be consigned to the dust-bin. There would be legal enforceability of road rates. Since it was all a bit of an unknown territory that transport was entering, legislation should provide that these arrangements would last five years in the first instance.

Progress was being made. However, the Prime Minister had already met Herr Hitler, returned home and announced that there would be 'peace in our time'. Politicians' agreements proved to be just about as effective as many of those for maintaining road haulage rates.

Notes

1. *CM*, 13/5/24, p.390.
2. *CM*, 23/12/24, p.561.
3. *CM*, 2/10/28, p.196.
4. *CM*, 9/ 10/28, p.230.
5. *CM*, 13/1/33, p.755.
6. *CM*, 7/10/32, p.236.
7. *CM*, 9/8/32, p.849.
8. *CM*, 15/6/34, p.589.
9. *CM*, 4/1/35, pp.714 & 715; 10/5/35, pp.432, 433.
10. Ibid.
11. *CM*, 22/2/35, p.41.

12. *CM*, 15/3/35, p.139.
13. *CM*, 5/4/35, p.251.
14. *CM*, 24/5/35, p.495; 31/5/35, p.528.
15. *CM*, 19/4/35, p.318.
16. Gilbert Walker, *Road and Rail*, p.62.
17. *CM*, 7/6/32, p.576.
18. *CM*, 26/7/32, p.816.
19. *CM*, 28/4/33, p.396.
20. *CM*, 18/8/33, p.l.
21. *CM*, 8/9/31, p.123.
22. *CM*, 14/4/31, p.288; 21/4/31, p.328.
23. *CM*, 10/11/31, pp.446/7.
24. *CM*, 16/6/33, p.626.
25. *CM*, 9/2/34, p.916.
26. *CM*, 9/3/34, p.134.
27. *CM*, 11/5/34, p.457.
28. *CM*, 3/11/33, p.402.
29. *CM*, 1/12/33, p.594.
30. *CM*, 3/8/34, p.824.
31. *CM*, 17/8/34, p.14.
32. *CM*, 3/8/34, p.826.
33. *CM*, 5/10/34, p.235.
34. *CM*, 14/12/34, p.583.
35. *CM*, 9/11/34, p.394.
36. *CM*, 25/1/35, p.798.
37. *CM*, 5/10/34, p.235.
38. *CM*, 10/5/35, pp.419, 420.
39. *CM*, 21/6/35, p.629.
40. *CM*, 19/4/35, p.316.
41. *CM*, 9/8/35, pp.870, 871.
42. Transport Advisory Council, Report on Service and Rates, Oct. 1937, p.45.
43. Ibid., p.46.
44. Gilbert Walker, *Road and Rail*, p.126.
45. Transport Advisory Council, Report on Service and Rates, Oct. 1937, p.60.

CHAPTER FIFTEEN

The End of the Beginning

Just a few short years after the period we have been discussing, the Prime Minister, then Mr Winston Churchill, referring to the course of the war, said that the British had not yet reached the end, nor even the beginning of the end, but had reached the end of the beginning. That description fits very aptly the position in the road haulage industry in the late 1930s. Forty years on from the repeal of the Red Flag Act there was a lively road haulage industry in existence with a substantial public haulage sector.

From the early years when it was a struggle to get the vehicles to go at all, the industry had achieved a fair degree of success by the beginning of the First World War. The message had been spread in those couple of decades partly by shows and parades. There was, for example, the Annual Parade in London organized by the CMUA since 1907. The sixth in the series, at Whitsun, 1912 – Monday 21 May to be precise – had 292 vehicles entered by the closing date back in January that year. These included 25 from E.W. Rudd Ltd, 20 from Pickford, and 16 from the Westminster City Council. McNamara, Milnes-Daimler (Hiring Dept), James Nelson & Sons Ltd, Joseph Rank, and Thomas Tilling Ltd each entered ten or more vehicles. The judges looked at the appearance and condition of the vehicles, taking into account the work they had done, and the drivers were questioned, too. The Westminster City Council won the Challenge Cup presented by *Commercial Motor* that year.[1] These parades attracted numerous personalities. The guest list at the 1911 parade had included the Prime Minister of Saskatchewan, the Chairman of the London County Council, and the Assistant Director of Transport of the War Office. The free lunch then provided left some 800 or 900 guests (including the drivers and their wives) well satisfied.[2]

A feature of these shows was that drivers themselves could enter for a special prize and in 1912 56 men did so. They were subjected to a three-hour written examination as well as a *viva-voce* at their own garages. Needless to say, the examiners' report could point to many failings amongst the examinees – some of the men, it seemed, were ignorant of the provisions of the Heavy Motor Car Order.[3]

There were other shows, organized at Olympia each year by the SMMT, for example, or held in connection with the major agricultural shows around the country. The Royal Show at Durdham Downs, Bristol, at the beginning of July 1913 had exhibits from a great many of the well-known builders –

Hallford, Yorkshire, Leyland, Mann, Sentinel, Tasker, Foden, Allchin, Burrell, Wallis & Stevens, Clayton & Shuttleworth, and Aveling & Porter. Most of those were steamers but the Leyland entry included a 40-h.p. petrol lorry for James Robertson & Sons, and the Bristol Tramways had three petrol lorries of from 1–3 tons.[4]

Another part of the publicity for the new form of transport was the various 'trials' organized to see what these vehicles could do. The Liverpool Trials at the turn of the century and the RAC 1000-mile trial of 1907 were landmarks, and as we have seen the War Department organized some for itself.

Then came war. The Great War of 1914–18 was truly a baptism of fire and the (still new) mode of transport was tried and tested in the most difficult circumstances imaginable, in the battlefield. In Britain the road transport industry struggled on, through shortages of vehicles, men and fuel; and difficulties of repair and maintenance. But road transport maintained its foothold through the fact that the railways were vastly overworked. Following the war there ensued a decade of learning (that is, for most operators; some had learnt pre war) the commercial skills necessary to make the industry a real competitor for the role of the nation's major land carrier. In those post war years the haulage industry was occupied almost entirely in tramp work. There were, as yet, few regular services to specific destinations. The industry was helped during this decade by the manufacturers who improved the vehicles, and administrators who improved the roads significantly. Perhaps it is not too much to say that they were helped, too, by railway management with traditions of a century of monopoly and by legislators determined to keep that monopoly under control. It must be pointed out that following the 1921 Act the railway managers had a great deal on their hands as they merged over 100 small companies into four large ones, and as they revamped their classification and rates structure.

As we have seen, at the beginning of the post war period there were new entrants to the road haulage industry by the thousand. Men were coming out of the forces seeking ,jobs, gratuities in hand, and a flood-tide of surplus government vehicles to be bought cheaply. In addition, there were those provided by the vehicle manufacturing industry relieved of wartime controls and now getting back to peace time production. Now young haulage businesses perished in great numbers, although there is little record of most of them. Note must be taken that apart from the first few post war years when there was a very high rate of entry, the death rate of haulage firms through bankruptcy was probably no higher than amongst small businesses generally in the commercial sector.[5] Each departure would have eased the lot of those remaining. Whereas in the war men sacrificed themselves at times to save their comrades, there was no such chivalry in road haulage in the 1920s and 1930s. Operators would breathe only a sigh of relief on learning of the demise of a competitor.

The later part of the war had been a period of very considerable activity and control by the State to save the nation. In the late twenties and early thirties the interventionist mentality was still alive and well. Now the legislators saw their task as that of saving the railways from the combined effects of the economic depression, their own possibly dilatory management, competition of motor vehicles, and the considerable constrictions imposed by free-market-loving legislators of earlier years. Now monopoly had gone and competition prevailed. The Royal Commission examined the problem thoroughly and was defeated by it, and the government passed the buck to the transport industry in the shape of the Salter Conference. Salter was not discouraged, but with somewhat less examination of the problem, proposed remedies. Between them, these two august bodies got Parliament to legislate for speed limits, the condition of vehicles, compulsory third-party insurance, the hours of drivers, a scheme for 'fair wages', and for limitation on the total capacity of lorries on the roads. The *Annual Reports* of the then newly established LAs were very reticent about the very object of the latter legislation – the total capacity of vehicles licensed.

The road haulage industry, in the form of the bigger, better organized and established firms, was able to live with the situation created by the new legislation. Indeed they may well have benefited from it. The road haulage industry, in the form of small one- or two-vehicle firms, often could not live with it, and many went to the wall. So the industry became 'stabilized' if not 'organized'. The pundits of the 1930s often seemed to think of 'organization' in terms of the size and structure of the firms. The railways were 'organized' in that they consisted of only four large firms with strong central control and fairly predictable behaviour following on restrictive legislation, long tradition, tight discipline and rules. The four main-line companies worked closely together. Road haulage, on the other hand, consisted of thousands of small companies with little in the way of common agreement about policies, competing ruthlessly with each other. Many people thought that if only road haulage were 'organized', that is, consisted of large firms like the railways, most of the problems would disappear. An article by Mr E.B. Hutchinson, later to be Secretary of the Long Distance Road Haulage Association, appeared in *Commercial Motor* in January 1931. Mr Hutchinson argued for amalgamations on the grounds that fleets of fewer than 100 vehicles could not be operated economically. An amalgamation of small firms would produce one policy instead of many; would be financially stronger; would avoid unnecessary competition; would reduce costs by reducing staff, offices and maintenance services; and would offer a much greater chance of regular back loads.[6]

However desirable such amalgamations, they had not come about universally by the late 1930s. Certainly there had been mergers or takeovers.

We see Ryburn United in Yorkshire (formed in 1908) merging with Transport Services Ltd early in 1932 to form a combined fleet of 125 vehicles. Both companies had offices in Leeds, Bradford, Halifax, Hull, Manchester, Liverpool and London. The new firm had agencies in some seventy towns. Under the chairmanship of Mr E.B. Hutchinson, Ryburn opened a depot in Bradford for 200 vehicles.[7] A few months later the company, with its capital increased by £25,000, purchased Sureway Transport Co. of Manchester and the Sheffield Express Delivery Company.[8] In the summer of 1933 Ryburn took over Dawson Transport of Manchester with its daily service from Manchester to the North-east coast, and Aire and Tyne Parcels Service.[9] Then at the beginning of 1934 Ryburn United Transport Ltd were themselves taken over by Oswald Tillottson, Ltd.[10] Tillotson, originally vehicle builders, had already taken over other firms, for example Bouts in 1930. Mr C. Dunbar cites a company (also named Transport Services Ltd) floated in 1936, as eventually having 26 subsidiaries in various towns from Gateshead and Hull to Folkestone, from Sudbury (Suffolk) to Pembroke.[11] Mr Dunbar may well be right in saying that the LAs and the Tribunal 'enabled the industry to achieve a much higher degree of organization'.[12] Maybe he should have said 'obliged' rather than 'enabled'. However, by the beginning of the Second World War the industry still consisted mainly of a great number of small firms.

Apart from straightforward mergers, there were many working agreements. Red Arrow Deliveries, Ltd, of Yardley, Birmingham (Mr Dunbar's company) made arrangements with Huxham and Co. of Plymouth in mid-1934 to the effect that through-transit of parcels was available from the Midlands to Penzance. Indeed, Red Arrow's network of agreements at this time extended from Penzance to Stirling, and from Carmarthen to Yarmouth.[13]

Mr Dunbar, in his book, points, too, to what he calls 'loose groupings of tonnage carriers' – for example around E. Saunders of Harpenden. This group of carriers had an elected executive committee. Surplus work was passed over to other members of the group. A levy was charged on member firms to cover administrative costs.[14]

Size of firms was affected also by straightforward growth through the building up of business. There was the London firm of Cattermoles (Transport) Ltd, for example. This firm was founded in 1843 and just before the First World War had some 300 horses. The first motor vehicle was bought in the early 1920s and by 1935 the firm had 27 petrol lorries (and only 20 horses).[15] Similarly, Lewis's Stores (Liverpool, Manchester and Birmingham) had five motors and two horse-drawn vehicles in 1911 but twenty years on they were using 150 motor vehicles.[16] R.J. Weeks of London had grown from one vehicle at the end of the First World War to 350 by 1935.[17] There were even bigger fleets. United Dairies had over 500 vehicles in 1933[18] and Anglo-American Oil Co. were said, in 1932, to be running 3075 vehicles.[19] Whether replacing horses, winning traffic from the railways, or generating new traffic which previously had not been transported at all, expansion of firms was a common enough occurrence in the late twenties and in the thirties.

Another form of 'organization' was going on apace – that of national associations of vehicle owners. There had been a National Association of Traction Engine Owners and Users by the end of the last century and very soon after steam and petrol wagons got going at the beginning of the twentieth century there arose the Motor Vehicle and Wagon Users' Association. This latter body soon changed its name to the Commercial Motor Users' Association (CMUA) and for more than twenty years it was the only national body. There were any number of small local associations (like the Liverpool group working on rates which we saw in the previous chapter) or representing vehicle-owners in particular trades (such as sand, ballast and gravel). Of course, there was the rather larger London Haulage and Contractors' Association. A number of small associations came together just after the First World War to form the National Road Transport Employers' Federation. There was, too, a National Association of Furniture Removers and Warehousemen. But the picture at the end of the 1920s was of many small, local bodies (some say too many) and only limited national representation. The CMUA was made up predominantly of ancillary users.

As we saw in Chapter Eleven, when the Royal Commission was set up in 1928 the long-distance haulage people did not really have any organization which could argue on their behalf, so the Long Distance Road Haulage Committee of Enquiry was set up to collect information for that purpose. But at that stage it certainly could not have been called a national organization. It had comparatively few members and a very limited purpose. However, it was obvious that there were benefits to be derived from such a body and at the beginning of 1931 the Committee was busy drafting Articles of Association for a national body. At a meeting in London on 18 February 1931 at which about 100 people were present the Long Distance Road Haulage Association Ltd (LDRHA) was founded (though it was not formally registered as a company limited by guarantee until 10 Sept. 1931). This non-profit-making company would engage in propaganda for the industry, in legal defence of members, and in stabilization of rates, among other things. The Council of this new body consisted of the 13 original subscribers to the Memorandum (including names like Donaldson Wright, Gupwell, Hutchinson, Sewell and the Marstons) and 13 members representing the 13 regional areas. Mr E. C.Marston was elected chairman, and he pointed out that the Motor Hirers' Association and the CMUA had been approached to join in, but without success.[20] The Motor Hirers' Association mentioned was, in fact, the Motor Hirers' and Coach Services Association which, itself, had been formed by the merger of over 20 small local associations. Soon after the London meeting the

LDRHA started holding meetings of transport interests in the various industrial cities of the country and by May 1931 its membership was said to have reached 150 companies with 1500 vehicles.[21]

Just when the LDRHA was being registered as a company (Sept. 1931) there came the news that the Hauliers' and Aggregate Merchants' Alliance had changed its name to the Short Distance Road Hauliers' Alliance (SDRHA) with the intention of allowing in any short-distance haulier, of any commodity.[22] In 1932 came the formation of the British Road Federation (BRF) which was to campaign tirelessly for better roads. Although its membership included bodies representing firms directly engaged in transport, such as McNamara, the Motor Hirers, the LDRHA, the Furniture Removers, and the CMUA; and others one stage back, like the SMMT, there were also a number of members involved in road-building – such as the Cement Makers' Federation, the Asphalt Roads Association, the Road Machinery Manufacturers, and the British Road Tar Association.[23] Among the committees of the BRF was the Special Operators' Committee, superseding the old Standing Joint Committee of Mechanical Road Transport Associations which had worked for road transport interests for a number of years. All the bodies represented on the old Standing Joint Committee had representatives, too, on the new BRF Special Operators' Committee; as did the Motor Hirers and the LDRHA.[24]

At the beginning of April 1932 the short-distance and the long-distance hauliers' bodies decided to amalgamate under the title of the Road Haulage Association (RHA).[25] As yet, though, membership of the national bodies was proportionately small. In an industry with over 20,000 haulage contractors the combined membership of the RHA and the CMUA barely reached 2000. But membership of the RHA grew steadily. By the end of the year it had over 1300 members.[26] In May of 1935, when negotiations were going on for the merger of the RHA, the CMUA and the Motor Hirers into one 'National Road Transport Association' the RHA then had around 9000 members and the CMUA, perhaps 5000, (between them, more than half the industry). In the event, the CMUA did not proceed with the union but the other two came together as the Associated Road Operators Ltd, being registered as a company limited by guarantee in July 1935. The CMUA would continue its separate existence until after the Second World War.[27]

So, the industry was established and growing. Its effects were beginning to be noticeable in terms of location of industry. As early as the Chief Inspector of Factories' *Annual Report* of 1931, note was taken of the many new factories in Brentford, especially along the Great West Road. Fifteen new factories had been built in North Acton in 1931. Location here was clearly aimed at the London market and its port, but while the move away from the industrial regions of the Midlands and North was, perhaps, initiated by the availability of electrical power, it was certainly facilitated by the availability of road transport. Similarly in East Anglia, Lincolnshire and Worcestershire, there were eight new factories that year which could be established in the heart of the fruit- and vegetable-growing areas, given the convenience of motor lorries.[28] Other effects were being noticed, too. To the shopper in the village perishable goods such as meat, fish and fruit became more readily available and prices were evened out as between town and country, between one place and another. Indeed a greater range of goods was becoming available, and everywhere shops and factories were keeping lower stocks of goods and materials, firm in the knowledge that they could be supplied in a day. Such rapid transport clearly facilitated an expansion of markets. One writer even noticed the decline in droving of herds of cattle or sheep along the roads (and perhaps also those famous flocks of turkeys walking from Norfolk to London at Christmas).[29]

So by the middle of the thirties Britain had this substantial industry, rather larger than the railways in terms of employment, even if the public haulage sector was not yet carrying as much for hire or reward as the railways. Despite the frailty of the economy, despite legislation, despite the campaign of its competitor, the industry had carved out its own territory, to the benefit of the nation. *The Fourth Annual Report of the Licensing Authorities* – to 30 June 1938 – showed already more than half a million freight vehicles in use (see Appendix III). The greater part of these were the 365,025 vehicles operated as ancillary to some other trade or industry. Although the number of C licences had fallen slightly to 178,586 in June 1938 (suggesting some business failures or mergers?) in the year to that date the number of vehicles 'in possession' had increased somewhat. It is clear that the majority of these vehicles would have been used for fairly short-distance delivery work, displacing horses and lads with bicycles. For the most part, they would not have competed with rail. In addition to these clearly ancillary vehicles under C licences there were, in June 1938, a further 54,906 vehicles licensed under 34,767 B licences. These would work as ancillary vehicles at times, and at other times engage in public haulage. The idea was good, allowing the most efficient use of vehicles, but the LAs certainly worked hard at severely limiting the public haulage side of their work by applying restrictions to these licences. Then there were 9467 vehicles under 5430 A (contract) licences. These were vehicles operated by public hauliers under contracts of at least a year with particular customers. The arrangement would allow firms using the lorries to avoid the capital cost (and the management problems) of running their own fleets. Some of the vehicles may well have operated virtually like C licensed vehicles.

Finally there was the public haulage sector proper – under ordinary A Licences. Of these, there were 83,749 vehicles 'in possession' of which 10,145 were railway-owned and 73,604 owned by haulage firms. The railway lorries were mostly used to replace horses for local C&D work at railway stations, but some would have been used for the service of lengthy routes in agricultural areas, as we have seen earlier. It must be noted that the number of licences does not match the number of firms operating vehicles. It was quite common for firms to hold more than one type of licence – B and C, or A and B, or A and A contract, for example.

Another point that must be stressed, despite our discussion of mergers above, is the small number of lorries owned by most firms. According to the April 1936 Census figures of the MOT some 14,060 A licensed vehicles (just over 17 per cent of the then 81,000 so licensed) were run by firms having just one lorry. Just under 23,000 hauliers ran between one and four vehicles, and if we include larger firms we find that well over 60 per cent of the vehicles were run by firms with less than ten vehicles. There were the bigger firms. Some 7.4 per cent of A licensed vehicles (about 6000) were run by firms owning 100 or more. That is to say that only 7.4 per cent of 'A' vehicles were in fleets of such size as to gain maximum efficiency in the terms set out by Mr E.B. Hutchinson five years earlier.

The story is very similar in the case of B licences where nearly half the 52,799 vehicles (25,661 to be precise) were operated by firms with just the one vehicle each. Fleets of less than ten vehicles accounted for just over 90 per cent of the 52,000-odd vehicles. Only 2½ per cent of B licensed vehicles were in fleets of 25 or more. Clearly, while fleets of 100 or more would have been the most economically efficient to run, it would have been only exceptional firms that could have had enough traffic to justify that number of vehicles.[30]

To get a proper picture of the half-million road freight vehicles running in late 1938 it is not sufficient to look only at fleet sizes. Gilbert Walker, in his most informative book, analyses these vehicles by capacity. He shows about 29 per cent of the main category of freight vehicles (over 140,000) as not exceeding 1 ton. Above that, and up to and including 5 tons, covered another 69 per cent. A mere 1.85 per cent (just over 9000) exceeded 5 tons' capacity.[31] Given the number of vehicles used under C licences for (retail?) distribution, it is perhaps not surprising to see so many small vehicles. Most of the bigger vehicles would have been used by hauliers, as would the few remaining steamers (which are not included in these figures). To complete the picture, recourse must be had again to Mr Walker's considerable expertise. He points out that in 1936 the railways carried some 280,000 tons of freight of which 177,500 tons were coal. This would leave just about 100,000 tons of general merchandise and other categories. Mr Walker estimates that road freight vehicles, too, carried about 100,000 tons. Apart from coal, this suggests virtual equality between road and rail. Unfortunately there were no ton-mileage figures and one could not say which form of transport was ahead without considering the distance the freight was carried. Bearing in mind the substantial work done in retail or short-distance distribution it is highly likely that the average length of haul was greater on the railways, so that their ton-mileage would have been greater. Road haulage had not yet won the first position.

The position which the road haulage industry had achieved owed a tremendous amount to the hard work and sheer persistence of the innumerable owners and drivers – those who had succumbed as well as those who survived. As mentioned previously, it owed a great deal, too, to the improvement in the roads and it owed a lot to the increasing efficiency of the vehicle. There were still old vehicles around, of course. When Leyland advertised in January 1932 seeking the oldest petrol-driven Leyland still in service, offering a prize of 100 guineas, Carter-Paterson won with a 1908 model. This vehicle had done 380,000 miles up to April 1932, and was still doing 55–75 miles per day carrying lift-vans (containers) between central and suburban depots. Indeed they still had, at that time, 30 Leyland X-type lorries manufactured before 1913.[32] Carter-Paterson obviously must have found it economical to run these vehicles, but by 1932 manufacturers were trying harder than ever to improve their vehicles.

Apart from any other consideration the 1930 Road Traffic Act (which allowed vehicles up to 2½ tons to do 30 m.p.h. while those over that weight were allowed only 20 m.p.h.) clearly gave an incentive to tare weight reduction. Sainsbury's – the grocery firm – had switched over to lighter Bedfords to take advantage of the 30 m.p.h.[33] The chassis manufacturers tackled the problem using new metals and at first the body builders did little, but inevitably the heavy wooden bodies had to give way to much lighter bodies, made say, of aluminium.

Economy and efficiency depend on more than the design of vehicles. Cost per mile would clearly be lower for a vehicle doing 600 miles per week than for a pre-1914 lorry doing 150 miles a week. It would be lower too, for vehicles taxed at the rates prior to 'Salter' than after that body's recommendations were seized upon by a happy Chancellor of the Exchequer. The ups and downs of fuel costs cannot be ignored either. There is a noticeable interaction in the components of total operating costs. With the improvement of pneumatic tyres we note that greater weekly mileages become possible, thus spreading standing charges. Pneumatic tyres (at first used only on vehicles up to a couple of tons) gradually became practicable for bigger vehicles; up to 5-tonners, then 6- and then 8-tonners. The use of these tyres (on probably much better roads) reduced vibration and so led to lower maintenance costs, a longer vehicle life and so lower depreciation charges. Following the 1930 legislation with its provision for drivers' hours, the greater mileages being run would entail the wages of two men, so standing charges would rise. The cost differences for any two successive years would require several paragraphs of explanation. In an article in *The Manchester School,* vol. 18, 1950, Ralph Cropper sets out (p.246) figures calculated by K.F. Glover (for a lecture to the Royal Statistical Society). These show that for a 4-tonner doing 600 miles per week, and taking 1922 total costs, 10.78d. per mile, as being equal to 100, the figure for 1937 for a petrol-engined vehicle had fallen to 57 (6.13d. per mile); that is, in 1937 the all-in costs of a 4-tonner were only 57 per cent of what they were in 1922. The 1937 total cost per mile of a diesel-engined 4-tonner was lower than that of a 1937 petrol 4-tonner, being 5.45d. per mile (51 per cent of the 1922 petrol 4-tonner). Appendix IV of the present work gives a selection of cost figures from the tables regularly published in *Commercial Motor*. While those cost tables were frequently improved (for example by what was included or assumed) and so may not always be strictly comparable one year with another, they do indicate plainly the gradual reduction in the cost of running road haulage vehicles. We see in these figures many relevant points. The figures for petrol vehicles on solid tyres were shown only up to 600 miles per annum in 1921. In 1923 data for 800 miles were inserted and by 1931 costs for 1200 miles per week were being shown – albeit for a 96-hour week (which meant double wages). For vehicles on pneumatic tyres the 1921 figures cover vehicles only up to 2 tons. It was only in March 1928 that information about 4- and 5-tonners was introduced into the tables, and figures for 8-tonners came in two years later. We notice that, in 1921, the all-in cost per mile of a 2-tonner doing 600 miles per week was 15.11d. per mile whereas in 1931 the 8-tonner doing that mileage was costing only 11.88d. per mile. But for a really satisfactory appreciation of the data, the *Commercial Motor* figures quoted as well as the Glover figures would need to be compared with or deflated by some index of the value of the pound, such as the Cost of Living Index. However, it is clear that costs of operating bigger and better vehicles gradually fell well below those for the small vehicles just after the First World War.

To get bigger loads, vehicles with more wheels were used. By October 1935 6-wheeled rigid 10-tonners on pneumatics, doing 600 miles per week, were running at 10.46d. per mile. The same date saw artics costing comparable amounts. At 600 miles per week the 6-wheeled artic, with petrol engine and pneumatics, was shown as carrying its maximum load at 11.75d. But a similar vehicle, fully laden, with an 'oil' engine, was running the 600 miles weekly at 10.12d. Before the advent of the 'oiler', the steam wagon had been the beast of heavy burden. Back in 1921 a steamer on steel tyres would have carried its 8 tons for only 200 miles at 28.32d. per mile, whereas on solid rubber it would have cost 27.8d. and shod in this way it could do 400 miles per week for an all-in figure of 21.45d. Only seven years later we find data being quoted for rigid 12-tonners on solids – 800 miles per week for 13.3d., and in 1931 on pneumatics the 800 miles per week would have worked out at 12.18d.

To sum up, we compare 1935 costs with those for a 6-tonner, on solids, petrol-engined, at 600 miles per week in 1921. The 1921 figure was 21.46d. per mile. In 1935:

4-wheeled	6-tonner	solid tyres	petrol	9.75d
4-wheeled	6-tonner	pneumatics	petrol	7.58d
4-wheeled	6-tonner	pneumatics	oil	6.52d
4-wheeled	5-6 tonner	solids	steam	8.99d
4-wheeled	5-6 tonner	pneumatics	steam	8.99d
6-wheeled	6-tonner	pneumatics	petrol	7.75d
6-wheeled	6-tonner	pneumatics	oil	7.29d
5-, 6-, or 8-wheeled artic	6-tonner	pneumatics	petrol	7.27d
5-, 6-, or 8-wheeled artic	6-tonner	pneumatics	oil	6.24d
6-wheeled artic	max	solids	steam	11.61d
6-wheeled artic	max	pneumatics	steam	10.64d

It should be remembered that these figures, prepared by the leading road transport journal, were averages, taking all kinds of vehicles, working in all sorts of conditions and terrain, and carrying all sorts of loads. Furthermore it must be pointed out that when new kinds of vehicles came on the scene (artics or oil-engined vehicles, for example) the cost figures for them would be included only after *Commercial Motor* had been able to get sufficient data from widespread use to enable a proper figure to be calculated. The first appearance of cost figures for a particular type certainly cannot be regarded as the inaugural date of that type.

One very relevant aspect of this whole question of costs was the relationship of the payload to the gross weight being moved, or to put it slightly differently, the relationship between tare weight and payload. For much of the 40 years we have been discussing, the payload, on a rough rule of thumb, was just about equal to the tare. Admittedly, for a long time, manufacturers were a bit wary of specifying at all precisely what their vehicles were able to carry. Even when they did, a game went on, in which many hauliers would load a wagon well beyond the designated capacity on the assumption that the manufacturers had built in a good margin of safety. The manufacturers, in turn, realizing that overloading went on, would, indeed, provide for a bit of extra strength. The legislation of the early 1930s, however, with speed limits and taxation related to tare weight, brought a little bit of sanity into the situation.

If we examine the 'chassis specifications' published in *Commercial Motor* in April and May of 1920, perhaps the first thing we notice is that in a great many cases no tare weight was stated at all. It is hard to believe that it was not thought important, for no operator worth his salt would have been ignorant of the cost of moving dead weight around. Perhaps hauliers just had to take what they could get. One might guess what he could from other information in the tables, such as 'shipping weight, packed'. A Hallford for 3-ton net load, for example, did not have a tare weight shown, but the shipping weight was 4 tons. For those cases where a tare weight was stated it was given as 'tare weight, chassis' so there again guesses would have to be made about the weight of the body; a body built, no doubt mainly of wood and built for strength. Let us take a few examples. A Leyland for a 2-ton net load had a chassis tare of 2 tons 10 cwt (2½ tons). A 4-ton net load vehicle had a chassis weight of 3½ tons. Oddly, a 6-ton load did not seem to require much more in the way of chassis weight – only 3 tons 13 cwt (3.65 tons). Similarly a Thornycroft for a 5-ton payload showed a chassis tare of 3½ tons although the 'shipping weight, packed', was given as 5 tons 9 cwt (5.45 tons). Steamers of the time came close to having the chassis weight equal to the payload. Clayton, Foster, Leyland, Mann, Tasker and Yorkshire firms all provided wagons for a net 5-ton load, which had chassis weights within a couple of hundredweight of the 5 tons, that is, from 4 tons 18 cwt (4.9 tons) to 5 tons.[34]

When we come to 1934 we see a difference. An Albion K82 designated as for a 4-ton payload had a chassis weight of 56 cwt (2.8 tons). A Thornycroft 'Speedy' EE/SC6, also for 4 tons, had a chassis weight of 49.75 cwt (just 28 lb short of 2½ tons). Its tare was given as 63.75 cwt (3.1875 tons). No chassis weight is shown for a Foden 10-tonner but its tare was only 99 cwt (4.95 tons). This was an oil-engined vehicle and so would have been slightly heavier than one with a petrol engine. The slightly bigger Albion R59 with a petrol engine had a payload of 10–11 tons on its tare of 6 tons.[35]

An article, discussing the 1934 vehicle specifications generally, talked of the influence of taxation- 'not altogether beneficial'. On particular points the view was taken that

> The legislative encouragement given to the pneumatic tyre has certainly had a most beneficial influence and has, perhaps, done more than anything else to stifle the complaints as to the damage to property, noise, etc, which were prevalent when the solid tyre was the vogue. [Furthermore] if the taxation on petrol had, years ago, been as heavy as it is today, the steam wagon and battery-electric would not only have retained, but have strengthened their positions; but with the arrival of the oil engine … the hopes for these types cannot be considered so promising [oil engines would certainly have developed even without a petrol tax but it might have taken longer.][36]

As was pointed out above, new classes of vehicles do not appear in published statistics from the moment the vehicles come into use. Official statistics, too, have this characteristic. In trying to follow the path of the development of compression-ignition engines we find that the numbers registered are not shown separately from petrol engines before 1934. In that year, one of returning prosperity, 67,377 goods vehicles were registered for the first time. Of these there were 1715 'oilers', including

up to 2½ tons	210
3–4 tons	434
4–5 tons	552

The same registration figures included, also, 1621 6-wheeled rigids, 50 8-wheelers and 833 artics, though the figures for 'oilers' and those for multi-wheelers would often cover the same vehicles.[37]

In the mid-1930s, then, after 40 years of development we have already arrived at an industry reasonably recognizable from our viewpoint.

As was stated at the end of the previous chapter, the Prime Minister had come back from Munich (end of September 1938) to tell the public that there would be peace. What he told his colleagues and civil servants must have been different. In February 1939 the MOT issued a booklet to all operators, whether A, B or C licensed. That booklet, entitled, *Organisation of Road Transport for a Defence Emergency*, had a foreword by the minister, Leslie Burgin. He pointed out that in the event of an emergency defence forces, including civil defence, would have the first call on fuel supplies and ordinary commercial traffic would in all probability have to be rationed severely. But given some 200,000 operators of 500,000 vehicles, he foresaw difficulties. 'Under war conditions full use cannot be made of the industry if there are thousands of individuals each going his own way. Neither an army of soldiers, nor convoys of lorries can prosper under a debating society.' That was one way of describing the road haulage industry, but he had a point, nevertheless. He went on to summarize his plan which was detailed in the remainder of the booklet. The basic idea was that

> all classes of operators, whether working under A, B or C Licences should in peacetime (and without interfering in any way with their ordinary business) voluntarily form themselves into working groups for wartime purposes, choosing, as far as possible, their own leaders, through whom the government can secure the best use of road transport and the best use of fuel without which it cannot move.

He had had the benefit of advice from an Advisory Committee consisting of leading men in the road transport industry, with representatives of the railways and of the TGWU. Paragraph 6 of the booklet urged operators to join 'shadow groups' right away, on pain of having no voice in the selection of sub-district managers; and Paragraph 7 talked of groups of 25–100 vehicles in the same kind of work.

So the industry, just about established and getting to grips with licensing, had war, nationalization and denationalization, and the 1968 Act, all to look forward to – thirty years in the future which would be as challenging, exciting, exasperating and frustrating as the previous thirty years had been.

Notes

1. *CM,* 18/1/12, p.406; 25/4/12, p.145 and 30/5/12, p.264.
2. *CM,* 16/2/11, p.517.
3. Ibid., notes 1 and 2.
4. *CM,* 26/9/13, p.387.
5. A.A. Walters and C.H Sharp, *A Report on Traffic Costs and Charges,* p.276.
6. *CM,* 20/1/31, pp.802/03.
7. *CM,* 26/4/32, p.351.
8. *CM,* 2/9/32, p.70.
9. *CM,* 7/7/33, p.736.
10. *CM,* 2/2/34, p.880.
11. C.S. Dunbar, *The Rise of Road Transport 1919–39,* p.70.
12. Ibid., p.48.
13. *CM,* 10/8/34, p.856.
14. Dunbar, *Rise of Road Transport,* pp.66/67.
15. *CM,* 14/6/35, pp.602/603.
16. *CM,* 16/6/31, p.599.
17. *CM,* 10/5/35, pp.416/417.
18. *CM,* 3/3/1933, p.69.
19. *CM,* 12/1/32.
20. *CM,* 27/1/31; 10/2/31, p.880; 24/2/31, p.43; 22/9/31, p.162.
21. *CM,* 21/4/31, p.333; 26/5/31, p.502.
22. *CM,* 1/9/31, p.64.
23. *CM,* 7/10/32, p.232.
24. *CM,* 2/2/34, p.880.
25. *CM,* 5/4/32, p.249.
26. *CM,* 16/12/32, p.605.
27. *CM,* 10/5/35, p.412; 12/7/35, p.732.
28. *CM,* 12/7/32, p.741.
29. *CM,* 24/11/31, p.563.
30. G. Walker, *Road and Rail,* p.20.
31. Ibid., p.223.
32. *CM,* 12/1/32, ads p.32; 26/4/32, p.354.
33. B. Williames, *The Best Butter in the World,* p.78.
34. *CM,* 20/4/1920, pp.230–232; 11/5/20, pp.317–319.
35. *CM,* 27/4/34, pp.384–387.
36. Ibid.
37. *CM,* 1/3/35, pp.82/83.

APPENDIX I

Selected Data from *Commercial Motor* Vehicle Specifications (1920)

"THE COMMERCIAL MOTOR" CHASSIS SPECIFICATIONS.

Year—1920. Type—Steam Vehicles.

NAME OF VEHICLE AND MAKERS.	Net Load.	ENGINE. Bore and Stroke.	ENGINE. B.H.P. at Normal Speed.	Type of Boiler.	FUEL. Recommended.	FUEL. Usable.	No. of Speeds.	Final Drive.	Type of Wheels.	Size and Type of Tyres.	TRACK. Front.	TRACK. Rear.	Wheel Base.	Length Overall.	Length, Body Space.	Tare Weight, Chassis.	Price of Chassis with Tyres.
											ft. in.	ft. in.	ft. in.				£
ALLCHIN ... ... William Allchin, Ltd., Globe Works, Northampton	3 ton	3⅝ in. & 5½ in. × 6 in.	22	Loco.	Welsh Coal	—	2	Roller Chain	Cast Steel	Rubber 660 × 140 850 × 140	3 9	6 2	13 9	20 ft. 8 in.	10 to 11 ft.	—	Prices on application.
	4 ton	4 in. & 6½ in. × 7 in.	26	Loco.	Coal	Coke	2	Roller Chain	Cast Steel	Rubber 680 × 140 850 × 140	3 9	6 4	13 9	21 ft. 6 in.	11 to 12 ft.	—	
	5 ton	4¼ in. & 7½ in. × 8 in.	30	Loco.	Coal	Coke	2	Roller Chain	Cast Steel	Rubber 850 × 160 1050 × 160	4 0	6 6	13 9	23 ft. 1 in.	12 to 13 ft.	—	
ATKINSON ... ... Atkinson and Co., Frenchwood Works, Preston, Lancs.	6 ton	6¼ in. × 10 in.	40	Ver. Wat. Tube	Steam Coal	Coke	1	Chain	Cast Steel	970 × 160 1070 × 160T	5 5	5 0	10 6	20 ft. 6 in.	15 ft.	4 ton 18 cwt.	
	4 ton	6¾ in. × 10 in.	35	Ver. Wat. Tube	Steam Coal	Coke	1	Chain	Cast Steel	900 × 160 950 × 140T	5 5	5 0	10 0	18 ft. 6 in.	13 ft.	4 ton 15 cwt.	
	5 ton (end tip)	6½ in. × 10 in.	40	Ver. Wat. Tube	Steam Coal	Coke	1	Chain	Cast Steel	970 × 160 1070 × 160T	5 5	5 0	10 6	20 ft. 6 in.	12 ft.	4 ton 19 cwt.	
	3½ ton (end tip)	6¾ in. × 10 in.	35	Ver. Wat. Tube	Steam Coal	Coke	1	Chain	Cast Steel	900 × 160 950 × 140T	5 5	5 0	10 0	18 ft.	11 ft.	4 ton 17 cwt.	
AVELING AND PORTER .. Aveling and Porter, Ltd., Rochester	5-6 ton tractor	4½ in. & 6½ in. × 8 in.	21	Loco.	Coal	—	2	Spur Gears	W.I. and Steel	5 ft. × 1 ft. and 3 ft. 4 in. × 5 in. (Steel)	—	5 8	8 0	14 ft. 1½ in.	—	—	
BURRELL ... ... Chas. Burrell and Sons, Ltd., Thetford	5 ton	—	19	Loco.	Coal	—	—	Roller Chain	—	—	—	—	—	—	—	—	
CLAYTON ... ... Clayton and Shuttleworth, Ltd., Stamp End Works, Lincoln	5 ton	4 in. & 7½ in × 7 in.	35	Loco.	Coke or Coal	—	2	Roller Chain	Cast Steel	Rubber 720 × 160 860 × 160T	4 0	5 10¾	14 3	21 ft. 6 in.	12 ft.	4 ton 18 cwt. 3 qr.	
FODEN ... ... Fodens, Ltd., Elworth Works, Sandbach	3 ton	4 in. & 6¾ in. str'ke 7 in.	30	Loco.	Steam Coal	Coal or Coke	2	Chain	Cast Steel	Rubber 850 × 140 1030 × 140T	4 0	5 11	13 0	22 ft.	11 ft.	—	
	5 ton	4 in. & 6¾ in. str'ke 7 in.	35	Loco.	Steam Coal	Coal or Coke	2	Chain	Cast Steel	Rubber 850 × 160 1050 × 160T	4 0	5 11	14 2	23 ft.	13 ft.	—	
FOSTER ... ... William Foster and Co., Ltd., Wellington Foundry, Lincoln	5 ton (wagon)	4 in. & 6¾ in. × 7 in.	20	Loco. Belpaire Bx.	Coal	Coke	2	Chain	Steel	Rubber	4 1	6 0	18 6	23 ft.	12 ft. 6 in.	4 ton 19 cwt.	
	6 ton (tractor)	4½ in. & 6¾ in. × 9 in.	25	Loco.	Coal	Coke	2	Gear	Steel	Rubber or Steel	4 1	5 6	8 0	14 ft.	—	4 ton 19 cwt.	
FOWLER ... ... John Fowler and Co. (Leeds), Ltd., Steam Plough and Locomotive Works, Leeds	5 ton (tractor)	4½ in. & 7½ × 9 in.	25 (continuous)	Loco.	Coal	—	2	Spur Gear	Steel	Steel 3 ft. 0¾ in. × 5 in. and 5 ft. × 1 ft. (rubber opt)	4 6 (width)	5 11 (width)	7 11¾	13 ft. 10½ in.	—	5 ton	
GARRETT ... ... Richard Garrett and Sons, Ltd., Leiston Works, Leiston	3 ton	3½ in. & 5¾ in. × 8 in.	25	Loco.	Coal	Coke	2	Chain	Cast Steel	690 × 140 850 × 140T	4 6	6 8	12 10½	20 ft. 1¾ in.	10 ft. 6 in.	—	
	5 ton	4 in. & 6¾ in. × 7 in.	35	Loco.	Coal	Coke	2	Chain	Cast Steel	680 × 140 870 × 160T	4 6	7 5	13 4	22 ft. 2 in.	13 ft.	—	

"THE COMMERCIAL MOTOR" CHASSIS SPECIFICATIONS—STEAM VEHICLES (contd.).

NAME OF VEHICLE AND MAKERS.	Net Load.	ENGINE. Bore and Stroke.	ENGINE. B.H.P. at Normal Speed.	Type of Boiler.	FUEL. Recommended.	FUEL. Usable.	No. of Speeds.	Final Drive.	Type of Wheels.	Size and Type of Tyres.	TRACK. Front. (ft. in.)	TRACK. Rear. (ft. in.)	Wheel Base. (ft. in.)	Length Overall.	Length, Body Space.	Tare Weight, Chassis.	Price of Chassis with Tyres. (£)
LEYLAND ... Leyland Motors, Ltd., Leyland, Lancs.	5 ton (stand'rd)	4½ in. bore 6in. stroke	35	Water Tube	Coke	Welsh Stm. Coal	2	Double RollerCh.	Cast Steel Spoked	970 × 160 1060 × 160T	5 7¾	5 8	10 0	19 ft. 7 in.	13 ft. 6 in.	4 ton 18 cwt.	1,318
	5 ton (hand tip)	4½ in. bore 6in. stroke	35	Water Tube	Coke	Welsh Stm. Coal	2	Double RollerCh.	Cast Steel Spoked	970 × 160 1060 × 160T	5 8¾	5 8	9 8½	9 ft. 0½in.	12ft. 4½ in.	4 ton 19 cwt.	1,440
	5 ton (mec. tip)	4½ in. bore 6in. stroke	35	Water Tube	Coke	Welsh Stm. Coal	2	Double RollerCh.	Cast Steel Spoked	970 × 160 1060 × 160T	5 8¾	5 8	9 8½	19 ft. 0½in.	12ft. 4½ in.	4 ton 19 cwt.	1,470
	6 ton (stand'rd)	4½ in. bore 6in. stroke	35	Water Tube	Coke	Welsh Stm. Coal	2	Double RollerCh.	Cast Steel Spoked	970 × 160 1060 × 160T	5 8¼	5 8	11 3½	20 ft. 7 in.	14 ft. 6 in.	4 ton 18 cwt.	1,340
	6 ton (long)	4½ in. bore 6in. stroke	35	Water Tube	Coke	Welsh Stm. Coal	2	Double RollerCh.	Cast Steel Spoked	970 × 160 1060 × 160T	5 8¾	5 8	13 0	22 ft. 7 in.	16 ft. 6 in.	4 ton 19 cwt.	1,368
	8 ton	4½ in. bore 6in. stroke All 2 H.P. cyl.	35	Water Tube	Coke	Welsh Stm. Coal	2	Double RollerCh.	Cast Steel Spoked	970 × 160 1060 × 160T	5 8¾	5 8	13 0	24 ft. 1 in.	18 ft. 0 in.	4 ton 19 cwt.	1,418
MANN ... Mann's Patent Steam Cart and Waggon Co., Ltd., Pepper Road Works, Hunslet, Leeds	6 ton	4 in. & 6½ in. × 8 in.	28 to 30	Loco.	Coal	Coke	3	Roller Chain	Steel	Rubber 880 × 160 1070 × 160T	3 5	5 4½	13 5	21 ft. 6 in.	13 ft. 8 in.	5 ton	1,270 (stan. ty.)
	3 ton	3⅞ in. & 6⅛ in. × 6 in.	18 to 20	Loco.	Coal	Coke	3	Roller Chain	Steel	Rubber 850 × 140 1080 × 140T	3 6	5 2½	12 0	18 ft.	11 ft.	4 ton	1,125 (stan. ty.)
	5 ton (cart)	4 in. & 6½ in. × 8 in.	28 to 30	Loco.	Coal	Coke	2	Spur Gears	Steel	Steel 2ft.9in. × 6in 3 ft. 10 in. × 10 in.	3 5	4 5½	10 [illegible]	16 ft. 6 in.	8 ft. 6 in.	5 ton	1,150 (stan. ty.)
MARSHALL ... Marshall, Sons and Co., Ltd., Britannia Ironworks, Gainsborough	6¼ ton (tractor)	4⅞ in. & 8 in. × 9 in.	20	Loco.	Coal and Coke	Wood or Oil if specially made	2	Spur Gears	Steel built up	Steel 5 ft. × 12 in. wide	5 1	5 9	7 6	14 ft. 4 in.	—	—	Prices quoted on application.
RANSOMES ... Ransomes, Sims and Jefferies, Ltd., Ipswich	7 to 8 ton (tractor)	4½ & 7½ in. × 8 in.	16 to 20	Loco.	Coal	—	2	—	—	—	—	—	—	14 ft.	—	—	
ROBEY ... Robey and Co., Ltd., Globe Works, Lincoln	5 ton	4 in. & 7½ in., 7 in. stroke	25 to 35	Loco.	Nixon's Navigation	Coke	3	Chain	Pressed Steel Cast Centre	Rubber 860 × 160 1080 × 160T	3 6½	5 9½	12 11	21 ft.	12 ft.	4 ton 18 cwt.	
SENTINEL ... The "Sentinel" Waggon Works, Ltd., Shrewsbury	3½ ton hydraulic end tip	2 H.P. cyl. 6¾ in. 10 in. str.	30	Vertical Water Tube	Coke, Stm. Coal or Both	Any Coal	1	Roller Chain	Cast Steel	Rubber 720 × 160 771 × 140 T fitting	5 4⅞	4 10⅞	9 9	19 ft.	11 ft. 6 in. inside	4 ton 12 cwt. 3 qr.	
	4 ton	2 H.P. cyl. 6¾ in. 10 in. str.	30	Vertical Water Tube	Coke, Stm. Coal or Both	Any Coal	1	Roller Chain	Cast Steel	Rubber 720 × 160 771 × 140T fitting	5 4⅞	4 10⅞	9 9	19 ft.	13 ft. overall	4 ton 12 cwt. 3 qr.	
	5 ton hydraulic end tip	2 H.P. cyl. 6¾ in. 10 in. str.	35	Vertical Water Tube	Coke, Stm. Coal or Both	Any Coal	1	Roller Chain	Cast Steel	720 × 160 860 × 160T fitting	6 4⅞	6 0½	10 4½	21 ft.	13 ft. inside	4 ton 19 cwt. 3 qr.	
	6 ton	2 H.P. cyl. 6¾ in. 10 in. str.	35	Vertical Water Tube	Coke, Stm. Coal or Both	Any Coal	1	Roller Chain	Cast Steel	720 × 160 860 × 160T fitting	5 4⅞	5 0½	10 4½	20 ft. 6 in.	14 ft. 6 in. overall	4 ton 19 cwt. 3 qr.	
TASKER ... W. Tasker and Sons, Ltd., Waterloo Ironworks, Andover, Hants	5 ton & 3 ton trailer	4½ in. & 6½ in. × 7 in. stroke	25	Loco.	Welsh Smokeless	Coke	2 or 3	Chain	Steel	Rubber 880 × 160 1060 × 160T	To Suit Customer's Requirements					4 ton 18 cwt. 2 qr.	
	3 ton	4⅛ in. & 6¼ in. × 6 in. stroke	28	Loco.	Welsh Smokeless	Coke	2 or 3	Chain	Steel	Rubber 860 × 140 1050 × 140T						3 ton 10 cwt.	
WALLIS AND STEEVENS ... Wallis and Steevens, Ltd., Basingstoke	Tractor	4⅞ in. & 8¼ in. × 9 in.	24	Loco.	Welsh Stm. Coal	—	2	Spur Gear	Steel	Steel or Rubber	4 8	5 7½	6 9	13 ft. 2 in.	—	—	
	Wagon	4⅞ in. & 8¼ in. × 9 in.	24	Loco.	Welsh Stm. Coal	—	2	Chain	Steel	Steel or Rubber	4 9½	6 10¾	13 10	21 ft. 9 in.	—	—	
YORKSHIRE ... The Yorkshire Commercial Motor Co., Ltd., Pepper Road, Hunslet, Leeds	6 ton	4½ in. & 7½ in. × 7½ in.	35	Loco.	Coal	Coke	3	Roller Chain	Cast Steel	Rubber 860 × 160 1050 × 160T	5 4½	5 4½	12 8	20 ft. 6 in.	13 ft.	4 ton 19 cwt.	
	3 ton	4 ins. & 7 ins. × 6½in.	30	Loco.	Coal	Coke	3	Roller Chain	Cast Steel	Rubber 820 × 140 880 × 140T	5 3	5 3	11 0	17 ft. 8 in.	12 ft.	4 ton	

"THE COMMERCIAL MOTOR" CHASSIS SPECIFICATIONS.

Year – 1920. Type—Electric Vehicles.

NAME OF VEHICLE AND MAKERS.	Net Load.	BATTERIES. Type.	Voltage.	Capacity in Ampere Hours.	Mileage Cap. per Charge.	Weight.	No. of Speeds.	Final Drive.	Type of Wheels.	Size and Type of Tyres.	TRACK. Front.	TRACK. Rear.	Wheel Base.	Length Overall.	Length, Body Space.	Tare Weight, Chassis.	Price of Chassis with Tyres.
											ft. in.	ft. in.	ft. in.	ft. in.			
B.E.V. ... ... British Electric Vehicles, Ltd., Churchtown Works, Southport.	30 cwt.	Chloride 13MV8	25	193	15 to 20	6 cwt.	3	Chain	Solid	14¾ in. × 3½ in.	2 7	2 7	4 2	8 2	8 ft. 6 in. × 3 ft.	1 ton	Manufacturers have not quoted prices. These can be obtained on application.
	15 cwt.	Chloride 13MV4	25	120	15 to 20	4 cwt.	3	Chain	Solid	16 in. × 3 in.	2 8	2 8	4 7	7 7	6 ft. × 3 ft.	14 cwt.	
(Utility trucks)	13 cwt.	Chloride 13MV4	25	120	15 to 20	4 cwt.	3	Chain	Solid	16 in. × 3 in.	8	2 6	3 6	6 0	5 ft. × 3 ft.	15 cwt.	
EDISON .. .. Edison Accumulators, Ltd., 2 and 3, Duke Street, St James, London, S.W.1.	40 cwt.	A-8	—	300	40	1,818 lbs.	—	Bevel Gear	Steel Castings.	870 × 100 mm. 920 × 100 mm.	5 9 5 9	5 9 5 9	10 0 10 0	16 6 16 6	10 ft. 10 ft.	— —	
ELECTROMOBILE... ... ... Electromobile (Leeds), Ltd., Prospect Works, Otley, Leeds.	1 ton	Lead	80	160	40	—	4 forward, 2 reverse	Enclosed Gears	Wood	771 × 90	5 2	5 2	8 8	14 5	—	—	
	2 ton	Nickel Iron	60	225	40	—	4 forward, 2 reverse	Enclosed Gears	Wood	771 × 100 771 × 90T	5 2 5 2	5 2 5 2	9 8 9 8	14 6 14 6	— —	— —	
	3½ ton	Nickel Iron	60	290	35	—	4 forward, 2 reverse	Enclosed Gears	Cast Steel	771 × 140 771 × 100T	5 2 5 2	5 2 5 2	11 1 11 1	17 4 17 4	— —	— —	
	5 ton	Nickel Iron	60	323	30	—	4 forward, 2 reverse	Enclosed Gears	Cast Steel	771 × 160 771 × 120T	5 2 5 2	5 2 5 2	12 1 12 1	18 4 18 4	— —	— —	
GARRETT ... ... Richard Garrett and Sons, Ltd., Leiston Works, Leiston, Suffolk.	1½ ton	Ironclad Exide	88	193	40 to 45	2,024 lbs.	3 forward, 2 reverse	Roller Chain	Cast Steel	771 × 110 771 × 90T	5 6 5 6	5 4 5 4	9 10 9 10	15 0¾ 15 0¾	— —	2 ton 1 cwt.	
	2½ ton	Ironclad Exide	88	236	35	2,332 lbs.	3 forward, 2 reverse	Roller Chain	Cast Steel	771 × 120 771 × 100T	5 8½ 3 8½	5 4 5 4	10 3 10 3	15 6¼ 15 5¾	— —	2 ton 8 cwt.	
	3½ ton	Ironclad Exide	88	290	35	2,800 lbs.	3 forward, 2 reverse	Roller Chain	Cast Steel	771 × 140 771 × 110T	5 7½ 5 7½	5 5¾ 5 5¾	11 0½ 11 0½	16 3¼ 16 3¼	— —	2 ton 10 cwt.	
G.V. ... ... General Vehicle Co., Ltd., 43, Shoe Lane, Holborn Circus, London, E.C.4.	5 ton	Ironclad 13MV9	86	284	30	2,953 lbs.	3 forward, 2 reserve	Chain	Wood	36 in. × 7 in.	5 9	—	11 10	17 5	14 ft. 3 in.	6,595 lbs.	
	6 ton	Edison 60A12	72	450	30	2,698 lbs.	5 forward, 2 reverse	Chain	Wood	36 in. × 6 in.T	5 9	—	11 10	17 5	14 ft. 3 in.	6,595 lbs.	
	2½ ton	Ironclad 441MV8	86	253	35	2,650 lbs.	5 forward, 2 reverse	Chain	Wood	36 in. × 5 in.	5 5	—	11 1	15 9	12 ft. 8 in.	5,940 lbs.	
	3½ ton	Edison 60A10	72	375	35	2,172 lbs.	6 forward, 2 reverse	Chain	Wood	36 in. × 5 in.T	5 5	—	11 1	15 9	12 ft. 8 in.	5,940 lbs.	
	2 ton	Ironclad 441MV7	86	221	40	2,346 lbs.	5 forward 2 reverse	Chain	Wood	36 in. × 4 in.	5 1	—	9 5	13 11	10 ft. 8 in.	4,050 lbs.	
	2 ton	Edison 60A8	72	300	40	1,720 lbs.	5 forward, 2 reserve	Chain	Wood	36 in. × 3½ in.T	5 1	—	9 5	13 11	10 ft. 8 in.	4,050 lbs.	
	1 ton	Ironclad 441MV5	80	158	45	1,670 lbs.	5 forward, 2 reverse	Chain	Wood	36 in. × 3½ in.	5 0	—	8 8	12 7	8 ft. 1 in.	2,800 lbs.	
	1 ton	Edison 60A6	—	—	45	1,300 lbs.	5 forward, 2 reverse	Chain	Wood	36 in. × 3½ in.	5 0	—	8 8	12 7	8 ft. 1 in.	2,500 lbs.	
	½ ton	Ironclad 441MV5	86	158	45	1,325 lbs.	5 forward, 2 reverse	Chain	Wood	36 in. × 2½ in.	4 8	—	7 5	11 1	6 ft. 8 in.	2,165 lbs.	
	½ ton	Edison 60A6	—	—	—	930 lbs	5 forward, 2 reverse	Chain	Wood	36 in. × 2½ in.	4 8	—	7 5	11 1	6 ft. 8 in.	2,165 lbs.	
(Utility truck)	2 ton	Ironclad 121MV7	23	221	25	—	4 forward, 4 reverse	Worm	Steel	20 in. × 3½ in.	2 6	—	4 6	7 8	6 ft. 10 in.	2,850 lbs., with batt.	
(Utility tractor)	20 ton	Ironclad 241MV8	46	252	25	—	4 forward, 4 reverse	Worm	Steel	20 in. × 3½ in.	2 6	—	3 4	6 5	—	3,200 lbs., with batt.	
ORWELL ... ... Ransomes, Sims and Jefferies, Ltd., Orwell Works, Ipswich.	3½ ton	Ironclad Exide Cells 401MV8	80	258	25 to 40	1 ton 5 cwt.	4 forward, 1 reverse	Chain	Steel Disc	741 × 120	5 3	5 10½	10 1½	16 0	12 ft.	2 ton 11 cwt. 3 qrs.	
	2½ ton	Ironclad Exide Cells 401MV7	80	236	30 to 45	1 ton 4 cwt.	4 forward, 1 reverse	Helical Gear (front wh. drive)	Steel Disc	741 × 120 771 × 140	5 3 5 3	5 3 5 3	9 4 9 4	16 0 16 0	12 ft. 12 ft.	1 ton 14 cwt. 3 qrs.	

"THE COMMERCIAL MOTOR" CHASSIS SPECIFICATIONS.

Year—1920. Type—Petrol Vehicles—British.

NAME OF VEHICLE AND MAKERS.	Net Load.	ENGINE. No. of Cylinders.	ENGINE. Bore and Stroke.	ENGINE. B.H.P. at Normal Speed.	No. of Speeds Forward.	Final Drive.	Type of Wheels.	Section of Tyres. Solids–Dia. of Rim. Pneus.–Overall Dia.	TRACK. Front.	TRACK. Rear.	Wheel Base.	Length Overall.	Length, Body Space.	Tare Weight, Chassis.	Shipping Weight, Packed.	Dimensions, Packed.	Price of Chassis with Tyres.
			ins.					mm. mm.	ft. in.	ft. in.	ft. in.	ft. in.	ft. in.	T. C. Q.	T. C. Q.	ft. in.	£
ALBION... Albion Motor Car Co., Ltd., Scotstoun, Glasgow	20 cwt. or 16 seater	4	3½ × 5½	20	3	Bevel	Cast Steel	90 — 720 90 — 720 T	5 1	4 9½	11 0	15 10	12 1	1 16 2	2 13 1	16 3 × 5 5 × 6 2	—
	30 cwt. (hand tip)	4	3½ × 5½	20	3	Bevel	Cast Steel	90 — 720 90 — 720 T	5 1	4 9½	11 0	14 9	11 6	1 16 2	2 13 1	16 3 × 5 5 × 6 2	—
	50 cwt.	4	4½ × 5	32	3	Chain	Cast Steel	100 — 720 110 — 720 T	5 10	5 6	13 1	18 7	14 6½	2 9 0	3 10 0	18 10 × 7 4 × 6 8	—
	3 ton	4	4½ × 6	32	3	Chain	Cast Steel	100 — 720 120 — 720 T	5 10	5 6	13 1	19 7	15 6½	2 9 0	3 13 2	19 10 × 7 4 × 6 3	—
	3 ton (long)	4	4½ × 5	32	3	Chain	Cast Steel	100 — 720 120 — 720 T	5 10	5 6	14 5	20 11	16 10½	2 9 2	3 14 0	21 4 × 7 4 × 6 3	—
	3½ ton pantechnicon	4	4½ × 5	32	3	Chain	Cast Steel	100 — 720 140 — 720 T	5 10	5 7	14 5	21 11	17 10½	2 13 1	3 18 0	22 3 × 7 4 × 6 3	—
	3½ ton (hyd. tip)	4	4½ × 5	32	3	Chain	Cast Steel	110 — 720 140 — 720 T	5 10	5 7	13 1	17 0	14 3½	2 16 0	3 19 0	17 3 × 7 4 × 6 3	—
	4 ton	4	4½ × 5	32	3	Chain	Cast Steel	100 — 720 140 — 720 T	5 10	5 7	13 1	19 7	15 6½	2 12 0	3 16 0	19 10 × 7 4 × 6 4	—
	4 ton (long)	4	4½ × 5	32	3	Chain	Cast Steel	100 — 720 140 — 720 T	5 10	5 7	14 5	20 11	16 10½	2 12 3	3 16 0	21 4 × 7 4 × 6 4	—
	29 seater char-a-banc	4	4½ × 5	32	3	Chain	Cast Steel	100 — 720 110 — 720 T	5 10	5 6	14 5	21 3	16 10½	2 11 3	3 14 0	21 6 × 7 4 × 6 3	—
A.E.C. ... Associated Equipment Co., Ltd., Walthamstow, London, E. 17	3½ ton (inc. body)	4	mm. 100 × 140	30	4	U'dertype worm	Cast Steel	100 — 771 100 — 771 T	5 10	5 10	14 2	20 4½ 23 5	14 10 *17 10½	1 5 0	3 10 0	23 0 × 6 6 × 4 6 less wh'ls	—
	5 ton (inc. body)	4	ins. 5 × 6	45	4	Overtype worm	Cast Steel	120 — 860 120 — 860 T	5 8	5 8	14 2½	23 0	13 4	1 0 0	4 10 0	24 0 × 5 0 × 3 10 less wh'ls	1,175
AUSTIN... Austin Motor Co., Ltd., Northfield, Birmingham	1½ ton	4	3¾ × 5	25	4	Worm	Detachable	36 in. cushion for 30 in. dia. rims.	5 0	5 0	10 6	16 11	†9 7	1 18 0	—	—	725
BELHAVEN ... Belhaven, Ltd., Belhaven Works, Wishaw	3 ton	4	mm. 110 × 140	30/35	3	Chain	Cast Steel	120 — 741 120 — 741 T	5 2	4 9	14 0	21 1½	13 0	2 13 0	—	—	—
	3 ton	4	110 × 140	30/35	3	Internal Gear	Cast Steel	120 — 741 120 — 741 T	5 2	4 11	14 0	21 1½	13 0	2 17 0	—	—	—
BELSIZE ... Belsize Motors, Ltd., Manchester	12 cwt.	4	90 × 110	—	4	Bevel	Pressed Steel	815 × 105 pneu.	4 8	4 8	8 3	13 0	†6 6	0 16 2	—	—	475
BRITISH ENSIGN ... British Ensign Motors, Ltd., Hawthorne Road, Willesden Green, N.W. 10	4 ton	4	ins. 5 × 6	45	4	Worm	Cast Steel	120 — 720 120 — 885 T	5 5½	5 6½	18 6	20 5	15 4½	3 4 0	4 2 0	20 6 × 9 5 × 7 3	1,220

* Including near side step support for bus body. † From rear of driver's seat.

"THE COMMERCIAL MOTOR" CHASSIS SPECIFICATIONS—PETROL VEHICLES (contd.).

NAME OF VEHICLE AND MAKERS.	Net Load.	ENGINE. No. of Cylinders.	ENGINE. Bore and Stroke.	ENGINE. B.H.P. at Normal Speed.	No. of Speeds Forward.	Final Drive.	Type of Wheels.	Section of Tyres. Solids-Dia. of Rim Pneus.-Overall Dia.	TRACK. Front.	TRACK. Rear.	Wheel Base.	Length Overall.	Length, Body Space.	Tare Weight, Chassis.	Shipping Weight, Packed.	Dimensions, Packed.	Price of Chassis with Tyres.
			mm.					mm. mm.	ft. in.	ft. in.	ft. in.	ft. in.	ft. in.	T. c. q.	T. c. q.	ft. in.	£
BRITISH FOUR WHEEL DRIVE LORRY ... ... Super-Engineering Co., Ltd., 274, Uxbridge Road, West Ealing	3½ ton (and 5 ton trailer)	4	120×140	44	3	Bevel (all wheels)	Pressed Steel	180 — 720 180 — 730	4 8	4 8	10 5	17 6	12 0	3 5 0	4 5 0	18 0 × [illegible] 0 × 6 8	1,150
CALEDON ... ... Caledon Motors, Ltd., Duke Street, Glasgow	4 ton	4	120×140	40	4	Chain	Cast Steel	120 — 771 120 — 860T	5 6	5 8	14 3	21 6	13 8	2 18 0	4 0 0	—	1,030
	4 ton	4	120×140	40	4	Worm	Cast Steel	120 — 771 120 — 860T	5 6	5 6	14 3	21 6	13 3	2 18 0	4 0 0	—	1,050
	6 ton	4	120×140	40	4	Chain	Cast Steel	140 — 670 160 — 771T	5 6	5 10	14 4	22 4	14 0	3 5 0	4 5 0	—	1,300
CLYDE ... ... Mackay and Jardine, Ltd., Wishaw	25 cwt.	4	ins. 3½ × 5½	20	3	Worm	Cast Steel	915 × 105 pneu. 100 — 771 solid	4 0	4 9	10 2	15 10	†8 6	1 10 0	2 2 0	16 0 × 5 0 × 6 0	626
COMMER CAR ... ... Commercial Cars, Ltd., Luton	1½ ton	4	mm. 95×120	22	3	Worm	Cast Steel	34 in. × 4½ in. pneu. 120 — 720 solid	—	5 6	10 0	15 4	†8 0	1 13 1	—	—	—
	2 ton	4	100×120	25	3	Worm	Cast Steel	100 — 720 100 — 720T	—	5 6	11 0	16 4	†9 0	2 0 0	—	—	—
	Passeng'r (30 seater)	4	115×140	40	4	Worm	Cast Steel	120 — 771 120 — 850T	—	5 5½	14 3	21 8	—	2 15 1	—	—	—
	3½ ton	4	110×140	32	3	Chain	Cast Steel	120 — 771 120 — 771T	—	6 8½	13 9	19 0	†11 0	2 18 0	—	—	—
	5 ton	4	115×140	36	3	Chain	Cast Steel	120 — 720 140 — 850T	—	6 0¾	12 6	19 11	†13 0	3 12 0	—	—	—
DAIMLER ... ... Daimler Co., Ltd., Coventry	2-3 ton	4	95×140	30	4	Worm	Cast Steel	100 — 771 100 — 771T	5 3	5 3	11 6	17 11	13 2	2 9 2	3 6 0	17 8 × 5 0 × 4 4	1,050
	2-3 ton (long)	4	95×140	30	4	Worm	Cast Steel	100 — 771 100 — 771T	5 3	5 3	13 6	21 11	17 2	2 10 2	3 8 0	22 0 × 4 10 × 4 4	1,050
DENNIS ... ... Dennis Bros., Ltd., Guildford, Surrey	3½ ton	4	115×150	40	4	Worm	Cast Steel	120 — 720 120 — 881T.	5 6	5 6	13 0	20 6	†12 3	3 1 2	3 15 0	20 2 × 4 5 × 8 5	—
	Passeng'r (30 seater)	4	115×150	40	4	Worm	Cast Steel	120 — 720 120 — 881T	5 6	5 6	14 1½	21 10	17 6	3 0 2	3 14 0	21 2 × 4 5 × 8 5	—
DURHAM CHURCHILL ... ... Durham Churchill and Co., Sheffield	3-3½ ton (lorry)	4	ins. 5 × 6	45	4	Roller Chain	Wood	120 — 830 110 — 771T	5 4½	5 4½	14 9	22 6	13 6	3 2 0	—	22 6 × 7 0 × 6 0	—
	3-3½ ton (passenger).	4	5 × 6	45	4	Silent Chain	Steel Disc	140 — 720 140 — 850T	5 4½	5 4½	15 7	25 0	19 6	3 6 0	—	25 0 × 7 0 × 6 0	—
ENFIELD-ALLDAY ... ... Enfield-Allday Motors, Ltd., Sparkbrook, Birmingham	2 tons	4	mm. 100×130	25	3	Chain Enclosed	Steel Disc	100 — 720 100 — 720T	5 6	5 6	12 3	17 9	†10 0	1 13 0	3 2 0	18 6 × 7 3 × 5 6	852
GARNER ... ... Henry Garner, Ltd., Moseley, Birmingham	30 cwt. (with body)	4	ins. 3⅞ × 5	30	3	Internal Gear	Wood	ins. ins. 36 — 3½ 26 — 3T [illegible] Solids—for 30 in. dia. rims	5 7	5 7	11 6	20 6	†10 0	1 11 0	2 3 4	218 cu. feet	695
GUY ... ... Guy Motors, Ltd., Wolverhampton	2 ton	4	4 × 5½	35	4	Double Reduction	Cast Steel	mm. mm. 90 — 720 90 — 720T	5 0	5 0	12 4½	17 6½	12 9	2 2 0	2 19 0	425 cu. feet	995

† From rear of driver's seat.

"THE COMMERCIAL MOTOR" CHASSIS SPECIFICATIONS.

Year—1920. Type—Petrol Vehicles—British (contd.).

NAME OF VEHICLE AND MAKERS.	Net Load.	ENGINE. No. of Cylinders.	ENGINE. Bore and Stroke.	ENGINE. B.H.P. at Normal Speed.	No. of Speeds Forward.	Final Drive.	Type of Wheels.	Section of Tyres. Solids: Dia. of Rim. Pneus.: Overall Dia.	TRACK. Front.	TRACK. Rear.	Wheel Base.	Length Overall.	Length, Body Space.	Tare Weight, Chassis.	Shipping Weight, Packed.	Dimensions, Packed.	Price of Chassis with Tyres.
			mm.					mm. mm.	ft. in.	ft. in.	ft. in.	ft. in.	ft. in.	T. C. Q.	T. C. Q.	ft. in.	£
HALLFORD ... ... J. and E. Hall, Ltd., 10, St Swithin's Lane, E.C. 4	30 cwt.	4	100×140	25	3	Chain	Cast Steel	90 — 720 90 — 771T	5 4¾	5 2½	10 10	16 6	‡8 9½	—	3 2 0	17 6 × 5 0 × 4 6	—
	2½ ton	4	100×140	25	3	Chain	Cast Steel	100 — 720 100 — 771T	5 4¾	5 1	12 4	18 0	‡10 3½	—	3 10 0	19 0 × 5 0 × 4 6	—
	3 ton	4	110×140	32	4	Chain	Cast Steel	120 — 720 120 — 850T	6 0	5 10½	0	19 1½	11 1½	—	4 0 0	20 0 × 5 0 × 4 6	—
	4 ton	4	110×140	32	4	Chain	Cast Steel	130 — 720 100 — 850T	6 0¾	5 11½	13 6	20 7½	‡12 7½	—	4 10 0	21 6 × 5 0 × 4 6	—
	5 ton	4	120×140	40	4	Chain	Cast Steel	140 — 720 140 — 850T	6 1½	6 0½	13 0	23 1½	‡14 1	—	5 0 0	23 0 × 5 0 × 4 6	—
HALLEY ... ... Halley's Industrial Motors, Ltd., Yoker, Glasgow	3-3½ ton	6	ins. 3½ × 6	35	4	Worm	Cast Steel	120 — 771 120 — 771T	5 6¾	5 1½	13 4	21 5	‡12 6	2 19 0	—	21 11 × 4 1 × 3 9	—
	3-3½ ton (long)	6	3½ × 6	35	4	Worm	Cast Steel	120 — 771 120 — 771T	5 0¾	5 1½	14 7	22 11	‡14 0	3 1 2	—	23 4 × 4 1 × 3 9	—
JACKSON HOLROYD ... ... James Whiteley, Ltd., Eagle Works, Well Lane, Halifax	30 cwt.	4	4 × 5	25	3	Doub.Red Spur-bevel	Cast Steel	90 — 720 90 — 730T	5 0	5 6	11 0	18 6	—	1 10 0	1 12 0	18 0 × 5 0 × 5 6	700
KARRIER ... . Karrier Motors, Ltd., Huddersfield	3 ton	4	5 × 6	50	4	Doub.Red Bevel and Spur	Cast Steel	120 — 720 120 — 881T	5 8	5 6	14 0	22 11½	‡14 0½	—	—	—	—
	4 ton	4	5 × 6	50	4	Bevel and Spur	Cast Steel	120 — 720 120 — 881T	5 8	5 6	14 0	22 11½	‡14 0½	—	—	—	—
	5 ton	4	6 × 6	60	4	Bevel and Spur	Cast Steel	140 — 720 140 — 881T	5 8	5 6	14 0	22 11½	‡14 0½	—	—	—	—
LACRE ... ... Lacre Motor Car Co., Ltd., Letchworth, Herts.	2½ ton	4	4.33 × 5	30	3	Chain	Cast Steel	100 — 720 100 — 780T	4 11	4 11	12 0	18 4	‡13 10½	2 3 0	2 15 0	18 0 × 4 7 × 3 5	900
	3½ ton	4	4⅞ × 5	38-45	4	Doub.Red Worm and Spur	Cast Steel	120 — 771 120 — 850T	5 6	5 6	13 0	21 6	‡13 10	2 12 0	3 8 0	21 9 × 4 10 × 4 0	1,100
	5 ton	4	4⅞ × 5	38-45	4	Doub.Red Worm and Spur	Cast Steel	140 — 720 140 — 850T	5 0	5 6	14 0	23 0	‡15 0	2 15 0	3 16 0	23 0 × 4 10 × 4 0	1,200
	Road Sweeper	4	mm. 69 × 120	15	2	Chain	Cast Steel	85 — 741 85 — 741T	4 10	—	8 9	12 0	—	1 6 0	1 16 0	12 0 × 5 0 × 4 6	650
LEYLAND ... ... Leyland Motors, Ltd., Leyland, Lancs.	2 ton	4	ins. 4 × 5	26	4	Worm	Cast Steel	100 — 720 100 — 771T	5 6	5 4½	11 9	19 1	‡10 6	2 10 0	3 2 0	18 10 × 3 9 × 3 8	—
	3 ton (standard)	4	4½ × 5	32	4	Worm	Steel Disc	110 — 720 110 — 771T	5 6	5 4½	13 1	21 1	‡12 6	2 10 0	3 2 0	21 6 × 3 9 × 3 8	—

‡ From rear of driver's seat.

"THE COMMERCIAL MOTOR" CHASSIS SPECIFICATIONS—PETROL VEHICLES—BRITISH (contd.).

NAME OF VEHICLE AND MAKERS.	Net Load.	ENGINE. No. of Cylinders.	ENGINE. Bore and Stroke.	ENGINE. B.H.P. at Normal Speed.	No. of Speeds Forward.	Final Drive.	Type of Wheels.	Section of Tyres. Solids: Dia. of Rim. Pneus.: Overall Dia.	TRACK. Front.	TRACK. Rear.	Wheel Base.	Length Overall.	Length. Body Space.	Tare Weight, Chassis.	Shipping Weight, Packed.	Dimensions, Packed.	Price of Chassis with Tyres.
			ins.					mm. mm.	ft. in.	ft. in.	ft. in.	ft. in.	ft. in.	T. C. Q.	T. C. Q.	ft. in.	£
LEYLAND (contd.)	3 ton (passenger)	4	4½ × 5	32	4	Worm	Steel Disc	110 — 720 110 — 771T	5 6	5 4½	16 2½	20 0½	—	2 10 0	3 2 0	19 9 × 3 9 × 3 8	—
	3 ton (overseas)	4	4⅝ × 6	40	4	Bevel	Steel Disc	110 — 881 110 — 881T	5 6	5 4	14 0	21 4	†18 6	3 0 0	3 18 0	18 10 × 3 10 × 3 9	—
	4 ton (standard)	4	4⅝ × 6	40	4	Bevel	Steel Disc	130 — 720 130 — 881T	5 6	5 4	14 0	21 4	†18 6	3 10 0	4 2 0	20 11 × 3 9 × 3 11	—
	4 ton (p'ss'ng'r)	4	4⅝ × 6	40	4	Worm	Steel Disc	130 — 720 130 — 850T	5 6	5 4	14 0	21 4	†18 6	3 10 0	4 2 0	20 11 × 3 9 × 3 11	—
	4 ton (long frame)	4	4⅝ × 6	40	4	Bevel	Cast Steel	130 — 720 130 — 881T	5 6	5 4	15 1½	23 7½	†14 6	3 10 0	4 6 0	23 11 × 3 9 × 3 11	—
	4 ton (passenger)	4	4⅝ × 6	40	4	Worm	Cast Steel	130 — 720 130 — 850T	5 6	5 4	15 1½	23 7½	†14 6	3 10 0	4 6 0	23 11 × 3 9 × 3 11	—
	4 ton (long w.b.)	4	4⅝ × 6	40	4	Bevel	Cast Steel	130 — 720 130 — 881T	5 6	5 4	15 10	24 11	†16 6	3 10 0	4 6 0	24 11 × 3 9 × 3 11	—
	4 ton (passenger)	4	4⅝ × 6	40	4	Worm	Cast Steel	130 — 720 130 — 860T	5 6	5 4	15 10	24 11	†16 6	3 10 0	4 6 0	24 11 × 3 9 × 3 11	—
	4 ton (overseas)	4	4⅝ × 6	40	4	Bevel	Steel Disc	130 — 881 130 — 881T	5 6	5 4	15 1½	23 7½	†14 6	3 10 0	4 6 0	23 4 × 3 9 × 3 11	—
	5 ton	4	5 × 6	48	4	Bevel	Cast Steel	140 — 720 140 — 850T	5 6	5 4	15 1½	23 7½	†14 6 †15 6	3 13 0	4 9 0	23 11 × 3 9 × 3 11	—
	6 ton	4	5 × 6	48	4	Bevel	Cast Steel	160 — 720 160 — 850T	5 6	5 5½	15 10	24 7½	†16 6 †16 6	3 13 0	4 9 0	24 11 × 3 9 × 3 11	—
MAUDSLAY ... ... Maudslay Motor Co., Ltd., Coventry	3 ton	4	4½ × 5	30	4	Worm	Cast Steel	120 — 720 120 — 881T	5 6	5 6	13 6	21 3	†12 4½	3 5 3	—	—	—
	passenger (28 seater)	4	4½ × 5 or 5 × 6	30 or 40	4 4	Worm Worm	Cast Steel Cast Steel	120 — 720 120 — 881T	5 6	5 6	14 6	23 0	†14 4½	3 5 3	—	—	—
	4 ton	4	5 × 5	40	4	Bevel and Spur	Cast Steel	130 — 720 130 — 881T	5 6	5 6	13 6	21 3	†12 4½	3 7 1	—	—	—
	5 ton	4	5 × 5	40	4	Bevel and Spur	Cast Steel	140 — 720 140 — 881T	5 6	5 6	14 6	25 0	†16 4½	3 11 0	—	—	—
McCURD ... ... The McCurd Lorry Manufacturing Co., Ltd., 71, Southampton Row, W.C. 1.	4 ton	4	mm. 114 × 140	40	4	Doub. Red. Worm	Cast Steel	120 — 720 120 — 881T	5 6	—	14 6	—	†18 0	2 15 0	—	—	1,350
NAPIER ... ... D. Napier and Son Ltd., Acton, W. 3	2 ton	4	ins. 3¾ × 5	35	4	Worm	Cast Steel	100 — 720 100 — 720T	5 0	5 0	10 6	16 5½	†10 6	1 19 2	2 14 0	17 2 × [illegible] × 4 6	850
PAGEFIELD ... ... Walker Bros. (Wigan), Ltd., Wigan	3½ ton (end tip)	4	4·72 × 5½	43	4	Worm	Steel Disc	120 — 720 120 — 720T	5 6	5 1½	8 0	15 9	†11 0	2 19 0	—	—	—
	3 ton (p'ss'ng'r)	4	4·72 × 5½	40	4	Worm	Steel Disc	120 — 720 120 — 720T	5 9	5 4½	14 6	21 0	†14 10	3 0 0	—	—	—
	4 ton	4	4·72 × 5½	45	4	Bevel and Spur	Cast Steel	120 — 720 120 — 860T	5 9	5 4½	13 8	20 2	†13 2	3 7 0	—	—	—
	5 ton	4	5 × 5½	50	4	Bevel and Spur	Cast Steel	120 — 720 120 — 850T	5 9	5 4½	14 9	21 3	†14 3	3 10 0	—	—	—
PALLADIUM ... ... Palladium Autocars, Ltd., Felsham Road, Putney, S.W. 15.	4½ ton (with body)	4	4½ × 5½	45	4	Doub. Red. Worm	Cast steel	120 — 771 120 — 881T	5 8	5 6	14 8	20 8	†12 5	3 0 0	—	—	1,165

† From rear of driver's seat.

"THE COMMERCIAL MOTOR" CHASSIS SPECIFICATIONS — PETROL VEHICLES - BRITISH (contd.)

Name of Vehicle and Makers.	Net Load.	Engine: No. of Cylinders.	Engine: Bore and Stroke.	Engine: B.H.P. at Normal Speed.	No. of Speeds Forward.	Final Drive.	Type of Wheels.	Section of Tyres. Solids: Dia. of Rim. Pneus.: Overall Dia.	Track: Front.	Track: Rear.	Wheel Base.	Length Overall.	Length, Body Space.	Tare Weight, Chassis.	Shipping Weight, Packed.	Dimensions, Packed.	Price of Chassis with Tyres.
								mm. mm.	ft. in.	ft. in.	ft. in.	ft. in.	ft. in.	T. C. Q.	T. C. Q.	ft. in.	£
G. SCAMMELL AND NEPHEW, LTD. ... ... Fashion Street, Spitalfields, E. 1.	7½ ton (tractor lorry)	4	ins. 5 × 5½	45	3	Chain	Cast Steel	100 — 741 120 — 771T (driving) 110 — 771T	5 4	5 4	To centre 10 0 centre to back 9 2	24 0	‡16 0	3 16 0	—	—	1.350
SCOUT ... ... Scout Motors, Ltd., Scout Works, Salisbury.	3 ton	4	mm. 114×140	32·4	4	Double red.	Cast Steel	120 — 720 120 — 720T	5 6	5 6	13 2	20 0	‡12 0	3 5 0	4 0 0	21 0 × 6 0 × 6 0	
	4 ton	4	114×140	32·4	4	Double red.	Cast Steel	140 — 720 140 — 850T	5 6	5 6	13 8	20 0	‡13 0	3 10 0	4 5 0	21 0 × 6 0 × 6 0	
STAR ... ... Star Engineering Co., Ltd., Wolverhampton.	30 cwt.	4	90×150	—	4	Worm	Steel Disc	90 — 720 90 — 720T	4 9	4 9	11 6	17 6	‡11 3	1 17 0	2 5 0	18 10 × 5 5 × 3 11	800
	50 cwt.	4	90×150	—	4	Double red.	Cast Steel	100 — 720 100 — 750T	5 0	5 0	12 6	20 6	‡13 8	2 2 0	2 18 0	19 0 × 6 8½ × 5 2	900
STRAKER-SQUIRE ... ... Straker-Squire, Ltd., Angel Road, Edmonton, N. 18.	5 ton	4	ins. 4½ × 6½	50-55	4	Worm	Cast Steel	140 — 880 140 — 860P	6 0	6 0	14 6	22 11	‡15 8	3 8 0	5 5 0	—	1225
THORNYCROFT ... ... John I. Thornycroft and Co., Ld. 10, Grosvenor Place, S.W. 1.	2 ton	4	4 × 5½	30	3	Worm	Steel	85 — 741 90 — 741T	5 2½	4 8	11 6	18 0	‡9 6	1 18 0	2 17 0	18 6 × 5 10 × 5 10	950
	3 ton	4	4½ × 6	40	4	Worm	Steel	100 — 881 110 — 881T	5 7	5 4	13 0	21 6	‡12 0	2 14 0	3 18 0	21 0 × 7 0 × 6 3	1075
	3 ton (p'ss'ng'r)	4	4½ × 6	40	4	Worm	Steel	100 — 881 110 — 881T	5 7	5 4	14 0	21 5	‡12 9½	—	—	—	1086
	4 ton	4	4½ × 6	40	4	Worm	Steel	120 — 720 140 — 881T	5 7½	5 6	13 7½	21 7½	‡13 6	3 5 0	4 9 0	22 0 × 7 0 × 6 6	1,150
	4 ton (p'ss'ng'r	4	4½ × 6	40	4	Worm	Steel	120 — 720 140 — 881T	5 7½	5 6	14 4½	23 7½	‡14 10½	3 5 0	4 9 0	—	1,160
	6 ton	4	4½ × 6	40	4	Worm	Steel	120 — 720 160 — 850T	5 11½	5 10	14 1½	23 8	‡15 0	3 10 0	5 9 0	24 6 × 8 3 × 7 0	1,225
TILLING-STEVENS ... ... Tilling-Stevens Motors, Ltd., Maidstone.	3 tn. 5 cwt. (with body)	4	mm. 105×125	25-30	4	Worm	Cast Steel	100 — 720 100 — 720T	4 10½	4 9	12 0	18 10	14 4	2 10 0	—	19 0 × 6 0 × 6 2	—
	P.E. 5 ton (lorry or passeng'r)	4	ins. 4½ × 6	40-45	(Petrol-electric)	Worm	Cast Steel	120 — 720 120 — 850T	5 10½	5 8	14 6	24 4	19 2	3 18 0	—	25 0 × 7 0 × 6 8	—
	P. 5 ton (with body)	4	5 × 6	45-50	4	Worm	Cast Steel	140 — 720 140 — 850	5 10½	5 8	14 6	24 4	19 2	3 10 0	—	23 0 × 7 0 × 6 8	—
VULCAN ... ... Vulcan Motor and Engineering Co., Ltd., Crossens, Southport.	30 cwt.	4	mm. 90×130	20·1	4	Over type Worm	Cast Steel	90 — 720 90 — 720T	4 8	4 8	11 5	16 10½	12 7	1 12 2	2 0 0	17 8 × 3 11 × 3 0	750
W. AND G. ... ... W. and G. du Cros, Ltd., Acton, London, W.3.	30 cwt. or 20 seater	4	95×140	25	3	Worm	Cast Steel	90 — 720 90 — 720T	5 0	4 7	10 6	16 2	12 2	1 14 0	2 12 0	16 2 × 6 2 × 4 10	—
	2 ton or 25 seater	4	95×140	25	4	Worm	Cast Steel	100 — 720 100 — 720T	5 0	4 7	11 3½	17 6	13 5	2 1 0	3 1 0	17 9 × 6 3 × 4 6	—
	2 ton (hand tip)	4	95×140	25	4	Worm	Cast Steel	100 — 720 100 — 720T	5 0	4 7	11 3½	15 6	11 5	2 1 0	3 1 0	—	—
WATSON ... ... Henry Watson and Sons, Ltd., High Bridge Works, Newcastle-on-Tyne.	3½-4½ ton	4	115×140	42	4	Spur Gears	Cast Steel	120 — 720 120 — 850T	5 0	5 0	13 0	19 6 21 0	—	—	—	—	1,075
	3½-4½ ton (char-à-bancs)	4	115×140	42	4	Spur Gears	Cast Steel	120 — 720 120 — 810T	5 0	5 0	14 6	23 0 23 0	—	—	—	—	1,100

‡ From rear of driver's seat.

"THE COMMERCIAL MOTOR" CHASSIS SPECIFICATIONS.

Year – 1920. Type—Petrol Vehicles—Foreign.

NAME OF VEHICLE AND DISTRIBUTORS.	Net Load.	ENGINE. No. of Cylinders.	ENGINE. Bore and Stroke.	ENGINE. B.H.P. at Normal Speed.	No. of Speeds Forward.	Final Drive.	Type of Wheels.	TYRE SIZES. Section of Tyres. R.-Dia. of Rim. M.-Overall Dia. All solids except where otherwise stated.	TRACK. Front.	TRACK. Rear.	Wheel Base.	Length Overall.	Length, Body Space.	Tare Weight, Chassis.	Shipping Weight, Packed.	Dimensions, Packed.	Price of Chassis with Tyres.
									ft. ins.	ft. ins.	ft. ins.	ft. ins.	ft. ins.	T. C. Q.	T. C. Q.	ft. ins.	£
A.A. ... ... A.A. Motor Lorries, 5-8, Broad Street, Birmingham	23 cwt.	4	ins. 3¼ × 5	—	3	Internal Gear	Wood	ins. ins. M 83 × 4 pneu. M 82 × 4	4 8	4 8	10 10	16 6	11 8	1 3 3	1 14 0	18 0 × 8 0 × 3 6	585
ACE ... ... Vigo Motor Trading Corporation, Ltd., 4, Vigo Street, London, W.	36 cwt.	4	3¾ × 5¼	30	3	Worm	Wood	M 84 × 3½ M 84 × 5	4 10	4 9½	12 0	—	†10 3	2 4 3	3 15 0	325 cu. ft.	745
	55 cwt.	4	4½ × 5½	36	3	Worm	Cast Steel	M 86 × 4 M 86 × 7	4 10½	4 10½	13 0 or Dump Body 13 0	—	†12 0	3 10 0	4 0 0	375 cu. ft.	1,148
AUTOCAR ... ... Agents: Gaston, Ltd., 212-214, Great Portland Street, W. 1	2 ton	—	—	—	3	Double Reduction Bevel-spur	Wood	M34 × 4 M34 × 5 or M34 × 4 M36 × 5 pneu.	4 10	4 10	8 1	—	†7 7	—	—	—	—
BERLIET ... ... L. C. Rawlence and Co., Ltd., 40, Sackville Street, W. 1	4 ton	4	mm. 110 × 140	45	4	Chain	Cast Steel	mm. mm. 140 — R 771 160 — R 850 T	6 0	6 0	14 0	22 0	†13 0	3 7 3	—	—	1,150 (with body)
BETHLEHEM... ... ... London and Midland Motors, Ltd., 445, Oxford Street, W. 1	30 cwt.	4	ins. 3¾ × 4½	25	3	Internal Gear	Wood	ins. ins. M 36 × 3½ M 36 × 3½ T	4 8	4 8	11 4	17 4	†10 6	1 9 2	2 8 2	272 cu. ft.	—
	2½ ton	4	4 × 4½	28	3	Internal Gear	Cast Steel	M 36 × 4 M 36 × 3½ T	4 8	4 8	12 0	19 0	†12 6	1 15 0	2 16 0	300 cu. ft.	—
	3½ ton	4	4¾ × 6	48	3	Internal Gear	Cast Steel	M 36 × 4 M 40 × 5 T	4 8	4 8	13 6	20 9	†13 9	2 3 3	3 6 3	335 cu. ft.	—
BRASIER ... ... Societe des Automobiles Brasier, 78, High Street, Marylebone	3½ ton (rapid)	4	mm. 100 × 160	32/35	4	Chain	Detachable Disc	mm. mm. M 935 × 153 pn. M 935 × 153 T pn.	5 7	6 2½	12 9½	20 1	†11 5½	3 10 0	—	—	1,250
	5 ton	4	100 × 160	32/35	4	Chain	Wood	140 — R 771 160 — R 850 T	5 7	6 2½	12 9½	20 1	†11 5½	3 10 0	—	—	1,350
BURFORD ... ... H. G. Burford and Co., Ltd., 16, Regent Street, S.W. 1	1 ton	4	ins. 3½ × 5½	21	3	Internal Gear	Wood	ins. ins. M 34 × 4 M 34 × 3 T	4 8	4 8	10 6	14 8	†8 0	—	—	—	585
	2 ton	4	4½ × 5½	30	4	Internal Gear	Wood	M 36 × 4 M 36 × 4 T	4 10	5 5	12 0	18 0	†10 9	—	—	—	695 + 3½ %
CLYDESDALE ... ... Whiting, Ltd., 334-340, Euston Road, N.W. 1	27 cwt.	4	mm. 89 × 127	—	3	Worm	Wood	M 34 × 3½ M 34 × 5	4 8	4 8	12 0	14 4	†9 6	—	—	—	—
	37 cwt.	4	105 × 133	—	3	Worm	Wood	M 36 × 3½ M 36 × 5	4 10½	4 10½	12 2	19 2	†10 11	—	—	—	—
	55 cwt.	4	105 × 133	—	4	Worm	Wood	M 36 × 4 M 36 × 4 T	4 10½	4 10½	13 7	19 8	†11 5	—	—	—	—
	4 ton	4	114 × 140	—	4	Worm	Wood	M 36 × 5 M 40 × 5 T	5 7	5 7	15 0	22 6½	†14 0	—	—	—	—
	5½ ton	4	120 × 152	—	4	Worm	Wood	M 36 × 6 M 40 × 6 T	5 9½	5 9½	15 0	22 6½	†14 0	—	—	—	—
COMET... ... ... American Motors, Ltd., Audrey House, Ely Place, Holborn, London	30 cwt.	4	3½ × 5	22·6	3	Worm	Wood	M 34 × 4 M 34 × 4	—	—	10 10	—	—	—	1 2 3	220 cu. ft.	—

† From rear of driver's seat.

"THE COMMERCIAL MOTOR" CHASSIS SPECIFICATIONS—PETROL VEHICLES—FOREIGN (contd.).

NAME OF VEHICLE AND DISTRIBUTORS.	Net Load.	ENGINE. No. of Cylinders.	ENGINE. Bore and Stroke.	ENGINE. B.H.P. at Normal Speed.	No. of Speeds Forward.	Final Drive.	Type of Wheels.	TYRE SIZES. Section of Tyres. R.—Dia. of Rim. M.—Overall Dia. All solids except where otherwise stated.	TRACK. Front.	TRACK. Rear.	Wheel Base.	Length Overall.	Length, Body Space.	Tare Weight, Chassis.	Shipping Weight, Packed.	Dimensions, Packed.	Price of Chassis with Tyres.
			ins.					mm. mm.	ft. in.	ft. in.	ft. in.	ft. in.	ft. in.	T. C. Q.	T. C. Q.		£
DAY-ELDER ... ... Foster and Tattersall, Ltd., 4, Great Marlborough Street, London, W.	30 cwt.	4	3¾ × 5	22·5	3	Worm	Wood	90 — R 711 125 — R 711	4 8	4 8	12 0	17 0	†10 0	1 12 2	—	—	725
								ins. ins.									
DEARBORN ... ... Watkins and Doncaster, Ltd., 95a, Gt. Portland Street, W. 1	30 cwt.	4	3¾ × 5¼	25	3	Worm	Wood	M 34 × 4 M 34 × 5	4 8	4 9	10 6	15 6	†8 0	1 6 0	—	—	600
	30 cwt. (long)	4	3¾ × 5¼	25	3	Worm	Wood	M 34 × 4 M 34 × 5	4 8	4 9	11 8	16 8	†10 0	1 7 0	—	—	650
	2 ton	4	3¾ × 5¼	25	3	Worm	Wood	M 34 × 4 M 34 × 7	4 9	4 11	12 6	18 3	†11 0	1 9 0	—	—	720
			mm.					mm. mm.									
DE DION ... ... De Dion Bouton, Ltd., 10, Great Marlborough Street, W.1.	3½ ton	4	100 × 140	25	4	Internal Gear	Cast Steel	120 × R 771 120 × R 771 T	5 5	5 3	13 5	20 1	†11 6	3 0 0	—	—	1,050
	5 ton	4	110 × 150	35	4	Internal Gear	Cast Steel	140 × R 771 160 × R 850 T	5 5	5 5½	13 6	20 6	†11 6	3 10 0	—	—	1,250
			ins.					ins. ins.									
FEDERAL ... ... Whiting, Ltd., 334-340, Euston Road, N.W. 1	1 ton	4	3¾ × 5	—	3	Worm	Steel Disc	M 35 × 5 pnu. M 36 × 6 pnu.	4 8	4 8	11 0	16 8	†9 3	1 11 1	—	—	—
	30 cwt.	4	4⅛ × 5¼	—	4	Worm	Wood	M 36 × 3½ M 36 × 3 T	4 9	4 10	12 0	17 2	†10 0	1 18 0	—	—	—
	2 ton	4	4⅛ × 5¼	—	4	Worm	Wood	M 36 × 4 M 36 × 4 T	4 10½	5 1½	13 0	18 2	†11 4	2 3 0	—	—	—
	3½ ton	4	4½ × 5½	—	4	Worm	Cast Steel	M 36 × 5 M 36 × 5 T	5 0½	5 7½	13 0	20 3	†11 0	3 2 2	—	—	—
	4 ton	4	4½ × 5½	—	4	Worm	Cast Steel	M 36 × 6 M 40 × 6 T	5 9½	5 10½	15 0	20 8	†13 0	3 12 1	—	—	—
			mm.					mm. mm.									
FIAT ... ... Fiat Motors, Ltd., 5, Albemarle Street, W. 1	Taxi	4	70 × 120	—	4	Bevel	Steel Disc	M 815 × 105 pnu M 815 × 105 pnu.	4 7	4 7	9 0	12 8	8 2	0 16 0	—	—	590
	10 cwt.	4	70 × 120	—	4	Bevel	Steel Disc	M 815 × 105 pnu. M 815 × 105 pnu.	4 7	4 7	9 0	12 8	8 2	0 16 0	—	—	490
	1 ton	4	80 × 140	—	4	Bevel	Steel Disc	M 815 × 105 pnu. M 815 × 105 T pnu.	4 8	4 8	9 4	13 9	9 10½	1 0 0	—	—	540
	30 cwt.	4	100 × 140	—	(4	Bevel	Steel Disc	M 880 × 120 pnu. M 880 × 120 T pnu.	4 7	4 7	10 1	14 11	10 10	1 5 0	—	—	800
	3½ ton	4	100 × 180	—	4	Chain	Cast Steel	110 — R 750 120 — R 900 T	5 6	5 5	13 0	18 6	14 6	2 9 0	—	—	1,010
			ins.					ins. ins.									
FORD ... ... Ford Motor Co. (England), Ltd., Trafford Park, Manchester	7½ cwt.	4	3¾ × 4	20	2	Bevel	Wood	30 × 3 pneu. 30 × 3½ pneu.	4 8	4 8	8 4	10 10	—	—	—	—	230
	1 ton	4	3¾ × 4	20	2	Worm	Wood	30 × 3 pneu. 32 × 4 pneu.	4 8	4 8	10 4	13 0	—	—	—	—	290
GARFORD ... ... Willys-Overland, Ltd., 151-3, Great Portland Street, W. 1	30 cwt.	4	3¾ × 5¼	27	3	Worm	Wood	M 36 × 6 pneu. M 36 × 6 pneu.	4 8	4 10	11 2	16 3	†8 8	1 16 2	2 8 0	213 cu. ft.	775
								mm. mm.									
G.M.C. ... ... Ancona Motor Co., Ltd., 78-82, Brompton Road, S.W. 3	1 ton	4	3¾ × 5	27·5	3	Bevel	Wood	M 34 × 5 pneu. M 34 × 5 pneu.	4 8	4 8	11 0	15 8	†10 0	1 4 3	—	—	—
								ins. ins.									
	2½-3 ton	4	4⅛ × 5¼	35	4	Worm	Wood	M 36 × 4 M 36 × 4T	4 10½	4 10½	13 2	20 1	†14 0	2 4 0	—	—	—
HURLBURT ... ... Metals and Engineering Co., 16, Albert Square, Manchester	2 ton	4	4 × 5¼	25	3	Worm	Wood	M 34 × 4 M 34 × 5	4 8	5 2¾	12 4	18 6¾	†11 4½	—	3 5 0	—	—
	3 ton	4	4½ × 5¼	30	3	Worm	Wood	M 36 × 4 M 36 × 4T	4 9½	5 2¾	14 2	20 6¾	†13 4½	—	3 16 0	—	—
	4 ton	4	4½ × 6	45	4	Worm	Wood	M 36 × 5 M 36 × 5 T	5 5	5 2¾	13 0 or 14 2	19 4½ or 20 6¾	†12 0 or †13 0¼	—	4 0 2	—	—
	5 ton	4	4½ × 6	48	4	Worm	Wood	M 36 × 5 M 40 × 6 T	5 5	5 4	13 0 or 14 2	19 0¾ or 21 0¾	†11 3 or †13 3	—	4 7 0	—	—

† From rear of driver's seat.

"THE COMMERCIAL MOTOR" CHASSIS SPECIFICATIONS.

Year—1920. Type—Petrol Vehicles—Foreign (contd.).

NAME OF VEHICLE AND DISTRIBUTORS.	Net Load.	ENGINE. No. of Cylinders.	ENGINE. Bore and Stroke.	ENGINE. B.H.P. at Normal Speed.	No. of Speeds Forward.	Final Drive.	Type of Wheels.	TYRE SIZES. Section of Tyres. R.—Dia. of Rim. M.—Overall Dia. All solids except where otherwise stated.	TRACK. Front.	TRACK. Rear.	Wheel Base.	Length Overall.	Length. Body Space.	Tare Weight, Chassis.	Shipping Weight, Packed.	Dimensions, Packed.	Price of Chassis with Tyres.
			mm.					mm. mm.	ft. in.	ft. in.	ft. in.	ft. in.	ft. in.	T. C. Q.	T. C. Q.	ft. in.	£
HURTU ... ... Ariel Motors and General Repairs, Ltd., 320-2, Camberwell New Road, S.E. 5	10 cwt.	4	75×130	25	4	Bevel	Steel Disc.	M 765 × 105 pn. M 765 × 105 pn.	4 3	4 3	9 8	13 2	8 1	0 18 0	0 18 0	210 cubic ft.	875
			ins.					ins. ins.									
INTERNATIONAL ... ... International Harvester Co., of Gt. Britain, Ltd., 80, Finsbury Pavement, E.C. 2	15 cwt.	4	3¾×5¼	—	3	Internal Gear	Wood	M 36 × 3½ M 36 × 3½	4 8	4 8	9 7	13 4	7 6	1 5 0	1 13 2	150 cubic ft.	465
	1 ton	4	3¾×5¼	—	3	Internal Gear	Wood	M 36 × 3½ M 36 × 4	4 8	4 8	10 8	15 0	9 0	1 6 0	1 18 3	163 cubic ft.	550
	30 cwt.	4	3¾×5¼	—	3	Internal Gear	Wood	M 36 × 3½ M 36 × 5	5 1	5 1	10 8	15 1	9 5	1 11 1	2 4 1	172 cubic ft.	660
	2 ton	4	4×5	—	3	Internal Gear	Wood	M 36 × 4 M 36 × 6	5 1	5 1	11 6	16 4	10 0	1 18 0	2 9 2	252 cubic ft.	770
MAXWELL ... ... Maxwell Motors, Ltd., 116, Gt. Portland Street, W. 1	25 cwt.	4	3¾ × 4½	30	3	Worm	Wood	M 32 × 4 M 32 × 4 or M 34 × 4½ pneu. M 34 × 4½ pneu.	4 8	4 8	10 4	15 10	12 2	1 5 0	—	—	530
			mm.					mm. mm.									
MERCEDES-DAIMLER ... ... Mercedes Concessionaires, Ltd., 21, Mercer Street, Long Acre, W.C. 2.	2 ton	4	110 × 150	40	4	Bevel	Cast Steel	100 — R 771 120 — R 771 T	5 0	5 0	12 8	13 0	—	1 0 0	—	—	900
	3½ ton	4	108 × 150	45	4	Bevel	Cast Steel	120 — R 771 140 — R 771 T	4 11	4 11	13 0	18 11	10 10	2 13 0	—	—	1,100
	5 ton (and 7 ton trailer)	4	120 × 160	50	4	Internal Gear	Cast Steel	120 — R 720 140 — R 850 T	5 1	5 1	13 7	19 8	—	—	—	—	1,200
			ins.														
OLDSMOBILE ... ... General Motors, Ltd., 136, Long Acre, W.C. 2	15 cwt.	4	3 11/16 × 5¼	25	3	Doub. Red.	Wood	M 880 × 135 pn. M 880 × 135 pn.	4 8	4 8	10 8	14 9¾	7 8½	1 0 3	1 12 2	4 0 × 4 1 × 15 4	545
								ins. ins.									
ONEIDA ... ... The British-American Motor Company, 11, Old Hall Street, Liverpool	25 cwt.	4	3¾ × 5	22·4	3	Worm	Wood or Cast Steel	M 36 × 3½ M 36 × 5	4 8	4 8	11 3	16 11¾	8 10	—	2 3 3	15 4 × 4 2 × 3 3	802
	35 cwt.	4	4 × 5¼	25·6	3	Worm	Wood or Cast Steel	M 36 × 3½ M 36 × 5	4 7¾	4 9½	12 0	17 7¾	9 6	2 4 0	2 17 2	17 6 × 3 6 × 3 5	867
	45 cwt.	4	4 × 5¼	25·6	4	Worm	Wood or Cast Steel	M 36 × 4 M 36 × 7	4 10	5 0	13 4	19 6¼	11 6	—	3 5 1	19 9 × 4 2 × 3 5	1,005
	3½ ton	4	4½ × 5½	33·5	4	Worm	Cast Steel	M 36 × 5 M 36 × 10	5 7	5 7	14 2	21 3¾	13 0	—	—	—	1,285
	5 ton	4	4½ × 5½	33·5	4	Worm	Cast Steel	M 36 × 6 M 40 × 11	5 8	5 9	15 0	23 0	14 9	—	—	—	1,635
PACKARD ... ... W. C. Gann and Co., 198, Piccadilly, W.1.	30 cwt.	4	4 × 5½	—	4	Worm	Cast Steel	M 34 × 3½ M 38 × 3½ T	4 7½	4 7½	10 6	—	9 1	2 1 2	—	—	—
	2 ton	4	4 × 5½	—	4	Worm	Cast Steel	M 34 × 4 M 34 × 4 T	4 7½	4 7½	12 0	—	9 1	2 5 0	—	—	—
	3 ton	4	4½ × 5½	—	4	Worm	Cast Steel	M 36 × 5 M 36 × 5 T	5 6	5 6	13 0	—	10 0	3 2 2	—	—	—
	4 ton	4	4½ × 5½	—	4	Worm	Cast Steel	M 36 × 5 M 40 × 5 T	5 7	5 7	13 0	—	12 0	3 6 2	—	—	—
	5 ton	4	5 × 5½	—	4	Worm	Cast Steel	M 36 × 6 M 40 × 6 T	5 9½	5 9½	13 0	—	12 0	3 17 0	—	—	—
	6 ton	4	5 × 5½	—	4	Worm	Cast Steel	M 36 × 6 M 40 × 7 T	5 9½	5 9½	13 0	—	12 0	3 19 3	—	—	—

"THE COMMERCIAL MOTOR" CHASSIS SPECIFICATIONS—PETROL VEHICLES—FOREIGN (contd.).

NAME OF VEHICLE AND MAKERS.	Net Load.	ENGINE. No. of Cylinders.	ENGINE. Bore and Stroke.	ENGINE. B.H.P. at Normal Speed.	No. of Speeds Forward.	Final Drive.	Type of Wheels.	TYRE SIZES. Section of Tyres. R.–Dia. of Rim. M.–Overall Dia. All solids except where otherwise stated.	TRACK. Front.	TRACK. Rear.	Wheel Base.	Length Overall.	Length, Body Space.	Tare Weight, Chassis.	Shipping Weight, Packed.	Dimensions, Packed.	Price of Chassis with Tyres.
			in.					in. in.	ft. in.	ft. in.	ft. in.	ft. in.	ft. in.	T. C. Q.	T. C. Q.	ft. in.	£
PIERCE-ARROW ... ... Gaston, Ltd., 212-214, Great Portland Street, W. 1	2 ton	4	4 × 5½	—	3	Worm	Wood	M 36 × 4 M 36 × 4 T	4 8	4 8	12 6 (Stand'rd) 15 0 (long)	—	†10 8 (Stand'rd) †13 6 (long)	—	—	—	—
	5 ton	4	4½ × 6	—	3	Worm	Wood	M 36 × 5 M 40 × 6 T	5 8	5 4	14 0 (Stand'rd) 17 0 (long)	—	†13 6 (Stand'rd)	—	—	—	—
RAINIER ... ... Easton, Lloyd and Co., Ltd., Broad Street Chambers, Easy Row, Birmingham	1 ton	4	3½ × 5	—	3	Worm	Wood	M 34 × 4½ pneu. M 34 × 4½ pneu.	4 8	4 8	10 6	17 3	†7 6	0 13 2	—	—	800
	1½-2 ton	4	3¾ × 5	—	3	Worm	Wood	M 34 × 3 M 34 × 4	4 8	4 8	11 1	17 6	†9 0	1 6 3	—	—	700
	2-2½ ton	4	3¾ × 5	—	3	Worm	Wood	M 34 × 4 M 34 × 6	4 8	4 8	12 3	19 0	†11 0	1 15 3	—	—	900
			mm.					mm. mm.									
RENAULT ... ... Renault, Ltd., 3, Keswick Road, S.W. 15	1 ton	4	80 × 140	—	4	Bevel	Wood	M 820 × 120 pn. M 820 × 120T pn.	4 6	4 6	10 5	14 8	10 0	1 5 0	1 15 0	18 6 × 6 0 × 6 0	730
	3 ton	4	95 × 160	—	4	Bevel	Welded Steel	M 955 × 155 pn. 965 × 155T pn.	5 5	6 1½	12 5	20 4	14 1	2 5 0	3 10 0	21 0 7 6 × 7 4 ×	1,050 1,085
	3 ton	4	90 × 140	—	4	Bevel	Welded Steel	120 — R 771 120 — R 850 T	5 6	6 0	12 5	20 4	14 1	2 10 0	3 15 0	21 0 × 7 6 × 7 5	975
REO ... ... Gaston, Ltd., 212-214, Great Portland Street, W. 1	15 cwt.	4	4½ × 4½	—	3	Bevel	Wood	M 34 × 4½ pneu. M 34 × 4½ pneu.	4 8	4 8	10 8	—	10 8	—	—	—	—
			ins.					ins. ins.									
REPUBLIC ... ... Republic Motor Trucks, 81-82, Bolsover Street, Great Portland Street, W. 1	1 ton	4	3¾ × 5	22·5	3	Internal Gear	Wood	M 34 × 3 M 34 × 4	4 8	4 8	10 4	15 3⅞	9 0	1 6 0	—	—	575
	30 cwt.	4	3¾ × 5	22·5	3	Internal Gear	Wood	M 34 × 3½ M 34 × 5	4 8	4 8	12 0	18 10⅞	12 0	1 8 3	—	—	606
	2½ ton	4	4⅛ × 5¼	27·2	4	Internal Gear	Wood	M 36 × 4 M 36 × 4	5 0	5 0	13 0 & 14 0	17 3⅞ & 21 10⅞	12 0 & 14 0	1 17 0	—	—	825
	3½ ton	4	4½ × 5½	32·4	3	Internal Gear	Cast Steel	M 36 × 5 M 36 × 5	5 5	5 6	13 9 & 15 5	20 0 & 21 8	14 0	2 16 3	—	—	1,100
SELDEN ... ... Gaston, Ltd., 212-214, Great Portland Street, W. 1	35 cwt.	4	3¾ × 5	—	3	Worm	Wood	M 34 × 3½ M 34 × 5 or M 34 × 3½ M 34 × 3 T	4 8	4 10	11 8	—	†9 6	1 10 2	—	—	—
	2½ ton	4	4⅛ × 5¼	—	4	Worm	Wood	M 36 × 4 M 36 × 3½ T	4 10½	4 10½	12 1	—	†14 2¾	2 7 1	—	—	—
	3½ ton	4	4½ × 5½	—	4	Worm	Cast Steel	M 36 × 5 M 36 × 5 T	5 6½	5 8	13 6	—	†16 3	3 4 1	—	—	—
	5 ton	4	4½ × 5½	—	4	Worm	Cast Steel	M 36 × 6 M 40 × 6 T	5 8¾	5 9½	14 2	—	†14 0	3 17 3	—	—	—
			mm.					mm. mm.									
SPA ... ... Vandys, Ltd., 27a, Pembridge Villas, Notting Hill Gate, W. 11	4 ton	4	95 × 200	35	4	Chain (enclosed)	Cast Steel	100 — R 720 100 — R 771 T or Steel tyres (front) 160 — 771 T (rear)	5 3½	5 4½	12 0	17 0	12 8	3 10 0	—	18 8 × 6 0 × 7 0	1,075

"THE COMMERCIAL MOTOR" CHASSIS SPECIFICATIONS — PETROL VEHICLES—FOREIGN (contd.).

NAME OF VEHICLE AND DISTRIBUTORS.	Net Load	ENGINE. No. of Cylinders.	ENGINE. Bore and Stroke.	ENGINE. B.H.P. at Normal Speed.	No. of Speeds Forward.	Final Drive.	Type of Wheels.	TYRE SIZES. Section of Tyres. R.–Dia. of Rim. M.–Overall Dia. All solids except where otherwise stated.	TRACK. Front.	TRACK. Rear.	Wheel Base.	Length Overall.	Length, Body Space.	Tare Weight, Chassis.	Shipping Weight, Packed.	Dimensions, Packed.	Price of Chassis with Tyres.
			ins.					ins. ins.	ft. in.	ft. in.	ft. in.	ft. in.	ft. in.	T. C. Q.	T. C. Q.	cu. ft.	£
STEWART ... ... Melchior, Armstrong and Dessau, London, Ltd., 14a, Great Marlborough Street, W. 1	15 cwt.	4	3¼ × 4½	25	3	Internal Gear	Wood	M 32 × 4 pneu. M 32 × 4 pneu.	4 8	4 8	9 2	—	†6 5½	1 1 2	1 7 3	184	450
	1 ton	4	—	30	3	Internal Gear	Wood	M 34 × 3½ M 34 × 4	4 8	4 8	10 10	—	†8 3½	1 5 1	1 14 3	225	505
	30 cwt.	4	3¾ × 5	35	3	Internal Gear	Wood	M 34 × 3½ M 36 × 5	4 8	4 8	11 8	—	†9 11½	1 10 3	2 1 1	265	626
	2 ton	4	4½ × 5½	40	3	Internal Gear	Wood	M 34 × 4 M 34 × 4 T	4 8	5 1	13 0	—	†11 0¾	1 19 3	2 1 3	300	845
	3½ ton	4	4½ × 5½	45	4	Internal Gear	Wood	M 36 × 5 M 36 × 5 T	4 10	5 10	13 9	—	†11 7¾	2 14 2	3 17 3	400	1,100
SULTAN ... ... American Motors, Ltd., Audrey House, Ely Place, Holborn, London	1 ton	4	3¾ × 5	—	3	Internal Gear	Wood	M 32 × 3½ M 32 × 4	4 8	4 8	11 0	—	—	1 4 0	—	—	—
	30 cwt.	4	3¾ × 5	—	3	Internal Gear	Wood	M 34 × 3½ M 36 × 5	4 8	4 8	11 0	—	—	1 9 0	—	—	—
TRAFFIC ... ... North-Western Motors, Ltd., Mersey Chambers, Liverpool	38 cwt.	4	3¾ × 5	22	3	Internal Gear	Wood	M 34 × 3½ M 34 × 5	4 8	4 8	11 1	17 8	†11 0	1 9 2	2 2 2	ft. in. 5 10 × 13 6 × 4 6	585
TWIN CITY ... ... Twin City Truck Co., 61, Gracechurch Street, E.C. 4	3 ton	4	4 × 5½	28	3	Internal Gear	Wood	M 36 × 4 M 36 × 7	4 10	4 10	12 6	19 2	†11 0	2 2 0	—	—	778
	3½ ton	4	4½ × 6	30/40	4	Worm	Cast Steel	M 36 × 5 M 40 × 5 T	5 6½	5 5½	14 0	21 8	†13 0	3 1 0	—	—	875
UNIC ... ... Unic Motors, Ltd., 18, Brewer Street, Buckingham Palace Road, S.W. 1	30 cwt.	4*	mm. 80 × 130	24	4	Worm	Steel Disc D't'ch'ble	mm. mm. M 820 × 120 pneu. M 820 × 120 T pn.	4 5	—	10 4	14 8	11 1	—	—	—	—
	3 ton	4	80 × 130	24	4	Worm	Steel Disc D't'ch'ble	M 935 × 135 pneu. M 935 × 135 T pn.	5 1½	4 2½	11 7	15 10½	11 10½	—	—	—	—
VIM ... ... F. G. R. Browne, Ltd., 13, Duke Street, St. James Street, W. ...	10-15 cwt.	4	ins. 3¼ × 4½	22	3	Worm	Wood	ins. ins. M 31 × 4 pneu. M 31 × 4 pneu.	4 8	4 8	9 0	13 2	6 9	0 19 0	1 11 0	—	455
WHITING MARK I ... ... Whiting, Ltd., 334-340, Euston Road, N.W. 1	1 ton	4	mm. 89 × 127	30	3	Internal Gear	Wood	M 33 × 4 pneu. M 32 × 3½	4 8	4 8	10 10	16 0	†8 6	1 5 2	—	—	—
	30 cwt.	4	89 × 127	30	3	Internal Gear	Wood	M 32 × 3½ M 32 × 5 T	4 8	4 8	10 10	18 0	19 6	1 7 2	—	—	—
	3½ ton	4	108 × 140	35	3	Internal Gear	Wood	M 36 × 4 M 36 × 4 T	4 8	4 8	12 6	17 9	†10 8	2 0 1	—	—	—
WILSON ... ... Duff, Morgan and Vermont, Ltd., 48, Dover Street, Piccadilly, W. 1	25 cwt.	4	ins. 3¾ × 5	24	3	Worm	Wood	M 35 × 5 pneu. M 35 × 5 pneu.	4 9	4 8	10 4	15 4	17 6	1 8 0	—	—	605
	45 cwt.	4	3¾ × 5	25	3	Worm	Wood	M 36 × 5 M 36 × 5 T	4 10	4 10	11 8	—	—	—	—	—	888
	3½ ton	4	4½ × 5½	30	3	Worm	Wood	M 36 × 4 M 36 × 4 T	4 10	4 10	12 0	18 0	†10 6	2 0 0	—	—	1,120
	5½ ton	4	4½ × 6½	30	3	Worm	Wood	M 36 × 6 M 36 × 5 T	5 6	5 8	15 4	20 6½	†12 3	3 0 0	—	—	1,415
	7½ ton	4	4½ × 6½	45	3	Worm	Wood	M 40 × 6 M 40 × 6 T	5 6	6 2½	15 4	20 6½	†12 8	3 7 0	—	—	1,618
WOLVERINE ... ... H. C. Motor Co., Ltd., 18, Great Portland Street	2 ton	6	3¾ × 5	22	3	Internal Gear	Wood	M 34 × 3½ M 34 × 3½	4 9	4 8	11 8	17 0	†9 2	1 11 1	2 4 3	17 0 × 5 10 × 3 0	700

†, From rear of driver's seat.

APPENDIX II

Summary of Haulage Firms listed in Roadway Goods Transport Guide No.1, 1931 (Selected Cities)

Table 1

Number of Firms with Specified Number of Vehicles (excluding trailers) and Tonnage Capacity (London)

No. of	*Tonnage Capacity*													
vehicles	1–	2–	3–	4–	5–	6–10	10½–20	20½–50	51–100	101–150	151–200	201–500	501–1000	1000+
1	82	7	4	2	18	6								
2		38	33	17	5	30	9							
3			12	25	11	21	19	2	1					
4				10	7	23	22	2						
5					5	13	23	15						
6						15	24	21	2	1				
7						4	13	15	2					
8						4	10	17	2					
9						2	2	21	1					
10							7	21	5					
11–15						1	10	39	34	2	1			
16–20								13	16		2	2		
21–50								5	19	17	11	21		
51–100										1	2	11	7	1
101–200												2	2	1
Over 200														2
Total	82	45	49	54	46	119	139	171	82	21	16	36	9	4

N.B. 45 firms omitted because of insufficient detail.

Table 2

Number of Firms with Specified Number of Vehicles (excluding trailers) and Tonnage Capacity (Birmingham)

No. of	*Tonnage Capacity*													
vehicles	1–	2–	3–	4–	5–	6–10	10½–20	20½–50	51–100	101–150	151–200	201–500	501–1000	1000+
1	8	2	1			2								
2		4	9	2	2	3	2	2						
3				5	2	3	4	1						
4				2	1	3	5	4						
5					3	4		2						
6						2		4	1					
7						1	1	3						
8							1	2	1					
9										1				
10							1	1						
11–15							1	3	4	3	1			
16–20								2	3	1	1			
21–50									6	2	1	4		
51–100														
101–200														
Over 200														
Totals	8	6	10	9	8	18	15	24	15	7	3	4		

N.B. 4 firms omitted because of insufficient detail.

Table 3

Number of Firms with Specified Number of Vehicles (excluding trailers) and Tonnage Capacity (Bristol)

No. of	*Tonnage Capacity*													
vehicles	1–	2–	3–	4–	5–	6–10	10½–20	20½–50	51–100	101–150	151–200	201–500	501–1000	1000+
1	8	3	2		1									
2		1	5	2		6	1							
3				2		3	4	2						
4					1	4	1							
5							3		1					
6							2	1						
7								1						
8							1	2	1					
9							1							
10								3						
11–15								1						
16–20									1					
21–50									1	1	2			
51–100												1		
101–200														
Over 200														
Totals	8	4	7	4	2	13	13	10	4	1	2	1		

N.B. No firms omitted because of insufficient detail.

Table 4

Number of Firms with Specified Number of Vehicles (excluding trailers) and Tonnage Capacity (Liverpool)

No. of	*Tonnage Capacity*													
vehicles	1–	2–	3–	4–	5–	6–10	10½–20	20½–50	51–100	101–150	151–200	201–500	501–1000	1000+
1	14	4	5	1		5								
2		5	3	3		6	6	2						
3			2	2	1	3	3	4						
4						2	4	4						
5						1	4	5	1					
6						2	2	7						
7						1		3	1					
8								1	1					
9							1		1					
10								1	2					
11–15								1	8	1	1			
16–20								2	1	2	1			
21–50								1	1	3	4	4		
51–100														
101–200														
Over 200														
Totals	14	9	10	6	1	20	20	31	16	6	6	4		

N.B. 17 firms omitted because of insufficient detail.

Table 5

Number of Firms with Specified Number of Vehicles (excluding trailers) and Tonnage Capacity (Manchester)

No. of	*Tonnage Capacity*												
vehicles	1–	2–	3–	4–	5–	6–10	10½–20	20½–50	51–100	101–150	151–200	201–500	501–1000	1000+
1	29	3	1	2	3	2	1							
2		9	9	5	3	9	5							
3			1	6	4	2	7	4						
4				2		5	3							
5					2	4	3	2	1					
6				1			1	6						
7							1	1						
8							2	4	2					
9								1	1					
10							1	1						
11–15							2	2	5					
16–20									1	2	1			
21–50									3	1				
51–100												1		
101–200														
Over 200														
Totals	29	12	11	16	12	22	26	21	13	3	1	1		

N.B. 16 firms omitted because of insufficient detail.

Table 6

Number of Firms with Specified Number of Vehicles (excluding trailers) and Tonnage Capacity (Sheffield)

No. of	*Tonnage Capacity*													
vehicles	1–	2–	3–	4–	5–	6–10	10½–20	20½–50	51–100	101–150	151–200	201–500	501–1000	1000+
1	13	2			1	1		1						
2		2	2	3	1	4	2							
3			1	4	1	3		1						
4						1		2						
5								2						
6						1		1				1		
7								3	1					
8							1	1						
9								1	1					
10														
11–15								1	4					
16–20														
21–50														
51–100												1		
101–200														
Over 200														
Totals	13	4	3	7	3	10	3	13	6			2		

N.B. 5 firms omitted because of insufficient detail.

Table 7

Number of Firms with Specified Number of Vehicles (excluding trailers) and Tonnage Capacity (Glasgow)

No. of	*Tonnage Capacity*													
vehicles	1–	2–	3–	4–	5–	6–10	10½–20	20½–50	51–100	101–150	151–200	201–500	501–1000	1000+
1	1		1	1		1								
2		2	1			4	1							
3				2		2								
4						1	1							
5							4	3						
6								2						
7						1		3						
8								1	1					
9								2						
10								1	2					
11–15							2	3	2					
16–20								1	3					
21–50									1	1	1			
51–100										1				
101–200														
Over 200														
Totals	1	2	2	3	-	9	8	16	9	2	1			

N.B. 8 firms omitted because of insufficient detail.

APPENDIX III

Selected Tables from 4th Annual Reports of Licensing Authorities (1937–38)

TABLE II.—Number of licences of each class, number of vehicles authorised thereunder, and average number of motor vehicles in possession per licence at 30th June, 1938, and at *30th June, 1937.*

AGGREGATE FIGURES—ALL TRAFFIC AREAS.

	Year	"A" Licences (including Short Term)			"A" Contract Licences.	"B" Licences (including Short Term).*	"C" Licences (including Short Term).	All Licences.		
		Railway Companies.	Others.	Total.				Railway Companies.	Others.	Total.
No. of Licences	1938	364	23,508	23,872	5,430	34,767	178,586	377	242,278	242,655
	1937	*386*	*24,085*	*24,471*	*4,417*	*34,589*	*186,734*	*399*	*249,812*	*250,211*
No. of Vehicles authorised :—										
(i) Motor Vehicles in possession ...	1938	10,145	73,604	83,749	9,467 (a)	54,906	365,025 (b)	10,257	502,890	513,147
	1937	*9,615*	*74,011*	*83,626*	*7,475* (a)	*53,775*	*362,380* (b)	*9,709*	*497,547*	*507,256*
(ii) Motor Vehicles to be hired ...	1938	45	403	448	15	147	6,638	45	7,203	7,248
	1937	*54*	*468*	*522*	*33*	*170*	*6,629*	*54*	*7,300*	*7,354*
(iii) Trailers in possession or to be hired	1938	4,714	7,189	11,903	368	1,508	10,197 (a)	4,721	19,255	23,976
	1937	*4,163*	*7,190*	*11,353*	*295*	*1,441*	*10,107* (a)	*4,166*	*19,030*	*23,196*
(iv) Trade Plates	1938	—	—	—	—	—	2,835 (a)	8	2,827	2,835
	1937	—	—	—	—	—	*2,939* (a)	*8*	*2,931*	*2,939*
Average No. of Motor Vehicles in possession per Licence	1938	27·87	3·13	3·51	1·74	1·58	2·04	27·21	2·08	2·11
	1937	*24·91*	*3·07*	*3·42*	*1·69*	*1·55*	*1·94*	*24·33*	*1·99*	*2·03*

* No Railway Companies operate vehicles under "B" licences.

(*a*) Includes under 20 for Railway Companies.

(*b*) Includes under 100 for Railway Companies.

TABLE VIII.—Classes of Goods Authorised to be carried for Hire or Reward under "B" Licences over Permitted Zone of Operation in all Traffic Areas at 30th June, 1938, and Totals at *30th June, 1937*.

Classes of Goods.	Permitted Zone of Operation.											Totals.	
	Goods not limited to Specified Persons.						Goods for specified persons, whether distance is limited or not.	Goods to specified destination.	Goods in one direction only.	Goods lifted within a specified district.	Special limiting conditions not falling within any of the previous categories.		
	Not exceeding 10 miles.	Exceeding 10 but not exceeding 20 miles.	Exceeding 20 but not exceeding 30 miles.	Exceeding 30 but not exceeding 50 miles.	Exceeding 50 but not exceeding 100 miles.	Exceeding 100 miles and unlimited.						1938.	*1937.*
General goods	2,969	6,437	3,856	2,009	687	315	443	142	33	181	330	17,402	*17,556*
Agricultural products, feeding stuffs for animals and poultry, fertilisers, implements and farm requisites	742	1,123	1,034	893	281	129	405	168	51	118	97	5,041	*4,971*
Alcoholic and other beverages	31	55	33	34	17	12	175	6	2	5	3	373	*364*
Builders' materials and plant, road making and repairing materials, sand, ballast and gravel, and excavated materials and rubbish ...	2,012	3,548	2,234	1,351	373	182	1,603	106	31	101	170	11,711	*11,273*
Camp and sports equipment and toys	14	31	46	78	66	130	72	17	3	8	23	488	*491*
Chemicals, drugs, dyes and explosives	24	32	29	22	15	7	116	4	1	1	4	255	*246*
Clothing and drapery	24	14	22	14	7	3	24	—	—	—	3	111	*108*
Coal, Coke, and patent fuel	3,737	982	322	184	45	43	928	69	21	63	51	6,445	*6,176*
Cotton and Cotton goods (other than clothing and drapery)	29	52	56	68	14	2	110	6	1	2	4	344	*345*
Dairy produce and requisites (other than milk)	26	52	41	40	14	5	30	30	3	11	7	259	*277*
Electrical goods and apparatus	5	28	20	15	11	3	80	2	—	—	—	164	*165*
Empties	12	7	11	14	6	10	30	33	56	5	15	199	*186*
Factory and other waste	92	48	21	14	7	4	36	8	1	1	1	233	*226*
Fish, ice, poultry and game	143	131	75	67	24	23	80	86	17	42	49	737	*748*
Fishermen's gear and requisites	12	11	17	15	13	7	5	3	2	6	15	106	*101*
Food products and canned goods, groceries and provisions, bread and confectionery	285	183	140	103	42	9	226	19	7	12	18	1,044	*1,056*
Fruit, flowers and greengrocery and garden produce, materials and requisites (including nurserymen's produce and requisites) ...	467	497	256	224	69	42	298	232	91	61	69	2,306	*2,314*
Furniture and household effects (including personal effects)	1,694	2,073	1,847	2,319	941	1,686	371	71	71	781	513	12,367	*12,332*
Grain, flour and millers' products	59	93	77	53	18	9	114	31	13	26	9	502	*494*
Iron and Steel (crude, pig, blooms, billets, and ingots) and Ore	104	48	19	21	15	3	32	4	—	—	3	249	*240*
Iron and Steel (bars, plates, sheets and manufactured articles)	64	58	35	30	23	10	122	10	1	—	5	358	*348*

TABLE VIII (continued)

Classes of Goods.	Permitted Zone of Operation. — Goods not limited to Specified Persons. — Not exceeding 10 miles.	Exceeding 10 but not exceeding 20 miles.	Exceeding 20 but not exceeding 30 miles.	Exceeding 30 but not exceeding 50 miles.	Exceeding 50 but not exceeding 100 miles.	Exceeding 100 miles and unlimited.	Goods for specified persons, whether distance is limited or not.	Goods to specified destination.	Goods in one direction only.	Goods lifted within a specified district.	Special limiting conditions not falling within any of the previous categories.	Totals. 1938.	Totals. 1937.
ronmongery and hardware	21	27	31	21	5	4	49	2	—	1	2	163	160
ivestock	160	454	595	630	339	328	143	224	11	142	145	3,171	3,069
achines and machinery	94	140	152	178	95	72	328	16	5	8	22	1,110	1,075
eat	101	102	95	72	23	9	64	23	6	11	8	514	527
etals, other than Iron and Steel (bars, plates, sheets and manufactured articles)	15	30	21	17	7	7	87	4	1	—	—	189	188
ilk	61	89	73	49	14	9	82	34	10	5	8	434	429
onumental masonry and sculpture	18	33	23	47	21	17	118	2	1	4	4	288	288
usical instruments and radio apparatus ...	13	36	47	48	20	37	47	5	1	6	7	267	264
aint, oils, tar, varnish, glue, etc.	45	55	35	20	20	8	104	4	4	5	3	303	298
aper, cardboard and paper-making materials and waste paper	24	30	25	23	12	5	70	12	1	1	5	208	204
arcels and luggage	188	104	71	85	41	39	112	32	5	30	68	775	741
st Office mails	151	23	9	10	3	16	64	4	1	2	46	329	257
ttery, glass and earthenware	21	29	16	19	18	9	61	6	2	—	3	184	185
inted matter and stationery (including books and newspapers)	71	68	37	34	10	25	83	16	2	12	11	369	351
rap metal	117	112	64	59	23	6	87	13	2	1	5	489	486
gar Beet, Beet pulp and Molasses	20	46	39	22	6	3	11	130	10	24	4	315	326
xtiles, raw material and products (other than cotton, wool, clothing and drapery)	54	83	67	49	21	10	87	8	—	2	6	387	391
eatrical scenery and equipment, and show and fair ground tackle and equipment ...	9	17	8	17	11	19	18	2	3	1	4	109	98
ood and manufactures thereof	217	320	253	249	88	58	281	31	12	19	28	1,556	1,477
ol and woollen goods (other than clothing and drapery)	19	62	57	61	16	5	30	10	1	2	8	271	274
ods (not defined) for specified customers ...	57	50	56	77	37	57	3,708	17	8	10	26	4,103	3,881
ods of customers to whom vehicle is hired ...	5	8	11	11	6	58	31	—	—	2	152	284	253
scellaneous (not included above)	141	190	116	131	87	127	318	43	15	18	45	1,231	1,159
Totals 1938	14,167	17,611	12,092	9,497	3,611	3,562	11,283	1,685	506	1,730	1,999	77,743	
1937	*13,290*	*17,464*	*12,061*	*9,488*	*3,525*	*3,587*	*11,210*	*1,739*	*531*	*1,716*	*1,787*		*76,398*

APPENDIX IV

Selected Data from *Commercial Motor* Cost Tables (1921–35)

Notes: The 'pence' in these cost tables are pre-decimal, i.e. £1 = 240 pence, which means that 1 modern penny (1p) = 2.4d. (old pence).
The 'cost-per-mile' figures are calculated on a 48-hour working week unless otherwise stated.

EXAMPLES OF OPERATING COSTS (i.e not including Establishment Costs/Profit). Selected from tables published in *Commercial Motor.* Pence per Mile

Petrol vehicles
Solid Tyres

Date of Pub'n	*Vehicle Capacity*	*Weekly Mileage* 200	400	600	800
11/1/1921	2T	17.47	13.64	12.36	–
	4T	22.62	18.27	16.81	–
	6T	27.59	22.99	21.46	–
27/11/1923	2T	11.02	7.88	6.81	6.31
	4T	13.42	9.95	8.79	8.22
	6T	15.89	12.34	11.16	10.56
23/3/1926	2T	10.60	7.60	6.60	6.10
	4T	13.30	9.90	8.77	8.20
	6T	15.20	11.70	10.53	9.95
14/12/1926	2T	10.55	7.46	6.46	5.95
	4T	13.68	9.98	8.78	8.18
	6T	15.43	11.73	10.43	9.83
20/3/1928	2T	10.60	7.26	6.16	5.60
	4T	13.12	9.22	7.92	7.32
	5T	14.00	10.00	8.67	8.00
	6T	15.00	10.96	9.61	8.94
15/5/1928	2T	10.98	7.64	6.54	5.98
	4T	13.65	9.75	8.45	7.85
	5T	14.60	10.60	9.27	8.60
	6T	15.70	11.66	10.31	9.64
4/3/1930	2T	10.11	7.04	6.02	5.51
	4T	14.64	10.64	9.30	8.64
	5T	15.54	11.51	10.17	9.50
	6T	16.71	12.61	11.24	10.56
	8T	19.38	14.18	12.77	12.07
14/7/1931	2T	9.72	6.71	5.70	5.20
	4T	13.82	9.95	8.67	8.01
	5T	14.61	10.70	9.40	8.75
	6T	15.63	11.67	10.34	9.78
	8T	17.38	13.25	11.88	11.19

Mileage		*200*	*400*	*600*	*800*	*1000*	*1200*
14/7/1931	2T	–	8.69	7.02	6.19	5.69	5.36
96 hour	4T	–	12.10	10.09	9.09	8.48	8.08
week	5T	–	12.86	10.84	9.83	9.23	8.82
	6T	–	13.82	11.78	10.76	10.15	9.94
	8T	–	15.41	13.32	12.27	11.64	11.23
13/10/1933	2T	8.95	6.20	5.28	4.82	–	–
	4T	12.89	9.01	7.73	7.07	–	–
	5T	14.41	10.18	8.78	8.07	–	–
	6T	16.06	11.43	9.88	9.11	–	–
	7T	16.81	12.14	10.59	9.81	–	–
13/10/1933	2T	–	–	6.47	5.72	5.26	4.96
96 hour	4T	–	–	9.16	8.15	7.55	7.14
week	5T	–	–	10.22	9.16	8.51	8.09
	6T	–	–	11.32	10.19	9.51	9.06
	7T	–	–	12.03	10.89	10.21	9.76
4/10/1935	2T	8.55	6.04	5.20	4.78	–	–
	4T	12.11	8.69	7.55	6.98	–	–
	5T	13.70	9.92	8.66	8.03	–	–
	6T	15.27	11.13	9.75	9.06	–	–
	7T	15.77	11.86	10.47	9.77	–	–
4/10/1935	2T	–	–	6.37	5.66	5.24	4.95
96 hour	4T	–	–	8.87	7.90	7.43	7.07
week	5T	–	–	9.98	9.02	8.44	8.06
	6T	–	–	11.07	10.05	9.44	9.03
	7T	–	–	11.79	10.76	10.14	9.73

Petrol vehicles
Pneumatic tyres

11/1/1921	2T	20.22	16.39	15.11	–	–	–
27/11/1923	2T	12.38	9.24	8.19	7.66	–	–
17/2/1925	2T	11.30	8.30	7.30	6.80	–	–
23/3/1926	2T	12.60	9.60	8.60	8.10	–	–
14/12/1926	2T	12.16	9.06	8.06	7.56	–	–
20/3/1928	2T	10.71	7.56	6.51	6.00	–	–
	4T	13.87	10.00	8.74	8.10	–	–
	5T	15.00	11.00	9.67	9.00	–	–

Mileage		*200*	*400*	*600*	*800*	*1000*	*1200*
15/5/1928	2T	11.07	7.92	6.87	6.36	–	–
	4T	14.37	10.50	9.24	8.60	–	–
	5T	15.57	11.57	10.24	9.57	–	–
4/3/1930	2T	10.33	7.27	6.24	5.73	5.43	–
	4T	14.79	10.92	9.64	9.00	8.61	–
	5T	15.44	11.54	10.24	9.59	9.20	–
	6T	16.40	12.43	11.10	10.45	10.04	–
	8T	18.60	14.46	13.08	12.39	11.98	–
14/7/1931	2T	9.74	6.72	5.72	5.22	4.92	–
	4T	13.76	10.01	8.76	8.14	7.76	–
	5T	14.36	10.60	9.32	8.70	8.31	–
	6T	15.11	11.29	10.00	9.37	8.98	–
	8T	17.05	13.06	11.73	11.07	10.67	–

Mileage		*600*	*800*	*1000*	*1200*	*1600*
14/7/1931	2T	7.04	6.20	5.71	5.38	4.96
96 hour	4T	10.20	9.21	8.62	8.26	7.76
week	5T	10.76	9.77	9.18	8.80	8.30
	6T	11.45	10.45	9.85	9.45	8.95
	8T	13.17	12.15	11.53	11.12	10.61

Mileage		*200*	*400*	*600*	*800*	*1000*
19/7/1932	2T	9.72	6.28	5.29	4.75	4.52
	4T	13.00	8.68	7.45	6.84	6.48
	5T	13.88	9.51	8.28	7.66	7.29
	6T	14.81	10.28	9.00	8.37	7.98
	8T	16.67	11.89	10.55	9.89	9.49

Mileage		*800*	*1000*	*1200*	*1600*
19/7/1932	2T	5.79	5.29	4.96	4.55
96 hour	4T	7.92	7.34	6.94	6.47
week	5T	8.74	8.15	7.76	7.27
	6T	9.45	8.85	8.45	7.95
	8T	10.97	10.35	9.94	9.43

Mileage		*200*	*400*	*600*	*800*	*1000*
4/10/1935	2T	8.01	5.44	4.58	4.15	3.90
	4T	10.14	7.10	6.09	5.58	5.28
	5T	11.27	8.02	6.93	6.39	6.06
	6T	11.98	8.68	7.58	7.03	6.70
Maximum load		13.10	9.52	8.32	7.73	7.37
Add for 5T trailer		5.83	3.68	2.96	2.61	2.39

Mileage		*800*	*1000*	*1200*	*1600*
4/10/1935	2T	5.03	4.60	4.31	3.95
96 hour	4T	6.57	6.07	5.72	5.31
week	5T	7.38	6.86	6.51	6.07
	6T	8.02	7.49	7.14	6.70
Maximum load		8.72	8.16	7.79	7.33
Add for 5T trailer		3.45	3.07	2.81	2.49

Rigid 6-wheelers (petrol)
Pneumatic Tyres

Mileage		*200*	*400*	*600*	*800*	*1000*
15/5/1928	2T	10.60	7.36	6.28	5.74	5.42
	4T	15.36	11.16	9.76	9.06	8.64
	5T	16.41	12.14	10.71	10.00	9.56
	6T	17.57	13.19	11.74	11.00	10.54
4/3/1930	2T	10.44	7.36	6.33	5.81	5.51
	4T	15.47	11.55	10.24	9.58	9.19
	5T	16.29	12.27	10.93	10.25	9.86
	8T	19.64	15.31	13.86	13.14	12.70
	10T	20.23	15.85	14.39	13.66	13.22
	12T	21.36	16.89	15.40	14.66	14.21
14/7/1931	2T	10.15	6.98	5.93	5.40	5.09
	4T	14.33	10.50	9.22	8.58	8.20
	5T	15.16	11.24	9.93	9.28	8.89
	8T	17.75	13.70	12.36	11.68	11.28
	10T	18.26	14.19	12.83	12.15	11.75
	12T	19.29	15.14	13.75	13.06	12.64
Mileage		*600*	*800*	*1000*	*1200*	*1600*
14/7/1931	2T	7.25	6.40	5.88	5.54	5.12
96 hour	4T	10.67	9.67	9.07	8.67	8.17
week	5T	11.37	10.36	9.75	9.35	8.84
	8T	13.80	12.76	12.14	11.73	11.21
	10T	14.29	13.24	12.62	12.20	11.68
	12T	15.19	14.14	13.51	13.08	12.56
Mileage		*200*	*400*	*600*	*800*	*1000*
13/10/1933	2T	9.01	6.08	5.11	4.62	4.33
	4T	13.00	9.23	7.97	7.34	6.97
	5T	14.43	10.38	9.05	8.35	7.95
	8T	17.59	12.96	11.41	10.64	10.15

	10T	18.58	13.93	12.38	11.60	11.14
	12T	19.82	14.83	13.15	12.33	11.84
Mileage		*800*	*1000*	*1200*	*1600*	
13/10/1933	2T	5.52	5.05	4.73	4.34	
96 hour	4T	8.43	7.83	7.43	6.95	
week	5T	9.43	8.81	8.40	7.88	
	8T	11.72	11.04	10.58	10.02	
	10T	12.68	12.00	11.55	10.98	
	12T	13.42	12.70	12.22	11.64	

Rigid 6- and 8-wheelers – petrol
Pneumatic Tyres

Mileage		*200*	*400*	*600*	*800*	*1000*
4/10/1935	4T	11.20	7.98	6.90	6.36	6.04
	6T	13.11	9.54	8.35	7.75	7.40
	8T	13.98	10.36	9.15	8.54	8.18
	10T	15.92	11.82	10.46	9.78	9.37
Maximum load 6 wheels		17.09	12.92	11.53	10.83	10.42
Maximum load 8 wheels		18.96	14.48	12.99	12.24	11.80
Mileage		*800*	*1000*	*1200*	*1600*	
4/10/1935	4T	7.35	6.83	6.49	6.05	
96 hour	6T	8.75	8.19	7.82	7.36	
week	8T	9.53	8.97	8.60	8.13	
	10T	10.84	10.22	9.80	9.28	
Maximum load 6 wheels		11.90	11.27	10.85	10.33	
Maximum load 8 wheels		13.31	12.65	12.21	11.66	

Articulated 6-wheelers
'Internal Combustion'

		Solid tyres				*Pneumatics*			
Mileage		*200*	*400*	*600*	*800*	*200*	*400*	*600*	*800*
15/5/1928	10T	27.49	18.19	15.09	13.54	27.60	18.30	15.20	13.65
	11T	28.25	19.05	15.84	14.28	28.55	19.35	16.14	14.58
	12T	29.01	19.66	16.54	15.00	29.42	20.10	16.95	15.40

4/3/1930	10T	22.82	16.14	13.91	12.80	22.45	15.92	13.75	12.66
	12T	23.78	17.04	14.81	13.68	23.65	17.08	14.88	13.79
14/7/1931	10T	21.22	14.89	12.78	11.72	20.72	14.55	12.49	11.46
	12T	22.11	15.74	13.61	12.55	21.80	15.58	13.51	12.47

Solid tyres

Mileage		*400*	*600*	*800*	*1000*	*1200*
14/7/1931	10T	18.94	15.48	13.45	12.71	12.02
96 hr week	12T	19.79	16.31	14.57	13.53	12.84

Pneumatic Tyres

Mileage		*400*	*600*	*800*	*1000*	*1200*
14/7/1931	10T	18.60	15.19	13.49	12.47	11.78
96 hr week	12T	19.63	16.19	14.49	13.47	12.78

		Solids				*Pneumatics*			
Mileage		*200*	*400*	*600*	*800*	*200*	*400*	*600*	*800*
13/10/1933	10T	23.34	16.00	13.56	12.33	21.90	15.07	12.80	11.66
	12T	24.24	17.00	14.51	13.28	23.03	16.11	13.80	12.66
Mileage		*600*	*800*	*1000*	*1200*	*600*	*800*	*1000*	*1200*
13/10/1933	10T	16.25	14.36	13.22	12.46	15.50	13.69	12.60	11.88
96 hr week	12T	17.22	15.31	14.16	13.39	16.50	14.66	13.57	12.84

Articulated, 5-, 6- and 8-wheelers

Mileage		*200*	*400*	*600*	*800*	*1000*	*1200*
4/10/1935	3T	9.39	6.59	5.66	5.19	–	–
	6T	11.40	8.30	7.27	6.75	–	–
	8T	13.27	9.80	8.64	8.07	–	–
max. load 6-wheeler		17.31	13.14	11.75	11.05	–	–
max. load 8-wheeler		19.93	15.40	13.89	13.14	–	–
4/10/1935	3T	–	–	6.93	6.15	5.68	5.37
96 hour	6T	–	–	8.59	7.74	7.23	6.90
week	8T	–	–	10.06	9.13	8.57	8.20
max. load 6-wheeler		–	–	13.17	12.12	11.49	11.07
max. load 8-wheeler		–	–	15.31	14.20	13.53	13.09

Steam Wagons

		Steel Tyres			*Rubber Tyres*		
Weekly mileage		*200*	*400*	*600*	*200*	*400*	*600*
11/1/1921	3T	21.06	15.51	–	20.73	15.18	13.32
	4T	23.05	17.45	–	22.41	16.81	14.95
	6T	25.67	–	–	25.19	19.49	–
	8T	23.82	–	–	27.80	21.45	–
27/11/1923	3T	–	–	–	14.45	10.55	9.25
	4T	–	–	–	15.25	11.35	10.05
	6T	–	–	–	17.55	13.60	12.29
	8T	–	–	–	19.43	15.43	14.09
23/3/1926	3T	–	–	–	14.38	10.38	9.05
	4T	–	–	–	15.30	11.28	9.93
	6T	–	–	–	18.18	14.06	12.73
	8T	–	–	–	20.05	15.87	14.48
14/12/1926	3T	–	–	–	14.70	10.40	9.00
	4T	–	–	–	15.73	11.33	9.83
	6T	–	–	–	18.22	13.72	12.22
	8T	–	–	–	19.97	15.37	13.87

Vehicles over 5 years old excluded from now on.

Weekly mileage		*200*	*400*	*600*	*200*	*400*	*600*	*800*
20/3/1928	3T	–	–	–	14.73	10.20	8.68	7.92
	4T	–	–	–	15.33	10.72	9.18	8.41
	5T	–	–	–	15.87	11.24	9.70	8.93
	6T	–	–	–	16.78	12.10	10.54	9.76
	8T	–	–	–	17.88	13.08	11.48	10.68
15/5/1928								
6 wheeler	10T	–	–	–	23.96	16.30	13.76	12.50
6 wheeler	12T	–	–	–	24.90	17.18	14.60	13.30
4/3/1930	5T	–	–	–	15.37	10.70	9.15	8.37
	6T	–	–	–	16.31	11.58	10.00	9.22
	8T	–	–	–	17.52	12.66	11.04	10.23
6 wheeler	10T	–	–	–	19.13	14.18	12.53	11.71
6 wheeler	12T	–	–	–	19.95	14.93	13.25	12.41
14/7/ 1931	5T	–	–	–	15.18	10.55	9.01	8.23
	6T	–	–	–	16.11	11.41	9.85	9.17
	8T	–	–	–	17.21	12.43	10.84	10.05
6 wheeler	10T	–	–	–	18.72	13.85	12.06	11.42
6 wheeler	12T	–	–	–	19.50	14.57	12.92	12.10

				Solid rubber tyres			
Mileage		*200*	*400*	*600*	*800*	*1000*	*1200*
14/7/1931	5T	–	13.46	10.95	9.69	8.94	8.43
96 hour	6T	–	14.32	11.79	10.52	9.76	9.26
week	8T	–	15.34	12.78	11.50	10.73	10.21
6 wheeler	10T	–	16.76	14.16	12.88	12.09	11.58
6 wheeler	12T	–	17.48	14.87	13.56	12.78	12.25
Weekly mileage		*200*	*400*	*600*	*800*	*1000*	*1200*
13/10/1933	6T	15.73	10.60	8.89	8.03	–	–
	7T	16.97	11.50	9.67	8.75	–	–
(6 wheeler)	10T	18.91	13.08	11.13	10.16	–	–
(6 wheeler)	12T	20.06	13.96	11.93	10.92	–	–
4/10/1935	5-6T	16.12	10.77	8.99	8.10	–	–
	7T	16.79	11.40	9.60	8.70	–	–
6 wheeler-maximum load		19.64	13.73	11.76	10.77	–	–
				Pneumatics			
14/7/1931	5T	15.06	10.56	9.07	8.32	–	–
	6T	15.78	11.22	9.70	8.94	–	–
	8T	17.05	12.40	10.85	10.08	–	–
14/7/1931	5T	–	13.47	11.01	9.77	9.03	8.54
96 hour	6T	–	14.16	11.66	10.41	9.66	9.16
week	8T	–	15.31	12.79	11.53	10.77	10.27
13/10/1933	6T	15.41	10.56	8.94	8.13	–	–
	7T	16.20	11.07	9.36	8.50	–	–
13/10/1933	6T	–	–	10.88	9.59	8.81	8.30
96 hr week	7T	–	–	11.30	9.96	9.16	8.62
4/10/1935	5-6T	15.31	10.38	8.99	7.91	–	–
Max load – 4 wheels		15.69	10.72	9.06	8.23	–	–

Rigid 6-Wheeler
Pneumatics

14/7/1931	10T	18.40	13.66	12.09	11.30	–	–
	12T	19.38	14.58	12.98	12.18	–	–
14/7/1931	10T	–	16.58	14.03	12.75	12.00	11.48
96 hr week	12T	–	17.48	14.91	13.63	12.86	12.35
13/10/1933	10T	17.62	12.21	10.41	9.50	–	–
	12T	18.48	12.86	10.99	10.06	–	–

13/10/1933 10T	–	–	12.35	10.96	10.13	9.57
96 hr week 12T	–	–	12.93	11.51	10.66	10.09
4/10/1935 max.load	17.96	12.53	10.72	9.82	–	–
4/10/1935 max load 8-wheeler	19.21	13.50	11.59	10.64	–	–
4/10/1935 96 hour week max load 6-wheeler	–	–	12.71	11.31	10.44	9.90
max load 8-wheeler	–	–	13.58	12.13	11.26	10.68

Articulated, 6 wheels

				Solid tyres			
Mileage		*200*	*400*	*600*	*800*	*1000*	*1200*
15/5/1928	10T	26.95	17.75	14.68	13.15	–	–
	12T	27.78	18.53	15.44	13.91	–	–
4/3/ 1930	10T	20.97	14.40	12.20	11.11	–	–
	12T	21.70	15.07	12.86	11.76	–	–
14/7/ 1931	10T	20.34	14.01	11.90	10.84	–	–
	12T	21.03	14.66	12.53	11.47	–	–
14/7/1931	10T	–	18.06	14.60	12.87	11.83	11.14
96 hr week	12T	–	18.70	15.23	13.49	12.45	11.76
				Pneumatic tyres			
14/7/1931	10T	20.19	14.02	11.96	10.93	–	–
	12T	21.21	14.99	12.92	11.88	–	–
14/7/1931	10T	–	18.07	14.66	12.96	11.94	11.25
96 hr week	12T	–	19.04	15.60	13.90	12.88	12.20

		Solids				*Pneumatics*		
Mileage		*200*	*400*	*600*	*800*	*200*	*400*	*600*	*800*
13/10/1933	10T	20.87	13.74	11.36	10.17	19.88	13.17	10.93	9.81
	12T	21.93	14.50	12.03	10.79	20.81	13.87	11.55	10.39
Mileage		*600*	*800*	*1000*	*1200*	*600*	*800*	*1000*	*1200*
13/10/1933	10T	14.04	12.18	11.07	10.32	13.61	11.82	10.75	10.03
96 hr week	12T	14.72	12.81	11.66	10.90	14.24	12.41	11.31	10.58

Articulated, 6- and 8-wheelers,

	Solids				Pneumatics			
Mileage	*200*	*400*	*600*	*800*	*200*	*400*	*600*	*800*
4/10/1935								
max load 6-wheeler	19.41	13.56	11.61	10.39	17.92	12.46	10.64	9.73
max load 8-wheeler	20.71	14.54	12.49	11.46	19.17	13.43	11.31	10.56
Mileage	*600*	*800*	*1000*	*1200*	*600*	*800*	*1000*	*1200*
4/10/1935 – 96 hr week								
max load 6-wheeler	13.60	12.12	11.25	10.66	12.63	11.22	10.38	9.81
max load 8-wheeler	14.48	12.96	12.04	11.43	13.50	12.05	11.18	10.59

Oil engines
(4-wheelers, pneumatic tyres)

Mileage		*200*	*400*	*600*	*800*	*1000*	*1200*
*8/9/1931	4T	12.96	9.12	7.84	7.20	–	–
	5T	13.47	9.61	8.31	7.71	–	–
	6T	14.12	10.18	8.87	8.24	–	–
	8T	15.76	11.65	10.28	9.60	–	–
*8/9/1931 96 hour week	4T	–	–	9.28	8.28	7.68	7.28
	5T	–	–	9.73	8.73	8.15	7.72
	6T	–	–	10.31	9.29	8.68	8.27
	8T	–	–	11.69	10.68	10.05	9.63

*NBThese figures for 8/9/1931 are estimates taken from an article in CM and not from regular CM cost tables

Mileage		*200*	*400*	*600*	*800*	*1000*	*1200*	*1600*
13/10/1933	3T	9.78	6.41	5.27	4.71	4.36	–	
	4T	11.62	7.66	6.34	5.68	5.28	–	
	5T	12.74	8.46	7.03	6.31	5.88	–	
	6T	14.10	9.37	7.79	7.00	6.52	–	
	7T	14.62	9.85	8.27	7.47	7.00	–	
13/10/1933 96 hour week	3T	–	–	–	5.69	5.16	4.81	4.35
	4T	–	–	–	6.76	6.15	5.74	5.23
	5T	–	–	–	7.39	6.75	6.32	5.78
	6T	–	–	–	8.08	7.39	6.93	6.45
	7T	–	–	–	8.55	7.86	7.40	6.92

4/10/1935	3T	8.54	5.74	4.81	4.34	4.06	–	–
	4T	9.50	6.43	5.41	4.89	4.59	–	–
	5T	10.42	7.13	6.03	5.48	5.16	–	–
	6T	10.96	7.63	6.52	5.96	5.63	–	–
	Max. load	11.99	8.37	7.16	6.56	6.20	–	–
4/10/1935	3T	–	–	–	5.29	4.82	4.71	4.11
96 hour	4T	–	–	–	5.88	5.38	5.04	4.62
week	5T	–	–	–	6.47	5.95	5.60	5.16
	6T	–	–	–	6.95	6.42	6.07	5.63
	Max. load	–	–	–	7.55	6.99	6.61	6.15
(Rigid 6-wheelers)								
13/10/1933	3T	10.65	7.08	5.90	5.30	4.95	–	–
	4T	12.40	8.35	7.00	6.33	5.92	–	–
	5T	13.66	9.27	7.81	7.08	6.64	–	–
	8T	16.98	11.77	10.03	9.16	8.64	–	–
	10T	17.55	12.32	10.57	9.70	9.19	–	–
	12T	18.82	13.19	11.31	10.38	9.81	–	–
Mileage		*200*	*400*	*600*	*800*	*1000*	*1200*	*1600*
13/10/1933	3T	–	–	–	6.29	5.74	5.37	4.91
96 hour	4T	–	–	–	7.40	6.78	6.37	5.85
week	5T	–	–	–	8.16	7.50	7.06	6.52
	8T	–	–	–	10.25	9.50	9.01	8.39
	10T	–	–	–	10.79	10.05	9.55	8.93
	12T	–	–	–	11.46	10.68	10.16	9.56
(Rigid 6- and 8-wheelers)								
4/10/1935	4T	10.61	7.35	6.26	5.72	5.39	–	–
	6T	12.09	8.49	7.29	6.69	6.33	–	–
	8T	12.82	9.16	7.95	7.33	6.97	–	–
	10T	14.45	10.32	8.95	8.26	7.85	–	–
Max.load 6-wheeler		15.40	11.20	9.80	9.10	8.68	–	–
Max.load 8-wheeler		16.95	12.45	10.94	10.19	9.74	–	–
4/10/1935	4T	–	–	–	6.71	6.19	5.84	5.40
96 hour	6T	–	–	–	7.68	7.12	6.75	6.29
week	8T	–	–	–	8.33	7.76	7.39	6.92
	10T	–	–	–	9.33	8.70	8.28	7.64

Max.load 6-wheeler	–	–	–	10.17	9.53	9.11	8.56
Max.load 8-wheeler	–	–	–	11.26	10.60	10.15	9.60

Articulated, 6-wheelers

		Solids				Pneumatics		
Mileage		*200*	*400*	*600*	*800*	*200*	*400*	*600*	*800*
13/10/1933	10T	22.71	14.54	11.82	10.46	20.85	13.38	10.90	9.65
	12T	23.59	15.32	12.57	11.19	21.73	14.16	11.64	10.38
Mileage		*600*	*800*	*1000*	*1200*	*600*	*800*	*1000*	*1200*
13/10/1933	10T	14.52	12.49	11.27	10.45	13.59	11.68	10.53	9.76
96 hr week	12T	15.27	13.22	11.99	11.16	14.34	12.41	11.25	10.47

Articulated, 5-, 6- and 8-wheeler

Mileage		*200*	*400*	*600*	*800*	*1000*	*1200*
4/10/1935	3T	8.89	6.07	5.13	4.66	–	–
	6T	10.43	7.29	6.24	5.73	–	–
	8T	12.15	8.65	7.48	6.90	–	–
max. load 6-wheels		15.74	11.52	10.12	9.42	–	–
max. load 8-wheels		18.21	13.62	12.09	11.32	–	–
4/10/1935	3T	–	–	6.40	5.61	5.14	4.83
96 hour	6T	–	–	7.57	6.72	6.21	5.86
week	8T	–	–	8.90	7.96	7.40	7.03
max. load 6-wheels		–	–	11.54	10.48	9.85	9.42
max. load 8-wheels		–	–	13.51	12.39	11.72	11.27

Bibliography

Acworth, Sir W.M. (1891), *The Railways and the Traders*, John Murray, London.

Aldcroft, D.H. (1968), *British Railways in Transition*, Macmillan, London.

Aldcroft, D.H. (1974), *Studies in British Transport History 1870–1970*, David & Charles, Newton Abbot.

Aldcroft, D.H. (1975), *British Transport Since 1914*, David & Charles, Newton Abbot.

Astor, J.J., Bowley et al. (1925), *Is Unemployment Inevitable?* Macmillan, London.

Bagwell, P.S. (1974), *The Transport Revolution from 1770*, Batsford, London.

Barker, T.C. and Savage, C.I. (1975), *An Economic History of Transport in Britain*, Hutchinson, London.

Beadon, R.H. and Fortescue, Sir J. (1930–31), *The Royal Army Service Corps* (Vol. I Beadon, Vol. II Fortescue), University Press, Cambridge.

Bonavia, M.R. (1954), *The Economics of Transport*, Nisbet & Co. and C.U.P. Cambridge.

Brunner, C.T. (1928), *The Problem of Motor Transport*, Ernest Benn, London.

Brunner, C.T. (1929), *Road Versus Rail*, Ernest Benn, London.

Clark, R.H. (1964), *The Development of the English Steam Wagon*, Goose, Norwich.

Cole, G.D.H. and Postgate, R. (1946), *The Common People 1746–1946*, Methuen, London.

Conradi, C.G. (1923), *Mechanical Road Vehicles*, McDonald & Evans, London.

Cornwell, E.L. (1960), *Commercial Road Vehicles*, Batsford, London.

Cornwell, E.L. (1963), *Commercial Vehicles*, Ian Allan, London.

Corpe, T.D. (1953), *Road Haulage Licensing*, Sweet & Maxwell, London.

Davison, Chas. St. Clair (1970), *History of Steam Road Vehicles*, Science Museum, London.

Dunbar, Chas. Stuart (1981), *The Rise of Road Transport 1919–1939*, Ian Allan, London.

Dyos, H.J. and Aldcroft, D.H. (1969), *British Transport – An Economic Survey from 17C.*, Leicester Univ. Press, Leicester.

Fenelon, K.G. (1925), *The Economics of Road Transport*, Allen & Unwin, London.

Fenelon, K.G. (1929), *Transport Co-ordination,* P.S. King, London.
Fenelon, K.G. (1933), *Railway Economics,* Methuen & Co., London.
Foster, C.D. (1963), *The Transport Problem,* Blackie & Son, London.
Glasgow, Geo. (1926), *General Strikes and Road Transport,* Geoffrey Bles, London.
Grupp, Geo. W. (1924), *Economics of Motor Transportation,* Appleton & Co., London and New York.
Gwilliam, K.M. (1964) *Transport & Public Policy,* Allen & Unwin, London.
Henniker, A.M. (1937), *Transportation on the Western Front, 1914–1918,* not catalogued.
Hogg, Ian (1985), *The British Army in the 20th Century,* Ian Allan, London.
Hughes, W.J. (1960), *A Century of Traction Engines,* P. Marshall, London.
Jackman, W.T. (1962), *The Development of Transportation in Modern England,* 2nd edn., Frank Cass & Co., London.
Geoffreys, W. Rees (1949), *The King's Highway,* Batchworth, London.
Kidner, R.W. (1948), *The Steam Lorry, 1896–1939,* Oakwood Press, South Godstone.
Klapper, C.R. (1973), *British Lorries 1900–1945,* Ian Allan, London.
Lloyd-George, David (1934), *War Memoirs,* Odhams Press, London.
Mance, H.O. (1940), *The Road and Rail Transport Problem,* Pitman, London.
Milne, Alastair (1955), *The Economics of Inland Transport,* Pitman, London.
Pelling, H. (1976), *A History of British Trade Unionism,* Pelican, London.
Phillimore, John (1920), *Motor Road Transport for Commercial Purposes,* Pitman, London.
Sargent, J.R. (1958), *British Transport Policy,* O.U.P., Oxford.
Savage, C.I. (1959), *An Economic History of Transport,* Hutchinson, London.
Seth-Smith, M. (1976), *The Long Haul,* Hutchinson, London.
Sharp, Clifford (1965), *The Problem of Transport,* Pergamon, Oxford.
Shrapnell-Smith, E. (editor) (1898, 1899, 1901), *Judges' Reports on Liverpool Trials of Freight Vehicles,* Winstanley & Watkins, Liverpool.
Sherrington, C.E.R. (1934), A Hundred Years of Inland Transport, Duckworth, London.
Stead, W.T. (1903), *How Britain Goes to War,* 2nd edn., Review of Reviews, London.
Strong, L.A.G. (1956), *The Rolling Road,* Hutchinson, London.
Taylor, A.J.F. (1977), *English History 1914–1945,* Book Club Associates and Oxford University Press, London.
Walker, Gilbert (1942), *Road and Rail,* Allen & Unwin, London.
Walters, A.A. and Sharp, C.H. (1958), *A Report on Traffic Costs and Charges,* Birmingham University, Birmingham.
Webb, S.&B. (1913), *English Local Government – The Story of the King's Highway,* Longmans, London.

Williames, B. (1994), *The Best Butter in the World,* Ebury Press, London.

Young, C.F.T. (1861), *The Economy of Steam Power On Common Roads,* Atchley & Co., London.

Official Publications

Select Committee of House of Commons on Tolls on ... Tolls to be Charged, 1831.

Departmental Committee of LGB on Regulations for purposes of Section 12 of Motor Car Act, 1903. Part I – Report, 1904. Cd 2069. Part II – Evidence, Appendix, Index. Cd 2070.

Royal Commission on Motor Cars – Vol. I Report, 1906. Cd 3080. Vol. II Evidence, Appendix, Index. Cd 3081.

Select Committee on Transport, 1918. Report – House of Commons Paper No. 136, Vol. IV. Minutes of Evidence – Paper No. 130, Vol. IV.

Select Committee on National Expenditure, 1918. 10th Report – House of Commons Paper No. 132, Vol. IV, p.95.

Departmental Committee of LGB on Construction and Use of Road Locomotives and Heavy Motor Cars. Part I – Report, 1919 HMSO, Cmd 5; Part II – Evidence, Appendix. Cmd 5.

MOT – Official Report of Conference with Members of Parliament 10/12/1919 and Statement By Sir Eric Geddes. HMSO, 1919. Cmd 493.

Committee on Road Conveyance of Goods by Railway Companies (Balfour–Browne Committee). HMSO, 1921. Cmd 1228.

Departmental Committee on Road Conveyance of Goods by Railways 1928. Royal Commission on Transport, 1928. First Report – The Control of Traffic on Roads, 1929–30, Cmd 3365; Third Report – The Co-ordination and Development of Transport, 1930–31, Cmd 3751. Minutes of Evidence.

Communications Received from Certain Organisatons with their Observations on ... the Final Report 1931–32. MOT. Cmd 4048.

Report of the Conference on Rail and Road Transport MOT 29/7/1932 (The Salter Report).

Report of the Committee on Regulation of Wages and Conditions of Service in the Road Motor Transport Industry (Goods) 1937 Cmd 5440 (The Baillie Committee).

Transport Advisory Council – Report on Service and Rates, 1937. MOT.

Transport Advisory Council – Report on the Proposals of the Main Line Railway Companies on the Conveyance of Merchandise by Rail, 1939. MOT.

Organisation of Road Transport for a Defence Emergency, 1939. MOT London.

Periodical Publications

Annual Reports of the G.P.O.
Annual Reports of the Licensing Authorities
Annual Reports of the Road Board
Annual Reports of the Railway Companies
Commercial Motor Magazine
Modern Transport
Municipal Year Books
Parliamentary Debates (*Hansard*)
The Times

Index